THE COMPLETE BOOK OF
GARDEN DESIGN, CONSTRUCTION AND PLANTING

DAVID STEVENS
LUCY HUNTINGTON
AND
RICHARD KEY

Edited by David Stevens

CASSELLPAPERBACKS

Acknowledgements

The publishers are grateful to the following for granting permission to reproduce the colour photographs and coloured artwork: David Stevens (pp. *i*, *ii* (both), *iii*, *iv*, *vii*, *viii*, *xi*, *xviii* (lower), *xx* and *xxv*); Peter McHoy (p. *v*); Richard Key (p. *vi*, *ix*, *x* (both), *xii* (both), *xiv* (lower) and *xvii*); Richard Balfour (p. *xiv*, top); Lucy Huntington (p. *xviii* (top), *xix* (both), *xxi*, *xxii*, *xxiii*, *xxiv* (both); *xxx*, *xxxi* and *xxxii* (both)); and Photos Horticultural Picture Library (p. *xxvii*, *xxviii* and *xxix*). All the remaining photographs were taken by Bob Challinor.

The publishers are also grateful to David Stevens for granting permission to reproduce Figures 1.1, 2.1, 2.3, 2.4, 2.5, 2.6, 2.7 and 2.8. All the remaining drawings were drawn by Nils Solberg.

First published in the United Kingdom in 1991
by Ward Lock

First paperback edition 1994

This paperback edition first published in 2002 by
Cassell Paperbacks, Cassell & Co
Wellington House, 125 Strand
London, WC2R 0BB

Distributed in the United States of America by
Sterling Publishing Co., Inc.
387 Park Avenue South,
New York, NY 10016-8810

A CIP catalogue record for this book is available
from the British Library

ISBN 1-84188-172-4

Text filmset by Chapterhouse Limited,
The Cloisters, Formby L37 3PX

Printed in Slovenia by Delo Tiskarna
by arrangement with Prešernova družba d.d., Ljubljana

THE COMPLETE BOOK OF
GARDEN DESIGN, CONSTRUCTION AND PLANTING

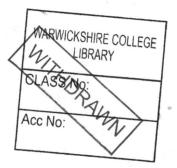

Contents

INTRODUCTION

There is a myth put about, more often than not by self-styled experts, that the making of gardens is a complicated subject, and as such the uninitiated need an abundance of equally complicated advice to make any headway at all. In fact nothing could be further from the truth and in reality commonsense should replace complication. The so-called novice is simply the acquisitor of a fresh air room, or series of rooms that adjoin his home. Assuming the latter means that the average garden user is very much aware that there is a valuable space available, often considerably bigger than the house, for a wide range of activities. The question is how to get the best out of it. Just where to start can be confusing and is made no easier by the wealth of information, often in piecemeal form, that is continually churned out by radio, television and for the greater part in magazines and books.

As far as books are concerned the problems are twofold. Firstly there are so many of them that making any kind of reasoned choice is well nigh impossible and, secondly, most authors home in on a particular aspect or speciality. In other words, to have access to a wide range of necessary information means that one has to buy an equally wide range of books.

In *The Complete Book of Garden Planning, Construction and Planting Design* we have made a positive effort to overcome this problem by taking you through all the essential stages of creating a garden, from the initial survey to the planting of the final shrub that sets the seal on the composition. Between these ends of the spectrum lies a wealth of necessary information and fact that if presented in a logical and stimulating sequence will allow a garden to be built and planted to reflect the personality and lifestyle of the reader. What's more, this sequence of planning and construction is not only fun but, if carried out correctly, will save a good deal of effort and hard-earned cash.

PERSONALITY

In many ways lifestyle is all important as gardens are all about personality. This is why no two plots, even if identical in shape, size and aspect, ever turn out the same. Gardens, too, are not only becoming smaller but also more crowded together, which means that ever more pressure and an associated need for privacy is placed on this invaluable space. The point is, quite rightly, that they are being treated more and more as 'outside rooms' and they are no longer necessarily a place in which to labour for long hours in order to grow vegetables, or simply to keep maintenance under control. Leisure time is at a premium for most families and, with both partners usually working, people want to spend their time enjoying their plot and certainly not being a slave to it.

Of course all these trends mean that an increasing number of requirements has to be levered into an ever smaller space, but with the right approach the phrase 'small is beautiful' takes on a refreshingly new aspect.

It is at this point that many people despair and it's small wonder when you think that the trauma, or at least hard work, of moving into a new home is compounded by the vision of a barren muddy plot, or perhaps an established garden just going to seed while you organize the spaces inside your home. The trouble is that while many of us are happy enough to organize the furniture and colour schemes in the sitting-room, or choose a range of kitchen units from the show home of a new estate, the ideas are less forthcoming when we move outside. In reality new homes are becoming increasingly 'fitted', from kitchen to bedroom, and it can only be a matter of time—and I believe a very short time—for this kind of built-in planning to include the garden. Be that as it may, for most of us the garden still does present a problem and to get the best from this vital space involves design.

WHAT IS GARDEN DESIGN?

To many people the whole subject of design and designers is slightly unreal, conjuring up pictures of idyllic gardens straight from the pages of glossy magazines. Professional design is seen as not only something inspirational but also beyond the reach, and pocket, of the average mortal. In fact good design is not difficult and is within the reach of anyone who is prepared to follow a well tried and tested set of rules. A worthwhile composition is inevitably simple and invariably unique, being tailored to a specific set of requirements that are in turn governed by the advantages and limitations of the basic site.

But the whole process of design starts long before you put pen to paper and the initial job will be to find out just what you have got and then what you want based on this initial fact finding. Only when you have this information should you set about moulding all these criteria into a sensible composition that is right for you.

Most gardens fail because this sequence is muddled, or development is carried out in a haphazard way. In part this is due to the proliferation of garden centres, nurseries and DIY stores, all of which offer the widest possible range of gardening goodies. Add to this the number of catalogues that regularly drop through the letter box, and the special offers in the Sunday supplements, and you can see that the temptation to make random purchases is hard to resist. How many of us, on the first fine day of spring, jump into the car,

arrive at the local garden centre and buy the first things that catch our eye. Once we get back home we are often hard pressed to know just where to plant the shrubs, position the pool or extend the patio. What's more, we probably paid scant attention to the eventual size or preferred habitat of plants and bought them for the simple reason that the bloom or leaf looked particularly attractive. Such an approach not only spells chaos but adds up to an alarming financial expenditure over the years, when up to 60% of plants can perish.

THE ADVANTAGES OF PLANNING

It's fair to say that garden planning is rather more than just creating a worthwhile composition. If you have a well thought out scheme it will allow you to construct the garden over a sensible period of time. The work can easily be broken down into phases and these can be simply related to a budget. The beauty of this approach is that you don't lose sight of the original concept—one reason why so many unplanned gardens end up looking a mess.

If you are unwilling or unable to carry out the work yourself, you will in all probability wish to get a contractor to build the garden. Without a design it will be almost impossible to get any kind of competitive quotation, as none of the firms will have a fixed plan to work from.

While on the subject of contracting, do be careful to select a good company as unfortunately the trade is riddled with 'cowboy' operators. If possible work from recommendation, but if this is impossible make sure you at least see examples of their work before they make a start. The extra effort could save you a good deal of heartache and hard-earned cash. It's also sensible to get two or three estimates as these can vary enormously depending on a particular company's work load, overheads and travelling distance from your garden. Once you have decided upon a contractor, get a firm quotation for the work involved.

DO IT YOURSELF

But most people will in all probability carry the work out themselves and where a design allows a contractor to make a realistic estimate, it will serve exactly the same purpose for you. It will in effect be your shopping list of all the materials and features needed. It will allow you to prepare and analyze your soil; it will indicate if drainage, additional topsoil, tree surgery or levelling are necessary. You will also be able quickly to count up the slabs needed for a terrace or patio, the number of bricks for a retaining wall, the area of turf for a lawn and so on. While all this may sound complicated to the new, or even long-time garden owner, it will in fact allow you to break everything down into that all important logical sequence.

This book sets out to remove the mystery that surrounds the making of a garden and to do this it is separated into the chronological order of design, construction and finally planting. In order to make this straightforward, I have asked two of my close friends and colleagues to undertake the two latter sections, while I shall be looking at the whole process of design, upon which the construction and planting are based. All three of us are not only professional but *practical* designers, with many years of experience dealing with plots (and clients) of every complexity.

DESIGN

The first stage of the project is design and here I shall show you how to assess just what you have got by carrying out a simple survey. We shall also look at making a checklist to see what you and the family like or dislike. Once the basic analysis is complete, we can move on to the fascinating and fun job of preparing the design. Over the years I have learnt a good many 'tricks of the trade', to make a small garden seem larger or an awkward shape less oppressive. There are of course many ways of

getting the best from your plot and we shall be looking at a number of examples, which will include those all important front gardens, to see just how they work and subsequently to show you how you can prepare a design that will fit you like a glove.

But the truth of the matter is that nobody wants a garden design; what they really need is the finished garden. In other words the design is simply a means to the end, albeit an important one.

CONSTRUCTION

Construction is therefore the next step in the creation of your outside room and here Richard Key takes you through all the necessary stages to achieve just that. He looks at and explains the importance and aesthetic differences of boundaries to give you shelter and privacy; he looks at the vast and increasing range of paving materials that are now available and shows how to lay them properly so that they provide value for money as well as a practical working surface.

Apart from the question of fencing, walling and paving, that form the 'bones' of the garden, there may be other hard surface features you have planned into the layout. Here we shall look at the various ways in which water can be handled, together with rock outcrops, cobble and boulder areas, and even swimming pools. Barbecuing is becoming increasingly popular in what seems to be a trend towards hotter summers, and these can be incorporated in a purpose-built area that includes overhead beams, awnings and seating. Lighting and power is another vital ingredient which is so often unimaginatively handled, but safety is paramount and is an area we look at in detail.

Then there are the furnishings of pots, statues and ornaments that bring all those 'hard landscape' areas to life, so we look at the options and how to maintain them.

Finally, there are the tools for the job and like any other trade the right selection and the correct maintenance makes life a whole lot easier. As well as being a designer Richard has a wealth of experience in contracting and his knowledge in this area is invaluable.

PLANTING

So far we have looked at design and construction but to most people it is plants and planting that really bring a garden to life. However, by now you will see that the making of a garden is a sequential job and although the planting is a vital element it is the last piece of the jigsaw. It is this that will draw the various elements of the design together, softening the crisp edge of paving and walling and providing colour and interest throughout the year.

While there are a number of talented 'plantspeople', very few of these are also good garden designers. Lucy Huntington is an exception to this rule and is able to clothe her gardens in the most stunning, and practical, planting schemes. Her expertise is vital to ensure that this book provides a complete picture.

But 'soft landscaping' includes other elements apart from planting. There is the question of lawns and the best method of constructing these. There is an increasing awareness of matters ecological, wild flower and naturalized areas, as well as drifts of ground-covering plants that will reduce maintenance to a sensible minimum.

To many, planting is a complicated headache and this is so often where the garden goes badly wrong. What do all those Latin names mean? What grows best on chalk or acid soil? How big will a particular shrub, conifer or hardy perennial grow? Like the basic design, a planting plan will allow you to plant material, if necessary, over a number of years, to suit your allocated budget.

That gardening is an art there is no dispute; the real point is that such art must be tempered and driven by practicality. This is just what we are going to show you.

PART I

CHAPTER 1

BASIC PLANNING

In the Introduction we discussed the advantages of planning a garden. We can now embark on the exciting job of creating a new and unique environment that will be tailored to what you and the family need.

The problem of more haste less speed is nowhere more apparent than in this design stage and, before you even think of putting pen to paper, there are a couple of important questions that you need to ask yourself. Both of these involve fact finding. The first is to find out exactly what you have in the garden already, together with all the relevant measurements; and the second revolves around what you want to see in the finished composition. The easiest way to gather this information is by checklists which will help you to crystallize your thoughts and avoid leaving out any important facts that might affect the design later on (Table 1.1). To check what you have got involves a simple survey, and before you panic about not being able to use a theodolite and other complicated equipment, it's worth pointing out that this is a relatively simple, but vital, process. The equipment you will need is a clipboard and several sheets of clean paper, pencil, a long tape measure — preferably 30 m (100 ft) — several bamboo canes for anchoring the latter, two metal pins tied to a long length of twine approximately 100 m (330 ft) long, a child's magnetic compass and finally, if the garden has a slope, a spirit level, a pole about 1 m (3¼ ft) long, and a plank.

Always use the right tools. All too many gardens are planned, on the back of an envelope, which means nothing can be designed even remotely to scale. Unfortunately some garden contractors still do this and the results speak for themselves.

TABLE 1.1 BASIC PLANNING CHECK LIST

WHAT DO YOU HAVE?	ANSWER
Any good or bad views	
Boundaries — type of fence or hedge	
Surfaces — gravel, concrete, brick etc	
Soil — acid/alkaline, heavy/light	
Interior floor/wall colours/materials in rooms adjoining garden	
Any changes in level	
Existing trees/planting	
Any other details	

WHAT DO YOU WANT? (tick as appropriate)

Annuals		Swings/slide	
Roses		Dining area	
Herbaceous		Barbecue	
Shrubs		Pergola	
Ground cover		Paddling pool	
Vegetables		Compost/bins	
Fruit		Bonfire area	
Greenhouse		Boat/caravan standing	
Shed		Anything else	
Pond/pool			
Sandpit			

How much maintenance can you manage?	
Number/ages of children	
Pets	

ANYTHING YOU DO NOT WANT

CARRYING OUT THE SURVEY
What do you have?

To make life easier, don't try to measure the back and front garden at the same time as this can become confusing. On a sheet of clean paper draw in the shape of the house at the bottom of the page, making this large enough to be able to pencil in clearly all the relevant measurements. Mark in the positions of doors and windows, projecting bays, patio doors, a possible conservatory, and so on. Next draw in the boundaries, using as much of the page as possible, showing any approximate angles to the house and indicate what the boundaries are, such as fence, wall, hedge etc.; and also the type of boundary, which could be close board or panel, brick or concrete block, beech or conifer (Fig. 1.1).

Indicate the position of any existing trees or planting and remember that certain types of plants, such as hardy perennials or bulbs, may not be visible at certain times of year. If you can identify the tree and shrub species, then so much the better. It will also be useful to indicate the dimensions of a shrub group and the size of the canopy of a tree. Mark these on the plan, as trees in particular cast shade and the extent of this will be dependent on the spread of the branches.

Show manholes or drains that impinge on a paved area or are an obvious problem in the main part of the garden. Show an existing paved area, path or patio. Mark any obvious changes of level and anything else that is present, even if it seems trivial or not necessarily worth keeping.

With regard to the latter, even apparent eyesores or the most unlikely objects can become a worthwhile part of the composition to come. Trees are a typical example and I am often asked to sweep away old fruit trees, well past their prime. The fact that they could quite possibly fruit again with correct pruning is immaterial; what is more important is the gnarled outline, which if worked into the overall garden pattern can become a real focal

point or pivot. Old unkempt hedges are another favourite for a slash and burn policy in a new garden, particularly if they partly straddle the space. Keep them, at least for the time being, and see how they could fit into the design. If this is possible, they can be cleaned up, the stems thinned and the whole thing worked into a delightful living trellis, or regenerated to form a screen for some of the more unsightly but practical elements of a garden.

Remember that trees and larger plants take many years to grow and as such are almost priceless. Conversely they take minutes to fell and that can be simply irresponsible.

TAKING MEASUREMENTS

The first job will be to run your tape across the back of the house, parallel with the building, from one boundary to the other. Once you are clear of the building make sure the tape carries on in a straight line by sighting back along it. Now take *running* measurements from the boundary to the house and then on across the face of the building, taking in doors, windows and any other relevant features. Clearly mark the end of the house and then carry on to check the final distance of the opposite boundary. The point is that when you come to transfer these running measurements to a scale drawing later on, it will be far easier to move across the page in a similar way, rather than having to work out the individual distances between windows or the end of the house and the boundary.

Next take your tape and run it from one end of the house, at right angles to the building, towards the bottom of the garden. Mark off any relevant points on the way such as the edge of an existing paved area, the position of a tree close to a boundary, the junction of a fence and hedge and so on. If the tape will not reach the bottom of the plot, mark the end with a bamboo cane, reel in and start again, making a note on your plan of this 'change' point. Quite often the boundaries will not be square with

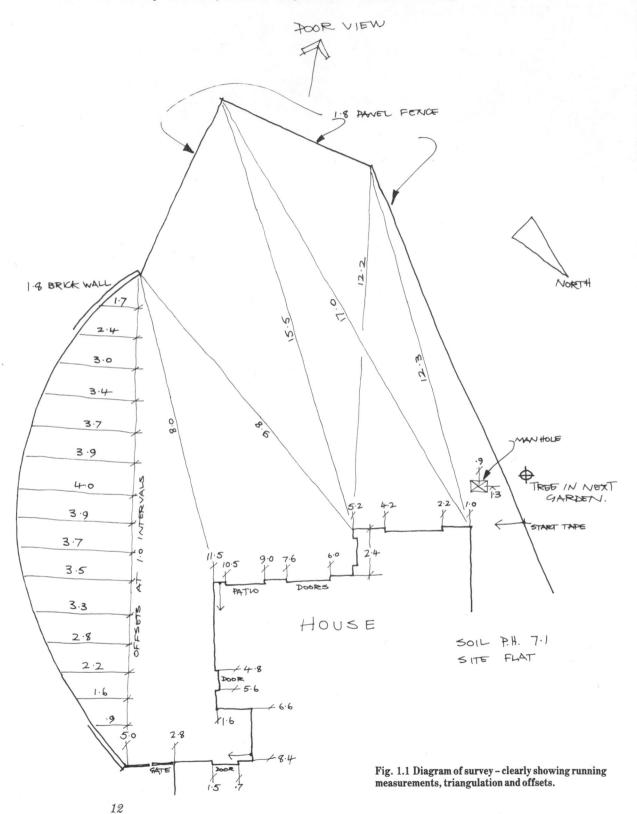

Fig. 1.1 Diagram of survey – clearly showing running measurements, triangulation and offsets.

the house, or there may be a tree or number of trees that you have difficulty in locating accurately by the simple method of running the tape up and across the garden. In this case you will need to use the simple technique of *triangulation*.

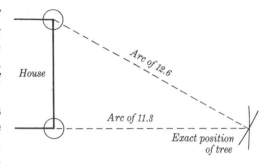

Triangulation involves taking measurements from two known points — the ends of the house, or the corner of the house and garage, will often be ideal — to the object in question. When you come to prepare the scale drawing it will be a simple job to scale off the radii involved, swing two compass lines and where the arcs intersect, accurately show the tree or corner of the garden (Fig. 1.2).

Fig. 1.2 Triangulation can be used to fix the position of a tree or angled boundary by taking measurements from two known points and then transferring them to a scale drawing, using a compass to swing two intersecting arcs. Where these meet is the exact position of the feature concerned.

On an even more complicated note, one or more of the boundaries may curve but here again the technique for accurate measurement is simple. Firstly plot the two ends of the boundary and then run your line tightly between these, fixing it with the metal pins. At 1 m (3¼ ft) intervals, run your tape at right angles from the line out to the boundary and clearly show the distances on your survey drawing. These are known as offsets and it will be a simple job to plot them to scale later on, and this will clearly indicate the curve. This same technique can be used to plot an irregularly shaped border or pool by running offsets from a known line to the feature in question.

CHANGES IN LEVEL

Changes of level in a garden can be a real bonus in design terms and will allow you a good deal of scope later on for a number of features. However it will be vital to plot these as they will affect just what goes where, and accurate levels will allow you to estimate accurately any materials needed for construction.

Where a garden slopes gently it can be sufficient to take a sighting back from the lowest area to a fixed point on the house and measure the drop with a tape. This can only be an approximate measurement and where the falls are steeper and more complicated a more accurate method will utilize that plank, spirit level and pole (Fig. 1.3).

Start at the top of the slope by laying the plank on the ground, place the pole at the other end and raise the plank to near horizontal. Place the spirit level on the plank and centre the bubble. Mark the height of the plank on the pole and measure the distance from the mark to the ground. Once this is complete remove the plank from its original position, place it in the position occupied by the pole and repeat

Fig. 1.3 Ensure plank is level and measure vertical distance.

the whole operation as many times as necessary to get down the slope. Add all the vertical measurements together and you will have a pretty accurate idea of the fall involved. It will be a good idea to plot these level survey lines on your main garden survey, as they may be invaluable for making a contour drawing later.

Of course there are some gardens that are really complicated, having steep slopes and awkward cross falls. If this is a mature plot there is also the possibility of existing vegetation, trees and other established features that will add to the confusion. Some gardens are not simply rectangular but have boundaries at acute angles or even 'dog-legs'. If this is the case and you feel that the completion of a survey is really beyond you, then it can be well worthwhile calling in a professional surveyor. He or she will have all the necessary equipment to make the task a whole lot easier and they will also draw the survey up to scale so that you have the basis for preparing your design. Like all professionals, your surveyor will make the job look simple but the fee will be well worth it if in reality the job would be impossible for you to carry out accurately.

VIEWS

Views can be either positive or negative but all gardens have them to a greater or lesser degree.

On the credit side a view can be the making of a garden, bringing the wider landscape into what may be a very limited space. In an ideal situation it might be a range of hills that rises above a simple close board fence. In such a situation the design will call for the fence to be screened in some way and the view emphasized by the careful positioning of trees or taller shrubs. Remember that a wide open view is often far less effective than one that is concentrated or at least focused. Close to the coast, it might be the glimpse of a cliff or the sea between neighbouring buildings, where

the same principle will apply of blocking out the houses and channelling the vista in the required direction.

In an urban situation things may seem a little more mundane but a church tower or the facade of a handsome period building may be well worth drawing into your composition. Coming down the scale again, you may simply be surrounded by neighbouring gardens that have attractive trees or particularly good planting. There will be little point in screening these out or having an immediately obvious boundary. It will be far better to minimize the division by using a fence through which the view can run, and capitalizing on someone else's good taste or fortune. In fact there is nothing new in this approach and it was one of the tricks of the trade employed by the great landscape designers of the eighteenth century, in particular Capability Brown and Humphry Repton. Their palette may have been a little larger but the principles were just the same.

It may be that you have a large country garden and in this case the ha-ha, or sunken boundary may allow you to borrow the adjoining land visually and make it appear to be your own.

All this is very well but for many of us the prospect is rather less promising and the surroundings can be at best mundane or at worst frankly awful. More often than not this will be in town, and here the bad view can be anything from the back of a factory to a neighbour's garage. New estates are becoming ever more crowded and the problem of overlooking first or second floor windows can be a particular problem. These can be screened in a number of ways, either by tree or high shrub planting on the boundaries or by overhead beams running out from the house. These can be particularly useful, not just for their screening potential but in their ability to act as host for fragrant climbers that will in turn cast dappled shade on a patio or sitting area below. A pergola or arbour can act in exactly the same way, screening a certain spot within the garden from outside views.

Sometimes, as in my own garden for instance, there may be a good view that is screened by planting that has grown up over the years. In fact I had good and bad in about equal portions and so with judicious thinning I opened up a fine vista by removing a group of old elder and overgrown laurel, but managed to retain enough cover to eliminate the corner of an intrusive housing estate some distance away.

So whether a particular one, or number of views are good or bad, it is essential to check them out and mark them clearly on your survey drawing so that they can be emphasized or screened when the design is prepared. It is also important to see just where they are most apparent, and this will often involve taking a view from the kitchen or sitting-room windows.

Remember too that such views may well change with summer and winter. Trees in particular will provide a greater or lesser degree or screening (and incidentally shelter) and it could be well worth considering a mix of evergreen and deciduous should space permit.

PREVAILING WINDS

The presence of a good or bad view can, as we have just seen, be dependent on screening and shelter. Just what form that shelter takes can range enormously from a solid structure such as adjoining buildings, walls, fences or a dense hedge, to the more open texture of a group of shrubs or trees. It is a fact in this country that it is a lack of shelter that often prevents us from using the garden and it's worth remembering that there are many gloriously sunny days in the winter when it is quite possible to sit outside as long as the screening is sufficient. One has only to look at the success of conservatories in recent years to see how true this statement is.

Very often wind will blow more frequently from one direction than another, and this is known as the prevailing wind. Such winds are more constant in coastal and rural areas than in town or the suburbs, where surrounding buildings can complicate the pattern by deflecting the main flow. Having said that, you will probably find that on your local housing estate the wind may be often funnelled in a particular way around a corner or between buildings. In other words, make a note of this on your survey drawing as it may well determine where you sit and where shelter is positioned, to benefit both plants and people.

Within your garden any wind blowing along the face of a wall will tend to accelerate, while a wind meeting a fence or wall square on will be deflected up and over the barrier and then turn in upon itself on the other side, creating a good deal of unpleasant turbulence.

The best kind of wind break is a 'permeable' screen. This can take the form of planting and if space permits an outer barrier of trees, backed up with shrubs and ground cover, can provide shelter in a horizontal direction for up to 10 times the height of the screen. If space is limited, as it is in many small gardens, then a slatted fence with gaps of approximately 10 mm between boards will be a very effective filter. On a very contemporary note, there are a number of synthetic materials coming onto the market that consist of a woven polyester material stretched between lightweight alloy posts. These have the effect of not only dramatically reducing the force of the wind but also of being translucent. This means that plants can be grown on the shady side without the problems of dense shadow cast by a conventional wall or fence. Such materials are also being produced in different colours which opens up all kinds of fascinating plant combinations that can tone or contrast with the surrounding boundaries.

MICROCLIMATE

Although Lucy will be dealing with the subject of microclimate in rather greater detail in Part III of this book (see page 148), it is an aspect that must, if identifiable, be included in the initial survey as it can affect just what you grow where.

The most common microclimatic problem is a 'frost pocket' and this is an area where particularly cold air can gather, often in contrast to other parts of a garden. Such conditions can occur on a hillside where a depression or the presence of a group of buildings can prevent this colder, heavier air draining away. Sometimes the problem can be overcome by opening a gap in a dense hedge or fence, replacing this with a more open mesh. Similar conditions can be found at the bottom of a slope and here it can be more serious as the cold air has no escape. Such a situation is not always immediately obvious but intelligent observation can forestall a problem. If such conditions occur it will be necessary to grow hardy plant material and avoid particularly tender species.

There are of course broad climatic bands and areas that stretch across any country and these can often be modified by changes in altitude and the proximity of the coast, producing local conditions that vary from the regional average.

The west coast of Scotland in the UK is at a relatively high latitude but the fact that it is washed by the Gulf Stream means that it is virtually frost free, and all kinds of tender plants thrive. Just a few miles inland these conditions are lost and the climate reverts back to the area norm.

Rain shadows

A little earlier in the survey process we looked at the importance of checking a prevailing wind. This will not only often determine where we sit but it will also have the effect of deflecting rain as it hits the roof and face of a building, or a garden wall. In other words, if rain is driven at an angle to an obstruction, the latter will provide shelter in its lee and this area may receive far less moisture than the rest of the garden. The more the roof overhangs the more obvious this problem will

be. Such dry areas can be particularly difficult, if not impossible for plants, and so it will be well worth assessing any possible rain shadows and marking them accordingly on your survey drawing.

SOIL TYPES

The soil that surrounds your house is vitally important and will determine what you can grow. It is made up of two broad parts: topsoil which is 'alive' with bacteria, insects and nutrients, and subsoil which is inert and 'dead' as far as being able to support plant growth.

The depth of topsoil can vary enormously, ranging from a very thin layer on a rocky hillside to many metres or feet in a fertile river valley. In most gardens an ideal depth is between 30–45 cm (12–18 in). Unfortunately, on many new housing estates this fertile layer can be buried beneath a layer of subsoil that was dug out from the building foundations. If this is the case, it will have to be removed and you will have a perfect right to ask the builder to do this for you.

Another problem in a brand new garden can be compaction by heavy machinery. Not only will this make the ground almost impossible to cultivate but it will also hinder drainage. Again, the developer should ensure that such ground has been 'ripped' and an adequate layer of topsoil spread. In less severe cases a deep rotovating can be sufficient and such machines can be easily hired.

There is a common fallacy that a 'heavy' or clay soil is infertile. In fact the opposite is the case and although it may be difficult to work, the sticky nature of the soil granules helps to retain nutrients and encourage plant growth. The incorporation of organic matter such as leaf mould or compost will lighten a heavy soil and help bind together a light sandy type. It is worth mentioning that peat was until recently recommended for soil conditioning as it is excellent in this respect; however, with the recent environmental problems of peat extraction, a substitute should always be sought. There are a number of alternatives already appearing on the market in quantity that include granulated bark and coconut husks.

Is your soil acid or alkaline?

Apart from the texture of the soil varying, it will also have a greater or lesser acidity. This is known as a 'ph' value and means quite simply that different plants thrive on different types of soil. A good example is the fact that rhododendrons, azaleas, camellias and pieris are a few of the shrubs that enjoy acid soils, whereas clematis, buddleia and weigela are happy on shallow soils over chalk. Part III will explore this subject in greater detail later on but it will be vital to check your soil type when carrying out the survey. This is easily done with a simple and inexpensive kit that can be bought from virtually any garden centre or shop. The real point is that it is unwise to grow acid lovers in chalk, and *vice versa*, as they will not be happy and in extreme conditions will die. Most container-grown plants will tolerate the wrong soil for a year or possibly two as their roots are contained within a specially prepared root ball. After that they will show signs of distress.

It is virtually impossible to change a soil type, even with the importation of fresh soil, as sooner or later chemicals will wash through from the underlying and surrounding layers. If you are really keen to grow, say, acid lovers in a chalky area, then it will be well worth while thinking of building completely self-contained raised beds.

THE WATER TABLE

This is a natural level of water in the ground and can be seen quite easily if you dig a pit in the garden, when sooner or later water will fill the bottom of the hole. This level will rise and fall with the amount of rain and so usually varies between summer and winter. However, it can be changed simply by the building of

houses or the alteration of a drainage pattern, by adjusting levels or the construction of a nearby major feature such as a road.

A high water table means that the ground can become waterlogged and this will be detrimental to plant establishment or growth. On the other hand a low water table means a lack of moisture and plants are at risk of starving to death through a shortage of vital nutrients. While watering or an irrigation system can cure the latter, you may need to consider drainage to cure water-logging – something that we look at in closer detail in Chapter 3.

ASPECT AND ORIENTATION

Perhaps the most important survey item is to establish just which way the garden is orientated. This will show where the sun rises and sets and this in turn will determine the best places to sit as well as the suitability of certain plants and crops for particular positions in sun or shade.

The easiest way to check north and south is to remember that the sun shines from the south at midday, rising in the east and setting in the west. If you are unable to see the sun, and for the most accurate measurement, use a simple magnetic compass. Remember too that the sun swings higher in the sky during the summer, while in the winter it will be much lower and cast longer shadows.

It can be invaluable to mark the passage of the sun on your survey, showing it as an arc passing from one side of the page to the other. In this way you will be able to see which parts of the garden receive sun at what time of day. If you have tall trees, high walls or adjoining buildings make a note of the shadows they cast as this will certainly have a bearing on the design.

WHAT WOULD YOU LIKE?

Everything that we have just done is absolutely vital and like any other job it is the preparation that is the single most important element. But the survey was more than just gathering information. It should have allowed you to get a real 'feel' of the garden and you will almost certainly know a great deal more about it now than you did at the beginning. It will also be certain that you are starting to get some positive ideas about how you want to use this outside room. But it is still too early to get on with the design and the next job will be to crystallize those thoughts about what you want.

The easiest way to do this is by drawing up a checklist and make sure that the whole family takes part. Don't worry if it seems to get too big, you can always thin things down later. The important point is not to leave anything out as it is virtually impossible, not to mention expensive, to add a major feature or item once the garden is built.

There is no typical family list, as we have already seen that all gardens turn out differently owing to that prime factor of personality. However you may want such items as a patio or terrace for sitting, dining and dry shod play, possibly a barbecue and built-in seating, a pool, lawn, play equipment, vegetables, fruit, borders for growing trees, shrubs and hardy perennials, a pergola or arch, paths, greenhouse or shed. Don't forget that many families have pets. Keen bird fanciers will want an aviary, others will need a dog run, rabbit hutches and so on. For my own part, I keep rare chickens and the runs have to be screened in a suitably aesthetic and fox proof way! So the list goes on and remember that the garden will have to contain the ugly and practical as well as the beautiful. This means that the dustbins will need to go somewhere, perhaps in a neat store close to the back door. How about the washing — would you prefer a long line or rotary type? The compost will be an invaluable item and so too will be a bonfire or incinerator.

Sometimes there is a need for a particular feature such as a large paved area for the parking of a boat or caravan, or car

maintenance for an enthusiast. Some people will want to grow specialist plants that will involve a major feature such as a rockery or heather garden. Fish too play their part and species like Koi carp will need an ample spread and depth of water.

Apart from the things you like, what about what you *don't* like? This could include poisonous plants; or a particular type or colour of plant. Pools and any other type of water feature can be a problem if you have a young family; while some types of paving can figure high on some people's dislikes.

One of the most important questions I ask clients is whether or not they are keen, average or lazy gardeners, and don't worry if you come firmly down on the side of the latter — a garden is there to serve you and never the other way about! Many first time gardeners set out with the best intentions and have little idea of the amount of time and effort a complicated garden can involve. Look at your lifestyle, see what your other hobbies are and set time aside for the garden accordingly. Another point worth bearing in mind is that a garden matures and knits together. This means that when first established, with young, small plants, there will be a reasonable amount of maintenance to do, even if using bark mulches and other labour-saving techniques. If you can spare the time in the initial seasons to keep weeds under control and generally keep the garden tidy, you will be surprised just how quickly things establish. Ongoing maintenance really is on a sliding scale and it can be immensely rewarding to see your design take shape and come to life with less and less work to do!

BUDGET

Another vital question is just what you are prepared to spend. Many people are quite unaware of what it takes to build a garden and it can be well worth while getting a 'feel' of the various paving, planting and incidental items by visiting nurseries and garden centres.

Remember though that a good garden is an equally good investment and if built well will provide a lifetime's service. It is in fact one of the few things in this world that actually improves with age, and that initial outlay will be money well spent.

In other words be realistic and allocate sensible funds that can be spread over several years if necessary. It is far better to build a straightforward and sensible composition that you can afford than embark on an impossibly complicated scheme that will not only founder but cost you a small fortune in the process.

As a final thought, remember that a well designed garden will be a flexible garden. The whole process of survey and analysis will allow you to organize both your thoughts and the space available into a worthwhile pattern.

Having said that, gardens and the criteria they fulfil, may well change over the years. It is quite possible to build a basic layout that can have the facility for 'bolting on' additional features as time and cash allow. In an extreme case the garden could start life as a budget composition for a young couple, move through a middle stage when a growing family would make full use of both the basic and new facilities and culminate as a plot for an older couple who have more time and cash to spend but wish maintenance to be reduced to an absolute minimum. In other words the garden is an infinitely flexible vehicle for the widest possible range of activities. Get the framework and the criteria right and you can embark on the most fascinating of projects, the creation of your outdoor room.

CHAPTER 2

DESIGNING THE GARDEN

Designing a garden should not only be easy but fun, and a great deal of the work that we have carried out for the survey will encourage both these ideals.

The problem with too many designs and designers is that they suffer from over-complication. A poor designer will try and justify his or her worth by trying to cram as many features, focal points and trivia into a scheme as possible. The end result is of course chaos. A good, well thought out design is both straightforward and simple; it is tailored to the owner of the garden and it will serve them well as a result.

Of course simplicity does not eliminate originality or subtlety. What it does do is to integrate these into a strong and positive framework. As we carried out the survey and thought about what we wanted to see in the finished garden it is inevitable that ideas started to form, but before we start to get these down on paper we need to prepare a scale drawing of the garden based on the measurements and other information that we have gathered.

PREPARING A SCALE DRAWING

The very word scale implies accuracy and this part of the design process is vital if you are going to be able to plot out your features and estimate materials properly for construction.

The easiest way to work will be on tracing paper laid over a sheet of graph paper but first of all we need to understand just what 'working to scale' means. Quite simply a square or number of squares on the graph paper represents a given, but much larger square in the garden. If the garden is of an average size, 1 cm on the drawing can represent 1 m on the ground ($\frac{1}{8}$ in = 1 ft). As there are 100 cm to every metre this scale is known as 1:100. If the garden is smaller, then you could use a scale of 2 cm to represent 1 m ($\frac{1}{4}$ in = 1 ft), and this scale is called 1:50. If in doubt as to which scale to use, add up the length and width of the garden from your survey and see if this will fit on your sheet of paper when translated into your preferred scale. As a general rule it will be easiest to use A3-sized paper to prepare the design.

The first job is to stick your sheet of graph paper down onto a smooth clean surface – if you have a drawing board then that will be ideal – using drafting tape or Sellotape. Next stick a sheet of tracing paper over this, making sure that the two sheets are square one with the other. Working with a pencil and in order to make the job of scaling off the measurements from your survey easier, mark each metre square with a number, starting at one and running both up the side and across the bottom of the page. In other words you will have approximately 1–25 running across the page and 1–35 running up the page. This would assume you are working to 1:100 ($\frac{1}{8}$ in = 1 ft) on a sheet of A3 paper. If you are using 1:50 ($\frac{1}{4}$ in = 1 ft) then you will have half the numbers.

Next start to transfer those running measurements you made on the survey to tracing paper and you will see the shape of the house, the boundaries, positions of existing features, manholes and paving start to take shape.

If some of those boundaries were at an angle to the house or if there were trees or other features that you had to fix by 'triangulation', then you should use the following technique.

Select the feature, a tree perhaps, check the survey measurement and extend the pair of

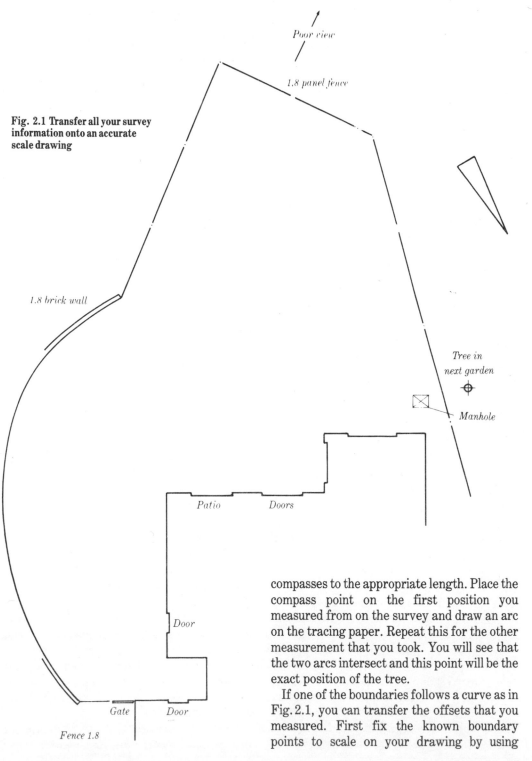

Fig. 2.1 Transfer all your survey information onto an accurate scale drawing

compasses to the appropriate length. Place the compass point on the first position you measured from on the survey and draw an arc on the tracing paper. Repeat this for the other measurement that you took. You will see that the two arcs intersect and this point will be the exact position of the tree.

If one of the boundaries follows a curve as in Fig. 2.1, you can transfer the offsets that you measured. First fix the known boundary points to scale on your drawing by using

21

running measurements or triangulation. Next join these two points by a straight pencil line and divide this pencil line into 1 m intervals as you did in your survey. From each 1 m point, measure off the appropriate distance at right angles to the offset base line and you will find that you have lines of different lengths set in an arc. Once these are joined together the curve of the boundary will be set out to scale. This same technique can be used to reproduce any irregular-shaped object such as a pool or plant bed that you surveyed by the offset method.

Once all the measurements have been transferred you can start to add in all the other survey information, which will include the types of boundary, a good or bad view, a prevailing wind and any other existing features. If there is a slope or number of slopes in the garden, it can be useful to mark these in relation to a fixed point close to the house. A manhole or drain cover outside the back door is often ideal. Surveyors call this a 'datum' point and it can be useful to assume this to be set at 0.0. This will mean that all points lower will be a minus measurement, say − 45 cm (− 18 in) or − 1.8 m (− 6 ft). A slope up from the house would be a plus figure. If you used the simple method of a post, plank and spirit level during the survey (see page 13), then the vertical measurements can be easily added up and plotted in their relative positions on the survey drawing.

Finally don't forget to mark in that North point. It is the single most important piece of information on the plan.

Once the drawing is complete take plenty of photocopies and file the original away for safe keeping — you may need it for more copies later! Before you start on the design — and you are probably wondering if you ever will! — we need to lend some thought to the possible advantages or limitations of the plot and how this will not only determine what you want but how it may fit into the surrounding environment. This will suggest the 'character' and style of the finished composition.

STYLE

Style exists on a number of levels, the two most important of which relate to the kind of garden you wish to create and the way in which that composition co-exists with the surrounding landscape.

Many people ignore the local character of their area and build both houses and gardens that are at odds with traditionally used materials or styles. The perfect example is someone who insists on using water-worn limestone in a suburban rockery set in the heart of Surrey. Not only does this kind of stone look totally out of place but the transport costs in getting it to its destination are virtually prohibitive. A lot of this thinking is down to 'fashion', which is a transient thing and has little to do with style. Another problem, which we have discussed earlier, is the simple fact that we are spoilt for choice when visiting a garden centre. It only needs a good display of a particular feature or group of plants and many people will copy it without first thinking if it will really relate to what they have got back home or in the surrounding area.

The most obvious examples of an indigenous style would be found in a typical Cotswold or Cornish village. Here you would find local stones being used for both buildings and boundary walls, most likely with paving to match. What's more, in such areas there may well be planning conditions that lay down very strict guidelines as to what you can or cannot use. The point is that this kind of environment looks comfortable, simply because all the materials are of a kind and this provides continuity.

Taking the concept a stage further, uniform precast concrete slabs would look quite out of place as the terrace of a fine period home where random York stone would look far better. Those same concrete slabs, however, would look fine leading out from sliding doors in a contemporary house.

What could be worse than when some people reverse this concept and use ghastly white concrete balustrade outside a suburban semi. Not only can they not afford the real thing but they lack the wit to see that this kind of feature needs the scale of a fine house or spacious terrace to set it off. This is the 'Keeping up with the Jones's' syndrome at its least attractive, and is the antithesis of good style.

To be fair, though, these are extremes and most of us live a rather more simple life style in quite modest surroundings. Even so, there are many ways in which we can visually unify both house and garden while at the same time respecting the style of our locality.

UNITY

There are several ways in which we can create or strengthen the link between house and garden and the most obvious of these is to extend the use of materials. A natural choice, where a house is built from brick, is to use the same material in the adjoining terrace or patio areas, either in their entirety or teamed with another material to provide a change of texture. Another example might be to continue the use of a floor material such as slate, stone or quarry tiles from inside to out. If you can do this by keeping the levels virtually the same, and also incorporate a large area of glass, then the visual disruption will be kept to a minimum. Of course this link need not necessarily use 'hard landscape' materials: those same sliding glass doors could have a bold collection of house plants on one side with an adjoining shrub bed to the other. There are even plants, such as *Fatsia japonica* that will thrive both inside and out, which would reinforce the picture.

In many urban housing developments properties are either terraced or built very close together. Here you may find that you have the benefit of a wall that extends the line of the house out into the garden. This might be of brick or concrete blocks but in either case it will give you the option to paint the wall and extend a colour scheme from the rooms inside. In fact the development of 'patio' doors and

large areas of glass has provided endless opportunities to link inside and out, but don't just think in visual terms, there is the sound of rustling grasses and the perfume of fragrant climbers that can be used subtly to enhance our inside living space.

SCALE

As well as considering the use of paving, walls and planting in the immediate area of the house as a link between house and garden, we should also address the matter of scale. So often a house and garden is dwarfed on the one hand by an adjoining larger building, or does itself dominate an empty plot. The question here is how to redress that balance. It could be that a carefully positioned group of trees would help to solve either problem by bringing the garden into scale with its surroundings. Closer to the house raised beds, overhead beams and groups of planting will all help to draw the eye away from the adjoining building and more into scale with the garden. Beams in particular can also be useful for screening overlooking windows and thus reduce the dominance of the building in question. Further away from the house a pergola, screen or summerhouse would do much the same thing.

USING SHAPES

Most garden designs start with the paved areas right outside the house and it makes sense to keep these 'architectural' in shape and character, reinforcing those links that we have just considered. Here you might use a crisp rectangular pattern of paving, raised beds, built-in barbecue, water feature and walling. Many people are afraid of using rectangles in the garden but if they are used with imagination, one shape overlapping or interlocking with another, then the interest and permutations are endless. Once you move down the garden, then you can start to use those strong flowing curves that will naturally provide a feeling of space and movement, and detract from what are almost invariably rectangular boundaries.

These of course are guidelines and it may well be that you can use a rectangular pattern at a distance from the house or indeed for the whole garden. Similarly you can on occasion use curves close to the building. The real point is to make sure that whatever pattern you use sits comfortably in that position.

FORMAL AND INFORMAL STYLES

Both of these are terms that are often misunderstood, being used to describe a mood rather than a specific style.

Symmetry

Formal gardens are usually laid out *symmetrically*, so that one side or end mirrors the other along a central axis. Such a pattern tends to be static and can look at its best surrounding a period building as a set piece. In this case it can echo very effectively the architecture of the house and provide a vital link with it. Smaller formal gardens can be surrounded by walls or hedges, possibly to form a self-contained area or 'room' that would be ideal for a specific theme such as roses or herbs. Although such gardens can be superb if handled correctly, they do not sit comfortably outside most contemporary homes and by their nature are impractical in a family setting.

Asymmetry

On the other hand, asymmetric or more informal styles are rather different, relying on balance rather than reflection, and can be simply explained by imagining weights on either side of a fulcrum. *Equal* weights will need to be set at equal distances from the fulcrum while *unequal* weights will balance with the heavier closest and the lightest furthest away (Fig. 2.2).

If you now think of this principle in terms of garden design it will mean that one feature can

be balanced or offset by another in a different position. In other words a terrace with raised beds and overhead beams to one side of the house could need balancing by a tree or number of trees at the bottom of the garden on the other side. Alternatively, a rock outcrop that forms a major feature in one position might need the counterweight of a summerhouse or arbour elsewhere in the garden. All this is to do with what looks and feels 'right' and stems from the very early design thinking of the Greeks and later Renaissance artists. They used the principle of the 'golden section' which involves the mathematical division of a line or construction of a rectangle in a particularly pleasing visual pattern. Much later Corbusier used these principles in his architecture and Mondrian in his painting.

All this is pure design and can apply equally well to any field — fabrics, wallcoverings, furniture, buildings and so on. Gardens are no different and it is worth remembering that good design is both straightforward and visually honest, which means that you need to forget a lot of the preconceived ideas you see about you or read in books! A great deal of design is to do with pattern making, and the

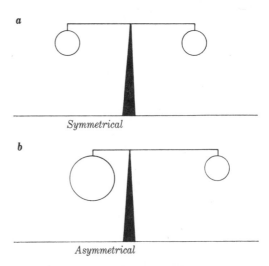

Fig. 2.2 (*a*) Both weights are equal and are positioned at the same distance from fulcrum — both balance. (*b*) Weights are unequal and are positioned at different distances from fulcrum — both balance.

same patterns that are used to make a collage or produce a carpet can be successfully applied to gardens.

PRODUCING THE OUTLINE DESIGN

At last the moment of truth has arrived. All that theory and information gathering can now be put to the best possible use, the creation of a garden.

The first job will be to look at the list of things that you wanted and put these in order of precedence so that a terrace and patio might be (1), lawn for play (2), vegetables (3), pergola (4), and so on. Once this is done you can start to rough in very simply onto one of those copy drawings, what goes where. There is no need for detail at this stage, as we are primarily concerned with allocating space.

While you do this, refer back to the other survey information that you gathered and see if it will modify your decision making. For instance a terrace or patio will usually be best located adjacent to French windows or patio doors, provided the area is in sun for a reasonable part of the day. If the rear of the house faces north on the other hand, and is in shade, then you might well consider the terrace in another sunnier part of the garden, linked back to the house by a path.

Certain garden features relate to one another and because of that can be grouped together. An obvious example might be the dustbins, oil tank and log store, which could all be housed in a simple purpose-built structure close to the back door. Such a store should, if possible, echo the style of the house or perhaps an adjoining fence when similar panels or boards could be used.

The shed or greenhouse could share common ground with the compost and incinerator. All of these would form a working area and will be positioned so that they have plenty of access for barrows, mowers or other large tools.

Play equipment is not always the most visually attractive element in a garden but, again, swing, slide and climbing frame might share common ground, so allocate space accordingly.

Very often front gardens are thought of in quite separate terms to the back but don't think that they *have* to be solely used for cars and paths to the front door. Many front gardens, particularly of houses built before the 1950s, are ample in size and set well back from the road. It can often happen that they are a deal sunnier than the back and I have seen and planned many a layout where sitting areas, pools and even vegetables were well sited in this invaluable area. Of course privacy can be a problem, both from the road and casual callers, but this can usually be solved by the use of screens or planting. The point is that you should have an unblinkered approach to garden design and if something that is commonly positioned to the rear of the house sits more comfortably in the front, then think of doing just that.

The provision of shelter is another vital aspect and you marked the position of prevailing winds and bad views on your survey. Now is the time to rough in just where shelter is needed and you can also start to think whether the screen should take the form of a fence, wall, trellis or planting. In some instances it could be a combination of these.

These days noise is becoming an increasing problem, perhaps from traffic, a nearby factory or even a school. By the planning of contoured banks, supplemented with dense screen planting, the problem can be greatly reduced.

Although we have already thought of positioning the terrace in a sunny position, there are other features that enjoy these conditions. If you are thinking of a pool, rockery or vegetable garden, all three will need to be sited accordingly. Many kinds of planting on the other hand thrive in shade and you might wish to allocate space for such beds in a quite different part of the garden.

By now your plan will have features roughed in at various points, perhaps all over! Don't

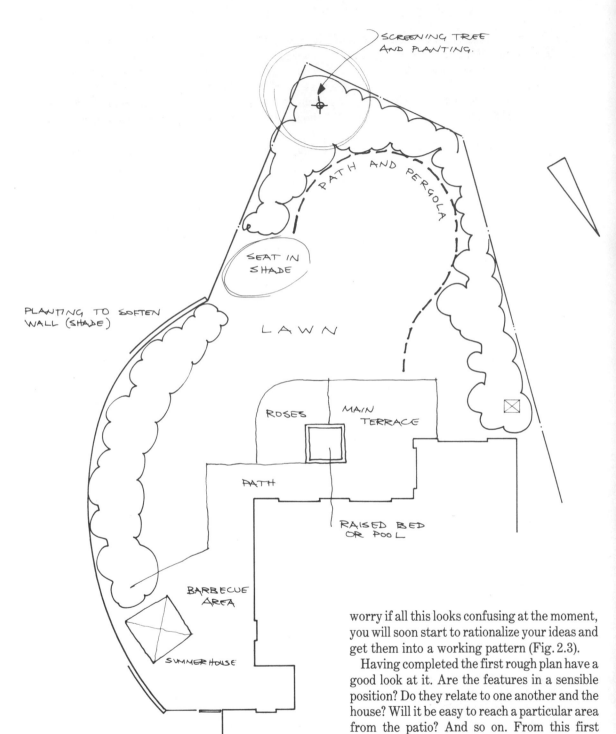

SCREENING TREE AND PLANTING.

PATH AND PERGOLA

SEAT IN SHADE

PLANTING TO SOFTEN WALL (SHADE)

LAWN

ROSES

MAIN TERRACE

PATH

RAISED BED OR POOL

BARBECUE AREA

SUMMER HOUSE

Fig. 2.3 Rough design. Initially just rough out what features you want and where they should go. There is no need to be specific at this stage and you can try as many variations as you like.

worry if all this looks confusing at the moment, you will soon start to rationalize your ideas and get them into a working pattern (Fig. 2.3).

Having completed the first rough plan have a good look at it. Are the features in a sensible position? Do they relate to one another and the house? Will it be easy to reach a particular area from the patio? And so on. From this first rough produce another but never throw any of your efforts away, as they will show you a sensible progression towards the end result.

Remember that although a professional designer works quickly, through experience, you have the advantage of knowing your requirements and the site inside out. You have also got time on your side so don't worry about making decisions too quickly.

PREPARING THE FINISHED DESIGN

Once you and the rest of the family are happy with the rough drawing you can think about producing the finished design. The materials you need are the same as for the preparation of the scale drawing and you will need to stick a sheet of tracing paper down over one of the copies of your scale drawing. Trace out the outline and when this is finished remove the original scale drawing and replace it with a sheet of graph paper, aligning this up with the outline of the house. Remember that you drew the original plan to a set scale of, say, 1:100 (⅛ in = 1 ft) or 1:50 (¼ in = 1 ft). This will mean that a number of squares will equal 1 m or 1 ft on the grid. More importantly, you will also be able to see just how big a paving slab will be. For instance a 600 mm × 600 mm (2 ft × 2 ft) precast concrete slab might measure four or sixteen squares. If you start from the corner of the house you can quickly draw a grid of paving slabs to represent the approximate area of a terrace or patio. Such a grid, being square with the building, will have a direct relationship with it. If you now start to incorporate panels of an alternative surface, such as brick paving or slabs of a different size, you will start to see a pattern emerge. Now is the time to position a barbecue, built-in seating and overhead beams, to cast light shade and possibly screen that bad view. A sandpit might be needed and will be best sited outside the kitchen window. By raising this you could fit a wooden cover to discourage nocturnal visitors and later it could double as a pool or raised bed. Think about the position of lighting and the provision of a power line that might be needed further down the garden for a shed, greenhouse or waterfall.

If there is a slope on the garden you will need to keep the patio flat, incorporating wide generous steps either up or down as you move away from the house.

As far as size is concerned, a terrace should be a minimum of 3.6 m (12 ft) square, approximately the size of an average room inside your home, and remember that it needs to be large enough for all kinds of activities that include sitting and dining, household chores such as the preparation of vegetables or the ironing, play and maintenance of bikes, boats and anything else that takes a growing family's fancy!

USING CURVES IN THE GARDEN

An architectural approach is often ideal close to the house but further down the garden you can afford to loosen the design up, using strong flowing curves to provide a real feeling of space and movement. One of the reasons why many gardens seem to lack any definite purpose is down to the fact that what curves there are seem to be built up from meaningless wiggles and arbitrary lines that simply link one point to another. When you think of using curves, and you can see plenty in the designs I have shown, use a pair of compasses when preparing the scheme and allow one shape to positively sweep into the next. In this way you can build up a real rhythm and this in turn will create a feeling of greater space.

This kind of curve is also easy to set out on the ground by scaling off the appropriate radius point, marking this with a cane, and swinging a line accordingly, marking the curve with a trail of sand. Such curves often look severe on the drawing, but when they are softened by mature planting they look perfect, in contrast to a serpentine wiggle which ends up looking a mess.

POSSIBILITIES WITH LEVELS

There is no doubt that a sloping garden has enormous potential, even though it can be more expensive to build than one on a level site. As a general rule, the smaller the garden the simpler the design needs to be and in this case too many retaining walls and changes of level produce an over-complicated result.

Remember that simplicity is one of the key elements to good garden design and if you do terrace the garden, and it's not always necessary, try to create level platforms of generous size that relate to one another in a positive way.

If you build retaining walls and steps then choose materials that are compatible with other parts of the scheme. If you use brick then match this with raised beds, free-standing walls and paving found elsewhere, which should in turn link with that of the house. Remember that there is nothing worse, or more dangerous, than mean steps; always make them easy going and as wide as possible.

Steps are not the only way up a slope and a ramp can be useful for mowers, barrows and wheeled toys, and also a lot easier for elderly or handicapped people. If the area slopes gently, capitalize on this by designing sweeping lawns and borders, remembering that you can balance the lower side of a garden by using a particular feature such as a summerhouse or arbour or alternatively taller planting and trees.

SURPRISE

Surprise is a major element in garden design, often making an area feel larger than it really is and certainly introducing greater interest. It may be that your plot has a 'dog-leg' shape, in which case part of the garden will be naturally out of sight at any one time. More often than not, however, you may wish to divide the space up by a wing of hedging, walling or planting, trellis or a pergola. All of these will have the effect of breaking a sight line and if you direct feet and eye around or through a feature, you will naturally move from one area or 'garden room' to the next. Very often you can constrict the garden at a certain point with planting

drawing in to either side. This will have the effect of increasing tension as you approach the narrower section and releasing it as you move into the space beyond. This is known as a 'tension point' and is another useful element in building up the overall garden pattern.

LIGHT AND SHADE

The importance of light and shade as an element of garden design has long been recognized in 'bright light' countries and in particular around the Mediterranean. Here the shadows are hard and crisp and if cast across a space by walls or trees make a positive visual division. Of course they also produce shade and this is another important element in a hot climate. In a more temperate climate both the light and shadows are softer, but in many ways this is an asset as it allows one to use shadow in an altogether more gentle way.

By positioning a tree to the south of one side of a long lawn, you will throw a tracery of shadow across the grass. If the tree is placed on that 'golden section' that we discussed earlier, it will look completely right but the shadow will also divide the lawn across this line and by doing so create its own 'tension point'.

Arches and pergolas also cast shade and to walk the length of the latter on a hot summer's day in a cool tunnel away from the sun can be delightful. While sun worship is fine for many of us, some people have the opposite view and in any garden there should always be a place to sit in the shade when the temperature rises to an unacceptable level. This being the case, think of positioning a seat or arbour accordingly; each will act as a focal point in its own right and be well used.

MAKING A MODEL

By now you should be happy with your design, although you will have probably modified it a number of times to reach that end result. Many people, though, have difficulty in reading plans and it can be very useful to build a simple model that will allow you to view the design three dimensionally.

This is a straightforward job and you will need a base of thick card, thinner card to make the features, sellotape or glue, pencil, rubber and felt-tipped pens.

The first thing to do is draw the garden plan *to scale* on the thick card. If the garden slopes and the patio is raised from the rest of the garden cut out the shape, again to scale, attach flaps and glue this to the base board at the appropriate height. Use this same technique to make raised beds, barbecues and built-in seating. Draw in the shapes of beds and borders and show the planting in simple cubes that will indicate the approximate mass. Make simple cardboard trees and stick them in position after moving them about to gauge the best situation.

Colour the model up to indicate paving, lawn, planting and water. If you have a family and you are not too keen on model-making, hand it over to the kids, they will love it!

Once the model is complete you can sight along it so that it would simulate the real eye line when built. Curves tend to look far tighter when viewed three dimensionally and this technique really can bring your design to life.

DIFFERENT SHAPES OF GARDEN

Gardens, like people, are all quite different. In part this is because every person or family has specific requirements and this in turn will mean that the ensuing design reflects those characteristics.

But apart from the question of personality, there is the physical aspect of the site which will include changes of level, views and, most importantly, the shape of the garden itself. The latter will have a strong bearing on the way in which the design is planned and this is an area where the expertise of a professional designer can be of real help. The point of course is that designers meet plots of every conceivable shape and from experience they build up a number of 'tricks of the trade' that allow them to deal with a great variety of problems effectively.

Long narrow gardens

You have only to take a train journey into any of the major cities in the UK to see thousands of long narrow gardens, usually adjoining properties built between the wars or before. You will also almost certainly see just how *not* to deal with them! So many times people emphasize rather than detract from the shape by running a path right down the middle, flanking this with a border and washing line and then planting a narrow strip right around the perimeter. The effect is not unlike dressing a tall man in a pin stripe suit.

In fact, such a garden is the ideal subject for creating a series of 'rooms', each having a different purpose or theme and each divided from the next in a variety of ways. My own garden (Fig. 2.4) is just one of these, being some 100 m (330 ft) long and barely 10 m (33 ft) wide.

It usually makes sense if the rear of the house is sunny to plan a paved area large enough for sitting and dining and general relaxation. Here you can build a barbecue, raised beds and pool, as well as soften the hard landscape with planting. If the garden slopes then you will have the opportunity of creating broad generous steps into the next room, which could be given over to lawn and play. This could be screened from the next area by a wing of planting and this space could be given over to vegetables, utility and fruit.

In this way we have broken the space up into three separate areas and by so doing created a far greater feeling of space.

Square gardens

Where long narrow gardens have positive movement up and down their length, square gardens are static. This makes them one of the most difficult shapes to handle as you have to find a way of introducing directional emphasis.

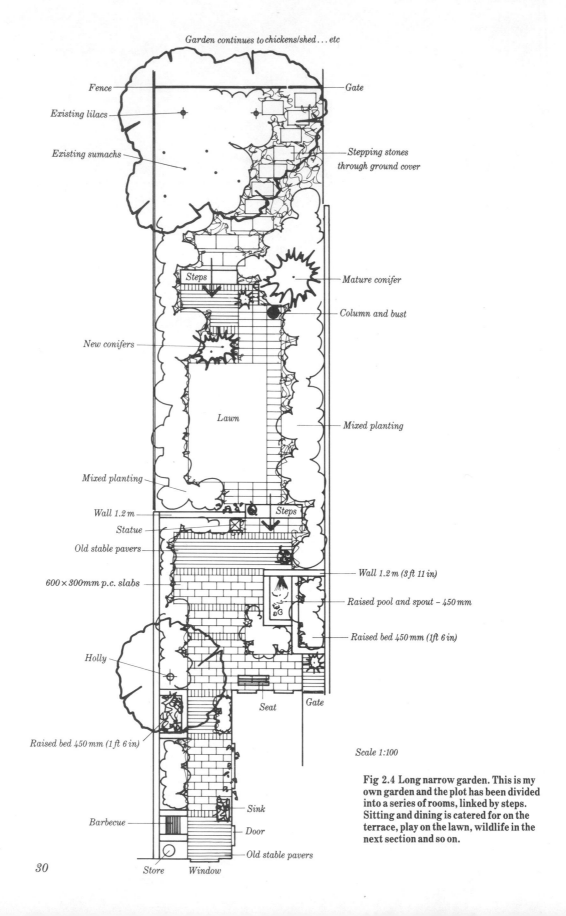

Garden continues to chickens/shed . . . etc

Fence

Gate

Existing lilacs

Existing sumachs

Stepping stones through ground cover

Steps

Mature conifer

Column and bust

New conifers

Lawn

Mixed planting

Mixed planting

Wall 1.2 m

Steps

Statue

Old stable pavers

Wall 1.2 m (3 ft 11 in)

600 × 300 mm p.c. slabs

Raised pool and spout – 450 mm

Raised bed 450 mm (1ft 6 in)

Holly

Raised bed 450 mm (1 ft 6 in)

Seat

Gate

Scale 1:100

Sink

Barbecue

Door

Old stable pavers

Fig 2.4 Long narrow garden. This is my own garden and the plot has been divided into a series of rooms, linked by steps. Sitting and dining is catered for on the terrace, play on the lawn, wildlife in the next section and so on.

Store   *Window*

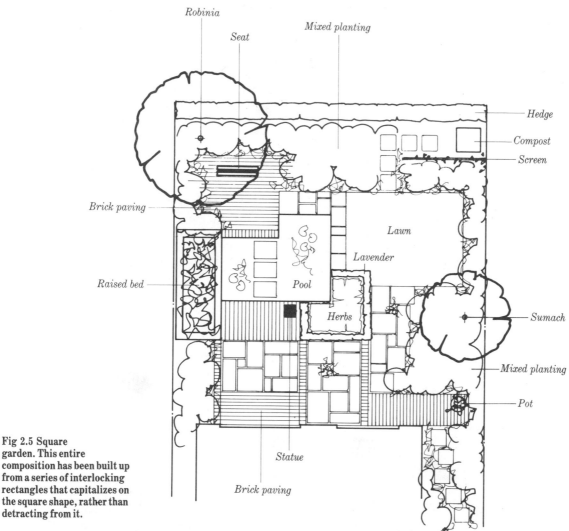

Robinia

Seat

Mixed planting

Hedge

Compost

Screen

Brick paving

Lawn

Lavender

Raised bed

Pool

Herbs

Sumach

Mixed planting

Pot

Statue

Brick paving

Fig 2.5 Square garden. This entire composition has been built up from a series of interlocking rectangles that capitalizes on the square shape, rather than detracting from it.

One way is to turn the whole design at an angle to the house of, say, 45°. This does two things. Firstly, it leads the eye away from the rectangularity of the plot and it brings diagonal lines into play. In geometric terms a diagonal is the longest line across a rectangle and by using this in a garden you immediately produce a feeling of greater space. The layout of the terrace or patio can be approached in just the same way as a paved area square to the house but a path leading away from it can sweep around the garden and set up an entirely different kind of pattern.

A second way to treat a square plot is to emphasize the inherent shape by building up a composition that is based on a series of interlocking rectangles (Fig. 2.5). This is a far more architectural approach but no less valid and it can look particularly handsome in an urban situation where hard landscaping can play a major role.

'Dog-leg'

'Dog-leg' gardens are the ones that disappear around a corner and by their nature can be full of mystery and surprise. The trouble is that many people fail to realize their full potential

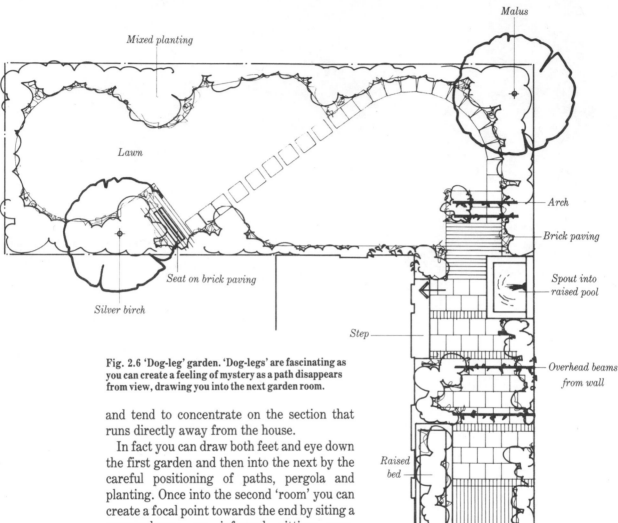

Malus

Mixed planting

Lawn

Arch

Brick paving

Spout into raised pool

Seat on brick paving

Step

Silver birch

Overhead beams from wall

Raised bed

Fig. 2.6 'Dog-leg' garden. 'Dog-legs' are fascinating as you can create a feeling of mystery as a path disappears from view, drawing you into the next garden room.

Brick paving

and tend to concentrate on the section that runs directly away from the house.

In fact you can draw both feet and eye down the first garden and then into the next by the careful positioning of paths, pergola and planting. Once into the second 'room' you can create a focal point towards the end by siting a summerhouse or informal sitting area, perhaps framed by an arbour. Such gardens (Fig. 2.6) are 'secret' and it can be a real asset for both children and grown ups to be able to get away by themselves for a while. Of course the area can also be host to any number of features that you wish to hide from the house, but if you do this don't just dump them down, make them a worthwhile part of the overall composition.

Triangular

Triangular gardens are not uncommon and are often formed where a house sits on a corner plot with the boundaries splayed in at an angle.

The main problem is preventing the eye from focusing on the apex of the triangle and the best way to do this is by disguising it in some way and then emphasizing some other feature that can become a major focal point (Fig. 2.7). A common mistake is to run borders in line with the boundaries so that they too come together at an apex. A more effective aproach would be to sweep the planting past in a strong flowing curve, perhaps utilizing the awkward space to house utility features such as shed, compost and incinerator.

Front gardens

While many people lavish time, money and a good deal of hard work on the back garden, the area to the front often tends to get entirely overlooked. This is a great pity as not only can it have real potential but it is the first point of contact for visitors and it can tell them a good deal about you before you even open the door!

Where the back garden is primarily for leisure and the cultivation of plants and possibly vegetables, the front is for access and the pace of life will be a good deal quicker here. Car-parking space will be a major element and

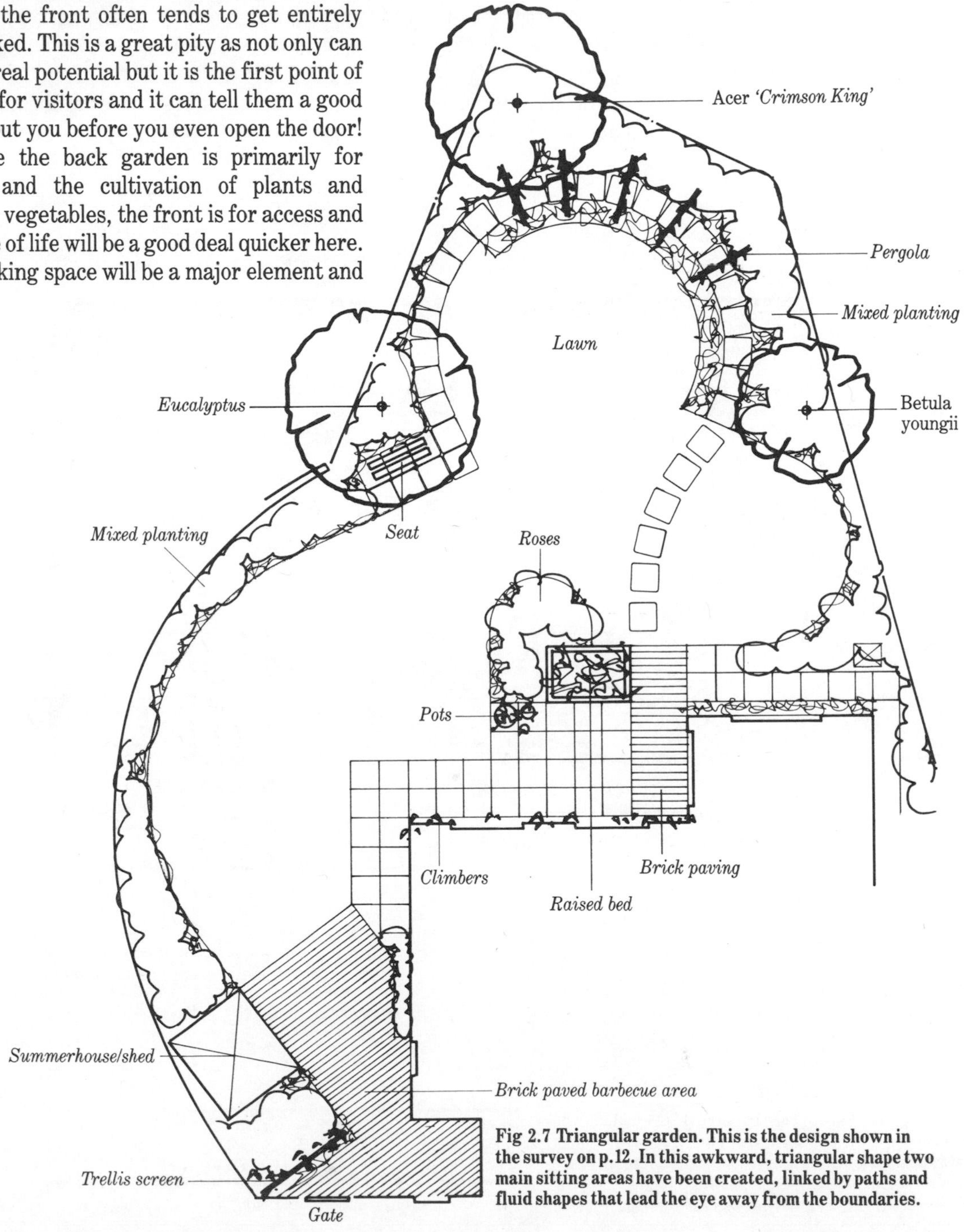

Acer *'Crimson King'*

Pergola

Mixed planting

Lawn

Eucalyptus

Betula youngii

Mixed planting

Seat

Roses

Pots

Climbers

Brick paving

Raised bed

Summerhouse/shed

Brick paved barbecue area

Fig 2.7 Triangular garden. This is the design shown in the survey on p.12. In this awkward, triangular shape two main sitting areas have been created, linked by paths and fluid shapes that lead the eye away from the boundaries.

Trellis screen

Gate

you will probably have to plan hardstanding areas as well as paths to the front door. As the space is usually smaller, there is a greater need for strength of purpose and simplicity. It makes sense to use a limited number of materials and have shared access for cars and people instead of a separate path and drive that will tend to 'chop up' the space. If the garden is established and you need to modify the pattern, try to match materials where possible. It may well be that the area is just too small to plan a lawn as well as the other features. Many of the most successful front gardens are a sensible combination of paving and planting that direct people in a subtle way towards the main entrance. Don't think that certain features are the sole domain of the back garden. Water in particular can look

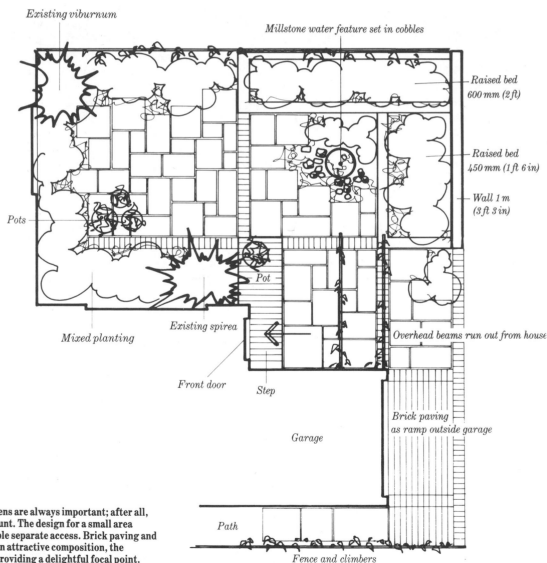

Existing viburnum

Millstone water feature set in cobbles

Raised bed 600 mm (2 ft)

Raised bed 450 mm (1 ft 6 in)

Wall 1 m (3 ft 3 in)

Pots

Pot

Mixed planting

Existing spirea

Overhead beams run out from house

Front door

Step

Brick paving as ramp outside garage

Garage

Path

Fence and climbers

Fig. 2.8 Front gardens are always important; after all, first impressions count. The design for a small area allows cars and people separate access. Brick paving and random slabs form an attractive composition, the millstone fountain providing a delightful focal point.

terrific in a raised pool close to the front door, as can arches or, if space permits, a pergola that will emphasize a main pedestrian route (Fig. 2.8).

When thinking of planting, pay particular attention to trees. Front gardens are usually small and the folly of planting a weeping willow or other forest species will be all too apparent in 10 years' time, both in terms of visual displeasure and possible structural damage.

Roof gardens

Of all gardens those on the roof are perhaps most charismatic. True, there are not too many of them but if you are lucky enough to own one then you have a Mary Poppins world at your fingertips.

Although the possibilities are considerable, things will not be easy up here with high winds and extremes of temperatures that can be the death of tender planting. Add to this difficult access, structural problems and the provision of irrigation and you will need a good degree of determination to create a garden at all.

The first necessity is safety and you will need to be sure that the roof is strong enough to take any planned structures or planting. As a general rule the edges of the area will be the strongest, together with any load-bearing columns or walls set below. If in any doubt whatsoever enlist the help of a qualified surveyor or architect; his fee will be well worth it and you can rest easy without the ghastly picture of a ton of wet compost arriving in your sitting-room unexpectedly!

Shelter is obviously important and here a permeable screen that will filter the wind will often be far more effective than a solid barrier. Toughened plate glass is an obvious choice and if you use this then fit it in panels of modest size with gaps between, so that the wind has a chance to pass through.

The floor will be another possible consideration and the existing surface can be anything from a bituminized felt to lightweight tiles. Neither of these look particularly attractive but conventional paving would in most instances be far too heavy.

Timber decking can be an excellent alternative and can be laid so that water can drain away underneath. Plastic turf, that can look dreadful at ground level, may be fine up here too, as it can be laid like carpet to fit easily any shape and solves that problem of irrigation! Plants will need to be tough and resistant to a degree of drought as things can dry up very quickly on a rooftop. Many Mediterranean plants are ideal and these can be grown either in raised beds containing lightweight compost or in a collection of pots or tubs. If you use the latter, make the containers as large as possible and try to stick to a specific theme of, say, terracotta or timber.

Always be careful where you position pots and never place them on a parapet where they could fall and cause injury below.

In all probability it will be hot at times and so a combination of overhead beams and awnings can be useful to break the force of the sun. White paintwork and furniture should be avoided at all costs because of the inevitable glare; cream or a pastel colour will be far more sympathetic.

As you can see, all the gardens we have looked at and discussed have quite different characteristics and need handling in quite different ways. The design process to achieve that end is the same however and if you follow the sequence that I have laid out, then you will have created a unique composition.

PREPARING THE GARDEN

We have already seen that the planning of a garden is very similar to planning any other room in the home. In terms of construction and 'do it yourself' most people are only too aware that to achieve a worthwhile result sound preparation is absolutely vital. Usually this initial work, hard though it is, will be covered up by the more spectacular finish and exactly the same principle applies to garden construction.

In other words there are very few short cuts to a good job and each one of these needs to be carefully planned if you are going to enjoy the finished composition to the full.

USING DIFFERENT LEVELS

In the last chapter we saw that the introduction of different levels can be a positive asset, helping to screen a bad view or soak up the noise of an adjoining road or playground. The creation of gentle contours can also add immeasurably to the interest of a flat site and this can be achieved either by the 'cut and fill' process, that takes soil from one place to form a dip and deposits it elsewhere to form a mound, or by the importation of soil to add to the existing ground level in selected places.

Apart from this, changes of level have other effects on the overall design.

a) A garden that slopes up from the house or a particular viewpoint tends to foreshorten the view and in consequence the garden looks smaller than it really is. With a slope down from the house the opposite occurs and the space can feel larger.

The steeper the slope the more obvious this is and in extreme cases it produces both visual and physical instability. You can counter the visual problem, at least to an extent, by using

trees and planting as a counterpoint on the lowest side or area. A rather better but more expensive solution would be to create a series of more level platforms, each one linked by generous steps. In an extreme situation, and I have done this a number of times, the whole garden can become a series of steps or platforms, each having a different purpose or theme. In general design terms, remember what we have said about keeping things 'architectural' close to the house and less formal as you move away. In other words you might use stone or brick steps and retaining walls to link with the adjoining building, and softly planted or grassed banks further away. In the more distant parts of the garden the levels can and almost certainly should return to their natural gradient so that they can blend into the surrounding landform and minimize the problem of merging into any adjoining gardens.

b) Retaining walls, and in particular steps, tend to focus attention and create a 'tension point' that can be an important factor in the design. Think about the position and the relationship of these features before they are constructed and make the most of them.

c) If you introduce steep banks or retaining walls into an area that previously had a steady slope or cross fall, you will find that shadows can be cast on the northern side. This could have an adverse effect on existing planting and should obviously be taken into account when planning new planting.

LOOKING AT THE EFFECT OF DIFFERENT LEVELS

If you wish to create level changes, have a good look around you before you start. Many historic gardens use levels in a dramatic and entirely practical way. The great landscape parks of the eighteenth century used subtle landshaping to perfection and often reinforced existing slopes and dips. Lakes were dug and the spoil used to create hillocks; trees were planted on rising ground to disguise boundaries, and the ha-ha (Fig. 3.1) eliminated the need for a fence and allowed park and garden to run together.

The lesson to be learnt is that level changes were handled with sensitivity and echoed rather than contrasted with the landscape.

In direct contrast the gardens at Dartington Hall, in Devon, are made up from a series of dramatic terraces and lead down to an arena which has sharply chiselled grass banks that spell out high visual drama.

In other words, if you stick to a definite theme or style in your own garden you are far more likely to succeed in terms of honest design.

EROSION

Another factor to bear in mind when creating slopes is the effect that erosion will have on them. In this country this will be almost entirely caused by water run-off, and the steeper the bank the more serious this problem becomes. The real solution is to get any bank planted or grassed as quickly as possible so that roots can bind the surface together and prevent topsoil being washed away. In extreme circumstances you can buy specialized plastic mesh that is fixed into the bank with long pegs, to stabilize the ground until planting takes over.

CUT AND FILL

The process of excavating soil from one part of the garden and depositing it in another is called 'cut and fill' and can be used not only when you construct level platforms that have been formed on a slope (Fig. 3.2) but also to create those contours that we talked about earlier.

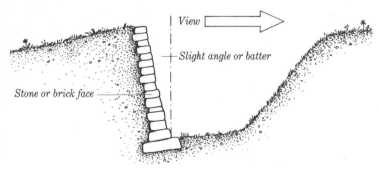

Fig. 3.1 The ha-ha allows park and garden to become a single visual entity.

When digging or moving soil, remember to keep the fertile topsoil separate from the infertile subsoil. It can be useful to make a stack of topsoil but don't leave it there for more than about six months as it can deteriorate and lose its fertility. The depths of topsoil necessary for different kinds of planting, and how to recognize it, is covered later in the section on 'soft landscape'.

Depending on the scale of the job, you can either carry out soil shifting by hand, with a spade and barrow (which was precisely the method used by Capability Brown), or you can hire one of those small mechanical diggers that are narrow enough to fit through an average side gate. It would be fair to say however that although these machines can be terrific in the hands of an expert and carry out a vast amount of work, they are not so accommodating for the first-time user. In my experience it takes two or three days to become even moderately competent and by then it's time to take it back!

Like most heavy jobs around the garden you don't want to try and do it all at once, so a

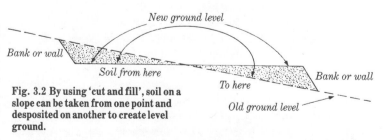

Fig. 3.2 By using 'cut and fill', soil on a slope can be taken from one point and desposited on another to create level ground.

project of any size needs to be tackled over several months, a bit at a time.

Another consideration is the simple fact that the cost of hiring a machine will be far more than if you do the job by hand; the real trade off is in the possible time saved.

A final thought is maintenance. A steeply sloping bank is obviously difficult to mow and if it meets the bottom or top of the bank at an acute angle there will be a section completely beyond the reach of the blades. In other words you will need to feather off any slope so that it marries gently into its surroundings.

CONTOUR DRAWINGS

You can with sufficient practice, or if you have a particularly good eye, plan and construct mounds and banks by eye. In order to be accurate and to be able to estimate the amount of topsoil you will need, the preparation of contour drawings will be a real help.

For the sake of simplicity these should be prepared on a separate copy of the scaled site plan. If you are plotting existing contours and you have already estimated levels in the garden by the method which we explained earlier (see page 13), all that is necessary is to join points of equal height by a line running in the appropriate direction. This will be a contour line and such lines are ideally plotted at 75 cm (2½ ft) or 1 m (3¼ ft) vertical distances. If you are designing mounds then you will need to draw a series of lines, one inside another, that join all points of equal height (Fig. 3.3a). Remember that distance will make a smaller mound close to the house look equal in size to a larger one further away and this is an important design consideration.

Slopes should always be gentle and a maximum gradient should be no more than about 30°. This means that the higher the mound, the greater the area it will cover, and for this reason there will be no necessity to construct soaring peaks that would in any event look totally wrong in a small garden. In fact a lack of space can be a real problem when

contouring ground but it can be a useful idea to hold the back of a mound in position with a retaining wall which will help maximize the space you have available (Fig. 3.3b). A flat contour drawing can be hard to visualize but if you plot a section from this, as shown earlier in Fig. 3.3a, then you will have a much better idea of how things will look. This same section, or a number of sections taken across the mound, will also help you estimate the amount of soil needed for the job.

The way to do this is to see that within contour lines there is a column of soil reaching down to the ground. Within the 50 cm (20 in) contour line that measures perhaps 150 cm × 150 cm (5 ft × 5 ft) on the contour plan, this column is 50 cm (20 in) high. To estimate the volume, multiply 150 cm by 150 cm to find the area (2.25 m²) and multiply this by the depth (50 cm) = $.5 \times 2.25 = 1.125$ m³. Repeat the operation for the ground within each contour line and add the totals together.

When constructing a mound, first peg out

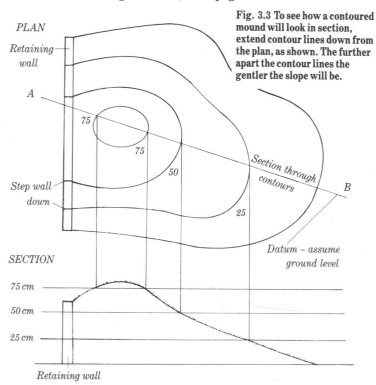

Fig. 3.3 To see how a contoured mound will look in section, extend contour lines down from the plan, as shown. The further apart the contour lines the gentler the slope will be.

PLAN

Retaining wall

A

75

75

50

Step wall down

Section through contours

B

25

Datum – assume ground level

SECTION

75 cm

50 cm

25 cm

Retaining wall

the shape working from your scale drawing. This is the time to make any final adjustments and if you use sand or canes the line can be easily moved slightly.

Build up the contours a layer at a time and tread each down firmly to consolidate the ground as you go. Check the work as it progresses against your contour plan and section and, when complete, rake the ground to remove any large stones and leave a suitable tilth for planting or grass.

Remember that in the final analysis the feature has to look and 'feel' right. There is no substitute for this and a good job done by eye may well turn out slightly differently than planned and be the better for it.

LEVELS AROUND TREES

If you alter the levels around mature planting, for instance around trees or shrubs, you will affect the latter by changing the height of the water table. Trees in particular are susceptible to this as water is gathered by the capillary rootlets that have grown at a quite specific level in the ground. If you need to build up the levels in the vicinity of a tree then you should build a wall around the trunk to the same level as the new ground and at least 1 m (3¼ ft) away from the trunk. This in effect will look like a well and it should always be kept clear of rubbish and debris. If the ground is heavy then it can be useful to lay a circular pattern of radiating drains to remove excess water; these can be connected to a ring drain that in turn connects into a land drain system. If the roots are only partially covered on one side of the tree then it can be sufficient to sweep the retaining wall around the higher side, horizontal drains allowing water to seep away through the face of the wall (Fig. 3.4). Some hardwood trees are particularly susceptible to changes of level and water table, oak and beech being good examples. In this case it can be useful to incorporate vertical tile drains, running down from the surface, to connect into the horizontal ring pattern.

If the ground level is to be reduced rather than built up then a platform should be left around the tree, held in position by either a retaining wall or bank. In general the root spread of a tree is roughly the same as the canopy above so any platform should conform to this outer limit — otherwise the capillary moisture-gathering roots, which tend to be at the end of the main roots, will be severed and death will result.

Smaller trees, shrubs and hardy perennials can usually be safely moved in the winter dormant season and replanted as soon as possible at the new ground level. They should be well staked, watered and fed.

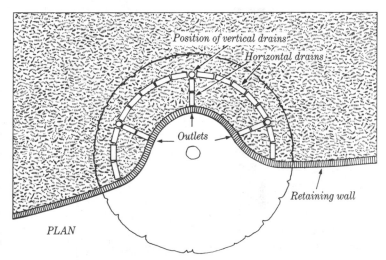

Fig. 3.4 **Be careful to minimize disturbance around mature trees. Good drainage around the roots, coupled with aeration, is essential.**

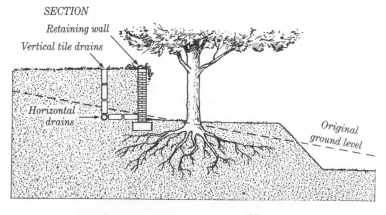

DRAINAGE

Problems with drainage are all too common in gardens but before immediately thinking of installing an expensive drainage system, which will treat the symptom and not the cause, just consider the latter.

Very often, on a new housing estate, the ground may have been compacted by site traffic and simply covered with a layer of topsoil. This is easily investigated by digging a few sample holes. Should this be the case then you have every right to ask the developer to deeply rotovate the ground for you and in most instances this will resolve the problem for good.

In some gardens, particularly if they are on a sloping site, water can be a problem coming through from a higher level. This can often be cured by running a drain around that part of the garden that adjoins the slope and this will have the effect of lowering the water table and prevent waterlogging (Fig. 3.5). With any kind of drain, however, there is always the problem

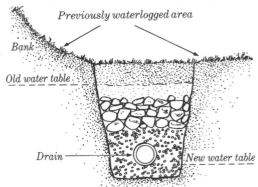

Fig. 3.5 By inserting a drain at the bottom of a bank you can effectively lower a water table and improve a previously wet area.

of where the water you have collected should go. It is hardly neighbourly to redirect it into the next door plot! The answer in most cases will be to construct a soakaway.

This is simply a pit approximately 1 m (3¼ ft) square and 1.8 m (6 ft) deep (Fig. 3.6). Strip the area of any topsoil and stack this neatly for re-use. Excavate the subsoil and preferably get

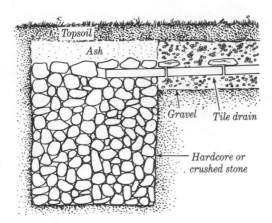

Fig. 3.6 Land drains should discharge into a soakaway if no other suitable outfall is available.

rid of it off site by hiring a skip. Fill the hole with clean hardcore or crushed stone and top this with a 15 cm (6 in) layer of clean ash or a sheet of 'terram', which looks and feels like a layer of felt. Both of these are permeable but will prevent soil from clogging the hardcore below. Replace the topsoil and finally turf over the area.

French drains

This is the simplest type of drain to construct and consists of a ditch filled with hardcore, topped with ash, terram or brushwood and then backfilled with soil. It is a quick and easy method but has a limited lifespan as it becomes clogged after a few years.

Tile and perforated plastic drains

Tile drains or perforated plastic drains are the most comprehensive type of drainage system and are either laid in straight lines or in a 'herringbone' pattern that will collect water over a larger area (Fig. 3.7). The depth at which you lay the drains, and the distance they are spaced, depends on the soil (Table 3.1).

Drains should run at a shallow gradient or 'fall' of approximately 1 in 200 and should run either into a ditch or a sufficiently large soakaway. Traditionally clay pipes were used

TABLE 3.1 SPACING AND DEPTH OF DRAINS		
SOIL TYPE	SPACING OF DRAINS	APPROXIMATE DEPTH
CLAY	4.55 m	60 cm
SAND	9.15 m	105 cm
LOAM	8.20 m	90 cm

and although this is still common practice, flexible plastic perforated pipes can also be used. Bed the pipes on an 8 cm (3 in) layer of gravel in trenches approximately 60–105 cm (2–3½ ft) deep, depending on the type of ground. If using tile drains, place broken crocks over the joints and then backfill with a layer of gravel 23 cm (9 in) deep. Finally fill the trench with topsoil, bringing this slightly proud of the surface to allow for natural settlement.

As we said earlier, poor drainage is often indicative of poor soil condition. The addition of organic material such as well rotted compost, leaf mould or manure will be of great help, as will ash and sand, which although without nutrient value, will act as a conditioning agent.

CULTIVATION

The reason we cultivate ground is to allow plants to develop quickly and healthily while at the same time being able to add fertilizers and various soil conditioners that in turn aid growth.

The best time to cultivate ground is in the autumn so that the frost and rain of winter can break the ground down into a friable tilth. Don't dig when the ground is solid with frost or waterlogged; it's not only much harder work, it can also damage the soil structure through over-compaction.

There are a number of ways to cultivate ground, the most straightforward of which is single digging.

Single digging

To carry out this method the ground is cultivated in strips (Fig. 3.8). First mark out the area involved and start by turning over the first trench to a spade's depth and removing this to a point where the final trench will finish. If you want to incorporate compost or manure then this can be forked into the bottom of the trench, turning the next strip over on top of it. While digging, remove all perennial weeds such as docks and bindweed. Work across the whole area, throwing the soil forward into the previously formed trench. The final job will be to replace the soil from the first trench into the last. As with all heavy jobs in the garden, take it easy and do a section at a time; there is no point in straining your back by trying to complete the whole job in a day.

Double digging

Double digging is hard labour and really only needs to be undertaken if the ground is virgin or there is a hard 'pan' of soil that is preventing adequate drainage. The job is similar initially to single digging in that the first spit of soil is removed and stacked for re-use at the end. The difference is that the trench so formed is then turned over to a further full spade's depth with plenty of manure or compost added. The second trench is turned into the first and the sequence repeated.

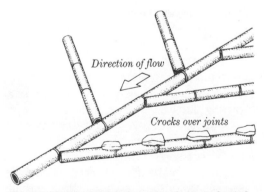

Direction of flow

Crocks over joints

Fig. 3.7 A herringbone drain can use clay or perforated plastic pipes and should discharge either into a ditch or soakaway.

Fig. 3.8 (*a*) The stages of single digging: this should be done every autumn. (*b*) The stages of double digging: this need only be carried out every few years. (*c*) The stages of deep-bed digging: work from a plank to avoid compressing the soil.

Both the above methods are suitable for vegetable growing and the cultivation of borders, but a method known as the 'deep bed system' is becoming increasingly popular for the former.

Deep bed system

This involves double digging as described above, incorporating ample organic material, but to avoid compacting the ground subsequently — and this is vital to the success of the system — the area is divided into narrow beds approximately 1 m (3¼ ft) wide. These can then be worked either from slightly raised boards laid across the beds or from narrow paths. This method means that you should only have to dig the beds every six or seven years, a real saving in effort. When the crops have been lifted, lightly cultivate the ground and add more organic matter.

Clean, sharp tools are vital for digging. Keep

them that way and when not in use they should be lightly oiled and kept in a dry place.

FERTILIZERS AND CONDITIONERS

Organic

We have already seen that the addition of organic material such as compost and well rotted manure is a real bonus both to condition the soil and provide fertility. For this reason a good compost heap or bin is an invaluable asset in any garden. Many materials make compost, including kitchen waste, prunings, flower-heads, annual (not perennial) weeds and lawn mowings, as long as you have not used a hormone weedkiller.

As far as conditioning is concerned, organic materials can also be used and these include seaweed, wood chips and sawdust. Spent hops and spent mushroom compost are also good conditioners but have a low nutrient value. A good all round organic fertilizer is blood fish and bone.

Inorganic

Inorganic fertilizers and conditioners can also be excellent but do not support the bacteria that keep the ground 'alive'. For this reason they are a supplement to be used with organics and not just by themselves.

Good conditioners on a heavy soil include ash and sharp sand.

Inorganic fertilizers are faster to react than organics and contain the three elements, nitrogen (N), phosphorus (P), and potassium (K). You will see this stated on the bottle or pack and always work to the recommended dosages, as applications that are too heavy can be detrimental.

Growmore is an excellent all round inorganic fertilizer.

IRRIGATION

Water is essential to plant growth and although we assume that rain is freely available, particularly in the UK, it is easy to forget that the country is also susceptible to drought. In addition, quite large areas of the garden can be denied water owing to the effect of being in the lee of an overhanging roof, wall or other feature.

Whether a lack of rain is therefore due to climate or a 'rain shadow', the provision of irrigation in some form will be vital.

In its simplest and cheapest form this will take the form of a suitably lagged outside tap, isolated by a stop cock, together with a hose that can preferably be wound in and out on a reel. In this case a watering can is essential to reach parts that the hose cannot. A can is also useful when you don't wish to unravel the hose.

A step up from the basic hose would be one of the excellent snap-together hose systems that have easy to fit connectors and a variety of spray heads, some of which can be loaded with liquid fertilizer that is diluted in the spray.

Perforated hosepipes used to be popular and are still available, but have been largely superseded by a wide range of oscillating and rotary sprinklers. Good water pressure is essential for these, otherwise they cover very little area.

The most modern systems are becoming increasingly automated and range from simple snap-together flexible pipes that can be laid through your borders and are operated by a simple timer fitted to your outside tap, to complex and fully fitted systems that are installed by experts to serve every part of the garden. These will include pop-up heads for lawns, trickle feeds for borders and drip feeds in specific areas that can include pots and hanging baskets. Computers are used to automate the whole operation and this will probably operate through a special header tank and feed lines, where fertilizer can again be incorporated.

Whatever your irrigation method, check with the local authority over licensing requirements, even for a sprinkler.

CONCLUSION

Everything we have talked about in this and the preceding chapters is concerned with planning and preparation. All of these jobs are straightforward and all are fun, provided you go about them in a logical sequence and take your time.

I'm sometimes asked to design gardens for disabled people, as though they are some kind of special case. It's true that some people have severe problems of mobility and reach, but remember that a garden is an individual and personal thing and most compositions, if planned with sensitivity, can be tailored to any requirement without looking in any way contrived.

Your garden is all about *you*, so now that you are aware of just what you want, let's see how to construct and plant it.

PART II

CHAPTER 4

WALLS AND FENCES

BOUNDARIES

The original purpose of a boundary was to provide protection from both enemies and wild animals. The need for enclosure changed over the centuries with the development of animal

Fig. 4.1 (*a*) Screening a bad view.
(*b*) Screening utility areas.
(*c*) Internal screens used to partition the garden.

husbandry and the subsequent necessity to keep animals within fields. Modern day living has given rise to a greater and more varied need for enclosure. Before deciding *how* you want to screen your garden, it is worth considering *why* you need to do so.

Security

Enclosure is still needed to provide security, although not to the extent of days gone by; today internal security is often more important, such as keeping young children and pets within the garden.

Privacy

Enclosure for privacy helps stop one's property being overlooked by both neighbours and passers-by. The anti-gossip panel (one single-solid fence panel) which is constructed adjacent to house walls, is an indication of the need for a sense of privacy today, due to the close proximity of modern housing.

Screening

It may be necessary to provide a wall or fence to screen a bad view (Fig. 4.1*a*); or conversely screening may be used effectively by either creating a window in a fence or an archway in a wall, to frame a good view. Internal divisions can also be used for screening utility areas (such as dustbins and compost — Fig. 4.1*b*), for privacy around sitting areas in overlooked gardens, and to add interest by separating parts of the garden to create a sense of mystery (Fig. 4.1*c*).

Environment

Enclosure may be used to provide a baffle against the sound of traffic or an adjacent factory, as well as to provide shelter against prevailing winds and adverse weather.

Demarcation

A fence may be used simply to mark the line of a property boundary; here posts may be used, often only at each end of the boundary if a clear line can be sighted between them (Fig. 4.2). It is unfortunate that Man finds it necessary to define his own area, particularly on well thought out, open-plan landscapes where the effect is all too often spoilt by dwarf conifers poorly spaced along the boundaries, splitting up what would otherwise be flowing areas of grass.

Choice of boundary

It has been shown that there are many factors which create the need for enclosure but there are also many points to consider when choosing the type of boundary. Design is a major influence on all garden construction and it is important that the type and style of boundary remains compatible with both the garden and house it adjoins. It would be incongruous, for example, to use natural stone walling around the garden of a modern brick house.

The locality of a property should also be considered and regional materials should be used for boundaries wherever possible. Even though gardens can be created as sanctuaries from the outside world, their boundaries form a common link with that world and therefore consideration should be given to those on the other side. It may be that the property lies in an area where natural stone is quarried and this is often reflected in local buildings and walls. To select a walling stone from another region on grounds of personal preference would not only be insensitive but probably prohibitively expensive, which leads us on to the next major influence affecting the choice of material.

Fig. 4.2 Marker posts used to delineate boundary lines.

Cost

In general, walling tends to be more expensive than fencing, especially if the job is to be contracted out, as the cost of labour will obviously have to be considered as well as that of the materials. This is particularly relevant with stone, which is far slower to work with than brick and also far more expensive. There is no doubt, however, that if the cost can be met, a well planned and constructed wall will set off the appearance of a property and offer many long term advantages over fencing.

WALLS OR FENCES?

Advantages of walls

1. Appearance — walls provide unity with both the property and locality and will usually enhance the appearance of both.

2. Privacy — walls create a solid barrier.

3. Screening — walls not only provide a visual barrier but also a far better sound barrier than fencing. They create a microclimate too by retaining warmth, and therefore less hardy plants may be grown against them.

4. Strength — well constructed walls are inherently stronger than fences and their life should be far longer, requiring little maintenance.

Disadvantages of walls

1. Cost — walls are more expensive than fences.

2. Construction — walling is a far slower and more complicated process than fencing as it includes the excavation of footings, the construction of piers and the laying of coping stones.

Advantages of fencing

1. Cost — fences are normally cheaper than walling.

2. Construction — fencing is a much simpler and speedier operation than walling.

3. Internal screens — fencing may be used to provide screens within the garden, usually of the trellis type which allows a partial view through it. When combined with planting, it gives a restricted view with a far softer appearance than a wall. The fence or trellis screen also allows a through passage of air, thus preventing turbulence on the leeward side and may be useful as a perimeter screen for exposed sites.

Disadvantages of fencing

1. Strength — fences are not as strong as walling and do not give such a good barrier to sound.

2. Maintenance — fences need regular maintenance and do not have such a long life as walling due to weathering. Posts may need renewing or supporting and, in time, the entire fence may have to be replaced.

THE LAW

It is most important to be aware of the law when considering the construction of walls or fences, as boundaries give rise to more disputes between neighbours than anything else. When replacing a wall or fence, it can normally be assumed that the existing construction followed the boundary line, although in some cases one neighbour may have gained some extra ground over the years. The deeds of the house should show the demarcation of boundary lines although, on occasions, the scale of the plan may be unrealistic, thus making it impossible to check the exact line.

The deeds should also indicate ownership of the boundary and this is normally indicated by the letter 'T' pointing towards the property to which the boundary belongs; if the boundary has joint ownership there will be 'T's pointing both ways and in this case it may be that the neighbours could share the cost of the new wall or fence.

It is important to check with the local authority any regulations regarding the height of boundary walls and fences before beginning construction.

In certain areas, permission will not only be required to construct an enclosure but the actual specification may also have to be agreed with the local authority, particularly if it adjoins a 'listed' building. Boundary enclosures that are adjacent to roads are of particular importance, for if they are over a certain height they may well impede sight lines and therefore be a danger to traffic.

The normal height limit for boundary fencing not requiring planning permission is approximately 1.8 m (6 ft). For peace of mind, it is always worth checking the legal position because if regulations are broken and walls or fences are erected without the necessary permission, you may not only be asked to take the construction down but may also incur fines during the time that it remains standing. It may be that retrospective permission is granted, often on the condition that planting is carried out as soon as possible to soften the initial starkness, but it is always far better to obtain approval at the outset.

The importance of consulting neighbours cannot be stressed too highly. It is essential to consider how the appearance of your neighbour's garden may be changed by any new structure, which may look good on your side but may turn your neighbour's narrow garden into a cold and shaded box. In this case, you may consider starting the fence line with a solid panel fence and then continuing the line with an open trellis or chain link fence, which will soon be made private with additional planting (Fig. 4.3).

Fences and walls often have a good or 'fair' face, for example close-boarded fences will have posts and arris rails on one side with flush feather-edge boards on the fair side, which is commonly set facing away from the owner's property, thus indicating ownership and offering the best view of the fence to the neighbour. This may also be the case with free-standing walls supported by reinforcing piers which may be set on the owner's side of the boundary, again offering the fair face to the neighbour (Fig. 4.4). It is also important to check whether any of your neighbour's plants will be affected by the new structure and to ensure that disturbance during construction is kept to an acceptable minimum. Ideally, consult your neighbour at all stages.

Fig. 4.3 (*a*) Ensure that your new fence or wall does not turn your neighbour's garden into a cold, shaded box. (*b*) A fence line starting with a solid panel and continuing with open trellis is more acceptable.

Fig. 4.4 Close board fence belonging to property *A*. Brick wall belonging to property *B*.

GENERAL CONSTRUCTION

Walls

There are several principles which should be followed for every type of wall, with the most important principle being that the wall is well planned and solidly built to fulfil its intended purpose. It should also be borne in mind that no matter how well the wall is constructed above ground level, it will not last long if it is built on inadequate footings.

Setting out

The line of an intended wall is transferred from the plan to the ground by positioning a peg at each end of the line. A nail is knocked into the top of each peg and a building line stretched taut between the two nails, indicating the centre of the proposed wall.

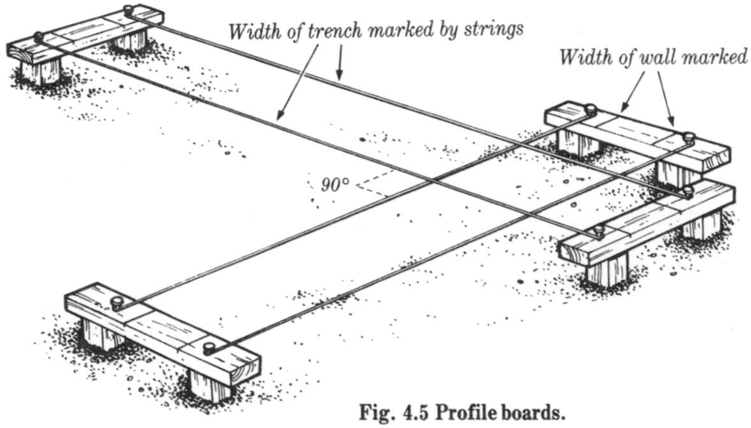

Width of trench marked by strings

Width of wall marked

90°

Fig. 4.5 Profile boards.

Profile boards, which are simple planks set level with a spirit level and fixed between two short pegs, are set approximately 1 m (3¼ ft) outside both ends of the building line. The line is then extended over the profile board and its position marked with a nail where it crosses the board. Measurements can be extended either side of this point to indicate the width of the wall, the width of the footing and the width of the excavation trench if that is to be different from the width of the footing. Further building lines can then be extended between the two profile boards and secured to nails where they cross those boards (Fig. 4.5). Sand may be dribbled along those lines so that it falls onto the ground and marks the lines of excavation. The strings should then be removed so as not to impede excavation, but the nails should remain in position so that the lines can easily be reattached when you start to build the wall.

Footings

The footings or foundation carries and spreads the load of the wall, and therefore its size and depth are influenced by both the height and width of the proposed wall as well as the type of soil. An insufficient depth of footings sitting on unstable soil can result in movement and the subsequent cracking of a wall. Generally, the foundation depth of walls of not more than 2.5 m (8 ft 4 in) must extend to 50 cm (20 in) below ground level, and in any case into firm subsoil. The width of the footings should be twice that of the wall and the top of the footings should extend to 15 cm (6 in) below ground level (two courses of brickwork) (Fig. 4.6). Walls that are half the above height and less may have a reduced depth and thickness of footings extending down to 30 cm (1 ft) below ground level, with the finished height of footings still at 15 cm (6 in) below ground level.

Placing footings

The trench for the footings is excavated to the right depth, as described above, which should be checked continually along the length of the trench to ensure that the correct amount of soil is excavated. This may be checked on short lengths of walling by holding a spirit level across the trench and measuring down with a steel tape. On longer runs, levelling equipment should be used with an assistant holding the levelling staff at various points along the trench.

It is important that, if the adjacent ground level is to change, all measurements are taken from a datum peg, which indicates the proposed finished ground level, and that measurements are not merely taken from the existing ground level (Fig. 4.7). When excavating the trench, ensure that the sides remain vertical and that no loose material is left in the trench bottom; also try not to dig out too much as it will then be necessary to backfill with concrete, which is not only expensive but hard work to mix.

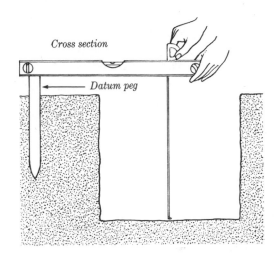

Fig. 4.7 Check trench depth from adjacent datum peg.

Pegs are then driven into the bottom of the trench to indicate the finished level of concrete and are placed level with each other at convenient intervals, which may be equal to the length of a straight edge. Concrete is next poured into the trench and roughly spread out across the pegs (Fig. 4.8) with a shovel prior to working it down into all the corners and levelling across the pegs with a straight edge, before finally smoothing the surface of the concrete with the back of a shovel or wooden float.

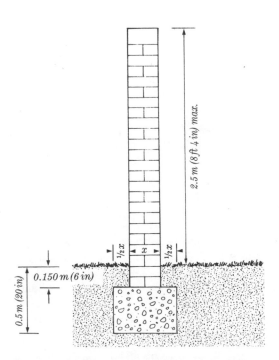

Fig. 4.6 Standard footings for free-standing walls of not more than 2.5 m (8 ft 4 in).

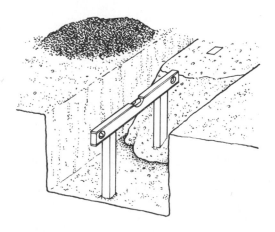

Fig. 4.8 Placing concrete footings.

49

Stepped foundation

On sloping ground it may be necessary to create footings which step up with the rise of the ground in order to avoid excessive digging out at the top end of a slope. The steps in the footing are planned by marking positions along the length of the building line equal to multiples of the building unit (bricks or concrete blocks), with the depth of the step being equivalent to the depth of the building unit. This will normally be two courses of brickwork, i.e. 15 cm (6 in) in the case of brick walls (Fig. 4.9). A simple board fixed with two pegs is put in as temporary shuttering to hold the concrete at the end of the stepped section and it is essential that any stepped footing overlaps the lower level, thus providing a continuous concrete strip.

Concrete footings should not be visible above ground level at any point and should normally run 15 cm (6 in) below finished ground level.

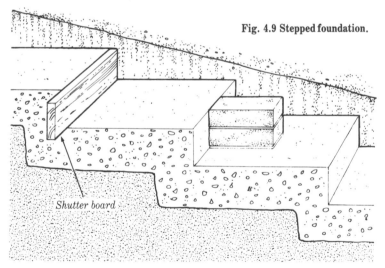

Fig. 4.9 Stepped foundation.

Shutter board

Concrete

Concrete is a self-setting mixture of cement, aggregate and water and is an extremely useful material in construction, not only for footings and foundations, but also for paved areas, especially when given a decorative finish. The cement normally comes in 50 kg (110 lb) bags and should be kept dry in a shed or garage if possible; or, if it is necessary to store it outside, it should stand on a board and be covered with polythene. Aggregate is best obtained as 'washed all in ballast' which is a mix of fine and coarse aggregate and is far more convenient to use than buying and mixing the separate grades. Water should be taken from a clean supply, which is especially important when mixing mortars for visible concrete surfaces, as any algae present may discolour the surface.

When mixing concrete, careful site planning is essential so as to avoid wasted time and energy. Store all materials close together with the concrete mixer next to the loose materials so that they may be shovelled straight into it, avoiding the need for unnecessary barrow runs. Cleanliness and site tidiness are all important so lay large polythene sheets on the ground with a sheet of plywood for materials over the top of them, standing the concrete mixer next to the materials, also on the ply sheet.

Never mix concrete directly on any paved surface unless it is old concrete that is to be broken up and removed, but, in particular, never mix up on tarmac as the stain will be permanent.

It is essential to gauge the materials carefully within the concrete mix, especially where visual appearance is important, as variations in the mix will alter the surface colour and texture. A mix of 1 part cement to 6 parts of 'all in ballast' is suitable for most concrete work and this means that one shovelful of cement should be used with six shovelfuls of ballast. Where the surface appearance of the concrete is more important, then a bucket will be a far more accurate gauge than a shovelful.

Important pointers

1. Mix up only enough concrete that can be used within one hour as it will then become

unworkable. Do not be tempted to water it down after this time, for although it will make the concrete easier to move, it will also make a far weaker mix. It is sensible to stick with small batches of concrete as overestimated amounts can easily be wasted.

2. If the concrete mix is left standing for any period of time, either in the barrow or on the mixing board, it will tend to settle with the water rising to the top, so turn it every so often with a shovel to ensure a consistent mix before using.

3. Concrete footings should always be covered over with polythene in order to keep moisture in and prevent the concrete drying out before it has fully hardened or cured; concrete should also be covered over if there is any likelihood of frost.

Mixing by hand

1. Always mix up concrete on a large board over a polythene sheet and never straight on to the polythene. It is not only annoying when the shovel continually snags on the polythene but the sheet is also likely to be torn by the shovel, allowing the water in the mix to drain through.

2. The materials should be gauged out into a pile on the board with enough mix to do two batches (i.e. for a mix of 1:6 then two shovelfuls of cement will be used together with 12 shovelfuls of ballast).

3. Mix the pile of materials thoroughly, turning the outside of the pile into the middle until an even colour has been produced throughout.

4. The pile should then be made to look like a small volcano and water is added to the 'crater'. The mix should be turned into the water, moving the pile round and round until all the concrete has been made workable. Try not to overdo the water, which will only weaken the concrete and make a sloppy mix that is difficult to use.

Mixing by machine

1. Ensure that plenty of coverings are placed both under and around the mixer as the concrete will tend to splash.

2. Put in approximately half a bucket of water followed by half the amount of ballast (six shovelfuls for two batches of a 1:6 mix) and mix thoroughly.

3. Add two shovelfuls of cement and mix until an even colour has been achieved, then add the remainder of the ballast and continue mixing.

4. Carefully add more water to give an even consistency which is not too sloppy.

5. Tip the concrete out into a barrow.

6. Switch off the mixer before scraping out the excess concrete with a shovel or brick trowel. *Never* try and do this when the mixer is running.

7. When all the mixing is finished, clean out the machine thoroughly, removing as much material as possible by trowel first before letting broken bricks turn around in the drum with a little water, which will help clean out the last of the mix. Tip the remains into a barrow before finally cleaning out with water. It is not good enough simply to throw a bucket of water into a dirty mixer as you will only end up with a drum full of slurry which is impossible to get rid of.

Ready-mixed concrete

This is the sensible solution for large runs of concrete footings or other concreting jobs, as not only will the exact mix required be consistent throughout the batch but it will also save an enormous amount of work. Concrete is delivered in a large truck so ensure that there is suitable access before ordering a load, and also ensure that everything is ready before the concrete arrives. If access to the site is good, it may be possible to pour the concrete straight from the lorry into the footings, so make sure that all the trenches are dug out ready. Taking delivery of ready-mixed concrete is not a one-man job as drivers will not wait while you barrow concrete to the far end of the garden, so if there are not enough assistants to move the concrete, it will have to be stockpiled. Be sure to have enough coverings and boards laid out and keep the pile of concrete covered with sheeting so that it does not dry out too quickly.

Take great care when estimating volumes for ready-mixed concrete so as not to be left with an excess.

Mortar

This is the mix that fills the gaps between bricks or blocks (and is also the bedding material for paving) consisting of cement, soft sand (for brickwork), water and a plasticizing agent. Hydrated lime can be purchased as a plasticizer but has the disadvantage of being unpleasant to use; also, as only small quantities are necessary, it is often wasteful on all but large jobs. Liquid plasticizers, which are far more convenient to use, entrap air bubbles into the mix and make it more workable.

It is particularly important to gauge the batches of cement and sand carefully in motrar as inconsistencies may not only affect the strength of the mix but may lead to colour variations throughout the wall. Additional colouring-pigment powders may be used to tone the mortar with the colour of a particular brick. Only small amounts of the powder are necessary to have a dramatic effect on the colour of the mortar so it is important to read the instructions carefully; it is also a useful exercise, when using mortar pigments, to build a separate small section of brickwork before starting on the actual wall, in order to see how the finished structure will look.

Mixing mortar
Mortar may be mixed by hand or machine along the same lines and following the same guidelines as set out for concrete mixing, with a suitable mix for most brickwork being one part cement to six parts soft sand, with additional plasticizer. Sharp sand may form part of the sand content when used for laying natural stone as in this instance a firmer mix and gritty joint may be called for. It should not be assumed that a high cement content in the mix will make for a stronger wall. Indeed too strong a mix may, in fact, cause the wall to crack. The mortar should be mixed thoroughly and only in sufficient quantity for one or two hours' work, especially in dry weather as after that time the mortar will become unworkable. The mix should end up like soft butter; if it is made too sloppy it will be difficult to handle and will spoil the face of the wall, and if the mix is too stiff then bricks cannot be bedded evenly and may end up being broken. By observing professional bricklayers you will note how the mortar flows off the trowel and the bricks are merely positioned against a building line with a gentle tap. Only when heavy blocks or stones are to be laid, which will compress mortar more than bricks, may a slightly stiffer mix be used.

WALLS

Free-standing walls

These are walls that are not attached to any other structure and are used to meet the various requirements of security, privacy, screening and shelter as set out at the beginning of this chapter.

It is essential that both suitable materials and sound construction techniques are used as this type of wall is more vulnerable to the elements; also, consider the factors set out under 'Choice of boundary' (see page 45).

Brick
Brick is probably the most commonly used material for free-standing walls as it forms an obvious link between brick-built houses and the garden; if the walling bricks are durable, they may also be used for paving and so the feeling of continuity is enhanced.

There is such an enormous variety of brick colours available that, even if the house brick is unsuitable for garden walling, there will be a good chance of finding another suitable brick that blends well with the house. Brick walls generally look good in most garden settings, especially when warm colours are used. The type of brick and method of wall construction will be influenced by both the style of the house and of the garden.

Brick walls have a practical benefit in that bricks take in the sun's heat during the day and release it slowly, making a good microclimate for fruit trees and other more tender plants.

TYPES OF BRICK

Most bricks are manufactured from clay but there is also a type known as calcium silicate bricks which are made from hydrated lime and sand. These are very pale and not suitable for external use.

There is a wide choice of clay bricks available in varied hues depending on what part of the country the clay was selected from and the length of time for which it was fired.

Be careful not to select bricks on their appearance alone as they come under several categories, some of which will be unsuitable for free-standing walls.

Common bricks These bricks may actually have good qualities of strength and weather resistance but do not have a good visual appearance and are therefore used for internal and underground building works. They are not suitable for garden walling.

Facing bricks This section comprises bricks that are manufactured for their appearance and are consequently available in a wide range of colours and finishes but also in varied strengths. This is the category of bricks that includes those used for external house walls, and whilst the temptation may be to extend the use of the house brick into the garden, it is imperative to check its quality first, as many are not suitable for exposed conditions. Many of these bricks have only one attractive, often textured, side which means that a half-brick wall constructed of such bricks can have only one good or fair face. This particular brick would obviously require good water-proofing characteristics of both coping stones and damp proof courses to keep the brick dry and prevent damage to its face by frost action. It would be an unsuitable brick to use for brick paving and therefore a degree of continuity would be lost if paving bricks were also required in the design.

The most suitable and attractive facing bricks for garden walls are normally those that are the same colours throughout, especially those known as 'multi-coloured' which are particularly attractive and are also well fired. They have a low water absorption capacity and offer greater frost resistance, thus making them a suitable brick for both paving and walling.

Engineering bricks These are very dense bricks, having been fired at high temperatures with a very low water absorption rate, together with a high load-bearing capacity. All these factors make the brick extremely useful and functional for below-ground work and for the formation of a damp proof course in a free-standing wall. The stark, often glossed finish of the brick is seldom sympathetic to garden walling, except in the most architectural situations, but it may be used to provide a crisp coping brick when it may offer a visual link to other areas of the garden where it may be used as a smart paving trim or for step treads.

QUALITY

Bricks are graded as follows for their suitability for different uses:

Internal These bricks are only suitable for internal work.

Ordinary These bricks may be used for outside work if they can be kept fairly dry by the use of copings and damp proof membranes, and when not used in exposed positions.

Specials These bricks are suited to extremes of conditions, i.e. in exposed areas and when in contact with wet ground.

Damp proof course

The purpose of a damp proof course, or d.p.c., is to keep moisture from penetrating a brick wall as excessive moisture can lead to frost damage on certain bricks, or the growth of algae on walls in very damp and exposed conditions. Efflorescence (the appearance of white salts on the face of brickwork) occurs with certain types of bricks due to damp, as salts are drawn up through the wall and left as a white powder on the face. Although unsightly, this is nothing to be concerned about and the powdery deposit will disappear in due course.

Walls become damp due to ground water rising into the brickwork which may be prevented by introducing a damp proof course into the lower courses of the brick wall. Coping stones, together with a damp proof membrane, may be incorporated in free-standing walls in order to prevent rain water settling on the top of the wall and subsequently saturating it. The damp proof course must therefore be an impervious barrier which is commonly formed by two courses of engineering bricks introduced at the bottom of the wall. Alternatively, two courses of half-lapped slates are set into the brick wall at 15 cm (6 in) above ground level. A strong mortar of 1:3 should be used to bed the damp proof course in both cases (Fig. 4.10).

Flexible strip damp proof courses such as bituminous felt should be avoided as adhesion is unsatisfactory, causing a weakness which may lead to the wall blowing over in a strong wind. It is, however, not always necessary to employ damp proof courses for garden walls if frost resistant bricks are used.

Expansion joints

Walls may move slightly along their length due to moisture expansion in clay bricks and to expansion and contraction with temperature changes. Any free-standing wall that is longer than 10 m (33 ft) requires an open gap movement joint of approximately 1–1.2 cm (⅜–½ in), which should extend from the top to the bottom of the wall and should not be overlapped at any place by either coping stones nor damp proof courses. Where total privacy is required, the joint may be sealed with an acrylic mastic, or alternatively a treated expansion joint board may be used.

Bonding

This is the term given to the interlocking pattern of bricks which, by staggering the vertical joints, subsequently spreads the load throughout the wall, increases strength, and also creates visual interest. There are three common bonds.

STRETCHER BOND

This is the staggering of bricks in alternate courses by half the brick length. This is the type of bond which is commonly seen in house walls today and must also be used in the construction of half-brick walls; if a full brick wall is required then two skins of stretcher

Fig. 4.10 Damp proof courses

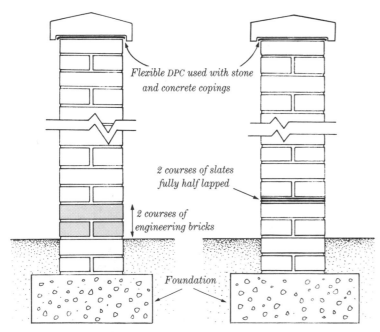

Flexible DPC used with stone and concrete copings

2 courses of slates fully half lapped

2 courses of engineering bricks

Foundation

bond brickwork must be constructed side by side and tied together with metal brick ties (Fig. 4.11).

ENGLISH BOND

This is used to construct a full-brick width wall and is stronger than two skins of stretcher bond; it comprises alternate rows of stretcher and header courses, requiring a half-header brick or 'queen closer' inserted on each header course to maintain the staggered bond. A variation is English garden wall bond which has a header course after approximately every third stretcher course (Fig. 4.12).

FLEMISH BOND

This is again used for full-brick width walls and is more attractive and less monotonous than English bond, incorporating alternate stret-

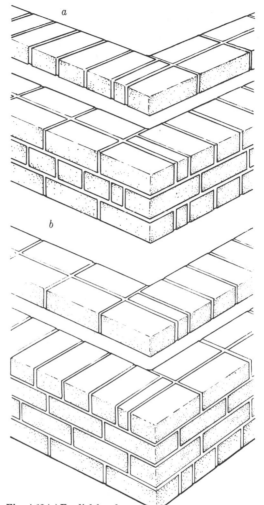

Fig. 4.12 (*a*) English bond
(*b*) English garden-wall bond.

cher and header bricks in every course with the use of 'queen closers' again, to maintain the bond pattern. Flemish wall bond is a variation in which one header brick alternates with every three stretcher bricks within each course (Fig. 4.13).

Pointing

'Pointing' is the technical term for the process of filling in joints with mortar, for instance when making good old walls. 'Jointing', on the other hand, is the finish given to joints during construction. The joints are finished to ensure

Fig. 4.11 (*a*) Full brick wall constructed from two skins of stretcher bond.

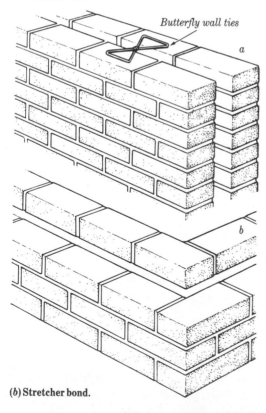

(*b*) Stretcher bond.

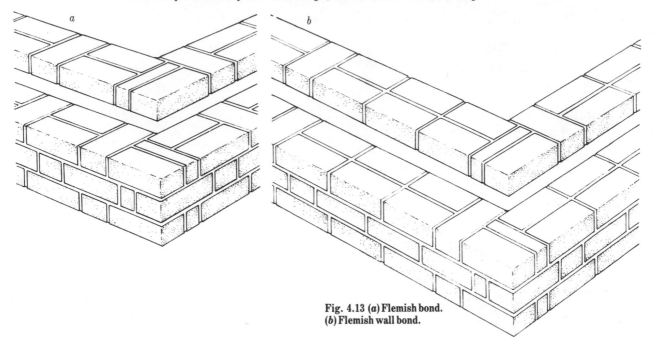

Fig. 4.13 (*a*) Flemish bond.
(*b*) Flemish wall bond.

a smooth, water tight joint and to enhance the appearance of the wall. The usual finishes (Fig. 4.14) are as follows:

Flush Mortar is scraped off level with the face of the brickwork.

Weathered The joint is filled and then a pointing trowel is run along the mortar to produce an angled joint.

Rubbed A rounded piece of steel, hosepipe, or old bucket handle is rubbed along the joint.

Recessed A piece of wood with a square end is used for raking out the joint to approximately 0.5 cm (³⁄₁₆ in) which creates an interesting shadow line and also sets off the brick. This type of joint should be avoided on bricks that are susceptible to frost damage, as water may become trapped in the joint.

Joints should be finished periodically during construction before the mortar becomes too stiff. Rub the vertical joints first and then the horizontal joints, filling any gaps in with mortar before rubbing smooth.

Coping

Copings are used to protect walls from vertical penetration of water and to shed water from the face of the brickwork, therefore preventing, in certain cases, any subsequent damage from frost action. There are purpose-made coping units available in stone, concrete and metal, as well as clay, of the size to allow an overhang of approximately 4 cm (1½ in) which incorporates a drip channel or 'throating' to keep water clear from the face of the wall. Certain stone copings, e.g. sand

Fig. 4.14 Jointing.
(*a*) Flush.
(*b*) Weathered.
(*c*) Rubbed.
(*d*) Recessed.

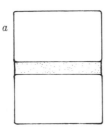

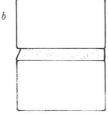

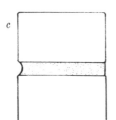

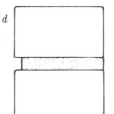

stone, and also concrete copings, may shrink slightly, allowing small cracks to form between each stone which let moisture through and so necessitates the use of a damp proof membrane (Fig. 4.15).

Two courses of tile creasing may be bedded under a brick on edge coping to create not only an impervious barrier but also a projection which will throw off rain water from the face of the wall. Coping units are often replaced with a simple brick on edge to give a lighter and more pleasing appearance, but it is not always possible to reuse the main walling brick as it may be too soft for a coping. A damp proof membrane must be incorporated at one course below the coping brick to prevent saturation; and it should not be cut back flush to the face of the wall as no water would be thrown off,

of both house and garden, whilst the height and thickness of the wall will be dictated by its proposed use and position within the garden.

When planning the height and thickness of the wall it is important to consider how they will affect the overall strength of the wall; it is unfortunate today that strength is often sacrificed for economy in the case of free-standing walls and many boundary walls on modern housing estates give testimony to this fact. False economy in the construction of free-standing walls will, at worst, put the safety of passers-by at risk and, at best, diminish the appearance of a wall; in general it does not cost much more to construct a safe wall.

Ideally, half-brick walls should be kept below a height of 90 cm (3 ft) and even at that height they should be supported by half-brick piers at

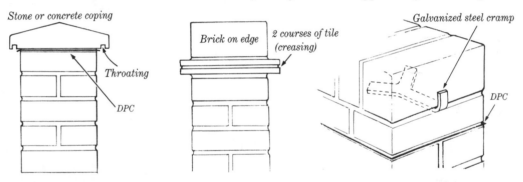

Fig. 4.15 Copings for brick walls.

resulting in the possible staining of the wall face. A strong mortar of 1:3 should be used for laying coping bricks and a galvanized steel clamp may be bedded at the stop end of a brick on edge coping to help hold in the end bricks, although this is not a visually pleasing finish.

Building a brick wall

DESIGN

It is important to consider the design and construction of a wall carefully. Thought must be given to the style, height and thickness of the wall as well as to the type of brick before starting work. The design and type of brick that is to be used may be affected by the style

every 1.8 m (6 ft) centres. Above that height it is advisable, and more pleasing in appearance, to utilize full-brick walls (21.5 cm/9 in) which may be constructed up to 2 m (6½ ft) in sheltered positions without reinforcing piers; or alternatively with an integral pier which is twice the thickness of the wall and spaced at 2.7 m (9 ft) centres, when used in more exposed positions (Fig. 4.16).

LAYING BRICKS

When setting out footings (see page 48), it is important to ensure that an allowance has been made for the piers as they are an integral part of the construction from the foundation to

Fig. 4.16 Design of brick walls.

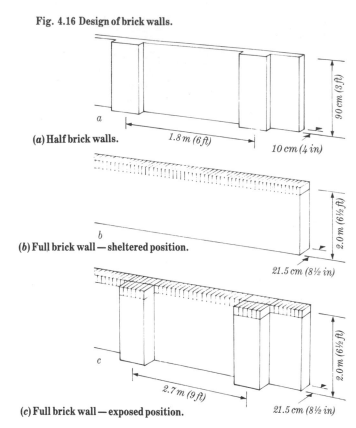

(a) Half brick walls.

a

1.8 m (6 ft)

90 cm (3 ft)

10 cm (4 in)

(b) Full brick wall — sheltered position.

b

2.0 m (6½ ft)

21.5 cm (8½ in)

(c) Full brick wall — exposed position.

c

2.7 m (9 ft)

2.0 m (6½ ft)

21.5 cm (8½ in)

the top of the wall. Mortar should be spread along the centre of the footing onto which the building line — indicating the face of the wall — will have been transferred.

If the proposed wall has a corner, then the corner lines should be marked out using a set square, and the brick corners (or 'quoins') should be constructed first, building out in two directions, checking the horizontal and vertical levels continually with a spirit level. If the wall is to step at any point then it is important that all construction starts at the lowest end of the wall. It is also important that the brick bonding is kept consistent and that joints do not begin to creep; ensure also that a 'queen closer' is laid when laying English and Flemish bond and that any damp proof course is inserted if necessary. A further check must be made by holding a spirit level diagonally across the face of the wall to be certain that the brickwork is

not beginning to belly outwards, in which case any bricks that are out of true should be gently tapped back with a trowel (Fig. 4.17).

Once the ends or corners are built up to a height of no more than 1 m (3¼ ft), the main face of the wall may be infilled by laying brick courses up against a building line which is pulled taut between the two ends of the wall and held in position by brick pins. The taut brick line is held a fraction from the face of the brickwork by a piece of paper known as a 'tingle'.

When laying bricks, mortar is spread with the brick trowel along the line of bricks prior to running the trowel through the mortar, thus creating a depression on to which the bricks may then be bedded. The bricks are then buttered with mortar at one end and tapped gently into place; there should be no need for the use of a spirit level at this stage apart from an occasional check for bellying along the face of the brick wall. The wall should be kept clean all the way to the top by scraping off any excess mortar with a trowel and reusing it to bed subsequent bricks. All coping courses, whether special units or brick on edge, are also laid to a string line along one face and tapped gently down into position.

The brick joints should be finished to give the desired effect as previously described and all brickwork should be covered over to protect it at the end of the day.

Concrete blocks

There is no doubt that concrete blocks are both underrated and underused in landscape construction, probably due to the assumption that they will create a sombre appearance. This is a pity as there are many advantages to their use. The blocks are either solid or hollow and are available in different sizes, one of the most common being the 45 cm × 21.5 cm × 21.5 cm (18 in × 9 in × 9 in) hollow block which allows for the provision of reinforcing rods and therefore makes it particularly suitable for use in retaining walls. One of the main advantages of using such a block is that it is equivalent in size

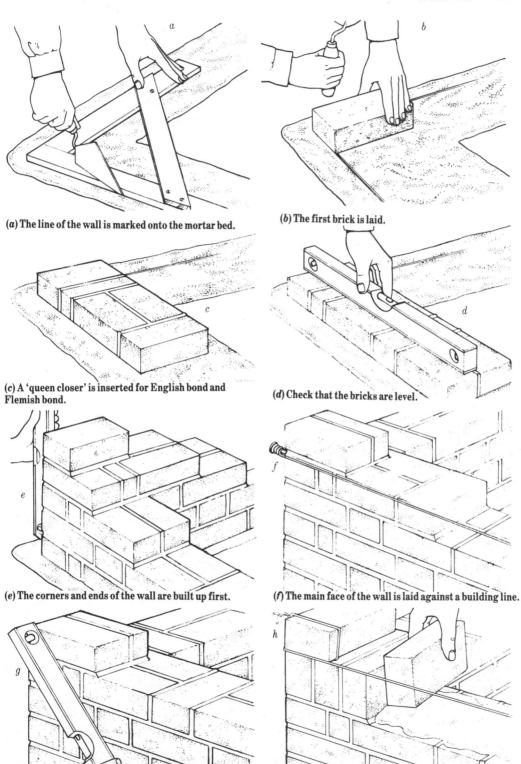

Fig. 4.17 Laying bricks.

(*a*) The line of the wall is marked onto the mortar bed.

(*b*) The first brick is laid.

(*c*) A 'queen closer' is inserted for English bond and Flemish bond.

(*d*) Check that the bricks are level.

(*e*) The corners and ends of the wall are built up first.

(*f*) The main face of the wall is laid against a building line.

(*g*) Check that the wall does not 'belly' outwards.

(*h*) Brick on edge coping.

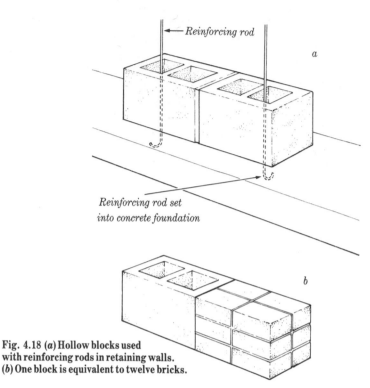

Fig. 4.18 (*a*) Hollow blocks used with reinforcing rods in retaining walls. (*b*) One block is equivalent to twelve bricks.

Concrete blocks are also relatively easy to lay and a wall of a good height may be constructed fairly quickly. Smooth or 'fair-faced' blocks can be colour-washed with masonry paint or rendered prior to painting if the blocks are rough and, when given a simple brick on edge coping, the effect can be crisp and architectural.

The disadvantages of concrete blocks are that as a large unit they must be sympathetically used in garden design so as not to look disproportionate when used in a low wall; they are also extremely heavy and their rough corners necessitate the wearing of gloves.

The construction detail of block walls can be linked to brickwork in the respect that blocks should be bonded, normally in stretcher bond. Any other bond would require half blocks to be cut throughout the wall which is both time consuming and unnecessary whereas stretcher bond only requires half blocks to be cut at the ends of a wall, or alternatively three courses of bricks may be laid here which looks attractive and avoids block cutting completely (Fig. 4.19).

to 12 bricks and is therefore far more economical in terms of material cost and also labour in both laying and mixing mortar (Fig. 4.18).

The general guidelines for height and strength of concrete block walls are the same as for brickwork, i.e. walls that are 21.5 cm (9 in) thick may be built up to a height of 2 m (6½ ft) in sheltered areas, without the need for reinforcing piers. Blocks should be laid in the same manner as described under 'Brickwork' (see page 57), building up the corners of the walls first before laying the infill blocks against a string line. A slightly stiffer mortar mix may be used for laying blocks as they are heavier units than bricks; the mortar joints may then be finished in any of the styles as shown for brickwork. There are various materials which are suitable for use as a coping for the block wall, including concrete paving slabs, timber and brick on edge, as well as the other types of coping described under the construction of brick walls.

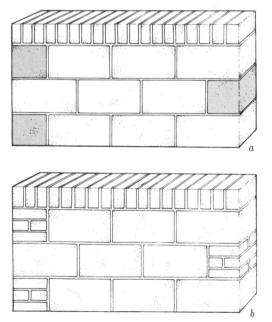

Fig. 4.19 (*a*) Half blocks used at the ends of a wall. (*b*) Bricks may be used instead of cutting the blocks.

Stone walls

Natural stone produces some of the most attractive walling when used in the right environment, obviously looking best in its local area but also in some country properties where there is no local stone. It need not be excluded from suburban areas either if used sympathetically, with low, planted garden walls looking particularly good.

Stone that is used for walling falls into two main categories:

Rubble This is available either straight from the quarry similar to small unshaped rockery stone. It is also available as squared rubble where the corners have been knocked off to make it into more regular-shaped pieces.

Ashlar This type of stone has been shaped or 'dressed' to a greater finish and is much smoother and more regular in appearance than rubble, having at least one good face; it is also more expensive to buy than rubble as it involves additional labour.

Most types of natural stone may be used for walling, with the softer, sedimentary types, e.g. sandstone and limestone, tending to be most common as they can be shaped and dressed and are therefore easier to work with; dense heavy rock such as granite would tend to be used for rubble walling as it is extremely hard to split and to shape.

Stone may be obtained through garden centres, stone merchants or direct from quarries and is sold by the tonne, so the amount you get for your money will be affected by the density of the particular type of rock. The amount of stone required can be estimated by relating either the square meterage of wall face or the cubic meterage of walling to one tonne of stone; a stone merchant would be able to advise you accordingly, depending on the type of stone that is selected. It is always worth looking at stone before purchasing, in order to check its quality and the mixture of sizes, as regular widths are essential for ashlar walling which is often used as a veneer to a regular unit of block or brick. Rubble walling should have a good mixture of large and small pieces normally in the ratio of five large pieces to one small piece.

RECONSTITUTED STONE

Reconstituted stone is made up of cement dust and crushed stone and should be used sympathetically in the landscape as some blocks come in gaudy colours and others are dreadful imitations of the real thing. Their main advantage is that they are far more economical and more readily available than natural stone. They are also manufactured in regular sizes which can then be laid to courses with the introduction of larger blocks or 'jumpers' to create a random effect. Reconstituted blocks are often used in building work, making use of crushed stone from the local quarries, and therefore a link of materials can be taken into the garden with the construction of block walls. It is important to ensure that the same reconstituted stone is used and also that the colour of the mortar joints blends well with it.

Walling techniques

Natural stone may be laid by a variety of methods normally influenced by whether it is rubble or ashlar blocks that are to be used.

RUBBLE

Rubble can either be random laid, i.e. with no attempt at coursing the stonework, or in a type of walling known as 'brought to courses' when squared rubble may be used and a regular course is introduced to the random pattern at approximately every 30 cm (1 ft). In both cases it is important that stones are laid with their bedding planes horizontal and that vertical joints are avoided. Rubble walls can be laid either dry, semi dry, or mortared (Fig. 4.20).

Dry walls This is the traditional dry stone walling seen criss-crossing hillsides and can be either random laid or brought to courses with rammed earth behind the stones to hold them firm and with occasional small stones left out in the face of the wall for planting pockets.

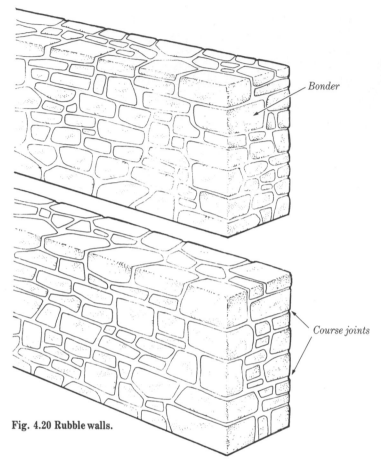

Fig. 4.20 Rubble walls.

cases the stone can almost be laid with the regularity of brickwork courses or, if a mixture of sizes are to be used, the occasional larger stone or 'jumper' can be inserted to break the regular coursing. Finely dressed stone will allow very narrow joints which, when brushed out, will give the impression of a dry stone wall (Fig. 4.21).

A stone veneer is a useful construction technique for wide, free-standing walls where the cost in constructing the wall in solid stone would be prohibitive. However, it is important to select the same width of stone when it is to be used for a cladding in this way.

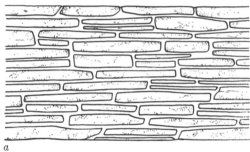

a

Fig. 4.21 (*a*) Ashlar walls. (*b*) Stone veneer.

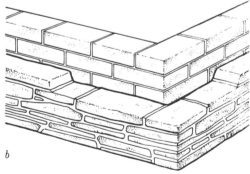

b

Laying stone walling

RANDOM RUBBLE

This construction technique is similar whether the wall is to be laid uncoursed or brought to courses; if the wall is to be laid semi dry then mortar instead of rammed earth will be placed behind the face stones. The construction is also

Semi dry wall The semi dry stone wall uses mortar instead of rammed earth to hold the stones firm and therefore creates a stronger wall and is more useful where walls of greater height are required. The mortar is not visible from the face of the wall and so the visual effect is still that of a dry stone wall.

Mortared walls This is an extremely strong type of stone walling which is constructed in a similar way to the above two types and can be random laid or brought to courses, but here the stones are bedded on mortar and the joints are pointed; raked joints look particularly good with stone work.

ASHLAR WALLS
Ashlar walls may be laid either as a solid wall or as a veneer to a brick or block wall. In both

similar for mortared walls except that, as has already been pointed out, mortar joints will be utilized and subsequently pointed. Semi dry and mortared walls should be used for constructions higher than 1 m (3¼ ft) as they are far stronger and will provide greater stability; concrete footings should also be laid for any mortared walls.

Coping stones are essential to keep water out of walls where mortar has been used, in order to prevent frost damage, but they may also be used on dry stone walls to provide a neat finish. Stone courses should always be laid horizontally but the coping stones should be laid so that the finished line of the wall is seen to follow the contours of the land (Fig. 4.22).

Rubble walls should be laid to a batter, that is to say the side faces lean in slightly from the vertical to provide extra stability, and the normal ratio of batter is 2.5 cm (1 in) of slope in every 60 cm (2 ft) of height. The width at the base of the wall is therefore calculated by assessing the width at the top of the wall (based on a double thickness of average-sized stones) and then applying the ratio of batter, as previously described, to the proposed height of the wall (Fig. 4.23).

Footings for low walls (up to about 1 m/3¼ ft) need a depth of approximately 30 cm (1 ft) of concrete, and should be approximately 45 cm (18 in) wide and allow for a depth of at least two stones below ground level. Dry stone walls, however, do not need concrete footings and may be laid straight on to rammed earth, allowing for the depth of at least four stones in the ground (Fig. 4.24). Timber profiles should be set up at each end of the rubble wall, corresponding to the batter of the proposed wall, between which taut building lines can be drawn as a guide for any horizontal coursing. A batter board should be placed against the wall from time to time in order to check that the correct angle of slope is being constructed.

The wall is built in rises of approximately 45 cm (18 in), starting with the two ends and

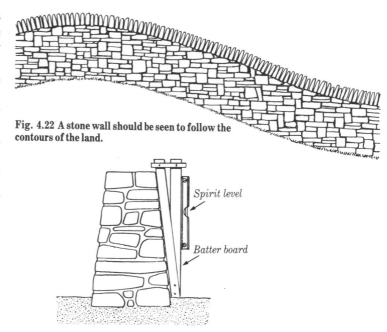

Fig. 4.22 A stone wall should be seen to follow the contours of the land.

Fig. 4.23 Checking the wall with a batter board.

Spirit level

Batter board

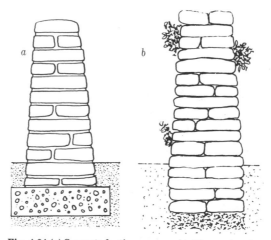

Fig. 4.24 (*a*) Concrete footings are required for mortared stone walls.
(*b*) Dry stone walls may be laid onto rammed earth footings.

ensuring always that the good face of the stone is kept to the outside. When the two ends have been built to the height of the first rise, the double skin of face walling is built against the string line, packing mortar and broken stone

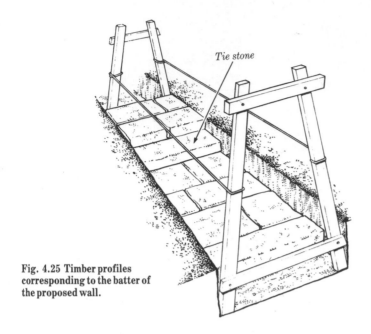

Fig. 4.25 Timber profiles corresponding to the batter of the proposed wall.

When a greater height of retention is required then the mechanics of construction become more crucial.

Although the major role of a retaining wall is functional, it may be utilized in the garden to create a number of interesting and varied effects. The obvious use of a retaining wall is to support an existing steep bank, whether by a single wall or a series of low walls or terraces. If there is sufficient space then terraces provide a more satisfactory solution to bank retention, especially when close to buildings. High retaining walls close to houses tend to create oppressive spaces which are often in shadow and therefore cool and damp; the rooms in the house that are close to the wall will tend to be permanently dark. By pushing the bank back in a series of terraces and low walls, the area will be opened up, allowing

into the middle of the wall, or using rammed earth in the case of dry stone walls (Fig. 4.25). When the first rise is completed the string line should be moved up which will act as a guide to keeping the stones horizontal and, if necessary, for when the stones are to be brought to courses. Larger stones should be used in the wider base of the wall and a very large stone or tie stone should be laid across the width of the wall every so often to aid stability; smaller stones will tend to be used in the narrower top section of the wall.

When the correct height has been achieved, the wall may be finished off in a variety of ways, with coping stones being essential for semi dry or mortared walls and useful on dry stone walls in order to keep the top courses of stones tight and to prevent them being dislodged (Fig. 4.26).

Retaining walls

The purpose of a retaining wall is to hold back earth where a change of level is created; this may take the form of a simple path edging at low level where soil is prevented from washing onto the path from a slightly higher level.

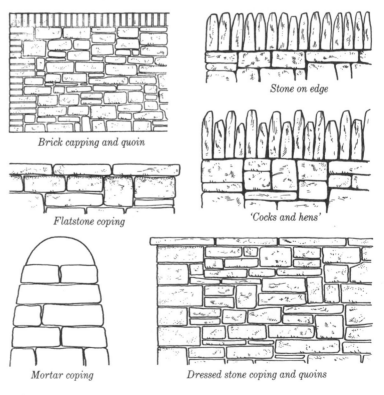

Brick capping and quoin

Flatstone coping

Mortar coping

Stone on edge

'Cocks and hens'

Dressed stone coping and quoins

Fig. 4.26 Coping methods for rubble walls.

The perfect outside
room, ample room for
sitting and dining,
with low maintenance
planting.

i

Above:
Steps should always
be generous and in
this garden they form
a major part of the
overall composition.

Right:
This empty pot is pure
sculpture and is the
perfect foil to the
adjoining planting.

Opposite:
Front gardens are
always important,
after all, first
impressions count.
Boulders keep feet
away from planted
areas while the urn
acts as a focal point by
the front door.

Old York stone and
brick paving provide a
mellow floor while
planting in containers
softens the transition
to the raised deck.

iv

more light into the house and creating a brighter more pleasing outlook (Fig. 4.27). The terraces will not only provide level areas for plants, which will soften the construction of the wall but will also make maintenance easier and be far safer for young children than the potential danger of high retaining walls.

Steps can be designed to form an integral part of the retaining wall, to form an interesting pattern; where there is sufficient space, a bold effect can be achieved by creating a broad flight of steps to retain the whole of a bank.

Retaining walls are also necessary in the construction of sunken gardens, where simple low walls may be all that is necessary to add an extra dimension to the garden. However, this type of feature should be avoided in areas with a high water table as, by lowering the ground, the water table is effectively brought closer to the surface, giving a strong likelihood of flooding.

One other use of the 'sunken' retaining wall is for the construction of a 'ha-ha'. This was the technique formerly used in large landscaped gardens where uninterrupted views of surrounding parkland were required while still maintaining a barrier against grazing animals. Walls and hedges were widely replaced by ditches and retaining walls to achieve the effect. If you are fortunate in backing on to open fields and parkland, the 'ha-ha' can be an effective technique, although some ground will be lost with this type of enclosure (Fig. 4.28).

Construction

There are three major criteria which are an influence on the construction of retaining walls. They are: ground pressure, drainage and expansion along the length of the wall.

GROUND PRESSURE

Ground pressure is exerted on the wall by the retained earth and increased when the height of earth to be retained also increases. Advice should be sought from an engineer or surveyor if it is necessary to construct walls higher than

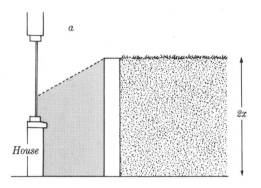

Fig. 4.27 (*a*) High retaining walls close to house create oppressive spaces.
(*b*) A brighter, more pleasing outlook will be created by terracing the bank.

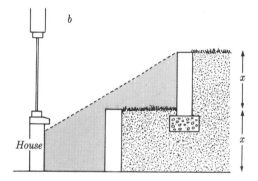

Fig. 4.28 The 'ha-ha'.

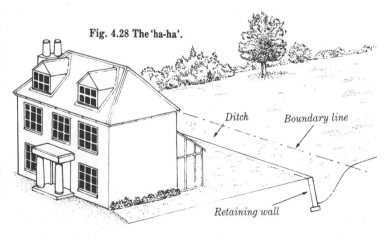

1–1.2 m (3½–4 ft), as inadequate construction may result in a retaining wall being pushed over due to the effect of ground pressure (Fig. 4.29).

It is insufficient to construct a single low

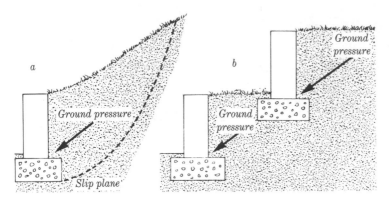

Fig. 4.29 (*a*) Ground pressure exerted by retained earth. (*b*) The effect of ground pressure is reduced by constructing a series of low retaining walls.

wall with a steeply rising slope behind it as retained slopes should not exceed 1:10. A stronger retention will be created by the construction of a series of low walls and level terraces; the ground pressure is then shared between all the retaining walls with the added advantages of terracing that have already been described. The effect of ground pressure is most pronounced at the base of the wall and so greater resistance can be provided by increasing the thickness of the wall at this point. The first six courses of a 1 m (3¼ ft) high brick wall should be one and a half bricks wide,

although a thickness of two bricks wide would be better. The top courses of the wall should be no less than one brick wide (Fig. 4.30). A similar profile can be constructed with an *in situ* concrete retaining wall. The concrete should be cast to a batter of 2.5 cm (1 in) in every 30 cm (1 ft) of height and may incorporate a toe at the base of the wall which will provide extra stability. Strength will also be increased by incorporating vertical, steel reinforcing bars at approximately 60 cm (2 ft) spacings along the wall. The appearance of such a wall will be greatly improved by cladding with a more decorative medium such as brick or stone, which also forms a more economical method than a solid wall construction in either of these materials.

DRAINAGE

The pressure on a wall is increased with a build up of ground water and therefore a facility for drainage must be incorporated. A granular fill of broken hard core, reject stones or gravel should be used as a backing to the wall, which will help water move down to a drainage pipe.

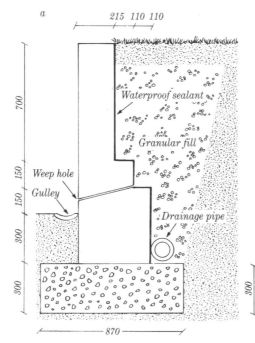

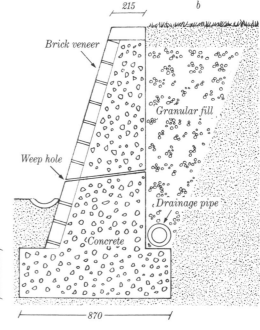

Fig. 4.30 (*a*) A typical construction detail for a 1 m (3¼ ft) brick wall. (*b*) A 1 m (3¼ ft) brick veneer retaining wall.

This pipe should be perforated (therefore allowing water into it) and set to a fall of approximately 1:50, leading to a separate soakaway. Although the pipe should be bedded on granular material, an impervious layer of polythene underneath will ensure that water goes into the pipe and does not seep under the wall.

Extra water pressure is relieved by the provision of 'weep holes', which allow water to pass through to the face of the wall and then into the ground at the front or into a gully drain in cases of extremely wet conditions. Clay drainage pipes are set into the wall with a slight incline to create the 'weep holes', or it may be sufficient in brick walls to leave some vertical joints open. Holes should be spaced at every 1–2 m (3¼–6½ ft) along the face of the wall, usually at a height of 15 cm (6 in) above the front ground level. Damp proof courses may be incorporated as previously described for free-standing walls but will only be of use if the back of the wall is damp proofed by painting on a waterproof sealant. Coping stones should also be laid to seal the top surface of the wall.

EXPANSION

Provision must be made for expansion along the length of retaining walls, as well as free-standing walls, with the same spacing of joints applying to both. Mastic joints would be beneficial, for although privacy is not a problem with retaining walls, a sealed joint would prevent water seeping through.

Choice of materials

There are many materials that can be used for retaining walls, whether on their own or as a cladding to another.

CONCRETE

It has already been shown that *in situ* concrete can be a useful material for retaining walls, especially as a backing to more decorative cladding which may link to other areas of the garden. Concrete blocks are also a useful

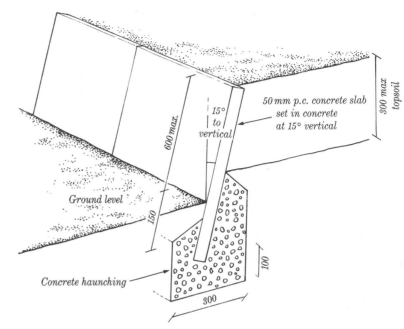

Fig. 4.31 Retaining wall in precast concrete paving slabs.

material, both as a backing and also as a facing material. Hollow blocks are particularly useful where extra strength is required, as vertical reinforcing rods can be set through them into a concrete footing. Precast concrete paving slabs also make a simple form of retention for low walls of approximately 60 cm (2 ft) high. The slabs must be set to a batter of 15° from the vertical and must be *haunched* with concrete as well as set into a concrete footing (Fig. 4.31).

BRICK

Bricks have the advantage of being used elsewhere in the garden and so provide continuity; they can be used for cladding or in a solid retaining wall when Flemish or English bond should be used for strength. As retaining walls tend to stay wetter than free-standing walls, it is important that extremely durable bricks are used.

STONE

When used in the right setting, low stone retaining walls look excellent. Stone walls

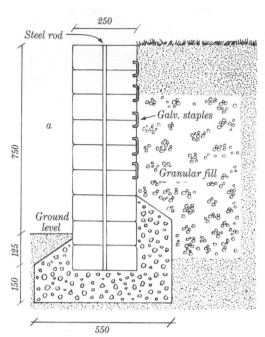

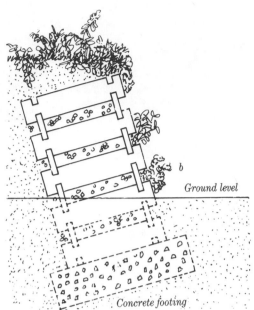

Fig. 4.32 (*a*) Typical construction for a 75 cm (2½ ft) sleeper retaining wall.
(*b*) Crib walling used as a low retaining wall.

must be built or 'set' to a batter and will look particularly good with plants growing in the crevices and tumbling over the top. Stone can also be used as a cladding to avoid the cost of a solid stone wall. Ashlar (see page 62) is commonly used in this construction as it can be obtained in fairly regular widths which are necessary when building against an inner brick skin.

Large clumps of rockery stone will provide an excellent retention for low banks. The weight of the rock itself will be sufficient to retain the soil without the need for foundations and mortar. Larger banks will require more room for construction as rock banks should be stepped back if they are to create a natural effect. This aspect is covered in more detail in Chapter 6.

TIMBER
Timber can make an extremely attractive and durable retaining wall as long as the wood has been well treated with preservative, otherwise it will rot quickly. Railway sleepers and telegraph poles, which both required good treatment for their original use, make

excellent retaining walls and they are a cheaper solution than using brick or stone. Both materials look good when laid horizontally and are bonded to avoid vertical joints. The horizontal timbers are often tied or bolted to vertical support posts, which are in turn concreted into the ground. Movement can be prevented at the end of a line of sleepers by drilling through the overlapping timbers and linking them with a steel rod set into concrete (Fig. 4.32*a*).

Another form of timber retaining wall is crib walling which is a manufactured system of interlocking pieces of timber. The wall is built to a batter and is backfilled with granular material for drainage. The open appearance of crib walling allows pockets of soil to be introduced so that plants may grow out and soften the face of the wall (Fig. 4.32*b*).

FENCES

Once fencing has been selected in preference to walling for enclosure, then the same cirteria that influenced that decision may be applied to choosing the type of fence.

Security

The need for security fencing around properties is a sign of the times. Some home-owners obviously have a greater need than others as indicated in their choice of high chain-link fencing. Most people, however, do not need such extreme anti-intruder fencing; it is more usual that the need for security is based on keeping children and pets within a property and that any fencing is more commonly constructed to prevent visual intrusion.

Privacy

The need for fencing to provide privacy has become more and more important. Modern developments and infill housing have pushed properties so close together and made gardens so small that fencing is necessary to offer the homeowner some degree of private space. However, the temptation to construct solid fences around such small plots should be avoided as this may create the feeling of living in a box. House developers favour anti-gossip panels adjacent to the house, where most privacy is normally required, before stepping down to an open type fence such as chain link. Planting against the chain link will offer more privacy, whilst also permitting glimpses of neighbouring gardens and so creating an illusion of greater space.

Larger properties, especially in the country, do not always have the same requirements for privacy. *Anti-gossip panels*, for example, are not relevant. Any solid fencing will tend to be for environmental reasons such as for a wind barrier around a swimming pool or sitting area.

Environment

There are two influences on fence type when considering the environment. One is the necessity of fences to combat harsh environmental conditions and the other is that the choice of fence is in character, not only with the site, but also the locality.

Fencing offers protection against prevailing winds, whether as a boundary enclosure or an internal screen. Slatted fences are the most effective barrier as they diffuse the wind, whilst solid fences create an eddy on the leeward side, pulling wind over and down to ground level at great speed. Fences can also help create areas of shade which may be necessary in an open, hot site. Here again, slatted fences are useful, by providing protection against the sun but also by casting an interesting dappled shadow. Noise protection from adjacent roads cannot be effectively controlled by fencing, as a greater density of material is necessary and therefore walling is more suitable. A screen constructed as a visual barrier to traffic at least offers the illusion of reducing noise levels.

The type of fence must also fit in with the style of property and its surrounding area. A picket fence may look fine around a thatched cottage with a country garden but would seem out of place around a new house on a modern development.

Demarcation

If it is necessary to define a boundary line without all the other constraints on fence type, then a simple line of marker posts may be all that is required. This is commonly seen on front verges, where sturdy boundary posts may also serve to deter unwanted car parking.

Design

It is important to consider the element of design both when choosing and constructing the fence. The fence must complement the general style of the garden but it is equally important that it looks good in its own right. A well constructed fence using the right dimension of posts and with adequate protection from moisture (i.e. post caps, panel cappings and gravel boards) will look well designed. Correct detailing of fences on slopes will also look well planned. It is essential that vertical elements do not follow the contours of a slope. Close board fencing for example, may be used on undulating ground, as the arris rails and gravel boards may be set off the horizontal but posts and feather edge boards must remain vertical. Do not try to make fence panels slope with an incline as not only would this make construction hard but the visual effect would be awful (Fig. 4.33*a*). Panels should remain horizontal and rise in steps to cope with the gradient (Fig 4.33*b*).

Although fencing is normally functional and may provide a backdrop to planting, there are fence panels available today which are decorative in their own right. These panels are normally of the open trellis type and are therefore often used in association with plants, for screening within the garden. The panels may come in a variety of sizes and patterns, including perspective panels which create the illusion of an archway in the trellis. The panels, which come in a wide choice of finishes, may combine with a complementary pergola system, thus creating unity and continuity of design (Fig. 4.34).

Cost

The budget for constructing the garden must also be considered when selecting the type of fence to be used. Solid fences tend to cost more, especially close boarded and other slatted varieties that need to be constructed on site.

In general, fences that require a lot of materials and on-site construction are the most expensive.

Planning and preparation

Fence construction requires careful planning with the most important aspect being initial discussion with your neighbour. It has already been mentioned that boundary lines are the cause of many disputes between neighbours and therefore it is imperative that any proposed alterations are discussed and agreed (in writing if possible) before commencing work. It is worth arriving at an amicable agreement, as your neighbour may even decide to share the cost of the new fence.

Once the position of the fence has been agreed, a simple level survey should be taken,

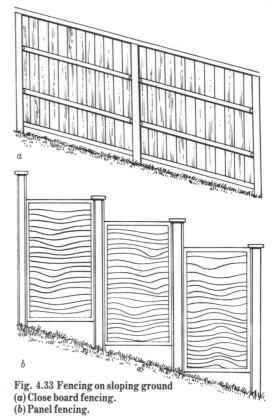

Fig. 4.33 Fencing on sloping ground
(*a*) Close board fencing.
(*b*) Panel fencing.

Fig. 4.34 Perspective panel.

to show whether the ground falls along the boundary line, as any changes of level should be incorporated into the fence plan. When using panel fencing along a boundary line with an even fall, any change of level may be taken up by equal steps on each panel. However, on gently sloping ground a pattern of three or four panels set level with each other before stepping down looks less fussy than a little step for every panel (Fig. 4.35).

An accurate measurement of the boundary line will determine the number of fence sections to be constructed and any cut panels or shorter sections of fence that may be necessary should be at the far end of the fence run, where they will be less obvious. Plan ahead, so that you are not left with a tiny section of fencing to infill; two sections of fencing cut equally look more pleasing than one that is at full size and one that is very small (Fig. 4.36).

It may also be that mature trees form part of the boundary line. In this case, the fence may be constructed up to the tree, taking care not to disturb too many roots when digging post holes, but no part of the fence should be attached to the tree, as nails and wire can cause damage.

Type of fence

Fencing may be classed as either 'open' or 'closed' and so the different types of fence available will be looked at under these headings. There are many construction techniques which may be applied to several styles of fencing and will therefore not be considered in detail for every type of fence that is listed.

Closed fences

PANEL FENCES

The fence panels used in this construction normally come in heights ranging from 90 cm (3 ft) to 1.8 m (6 ft). Panels may be increased in height, if necessary, by adding a trellis panel to the top or a gravel board to the bottom. The fence panels are available in varying degrees of quality which is obviously reflected in their cost. The cheaper panels are comprised of thin, interwoven strips of wood and should be avoided as they really are false economy.

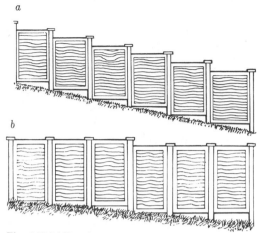

Fig. 4.35 (*a*) Stepping every panel.
(*b*) Stepping every three or four panels looks less fussy.

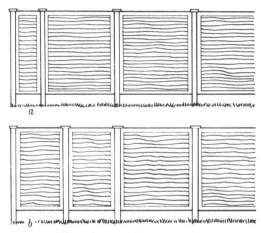

Fig. 4.36 (*a*) A tiny section of fencing at the end of a fence line looks unplanned.
(*b*) Two sections of fencing cut equally at the end of a fence line looks more pleasing.

Stronger panels are made up of thicker, over-lapping lengths of wood, secured to battens on the rear (Fig. 4.37). The panels may have a built-in capping or, if not, then capping strips should be purchased separately and fixed in order to protect the top of the panel. Good quality panels will be well treated, preferably by pressure impregnation and will often carry a guarantee. Most garden centres and builders' merchants stock good quality panels and the posts to go with them. Posts should be 7.5 cm (3 in) square and should be longer than

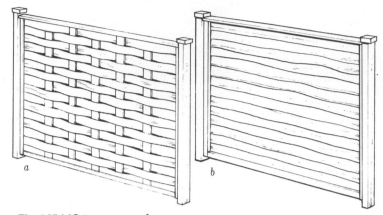

Fig. 4.37 (*a*) Interwoven panel.
(*b*) Overlapping panel.

the panel height by approximately 60 cm (2 ft), which allows for 55 cm (22 in) to be in the ground plus 5 cm (2 in) to extend above the panel and be finished with a post cap. Longer posts will be necessary to accommodate any steps within the fence line.

Constructing panel fencing — timber posts
The ground should be cleared along the proposed fence line, tying back any overhanging shrubs and clearing unwanted plant material. If there is any fall on the ground, construction should start at the highest end of the line to avoid digging panels into the ground. The first post should be set into a hole which has been dug approximately 30 cm (1 ft) square and to a depth of 60 cm (2 ft). Support the post on broken hardcore until it is the correct height

out of the ground, i.e. 1.9 m (6.2 in) for a 1.8 m (6 ft) panel, which allows for an extension above the panel for the post cap and a gap under the panel to clear ground level. Backfill the post with a fairly dry mix of concrete (1 part cement to 6 parts ballast) and ram firm; a broken broom handle makes a good tool for this job. Slope the top of the concrete away from the post to ensure good drainage and check that the post is vertical in both directions before securing it with a temporary strut. A builder's line can then be secured to the post and run along its boundary face to the far end where it is fixed, ensuring that the line does not snag, or you will end up with a crooked fence. Post holes may then be marked out using a spacer 1.875 m (6 ft 3 in) long, i.e. the distance from one post centre to the next. Successive post holes may then be dug, but it is wise to dig no more than three ahead in case your measurements have crept. The first panel is then secured to the first post with galvanized nails (three on each side of the panel) while the bottom of the panel is supported to level with a brick. The second post is then positioned against the panel ensuring that it is vertical in both directions and is flush against the boundary string line as well as protruding above the panel by 5 cm (2 in). Concrete is then firmed around this post and the panel is nailed to it as before (Fig. 4.38).

This procedure is continued to the end of the line, when it may be necessary to cut a panel to

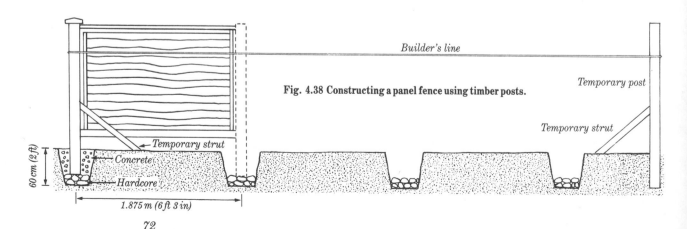

Fig. 4.38 Constructing a panel fence using timber posts.

fit. In this case the end battens of a panel are levered off and renailed to give a panel of the correct width. The excess is cut off, and the panel can then be fitted (Fig. 4.39). Post caps and fence cappings (if not part of the panel) should then be nailed on and every post should be temporarily strutted until the concrete has hardened (normally a couple of days).

Gravel boards are planks 15 cm (6 in) high by the length of a panel and are set flush under the bottom of a panel. They are secured to blocks which are nailed to the fence posts. If gravel boards are to be used, then the panel must be set 15 cm (6 in) above ground level to accommodate them, not the usual 5 cm (2 in); also extra long posts should be purchased. Gravel boards are essential if the fence needs to step by 15 cm (6 in) or more as this would leave an excessive gap underneath. Gravel boards will be bedded into the soil to fill the gaps and although they will obviously rot in time, they are both cheap and easy to replace. Similarly, they may be used on level sites when it is necessary to set fencing at ground level as fence panels would be expensive and awkward to replace if they were to rot (Fig. 4.40).

As an alternative to setting posts in concrete they may be bolted into manufactured metal sockets which have initially been driven into the ground. The idea is to hold the post above ground level and therefore prevent rot. In practice, however, they are almost impossible to fix square to a line and with a true vertical. They also provide an unstable support, especially for tall fencing so if they are to be used, the posts should first be fixed into the sockets which are then concreted into the ground in the normal way.

PANEL FENCES — CONCRETE SLOTTED POSTS AND GRAVEL BOARDS

The use of concrete makes an extremely strong and durable type of fence. The concrete gravel boards are particularly useful for sloping sites and where it is necessary to retain slightly banked areas of earth. The slotted

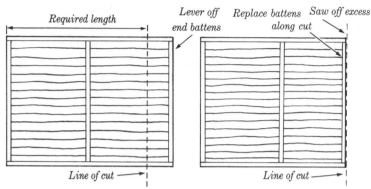

Fig. 4.39 Cutting a panel to fit.

posts also allow easy replacement of any damaged panels. This type of fencing, however, is more expensive than using timber posts and is much heavier work. Care should be taken not to crack the gravel boards or to damage the surface of the posts. It would also be wise to wear gloves, as the posts often have rough edges. Despite the use of concrete, this is not an unattractive fence in an urban or suburban situation, as long as the proportion of panel to gravel board is right. Gravel boards are either 15 cm (6 in) or 30 cm (1 ft) and can obviously be stacked one above the other; however, this should be avoided unless absolutely necessary on steep ground or when used as retention, as the overall appearance is too hard. It is far better to use a taller panel and less gravel boards than the other way around.

Construction The first post is set into the ground and concreted in as previously

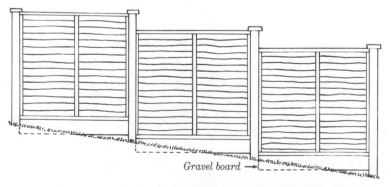

Fig. 4.40 Gravel boards used on sloping ground.

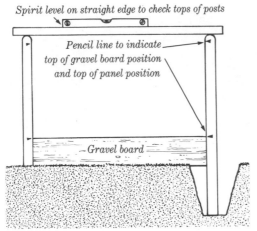

Spirit level on straight edge to check tops of posts

Pencil line to indicate top of gravel board position and top of panel position

— Gravel board

Fig. 4.41 Constructing a panel fence using slotted concrete posts and gravel boards.

described for timber posts. It is important however, that the correct height is left above ground level for both the gravel board and panel, and unlike the previous construction, panels are not put in at the same time and so cannot be used to fix the height of subsequent posts. Posts can be marked with pencil as a guide to indicate both the top of the gravel board and the top of the panel (Fig. 4.41). The gravel board is positioned and supported with broken tiles or wood blocks to level, prior to placing the second post in position. The second post must be checked in both directions and to make sure it is square to the line. The tops of the posts must also be level and this is best checked with a spirit level held on a straight edge. If the fence is to step down, then both the

Fig. 4.42 Inserting the panels between slotted posts.

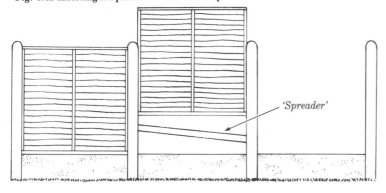

'Spreader'

gravel board and the following post must step down by the same amount. Successive posts and gravel boards are erected along the fence line, ensuring that if there is a fair and rough slotted face, then the fair face should point towards the house. The end gravel board may have to be cut with a stone cutter to complete the fence line, and if so, do make sure you wear goggles and gloves for protection against injury. The posts should then be left for at least two days so that the concrete hardens, before inserting the panels (Fig. 4.42).

Choose a calm day for slotting in the panels as it is pretty tricky to hold 1.8 m (6 ft) panels above a 1.8 m (6 ft) high fence on a windy day. If the posts have closed in slightly at the top, a length of timber (the length of a panel) may be eased between them so that they open up, allowing the panel to be slotted in; and then the 'spreader' can be removed. The panels should be tapped down to level and capped if necessary.

WATTLE HURDLES

Wattle and osier hurdles, made from woven hazel stems and willow stems respectively, form a good, if temporary, solid screen. The hurdles are traditionally used for sheep penning but have been adapted for garden use, looking particularly at home in rural settings as a backdrop to planting. Their life expectancy may be no more than five to ten years and so they form an excellent temporary fence whilst shrubs or hedges become established.

The construction of a hurdle fence (Fig. 4.43) is straightforward. Round timber stakes are driven into the ground and hurdles are secured to them with galvanized wire. Often the hurdles meet in front of the stakes so that the fence does not appear to be split into panels. Although wattle hurdles may bend slightly, it is best to treat them as rigid panels on sloping ground and therefore step them rather than try to follow the contours of the ground. It is almost impossible to put a spirit level to a hurdle (and not really necessary) so 'eye' them in to level as closely as possible.

CLOSE BOARD FENCES

This is an extremely strong type of construction which offers total privacy but is also fairly expensive. The fence may range in height from 1–1.8 m (3¼–6 ft), which may be extended with the addition of a gravel board. The fence is made up with either timber or concrete posts, normally 12.5 cm (5 in) square, which are joined by arris rails usually set into morticed joints, three rails being necessary for fences over 1.4 m (4 ft 8 in). The sections of post and rail are then clad with overlapping vertical boarding known as feather edge. A gravel board set underneath the boards not only gives extra protection but also gives a neat finish to the fence and helps support the feather edge when nailing it on (Fig. 4.44).

One advantage of close board fencing is that it can be constructed on a slight incline without stepping, and another is that individual boards can be replaced if damaged. All-timber constructions are normally used for gardens, although concrete posts and gravel boards will certainly last longer.

Construction The first post is positioned against the boundary line to the correct height above ground level and set in with concrete. Posts can usually be bought machine-morticed, which makes the job easier. A line is then run from this post to the end of the fence at a constant height above ground level to ensure that all posts are set in to the right height. It may be, for example, that the line is set to correspond with the height of the highest morticed joint. If the fence is to run level, post tops can always be checked with a straight

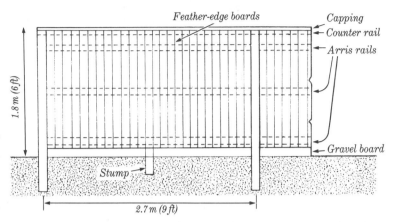

Fig. 4.44 Close board fence.

edge and spirit level. The post holes can then be marked using a 'spacer' from centre to centre of post positions, according to the width of clad panels which may vary from 1.8 m (6 ft) to 2.7 m (9 ft) for taller fences.

Arris rails are positioned and the second post is located on to them and set to vertical in both directions as well as against the straight line, before being concreted in. This process is continued down the line cutting the last set of arris rails, if necessary, to fit at the end of the fence. The gravel boards are then nailed on to the posts or, in the case of concrete gravel boards and posts, a right-angled metal cleat is used which is bolted to the board and post. Once the framework for the fence has been erected it should be left for a day or two so that the concrete goes hard, prior to cladding with the feather edge boards (Fig. 4.45). The boards are set vertically to overlap each other by about 2.5 cm (1 in) and nailed individually to allow for easier removal if necessary. A 7.5 cm (3 in) 'spacer' should be used giving approximately four boards per 30 cm (1 ft) linear run. Check the boards with a spirit level every so often to ensure that they remain vertical. Every alternate panel may have its feather edge boards turned around to give an interesting effect.

On wide-spaced panels of 2.7 m (9 ft), a small post known as a stump is driven into the

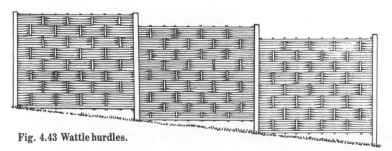

Fig. 4.43 Wattle hurdles.

75

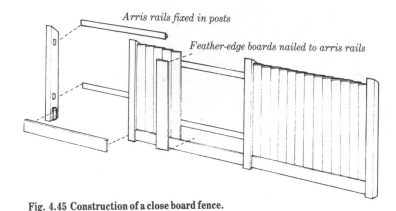

Arris rails fixed in posts

Feather-edge boards nailed to arris rails

Fig. 4.45 Construction of a close board fence.

ground under the lowest arris rail and nailed to it, to prevent it sagging. An additional finish is the use of a weathered capping which protects the top of the boards and provides a neat finish; this capping is nailed to a counter rail which is in turn set into a morticed joint in the post.

SLATTED FENCE

A whole variety of slatted fences may be designed to provide interesting architectural effects. The slatted fence is based on the same construction as the close boarded fence, but uses square section slats of different dimensions as opposed to feather edge. Planed or finely sawn slats of approximately 2 cm (¾ in) give a smart, crisp appearance which looks particularly good when a fine joint is left between each slat, creating an interesting light and shadow effect. More light is obviously let in with a wider joint but some degree of privacy will also be lost. These slatted panels look best if framed on top and bottom by broad

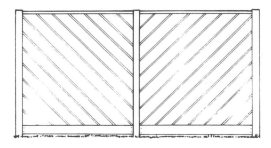

Fig. 4.46 Slatted fence using boards and diagonal pattern.

76

rails and if recessed from the face of the posts to give an extra shadow effect.

This type of fence allows for individual design enabling the fence to become a strong feature of the garden in its own right. Slats of varied widths can be combined and if no counter rail is used, the heights of the slats can be staggered to provide an unusual effect for the top of the fence. Broad slats, usually 15 cm (6 in), can be nailed on diagonally and then turned to the other diagonal for the next panel. This method involves a lot of cutting but again provides an interesting appearance. (Fig. 4.46).

HIT AND MISS FENCE

This is a version of ranch style fencing made of posts and boards but whereas ranch fencing has boards attached to one side only, the hit and miss fence is boarded on both sides for privacy. It is normally constructed to a height of 1.8 m (6 ft) to maintain privacy and looks particularly good with modern property and gardens as it has a very square and smart appearance. However, the horizontal boards make it easy to climb and therefore it is not a good security fence. There was a vogue for painting this type of fence white, which looks fine initially but soon looks tatty as the method of construction makes it very hard to maintain; the use of preservative gives a far more satisfactory appearance. The posts are 7.5 cm (3 in) square and the boards are usually 15 cm × 2.5 cm (6 in × 1 in), set at 15 cm (6 in) spacings up the posts. The boards on the rear side of the fence are set at the same spacings, but staggered to provide privacy. Light and air will pass through this type of fence, making it useful for plant protection and as a wind break (Fig. 4.47). The first post is set in concrete and strutted, prior to marking and digging subsequent holes. The lowest board is then nailed on and used to position the next post which should be set in to vertical and against the fence line. This process should be continued down the line using the lowest boards, tacked to the posts, to position the next upright along. After the

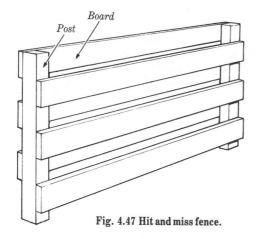

Fig. 4.47 Hit and miss fence.

concrete has set, the boards can be nailed on from the bottom upwards, using a 'spacer' to keep them the right width apart. Staggered joints at the posts make for a stronger fence.

Open fences

POST AND RAIL FENCE

This is a stock fence and is therefore used in rural settings where it follows the contours of the ground. Its equivalent for urban settings is the post and board, or ranch fencing, which is the same construction as hit and miss but with boards on one side only. Post and rail fences vary in height from 1.1–1.4 m (3 ft 7 in–4 ft 8 in) and usually look best with four horizontal rails. The posts are sawn rectangular 15 cm × 7.5 cm

(6 in × 3 in) sections in hard wood or treated soft wood. The rails are 10 cm × 3.8 cm (4 in × 1½ in) and are either nailed to the front of the posts or set into morticed joints for a stronger fence (Fig. 4.48). A more rustic type fence has half round posts driven into the ground with half round rails nailed on to them. The posts are normally at 1.8 m (6 ft) centres but may be at 2.75 m (9 ft 2 in) centres which would necessitate a central prick post. This post is of the same dimension as the rails and is driven in to a depth of 45 cm (18 in) and nailed on to the cross rails to prevent them sagging. The rails are usually set on the inside of the post so that livestock push them on to the posts not off, and are normally fixed with staggered joints for strength.

CONSTRUCTION

The first post is set into the ground to a depth of approximately 75 cm (2½ ft) and backfilled with rammed earth or concrete for extra strength. The end post is also set in and a line is pulled taut between it and the first post at a convenient height (normally the top of the highest rail). Post holes are marked out and dug using a rail from centre to centre as a 'spacer'. Set the second post and nail on the second rail, continuing this process along the fence to the end of the run (Fig. 4.49). Do not use the same rail as a marker unless you are

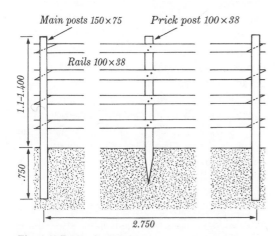

Fig. 4.48 Post and rail fence.

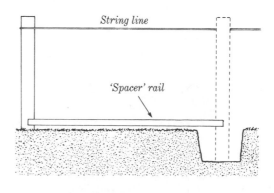

Fig. 4.49 Setting out a post and rail fence.

sure all rails are the same length. It is far safer to batch your rails into exactly the same lengths for each section and use one of them to mark out their relevant post. Double length rails can, of course, be used which would span two posts, giving a staggered joint and stronger fence.

CONTINUOUS BAR FENCE

Metal continuous bar fencing is another rural stock fence associated with large parkland estates. It is normally at a height of 1–1.2 m (3¼–4 ft) and consists of standard posts at 90 cm (3 ft) spacings with joiner posts at 4.5 m (14¾ ft) intervals. The standards have holes in them at regular spacings up the post to carry the continuous horizontal bars; the top hole is for a round bar with the rest being rectangular in section to take flat bars. The joiner standard has larger holes to take the overlapping bars, with short wedges holding the bars in on the joiner standard, and grub screws holding the top round bar in a tubular 'ferrel'. Stout posts or pillars are set into the ground at corners, whereas standards are normally driven. Curved tops may be available with standards for the attachment of barbed wire, although it spoils the look of this type of fence (Fig. 4.50).

Fig. 4.50 Continuous bar fence.

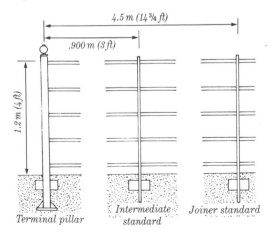

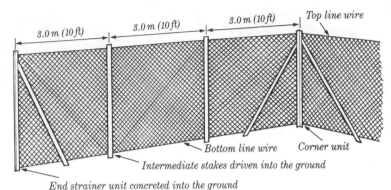

End strainer unit concreted into the ground

Fig. 4.51 Chain link fence.

CHAIN LINK FENCE

Chain link fencing is a good security fence which, even at low heights, is difficult to climb; it offers little privacy but forms a good backdrop to planting as it is so unobtrusive. It is commonly used as a property division on new developments, at a height of 90 cm (3 ft) which is its most revelant domestic scale. The fence is made up from a cladding of green or black plastic-coated galvanized wire mesh attached to lines of horizontal strained wire. The posts are either concrete, timber or more commonly angle iron; concrete posts look heavy and out of proportion for the fine mesh infill, whereas black angle irons are a better scale and less obtrusive (Fig. 4.51).

Construction of a 90 cm (3 ft) chain link with angle iron posts End 'strainer' units are set into the ground, at 90 cm (3 ft) above ground level, at each end of the fence run. The unit consists of an upright and strut which should be set at approximately 45°. Both post and strut will be concreted in and left for two or three days before line wire is attached. The fair face of the units should point away from the property, with the flat of the angle iron adjacent to the boundary line. Line wire is attached to barrel winders at each end, prior to passing through holes in the intermediate stakes which are set at 3 m (10 ft) intervals. The wire is then strained tight and subsequently fixed with a lock nut.

A stretcher bar is then pushed through the end of the chain link roll and bolted to the top and bottom of the strainer unit. The chain link is pulled tight to the far end and a stretcher bar is poked through the mesh just short of where it will be attached; this is so it can be pulled tight and bolted to the end unit. The cladding is secured to the line wire by twists of wire at every 15 cm (6 in) along the top and 45 cm (18 in) along the bottom; also if the bottom of the chain link is buried slightly, it offers a fairly good barrier for pets.

PICKET FENCE

The traditional picket or palisade fence is synonymous with the English cottage garden and looks out of place in an urban setting. It has the same framework as close boarded fencing and is clad with vertical pales, either white painted or stained. The fence is normally 90 cm to 1.2 m (3 to 4 ft) high and difficult to climb. It also has the advantage of being fairly pet proof, if the pales are kept close to the ground. There is no capping rail so the pales may be finished in a variety of designs, most usually pointed or round, which is matched to the finish of the post tops. The posts are 10 cm (4 in) square and are spaced at 1.8 m (6 ft) intervals. They should be set in concrete with rails of 7.5 cm × 5 cm (3 in × 2 in) in sections set into morticed joints. The pales, which range from 5–7.5 cm (2–3 in), are nailed on so that they finish flush with the top of the posts and are approximately 5 cm (2 in) from ground level (Fig. 4.52).

It is normal for the space between pales to be equal to or less than the pale itself. If equal, then a pale can be hooked over the top rail with a couple of nails and used as a spacer. The pleasing design of this fence has resulted in several preformed palisade panels coming onto the market, which are simply fixed by brackets on to the posts.

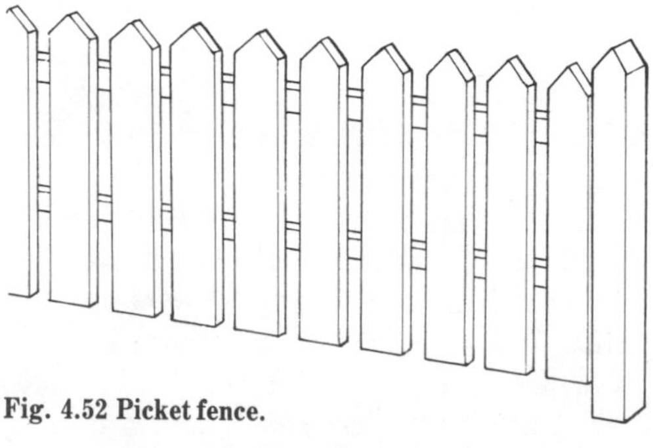

SINGLE RAIL FENCE

This is a simple demarcation fence offering no privacy but indicating a boundary and preventing a pedestrian cut-through without being obtrusive. The rails are 10 cm (4 in) square and set diamond fashion on to low posts 30 cm (1 ft) high, of the same dimension, with an open joint to suit. Rails will come together over posts (without being jointed) and are fixed with galvanized strips nailed over them on to the posts (Fig. 4.53).

Fig. 4.53
(*a*) Single rail fence.
(*b*) Single rail fence — fixing detail.

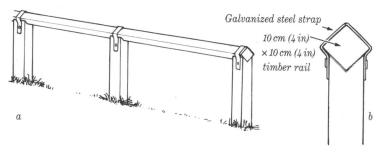

Galvanized steel strap

*10 cm (4 in)
× 10 cm (4 in)
timber rail*

a

b

POST AND CHAIN FENCE

This traditional construction performs the same demarcation role as a single rail fence. It looks good with a black painted iron chain fixed to white painted or treated posts at entrances to fine character properties (Fig. 4.54). It looks nothing short of pretentious however, when used anywhere else, and plastic should be avoided at all costs!

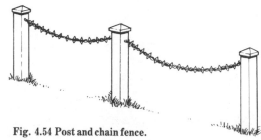

Fig. 4.54 Post and chain fence.

Fig. 4.52 Picket fence.

GATES

Careful thought must be given when choosing the type of gate and, indeed, as to whether a gate is needed at all. Many front boundaries are open plan or at least have low boundaries, affording no privacy, and yet a pair of gates is often constructed across the drive. These gates are usually left open to save opening and closing them every time the car is taken out — so, are they really needed?

Gates may of course be necessary for safety, to keep in children and pets. Metal gates or palisade gates, which have closer vertical pales, are normally the most suitable for this purpose. If driveway gates are necessary, consider combining one leaf of the gates for pedestrian access, eliminating the separate gate and often unnecessary front path.

Gates are often focal points and form a useful function in attracting you to the entrance area. For this reason they must be carefully detailed and in proportion with the surrounding enclosure. The style of gate must also be in keeping with the fence or wall; a wrought iron gate for example, set in a post

and rail fence, would look totally wrong. Any gate should be of simple design and look strong; it must not be flimsy, nor ornate. It is also extremely important that the gate posts or piers are strong enough to support the gate, without looking over designed. Posts should be set in the ground to a depth of at least 75 cm (2½ ft), while brick pier supports should always be reinforced.

Hanging Gates

Gates should, if at all possible, open into the property. This may, however, be a problem if the ground rises within the gateway, as an opening gate would obviously catch on the rising ground. A solution may be to create a level platform in the immediate vicinity. Regrading of the ground may therefore be possible or, alternatively, double gates may be used instead of a single leaf. Metal gates come with all the fittings attached as well as freestanding posts with integral hooks. Separate fittings have to be fixed to timber gates, making that a more complicated operation. There is a wide variety of hinges and catches available and it is essential to use a type that is strong enough for the particular gate.

METAL GATES

The hanging post should be concreted into the ground so that its bottom hinge fitting will leave the gate 5–7.5 cm (2 in–3 in) above ground level. Position the gate on to the post, supporting it underneath with a block, before levelling up the gate post in both directions. The gate should be temporarily propped while more concrete is firmed around the post. The gate should then be left in this position until the concrete has set, at which stage any additional fittings and locks can be put on (Fig. 4.55).

If a second leaf for a double gate is to be hung the same operation should be carried out leaving a 0.5 cm (³⁄₁₆ in) gap between the two gates. The gates should be squared up and levelled with each other, leaving them propped until the concrete has gone hard. It is often

Fig. 4.55 Hanging a metal gate.

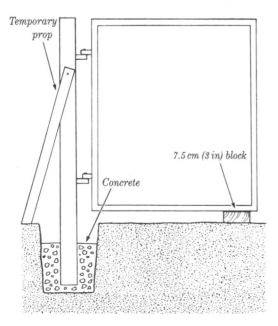

Temporary prop

7.5 cm (3 in) block

Concrete

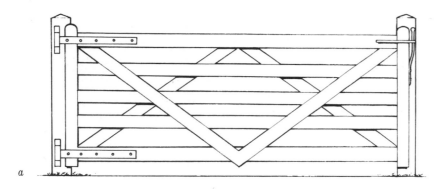

a

Fig. 4.56 (*a*) A typical design for a wooden field gate.
(*b*)a gate hung between posts will open to 90° only.
(*c*)A gate hung on the face of the post will open to 180°.

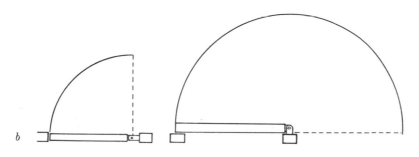

b

c

wise to leave gates slightly high at the centre, as they will inevitably sag.

WOODEN GATES — FIELD GATES

Unlike metal gates, the fittings must be secured to timber gates and posts before construction. Timber gates should normally be hung on the face of a post so they open 180°, for if they are hung between the posts they will only open to 90° (Fig. 4.56).

The posts for wooden gates should be sturdy, often 17.5 cm (7 in) square, especially in the case of field or driveway gates, which are extremely heavy. The posts should be set in the ground to the correct depth for the height of the gate, allowing for a 7.5 cm (3 in) gap

underneath. The width between the posts will be the length of the gate, less a slight overlap at each end. A gap of approximately 2 cm (¾ in) should be left between double gates. When the posts are firm, the top hanging bolt can be fixed — this is a threaded bolt for a field gate and it is first knocked through a pre-drilled hole and then tightened up. The gate can be hung on this and supported with a block under it at the far end. If the gate needs to be levelled up, the threaded bolt can be turned slightly so that the lower fitting can be located accurately. The bottom hinge fitting for a field gate is pointed and driven into a pre-drilled hole. The gate may then be hung and latch and bolt positions established.

CHAPTER 5

PAVING

The role of paving within the garden is to provide a firm, dry surface for heavily used areas which if left unpaved would soon turn to mud.

One of the most important functions of paving is to ensure good circulation so that the different areas of the garden can be reached without cutting across shrub beds or lawn; the linking together of these areas provides continuity which should be planned carefully to avoid the overuse of paths. It is important that, if pathways are to be used, they should be seen to be fulfilling a function and lead somewhere, rather than meandering aimlessly; that does not mean to say they need to be straight, but any curves in the path should be for a good reason (around a shrub bed, for example), or the temptation will always be to cut the corner. Twisting lines of stepping stones through lawns should be avoided at all costs as invariably it is the grass that is stepped on and not the slabs, resulting in stepping stones through mud; this can be minimized by ensuring that the slabs are large enough to step on and at close enough spacings so that they are not overstepped. A less fussy and more practical solution is to construct paths around the edge of a lawn adjacent to a shrub bed which will provide access around the garden, a mowing strip (avoiding the need for edging), and a firm base from which to maintain the bed. If joints need to be opened up between the slabs for paving around a curve then these may be planted with low carpeting plants to good effect. Pathways may also be used to help maintenance by providing hidden access along the face of hedges which are often difficult to reach when bordered by shrubs. Paving slabs set into planted areas will also give an unobtrusive link to house windows for cleaning and maintenance.

Functions of paved areas

There are three main areas within the garden that need to be paved, and these may be categorized as: relaxation, utility and access.

Paved areas for relaxation often form the link between house and garden and so must be carefully planned to ensure continuity is maintained between these two areas. Although patios are often constructed adjacent to the house, it may be that due to the position of the sun, the sitting area would be more useful elsewhere in the garden. In this case the need for good access and a visual link between materials is extremely important. Patios may serve some utilitarian purposes but invariably they are for entertaining, relaxing and children's play, and consequently should have a hardwearing but decorative finish.

Paving of utility areas for greenhouses, sheds, compost areas and dustbins must also be hardwearing, but without the need for such a refined finish. Driveways, however, must be extremely durable but also sympathetically designed as they form a large part of the garden and are usually on public view. The type of paving that is selected to provide access is influenced by both the amount of use for which it is intended and its position within the garden. The pathway between the house and garage that is used frequently should be paved with a decorative, hardwearing surface such as brick or paving slabs, whereas for a woodland path a softer material such as bark chippings may be preferable.

Size of paved areas

Consideration must not only be given to the type of paving but also to the size of any proposed paved area, such as for the patio, driveway or path. When planning a patio, decide how many people will need to be catered for and how much room tables and chairs will take up, allowing plenty of room around them to avoid walking through shrub beds in order to get past. Paved areas that are intended for sunbathing should be carefully planned to provide access around one or more sun-loungers which are generally 2 m (6½ ft) long. Young children need plenty of room for play; and paved tricycle runs will be made more interesting if they can extend around a garden. Junctions of patios and pathways should be staggered if possible, making it easier to circumnavigate the garden without cutting corners through shrub beds. It is also important when planning paved areas adjacent to the house, or a garden building, to allow enough room for passing by an open door without having to step back into a planted area. Doors that open out directly across pathways are potentially dangerous and should be avoided if at all possible; it is far safer if paths run a few feet in front of buildings with short paved links to the actual doorways.

Careful planning should be applied to driveways too, not only to ensure that there is adequate parking space but also to allow enough room for pedestrians to walk alongside cars without stepping on to plant beds or grass, and so that car doors do not open into adjacent walls or fences.

The influences on choice of paving

There are three major criteria which influence the choice of paving: practicality, aesthetics and cost.

Practicality

Thought must first be given to the use of any proposed paved area within the garden which will normally be for a driveway, patio or path; these three categories, which may obviously combine on occasion, can be looked at as three separate entities with different construction techniques and surfacing materials.

Driveways, which have a greater surface loading than either patios or pathways, require a far greater depth of base construction and are often surfaced in flexible materials such as interlocking bricks or tarmac, which spread any load throughout the drive surface. Such flexible materials also have the advantage of being able to flow around curves, which is often essential for driveways and could otherwise only be achieved by excessive and costly cutting of rigid units such as concrete paving slabs.

The surface finish of the paving material is also influenced by the proposed use of the area; textured paving is necessary for any ramped or potentially slippery areas under trees and also for children's gardens, where smooth and uneven paving should be avoided as a firm footing is essential. The texture of the paving material also has an effect on the speed of movement over its surface; smooth materials, such as tarmac, allow quick movement of traffic which can be slowed down by the introduction of an uneven, cobbled area. Paths which are frequently used should be surfaced in concrete slabs or bricks which are easy and quick to walk along; whereas crunchy shingle or loose pebbles, which necessitate a more leisurely pace, should be restricted to areas of less regular use.

Aesthetics

Continuity of design may be achieved by linking paving materials with both the house and the locality. Brick is particularly useful as many house bricks are suitable for both garden walls and as paving units. Local stone, or its equivalent in reconstituted stone, looks far more sympathetic for paved areas than imported stone flags or concrete slabs that are out of character with the region.

It is also important that the style of house and garden is not ignored when choosing materials as the mood and atmosphere of a property can easily be ruined by an incongruous choice of paving. As we stated in

Part I of this book, modern, regular-sized concrete slabs, for example, have an important function in many gardens but look sadly out of place adjacent to period homes, whereas natural stone or good imitation reconstituted stone slabs would look ideal. Paved areas usually look more effective when the design is kept simple with broad areas of the same surface being used, perhaps linked together by lines or edgings in a contrasting or toning material. Paving slabs or natural stone look equally good as large patio areas, with brick being the ideal small unit to provide the contrasting or toning link lines.

There is a wide and varied choice of materials available for use as paving if you are prepared to look further than the local garden centre. Stone suppliers, builders' merchants and stockists of reclaimed materials can be the source of inspiration for creating a variety of paved areas which differ from the usual square patios of concrete paving slabs often seen laid by builders at the rear of new houses. Those existing slabs need not be wasted as they may be used elsewhere in the garden for utility areas or pathways of less visual importance; a little more imagination can then be applied to the more decorative, paved areas with the possible use of bricks and stone or timber decking. Combinations of materials look very effective and may be used to create a particular theme, for example, timber decking with a beach area of loose pebbles can evoke an interesting coastal atmosphere.

Cost

If paving is to be carried out as a one man do-it-yourself operation then the only cost incurred will be that of materials; however, some paving jobs, for example laying tarmac, are not only almost impossible to carry out alone but are often best left to a reputable contractor, when there would obviously be a labour charge to be considered as well as material cost. Whichever way the project is to be carried out, it is important to bear in mind the hidden costs of hiring levelling equipment,

skips for spoil removal, concrete mixers and stone cutters, as well as the cost of all the necessary base construction material.

Choice of materials

It has already been shown that paved areas can be labelled as: patio, drives or paths and so the choice of paving materials will also be considered under those headings, with the understanding that certain materials will be quite suitable under more than one heading.

PATIOS

Patios can be surfaced in both man-made and natural paving, or a combination of the two may often be used to good effect.

Precast concrete paving slabs

There is a vast choice of concrete slabs on the market, which span the colour spectrum and range from the cheap soft-moulded versions to the more expensive and extremely dense, hydraulically-pressed slabs. Colours and patterns of paving slabs should be subdued rather than garish, so choose subtle buff or grey-coloured slabs laid to simple lines rather than gaudy red and yellow slabs laid to obvious chequer board patterns.

If possible, try to view some wet slabs before making your choice as they may appear totally different and unsuitable when in that condition. Also, try to view a broken slab, as the inside may give a good indication of the strength of material; soft slabs often comprise a great proportion of large aggregate stones bound together in an open textured, weak mix and are quite likely to crack when tapped into place, if they have not already become crazy paving on the back of the delivery lorry! Good quality slabs are extremely dense, comprising an even mix of fine, crushed stone and cement with well machined edges. These will provide a hardwearing paving unit for many years.

Be wary of taking slabs straight from the

factory as they may still be 'green', which means that they have not yet had sufficient time to cure and therefore may also crack when knocked into place.

Slabs may be given different surface treatments which affect both the appearance and their possible use; textured slabs, to provide a non-slip finish, are made by grinding the surface off their equivalent, smooth-topped version. The surface of riven slabs is often irregular and uneven, which although it makes the slabs tricky to lay, also helps to create a more convincing imitation of natural stone.

Paving slabs may be available in different size units which can be laid to form an effective random pattern, so eliminating the long lines of paving joints, and may be used to create a soft, staggered outline to patios. If a definite curved edge to a patio is necessary, then bricks may be laid either on the flat or on edge to form a neat border, against which cut slabs should be set. Bricks may also be used to create pattern lines through a paved area or as an infill to small square pockets, to give relief to large areas of random paving.

Paving slabs normally look best when laid in simple broad areas or with the introduction of brick lines and an edging trim. Patterns that are integral to the paving unit itself, such as slabs that imitate bricks or setts, look contrived and should be avoided.

Laying precast concrete paving slabs

BASE PREPARATION

The strength of the base is all important when it comes to laying paving; it is a total waste of time and money bedding expensive slabs on an inadequate foundation which subsequently settles and causes the slabs to break. Paving slabs are a form of rigid paving which relies on the strength of its own layers of construction to carry loads to the ground directly below. This is unlike flexible surfaces, such as inter-locking bricks, which spread the load over the underlying ground.

By far the best and strongest method of laying slabs is on a 5 cm (2 in) continuous mortar bed over a compacted layer of hardcore or lean mix concrete. A half-way measure is to bed slabs on five dots of mortar, one at each corner and one in the middle, which is a suitable method for extremely heavy slabs or natural stone flags which are almost self supporting but require the mortar dots to hold them at the correct level or fall. Laying slabs over sand may be cheaper initially but is really only a temporary job and should be avoided; eventually the sand will settle and wash out, causing the slabs to become unstable (Fig. 5.1).

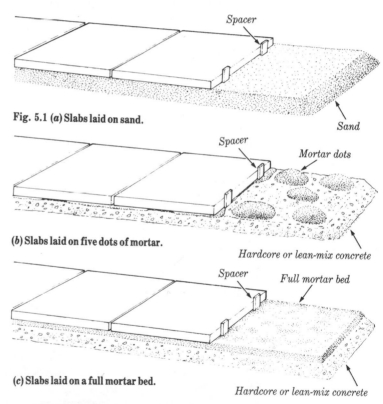

Fig. 5.1 (*a*) **Slabs laid on sand.**

(*b*) **Slabs laid on five dots of mortar.**

(*c*) **Slabs laid on a full mortar bed.**

The best type of sand to use in paving mortar is a fairly gritty material known as 'river-washed sand', which creates a mortar bed almost as firm as concrete. The hardcore may consist of any broken bricks or paving, which are both lumpy materials and therefore need to be 'blinded' or covered with a layer of ash or sand, to give a level base onto which to bed the slabs. It is more satisfactory to use a hardcore material with an even composition such as 'scalpings' (a mix of 2.5 cm or 1 in stones and quarry dust), which is also easy to spread and will provide a firm level surface, without blinding, when compacted by a vibrating plate compactor or hand rammer. A 7.5 cm (3 in) layer of hardcore is sufficiently deep under paving but this should be increased over any areas of soft ground.

Concrete should always be used as a base material when paving is to be laid in any areas of disturbed or made up ground; a weak semi-dry mix of concrete such as 1 part cement to 10 parts of all-in-ballast (known as lean mix) is sufficient and must also be compacted to create an even base for paving. It should be borne in mind that both scalpings and lean mix concrete will compact by about 15–25% respectively and this must, therefore, be allowed for when ordering the material.

The area to be paved should be marked out, allowing for a slightly larger area to be dug out than the actual size of the patio. The soil is then excavated from the proposed patio area either by machine or by hand, depending on the scale of the job. Try to save any topsoil for use elsewhere in the garden as it is expensive to buy in, but remove from site any subsoil or other excavated rubbish. Pegs that indicate the proposed finished level of the paving should be driven in around the outside of the area and used as reference points when digging out; pegs set into the patio area itself would only be in the way at this stage and are therefore set in when the soil has been roughly excavated. When fixing finished levels for paved areas, allow for the paving to slope gently away from house walls to remove surface water, and to be set at least 15 cm (6 in) below the house damp proof course where it abutts the wall.

The fall required for a paved area is often dictated by the type of slab to be used; a fall of 1:72 is adequate for most paving slabs but may be increased to 1:50 or 1:40 for slabs with an uneven and irregular surface. Pegs should therefore be set in along the house wall to finish 15 cm (6 in) below the damp proof course and used as reference points to fix the level of the outside edge of the patio; on large areas levelling equipment will make this a quick and simple job but for small areas it may be just as easy to use a straight edge and spirit level. The outer pegs will obviously need to be set lower than the pegs adjacent to the house and this is achieved by using a block of wood equal in depth to the proposed drop in level, set on the outer pegs as they are knocked down to level. When a level reading is shown from the house pegs to the outside pegs, remove the blocks of wood as the correct fall will have now been achieved (Fig. 5.2).

Begin digging out adjacent to a finished level, usually along the house wall, taking care not to dig too deep as any loosened soil will have to be removed and replaced with hardcore; a depth of approximately 16 cm (6½ in) should be allowed for paving construction consisting of a 3.7 cm (1½ in) paving slab bedding on 5 cm (2 in) of mortar over 7.5 cm (3 in) of compacted hardcore. This depth of construction will vary slightly depending on the thickness of the paving unit and must always be increased in areas of loose soil as a firm sub-base must be formed. Excavation should then continue in strips away from the house towards the outer pegs, checking the levels occasionally to ensure that the correct amount is being dug out. Pegs may then be set in to finished paving heights at approximately 1.8 m (6 ft) intervals along the excavated areas in the same way as previously described; this will provide enough reference points to dig out the rest of the soil to the correct depth. Be careful when using a fork to dig out as there is a tendency to go too deep, leaving a base of disturbed soil; a mattock is often a better tool to use as it will chip up soil to the correct depth, leaving a smooth and firm base.

Bear in mind, when estimating for the number of skips or grab loader lorries to take

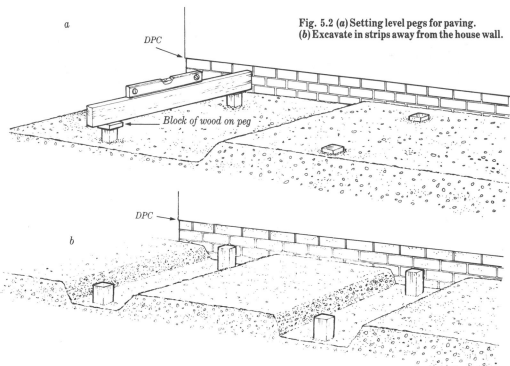

a

DPC

Block of wood on peg

Fig. 5.2 (*a*) Setting level pegs for paving.
(*b*) Excavate in strips away from the house wall.

b

DPC

away the rubbish, that loosened soil will bulk up in volume by 25% or up to 40% in the case of heavy clay.

After the area has been excavated, the matrix of level pegs should be checked in case any have been knocked during the digging out and any areas of loosened soil should be removed to leave a firm sub-base. Scalpings or lean mix concrete will then be wheeled in, tipped over the area and spread out with a shovel, after which it should be raked to the correct level prior to compacting with either a hand rammer or plate vibrator. It should be noted that scalpings will compact by 15% and therefore a depth of 8.7 cm (3½ in) should be spread initially to provide a finished depth of 7.5 cm (3 in). Again, the fact that this material will compact down should be borne in mind when calculating the volume to be ordered which will be the length of the area by the width of the area by the depth of the area (8.7 cm (3½ in)). Lean mix concrete will compact by 25% and so a depth of 10 cm (4 in) should be allowed for to provide a finished depth of 7.5 cm (3 in).

LAYING SLABS

A builder's line should be fixed along one side of the patio area and attached to level pegs, indicating both the exact edge of the paving and the correct fall over the surface from the house to the far edge. A second line should be fixed to pegs along the house wall to indicate the correct level; this is more accurate than relying on a brick joint which may vary in width. Care must be taken, when setting up the lines, that a right-angle is formed between them. The first slab is laid on the corner at the right angle between the two lines and is the most important slab as it sets the pattern for the whole of the terrace.

The paving slabs should be laid on a full bed of mortar which should be in the ratio of 1 part cement to 6 parts river-washed sand and should be just firm enough to support the slabs, but not so firm that they cannot be tapped down. Spread the mortar, using a brick trowel if necessary, and push each slab down and into it, leaving the finished surface just proud of the lines. The individual slab can then be tapped

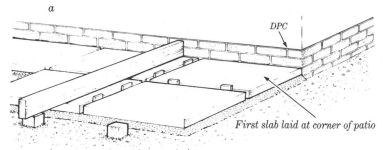

Fig. 5.3 (*a*) Laying paving slabs.
(*b*) Direction of slab laying.

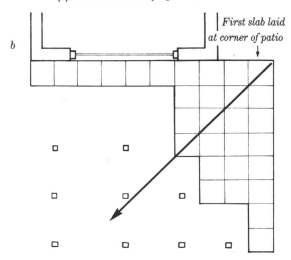

keep the correct spacings. Once the two paving lines have been laid the patio can be infilled, starting from the corner and fanning out, using a straight edge continually to check the finished levels across surrounding slabs and reference pegs.

Slabs may have to be cut to fit into a pattern, or against a wall, in which case use a slab cutter which can be hired and makes the job easy. Mark the slab with a pencil and lay it on a firm surface before cutting along the pencil line; most slabs can be cut straight through if supported on a couple of bricks or pieces of wood, thicker slabs should be cut around every face and then tapped each side of the cut until it breaks. Finally clean up the rough edges with a bolster.

Cutting slabs is not a very pleasant job so always wear a dust mask and goggles and consider your neighbours; if they have just painted their house or put the washing out, a large cloud of dust will not be appreciated, nor will the dreadful noise made by the slab cutter.

When the patio has been laid, all excess mortar should be scraped from the edge of the slabs before it goes hard; the whole area will need to be covered with polythene sheets to keep the rain out and the slabs should not be walked on for 24 hours.

JOINTING THE SLABS

Paving slabs may be either butt jointed (i.e. no gap between them) or mortar pointed, where the slabs are laid with an open joint which is subsequently filled with mortar. Butt joints are suitable for heavy, dense slabs such as those used for pavements, as there will not be a tendency for the slab to move, whereas lighter and smaller units may be held firm to each other with a mortar joint. There is also a possibility that weed growth may creep in to unpointed joints and therefore detract from the appearance of the patio; however, butt jointing can look effective in creating a sharp architectural appearance. To be successful, slabs with well machined edges should be used and great care taken in laying them as any

down gently to finished level, ensuring that it remains square to the lines and is set to the right fall; it may also be worth checking that one edge of the slab is not slightly raised by running a straight edge across it to an adjacent slab (Fig. 5.3). A carved piece of hardwood (e.g. holly), about 30 cm (1 ft) long with a handle, makes an excellent and long-lasting tool of just the right weight for tapping paving down; club hammer handles are often used for this job but the handle will soon split and be ruined.

After the first slab has been laid, subsequent slabs will be laid down both the lines, tapping to level and checking every now and again with a straight edge; if the slabs are to be jointed then small pieces of wood, the width of a joint, (normally 1 cm/⅜ in) are set between them to

speck of mortar left between the slabs will cause the jointing pattern to creep.

Many modern day slabs are manufactured to a unit size which are intended to be laid with a mortar joint in order to achieve certain paving patterns. The mortar joint not only provides a strong finish in helping to bond slabs together but also takes up any irregularities on the edge of the slab; many slabs, especially those that imitate natural stone, must have mortar joints to create the correct surface appearance and because their edges are so irregular they could not be successfully butt jointed.

The mortar used for jointing slabs should be a strong mix of about 1 part cement to 4 parts sand; the sand may be split into two parts sharp (not river washed) for strength and two parts soft so that the joint may be rubbed smooth. It is extremely important that the materials in a pointing mix are gauged carefully to ensure a uniform appearance throughout the patio. Joints for smooth and textured paving slabs are normally given a rubbed finish while riven slabs, especially the more uneven units, often look best with a twice-weathered finish (Fig. 5.4). Make sure that loose particles are cleaned out of paving joints before filling with mortar pushed in with a trowel, which is then drawn along the joint until the mortar is flush with the slabs. A crumbly consistency should be mixed for pointing, if it is too wet the slabs will stain. The joints are then finished with a bucket handle, or pointing trowel for a twice-weathered finish, and the paving should again be covered up until the next day when any crumbs of excess pointing mix may be cleaned off carefully with a trowel.

Natural stone

The types of natural stone available for paving include many sandstones, as well as the extremely durable metamorphic rocks, slate and marble.

Sandstone, which is available from many different regions, forms the ideal paving

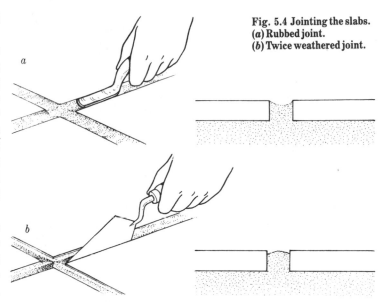

Fig. 5.4 Jointing the slabs.
(*a*) Rubbed joint.
(*b*) Twice weathered joint.

stone, especially when large, reclaimed flagstones from pavements are laid. These stones have a warmth of colour which looks particularly good in gardens when used in association with brick or gravel, and their solid appearance helps to create a sense of permanence sometimes lacking in modern paving slabs.

Second-hand flags should be viewed, if possible, before taking delivery as their surfaces may have been previously spoiled by oil or other pollutants; their thickness may also vary considerably from 5 cm (2 in) to 12.5 cm (5 in), which not only makes it difficult to estimate foundation depths but may involve four people to lift some of the flags.

It is always wise to order stone flags by the square metre to ensure that the patio area will be covered, as ordering by weight can be misleading with a material of such varied thickness.

New sandstone flags are available at extremely high cost and, although they tend to be of a more manageable size, they lack the more mellow, weathered appearance of reclaimed stone. New and second-hand stones are both available as crazy paving which, due to its small unit size and amount of necessary jointing, looks best used in pathways or small courtyards, but if it is to be laid for larger patios its appearance will be enhanced by setting the stones in a grid pattern of brick lines.

The advantages of sandstone flags must be carefully weighed against the disadvantage of material cost and difficulty in handling; this is particularly relevant if hired labour is to be employed, as laying stone flags is a time-consuming operation often requiring three or four people to lay one flag, therefore resulting in a high labour cost. Sandstone is the most durable of the sedimentary rocks for paving as many of the other available limestones, which are fine for walling, are far too soft and will suffer frost damage when set permanently on the damp ground.

Slate is an extremely durable material but its smooth and often stark appearance makes it hard to blend into garden use outside its native environment. Marble is totally unsuitable for domestic garden use as, apart from its high cost, it has a highly polished and decorative surface which looks more in keeping with the foyer of a bank or hotel than with a patio on which pots and garden furniture will stand.

Laying natural stone flags

The principles that have been outlined for laying concrete paving slabs should all be applied to laying natural stone and, although it tends to be a far heavier material, it is still sensible to provide a firm base of scalpings or lean mix concrete where applicable. Be sure to excavate foundations deep enough to allow for the varied thickness of stone, as it is far easier to build up with mortar under the occasional thin stone than scrape away continually at a sub-base in order to bed all the thick flags.

Natural stone flags have an irregular surface and therefore should be laid to a greater fall than paving slabs; pegs set to give a fall of about 1:50 should ensure that surface water gets away, although due to the nature of the material, there may be occasional low spots on individual slabs which will be slow to drain.

Stone flags are much heavier than their concrete equivalent and therefore should be laid on a much stiffer mix of mortar to avoid initial settlement. Natural stone is normally laid to a random pattern where it is important to build around a small keystone in an irregular pattern to avoid long, unsightly joints (Fig. 5.5). The stones are laid so that they are slightly proud of the adjacent paving and then tapped down to level with a mattock or pickaxe handle; smaller infill stones are bedded and tapped down with a club hammer on to a piece of wood, or a wooden tool as used for concrete slabs.

The irregular edges of the paving stones will require a wider joint which looks best if pointed with a strong mortar mix and given a twice-weathered finish to set off the stone.

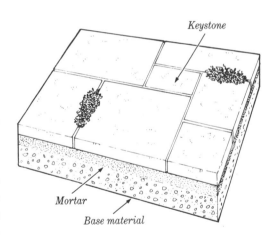

Fig. 5.5 Natural stone paving.

This is best done with a round-ended pointing trowel which tends not to dig into the mortar and is useful for smoothing off the peak left with a twice-weathered joint. The occasional joint may be left unpointed and backfilled with gritty soil and planted with alpines or other low plants. It should not be necessary to cut any slabs, except around an obstacle, as full slabs may be used in any size to form the random pattern. Full slabs may also be used to create a staggered edge to the patio, again avoiding the need for cutting.

Timber decking

Low timber decks created from slats of treated wood form ideal patios for sunny sheltered areas, looking particularly good when used in conjunction with loose pebbles to create that 'boardwalk beachside atmosphere'. The appearance of timber, which blends well with the garden setting, makes decking an ideal surface that also has the advantage of being warm underfoot. Low timber decks avoid the expense of creating foundations and are therefore ideal for sloping ground where there will be no need for expensive retaining walls. Treated timber should always be used and the individual slats should have an air gap between them to allow for drainage and ventilation in order to keep the timber dry; shaded areas for decking should be avoided as there would be a tendency for the timber to become slippery.

The size of timber used for the slats may be chosen to suit the design, with dimensions ranging from 2.5×7.5 cm (1×3 in) to 2.5×15 cm (1×6 in), and often a combination of sizes may be incorporated to create an interesting appearance. It would be wise to spread a sheet of dark polythene covered with shingle under any decking area before construction, to prevent weed growth, as subsequent maintenance would be difficult.

Construction

Low decks may be constructed simply by using either timber posts or 'brick sleepers' to support the joists and decking. 'Brick sleepers' are simply lines of brickwork approximately one or two courses high, depending on the finished height of the deck, laid on concrete footings and set at approximately 45 cm (18 in) spacings; a damp proof course membrane should then be laid along the brick lines before placing joists of either 5×7.5 cm (2×3 in) or 5×10 cm (2×4 in) along the brickwork. The deck slats will then be laid at 90° to the joists, with air gaps between them of 1 cm (⅜ in) and fixed with galvanized nails. (Fig. 5.6). If posts are to be used for support then 10×10 cm

$(4 \times 4$ in) timbers should be set in the ground in concrete to give the correct finished height. Bearers may then be bolted with coach bolts to the post in a neat half-lap joint to create a framework for the deck; joists will then be nailed to the bearers at the same spacings as for brick sleepers, before securing the deck boards. If bearers are set at close enough spacings then there will be no need for joists and the deck slats may be nailed straight on to the bearers. It is best to allow the decking timbers to be fixed and then trimmed back to the right length as this will ensure a neat finish to the deck edge. Steps up to the deck may either be of the same timber construction or alternatively large pieces of rock or timber logs may be used to create a bold effect.

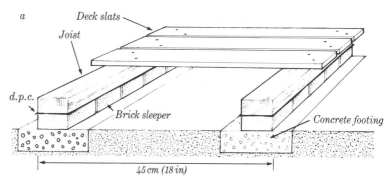

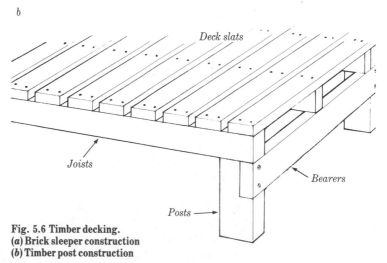

Fig. 5.6 Timber decking.
(a) Brick sleeper construction
(b) Timber post construction

Fig. 5.7 Laying concrete.

(a) **Setting out form work.**

(b) **Pouring and spreading the concrete.**

(c) **Tamping the concrete.**

(d) **Preparing an exposed aggregate surface.**

Cast concrete

Concrete is one of the most versatile of materials, as it is not only suitable in its functional role to create foundations but also in producing extremely hardwearing and often decorative paved surfaces. It is suitable not only for both driveways and paths but for any much-used areas near the house.

Laying concrete

Concrete should be placed in bays constructed from timber formwork which, if set to the correct spacings, may also combine to form expansion joints. The bays are constructed for concrete using timber which is 5 cm (2 in) thick; the depth of construction, and therefore the subsequent depth of the formwork, will depend on the use of the paved area. A thickness of 7.5 cm (3 in) of concrete over 7.5 cm (3 in) of scalpings would be sufficient for pedestrian areas, but should be increased to 15 cm (6 in) over 10 cm (4 in) of scalpings for areas that are to take light traffic. The boards should be nailed to the inside of driven timber pegs and set to the correct line and level to form the finished height of the paving; a fall of 1:60 should be allowed to drain the surface of all concrete paved areas. The bays should be constructed in areas with the longest dimension no more than 3–4 m (10–13 ft), at which point an expansion joint should be allowed for; this joint may be formed by using a treated fibre-board which will be pinned between each bay of concrete to take up any movement. The bays of concrete can be made more attractive by creating a grid pattern of brickwork, into which the concrete is placed, and so masking the expansion joint between the lines of brick (Fig. 5.7).

The concrete, which is normally one part cement to six parts all in ballast, is shovelled into the bays, left slightly proud of the finished level and tamped to the correct height with a thick timber board (approximately 15 × 5 cm (6 × 2 in)). This is used with a downward movement to compact the concrete and then with a sawing action to remove excess material and provide a level, riven surface. One of the most attractive non-slip surfaces for concrete paved areas is known as exposed aggregate; here the concrete is left to go almost hard prior to watering lightly with a hose or watering can, while at the same time brushing away the surface to expose the stone aggregate. It may be worth experimenting on a small, trial area before attempting to surface the whole patio with this method.

Concrete should be allowed to cure properly before it is hard enough to use and must, therefore, be covered with polythene sheets when the surface is just hard enough not to be marked, and kept covered for about three days. The sheets, which must be used with sacking or similar material if there is any danger of frost, should be pinned down around the edges with bricks and boards.

PATHS

Pathways may obviously be constructed from the same materials as patios but often a smaller unit will be used which is more in proportion with the size of the path and is more easily adapted to curves.

Brick paving

The importance of brick in providing unity between house and garden has already been clearly shown in its use for walling and patios, but bricks have a particular value for pathways where their unit size makes them useful for curved paths, and their various bonding patterns may be used to create both pleasing and functional designs.

Purpose-made brick pavers and good quality, well burnt facing bricks should be used for paving as they are hard, with low water absorption and will therefore not crumble as a result of frost action. Some multi-coloured stock bricks used for house building make excellent paving bricks, as do the hard and smooth finished semi-engineering bricks.

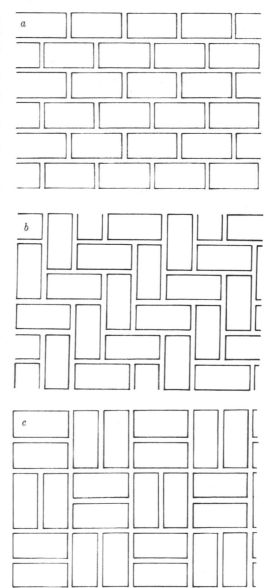

Fig. 5.8 Brick paving. (*a*) Stretcher bond/Running bond. (*b*) Herringbone. (*c*) Basket weave.

Bricks that may be used on all faces are particularly useful, as brick on edge may then be laid as a detail trim to a pathway laid as brick on flat. Blue stable pavers with a diamond or square pattern top make an excellent brick for paths and as a detail to other paving; they were once used for stable floors and are extremely hardwearing, with their patterned surface providing a good grip.

Interest may be provided by the various bonding patterns which include traditional herringbone and basket weave, as well as stretcher bond and running bond; the latter two bonds are a similar pattern but with stretcher bond being laid across the path to increase the appearance of width and running bond being laid along the length of the path to accentuate direction (Fig. 5.8).

Brick paths, like any other paved area, should be laid over a 7.5 cm (3 in) base of compacted hardcore; the bricks can either be bedded on to a semi-dry 1:4 mortar mix or, if the area is to receive a lot of wear, the bricks should be wet mortar-bedded and pointed. A suitable edge restraint should be constructed for either method to prevent the bricks creeping sideways and also to help set the infill paving bricks to the correct level. At this stage

a cross fall will be built in by setting one edge of the path lower than the other to give a fall of approximately 1:60, in order to remove surface water. The edge restraint may either be of treated timber, which may act as a temporary edging and so could be removed when the bricks have set firm, or more usually a brick-on-edge trim is used, set on a concrete footing, which gives a neat finish to the path. Once the edge restraints have set firm, a layer of mortar should be screeded between them, on to which the bricks should be placed so that they finish proud of the edging by between 0.5 and 1.5 cm (¼ and ½ in); the bricks can then be tapped into place with a straight edge laid across the two edges (Fig. 5.9). Once all the bricks have been laid the joints should be checked to ensure that they have not crept or opened up excessively. They can then be pointed with a dry 1:4 mortar mix, which may be brushed over the joints, ensuring that each

a Screed board   Screeded mortar bed   Hardcore   Temporary edge restraint

joint is filled to the top. Care should be taken not to use too wet a mix or the bricks will be stained. Alternatively, wet-laid bricks should be pointed with a wet mix which is well trowelled into the joint, both methods of pointing are then finished off with a rubbed joint.

Gravel

Gravel is available either as crushed stone (particularly suitable for use in association with its parent rock) or as a more rounded form known as shingle which is extracted from gravel pits. In either form, it is a particularly useful material in the garden, forming a relatively cheap surfacing material which is ideal for covering awkward shapes and curves. Gravel looks good as a foil to both buildings and plants and associates well with natural stone and man-made surfaces. The colour of shingle is suitably mellow but care must be taken when selecting coloured gravel as the appearance of some of the chippings can be garish.

Gravel is a useful material for security as it is hard to crunch across its surface quietly but it does have some drawbacks; when gravel is laid too thickly it is almost impossible to walk on

Fig. 5.9 Laying brick paving. (*a*) Screeding the mortar bed. (*b*) The bricks are tapped into place. (*c*) Brushing in a dry mortar mix. (*d*) Pointing with a wet mortar mix. (*e*) Both methods of pointing are then finished with a rubbed joint.

e

and so the trek to the front door becomes a real chore. It is just as awkward walking over a surface where the aggregate size of stone is too large, with the subsequent risk of a twisted ankle. Very small stones can also be a nuisance as they tend to transfer via shoe treads from the garden to the house and, if used for driveways, may be scattered everywhere. A sensible grade of gravel for paths and drives is in the a range from 1–2 cm (⅜ to ¾ in), laid to no greater depth than 2 cm (¾ in).

Although gravel is a self-draining surface, cross falls should be built in where possible up to about 1:40 to prevent puddling. Edge restraints of treated timber or brick should be used to prevent the material spreading sideways, unless it is to be allowed to drift over planting areas. The edge restraints should be set in as for brick paths prior to placing a 7.5 cm (3 in) base of scalpings (double this amount for driveways), which should be compacted with a vibrating plate or roller; a hand rammer may be used for small areas. A dressing of shingle will then be spread and raked out before being rolled into the scalpings, spreading and rolling a further layer until the correct level is reached. Periodic raking and rolling of the gravel will be necessary to maintain an even, tidy surface. (Fig. 5.10*a*).

Cobbles

Cobbles are smooth rounded stones and may range in size from 2–10 cm (¾–4 in); anything larger than this would be known as a boulder. They may be bedded flat to provide an interesting pathway, on end as more of a deterrent to access, or loose to create a pleasing beach effect. All cobble pathways should have a suitable edge restraint in order to keep the stones in bounds and to provide a finished level to which the stones may be set. A 7.5 cm (3 in) base of compacted scalpings should be laid under the cobbles, which in turn should be bedded as close as possible to each other on a 5 cm (2 in) bed of dry mortar and

Fig. 5.10 (*a*) Gravel path.
(*b*) Cobble path.

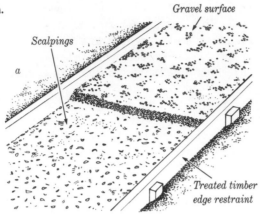

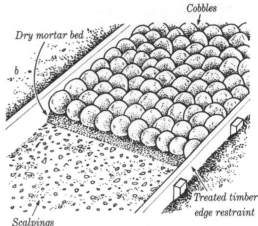

tamped down to level. The same dry mix can be brushed across the surface and watered in to help hold the cobbles firm. Hardcore may be omitted if cobbles are to be laid informally amongst planting areas so that plants can be allowed to grow through the gaps (Fig. 5.10*b*).

Timber

Timber in its various forms makes an ideal and often cheap, informal pathway, blending particularly well into woodland areas where other materials would look too hard.

Railway sleepers

Railway sleepers may also be used in such a setting to create an interesting and durable path. Lay the sleepers either horizontally, for a broad path, or lengthways for a narrower path. No hard core will be necessary under the sleepers due to their weight, but a layer of sand should be used to bed them to the correct level.

Log slices

Timber rounds or log slices, which are cut from fallen trunks of hard wood, make excellent stepping stones through planted areas and, again, should be bedded on sand in order to set them level. Chicken wire can be nailed over the surface of the slices to provide better grip if they become too slippery.

Bark chippings

Bark chippings form a superb medium for woodland paths where they may be used to dress the gaps between the above two types of unit, but also to form a soft pathway in their own right. Bark paths may meander through planted woodland areas without seeming too obvious, especially if the bark is used to dress the surrounding planting areas as well. A 7.5 cm (3 in) base of compacted scalpings should be laid underneath a 2.5–5 cm (1–2 in) dressing of bark to prevent the pathway becoming muddy. As the bark may often be allowed to drift across the surrounding beds, an edge restraint will not always be necessary unless a definite edge is required against a lawn.

DRIVEWAYS

Many of the materials used for paths and patios may be equally suitable for driveways, with the major difference being the depth of construction underneath them to carry the greater loads. Rigid paving with mortar-bedded units can be a time-consuming and expensive operation when used on large driveways, but may be more practical for small drives or courtyard areas when materials such as granite setts may be used to good effect. Drives, however, are commonly constructed

Any garden is a combination of features; the rocky stream
here forms a perfect background to the mixed planting
and paved area.

Finely sawn timber slats may be used to create an elegant fence.

Different types of paving have been neatly separated here by a darker band of brick.

This crisp precast concrete paving has been laid in bands with a wide joint between each to provide directional emphasis.

**Timber decking and beach pebbles are used to good effect
in this small urban garden.**

Above:
This attractive flight of steps has been designed using the unusual combination of brick treads and timber risers.

Opposite:
Raised beds and pools lift the feature closer to eye level and also make maintenance far easier.

Right:
Informal lines of rock have been used to make simple steps through this rock garden at the Royal Horticultural Society's Wisley garden.

This millstone water feature is particularly useful for a small family garden as it is relatively safe and requires little or no maintenance.

Below:
A bog garden, pebble beach and native planting complement this informal pool.

from flexible surfaces which spread the load, such as tarmac or shingle. Also growing in popularity is the modern interlocking brick, which is available in clay or concrete and creates an extremely hardwearing and attractive surface for driveways.

Tarmac

Tarmac is a sealed, flexible surface normally made up of two layers over the base construction. The two layers are the base course tarmac, which takes the load, and the wearing course tarmac, which provides a waterproof and flexible surface. Tarmac, which is also known as coated macadam, consists of stone aggregates of various grades which are coated with a binder of either bitumen or tar; a fine smooth material known as asphalt is also available as a surfacing material of a similar appearance to tarmac but is more commonly used for roads and areas of heavy traffic. Asphalt is, however, available in bags from builders' merchants for use as a surfacing material for small pathways, or for patching in damaged areas.

Tarmac is the material that is normally used for driveways and may also be laid as a wearing course over well compacted bases for pathways. Suitable edge restraints must be constructed to retain the drive prior to treating the sub-base area, to prevent weed growth. A 15 cm (6 in) base of compacted scalpings should then be laid prior to spreading a 5 cm (2 in) base course of open textured coated macadam, raked to the correct level and compacted with a vibrating roller which should be kept wet to avoid picking up the tarmac. The drive is finished with a 1.5–2 cm (½–¾ in) layer of wearing course, which is a much finer material made up from coated 0.5 cm (¼ in) aggregate. This is again raked and rolled to the finished level (Fig. 5.11).

An additional finish may be given to the tarmac drive by omitting the wearing course and spraying bitumen emulsion over the base course prior to spreading and rolling in a pea

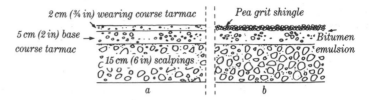

Fig. 5.11 Flexible paving. (*a*) Tarmac wearing surface. (*b*) Shingle wearing surface.

grit shingle. This provides a very attractive textured surface which may tone more with the surrounding landscape than tarmac, but it should be avoided in tight turning areas as car tyres may skid on the shingle and expose the black sub-surface.

Laying tarmac is not an easy job as timing is critical to ensure that the hot tarmac is laid straight away before hardening. Tools must also be kept hot to ease the spreading of the material; achieving good, level surfaces of wide areas of driveway is awkward and any irregularities will be hard to alter and will always be evident. It is, therefore, often wise to employ a reputable contractor to carry out the surfacing work, whilst saving some money by laying both the edge restraints and foundation yourself.

Granite setts

Granite, which ranges from grey to pink, is an extremely hard and durable igneous rock making it suitable for use as a paving material. Granite setts are normally available in 10 cm (4 in) cubes or as random length rectangular blocks and may be obtained as newly quarried and extremely expensive imported stone or as second-hand reclaimed stones which have formerly been used on old roadways. Sandstone and limestone setts can also be obtained, offering a smoother finish but lacking the hardwearing qualities of granite.

Setts not only make strong edge restraints and trim to other drive materials such as tarmac or gravel, but form an excellent surface themselves, looking especially good

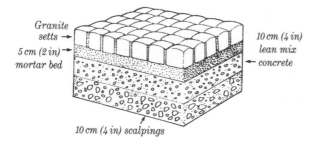

Granite setts → | 10 cm (4 in) lean mix concrete

5 cm (2 in) mortar bed →

10 cm (4 in) scalpings

Fig. 5.12 Granite sett paving.

when used for small driveways where a great speed of movement is not essential. The setts may either be laid in stretcher bond pattern, in which case the rectangular, brick-shaped units are used, or in the traditional fan-shape or fish-scale pattern for which the small cubes are more suitable. The introduction of brick to provide a contrast in colour and texture may enhance the pattern of the setts and be particularly useful in increasing the visual interest of large areas.

There are modern equivalents to granite setts available today that are manufactured from reconstituted stone in varying tones. They do not have the timeless appearance of natural stone, but provide the same degree of interest in surface pattern at a far more reasonable cost, especially when used for large areas.

Laying granite setts

Granite setts should be butted tightly and laid on a strong 1:3, 5 cm (2 in) mortar bed over a 10 cm (4 in) lean mix concrete base, which in turn overlays the sub-base of 10 cm (4 in) compacted scalpings. A dry mix of 1:6 cement and sharp sand mortar should then be brushed into the joints and lightly watered in. A stronger wet mix should be used to point the setts when they have been used to form drainage gulleys within the driveway, so that a completely water tight joint is formed (Fig. 5.12).

The appearance of quite severe crossfalls of at least 1:50 on granite sett driveways is

acceptable and is certainly necessary to drain such an uneven surface. Edge restraints may be constructed from large granite setts or from a different material, such as brick, which will provide an interesting and contrasting trim to the driveway.

Clay paver and concrete block flexible paving

The use of clay pavers and concrete blocks for flexible paving offers both a structural advantage and economy of installation over rigid paving. It also provides a surface which is easy to lay and pleasing in appearance.

Clay pavers may be slightly more sympathetic to a garden setting than concrete blocks, often toning closely with the house bricks and having a finer surface texture than concrete which tends to be coarse. The scale of either unit is more suited to a domestic driveway than tarmac, whilst retaining the same advantages of a flexible surface. The individual pavers or blocks are extremely durable and are finished to provide a skid resistant surface. Their small unit size also allows them to form curved driveways and to be laid easily around manholes or other obstacles. Flexible paving may be laid to inclines of up to 1:10 without a problem, whereas loose gravel surfaces may wash down on such slopes; any steeper inclines than 1:10 should be paved with the same unit but mortar- bedded as rigid paving.

The rectangular paving units are normally 20 cm × 10 cm (8 in × 4 in), making them easy to lay in a variety of brick bonds. Most patterns can be laid as previously described under brick paving but the strongest pattern for driveways is herringbone, especially when laid at 45° to the main direction of traffic.

The paving should be laid to provide a crossfall of 1:40 towards drainage channels as, despite some initial seep of surface water, the joints become sealed with dirt after two or three weeks and so the surface should be drained as for any other paved area. Separate drainage channels should be constructed to remove surface water and may be made from the same bricks or from special units to match. These bricks should be mortar pointed and set to provide a fall of 1:100. Edge restraints should be provided to prevent sideways movement of the blocks and to retain the bedding sand; this may be done by existing walls or paved areas, or by laying special kerb units to match the blocks.

Pavers and blocks are fairly easy to lay and unlike tarmac, where speed is of the essence, pavers and blocks may be laid at your pace over a period of time. Tarmac may also incur surface problems due to hot weather causing soft spots, or frost which may lift the surface. Any necessary surface repairs due to either of these reasons or due to subsequent excavations to services will always be visible. On the other hand, damaged blocks or pavers can simply be lifted out, and sections of paving replaced, without any evidence of disturbance.

Tarmac is a cheaper construction than flexible pavers or blocks and is sensible for extremely large areas, but for most domestic driveways that saving in cost is outweighed by the ease of block construction and repair work, as well as overall appearance.

Laying flexible paving units

The area to be paved should be excavated to allow for a 10 cm (4 in) sub-base of scalpings, a 5 cm (2 in) bed of sand and a 5 cm (2 in) depth of paving; blocks are usually 6.5 cm (2½ in) but will compress by 1.5 cm (½ in) into the bedding sand.

A suitable edge restraint must be constructed along the sides of the drive and should be set onto concrete footings and haunched with concrete; the edging may finish flush with the drive or be raised, if necessary, for retention of a bed or if it is to combine with a drainage channel. When bedding the edge units, make sure that the foundation concrete is not 'haunched' or ridged up at the front or it will then impede the laying of the surface units. Movement joints should be left in a line of edgings at approximately 6 m (20 ft) intervals, although there is obviously no need for such joints in the drive itself as it is a flexible not rigid surface (Fig. 5.13).

The sub-base layer of scalpings is then spread and compacted with a vibrating plate compactor, building in any cross falls and cambers at this stage so that an even thickness of bedding sand may subsequently be spread. Sharp dry sand should be used, spread and screeded to the correct level, using a cambered screed board if necessary. As an alternative, 75% of the bed depth could be spread and compacted prior to spreading and screeding the top 25% which may be left loose. It may be necessary, on wide driveways, to set up

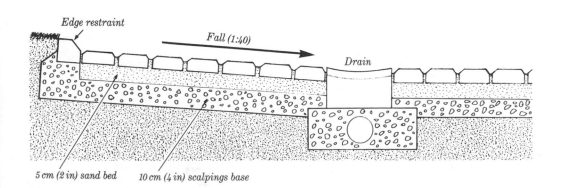

Fig. 5.13 Block paving construction.

intermediate level rails on the sub-base, up to which the sand must be screeded. Once the sand has been brought to level, it should not be disturbed and it is also a good idea to protect it from the rain with covers. It is useful, when laying the drive, to work towards the stockpile of sand so that it does not have to be carried over newly laid bricks (Fig. 5.14).

Start to lay paving from a base line, butting the blocks closely to each other so that they form a tight interlock. One of the commonest and strongest bonds for driveways is 45° herringbone which is awkward to start off at a base line, so manufacturers have produced a triangular starter unit which allows the pattern to begin from a flat line. Blocks are laid from one side of the drive to another and then back again with this bond pattern, whereas 90° herringbone follows a 'nose' of paving up the driveway; with this pattern a string line is set at 90° to the base line on wide driveways so that two people may lay blocks either side of the line (Fig. 5.15).

A 1 m (3¼ ft) strip of screeded sand should always be prepared ahead of the laying face and supplies of blocks should be brought in and stacked no nearer than 1 m (3¼ ft) back from the laying face. Manufacturers normally advise the mixing of blocks from different packs to avoid possible colour banding across

the driveway. It is also a good idea to check the alignment of the blocks now and again to ensure that the pattern has not crept and that it still runs true to the line.

Infill blocks should be cut on a regular basis to complete the interlocking surface prior to compaction; clay pavers should be cut with a hand held or bench disc cutter whereas concrete blocks may be cut with a block splitter. Once a broad band of paving has been laid, the surface should be compacted up to 1 m (3¼ ft) from the laying face, using a vibrating plate compactor with a rubber sole plate. Concrete blocks are first vibrated before fine dry sand is spread and the surface is compacted again, whereas clay pavers are sanded prior to any compaction. This procedure should be carried out two or three times and, when completed, a fine layer of sand may be scattered over the surface which will work down into any gaps in the joints. The driveway will then be ready for immediate use.

EDGE RESTRAINTS AND TRIM

Edge restraints and trim, when used in association with paving are often interchangeable, with the main difference being that edge restraints have a functional necessity to retain both flexible surfaces and adjacent soft

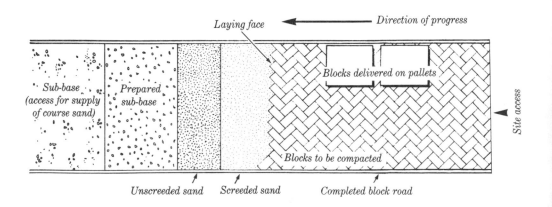

Fig. 5.14 Site layout for block paving.

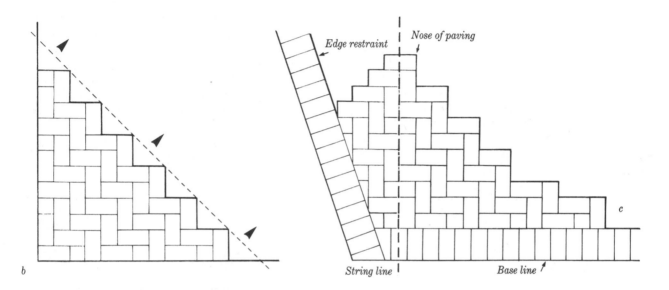

Fig. 5.15 (*a*) Laying direction for 45° herring bone pattern.
(*b*) Laying direction for 90° herring bone pattern.
(*c*) 90° herring bone pattern laid to follow a 'nose' of paving up the driveway.

landscaping whereas trim may be used simply for aesthetics.

Paving trim may be used to define the edge of a patio or to link two different types of paving; it may also be used for more practical purposes such as masking expansion joints, forming drainage channels and creating mowing strips. As with other construction materials, careful consideration should be given to the choice of trim which must be durable and cost effective, as well as complementing the style of paving and the surrounding area; scalloped or rope top edges and any other unnecessarily fussy finishes should be avoided. Only use trim where there is good reason to do so; for example a mowing edge set between grass and a rock outcrop may spoil the intended natural effect and therefore the edging trim should be omitted and the

extra maintenance accepted. Equally, path edging, so commonly seen standing proud of the adjacent lawn, serves no useful purpose and maintenance would be far easier if it were either set flush or removed completely.

Types of trim

Brick

The small unit size and the aesthetic value of brick make it one of the most versatile materials to use for trim. When used as a paving trim, brick is laid either flat or on edge, set on to a concrete footing and haunched up. It is also useful for curved patios to form a neat edge for cut slabs or may be used to create drainage channels or mask expansion joints in paving (Fig. 5.16).

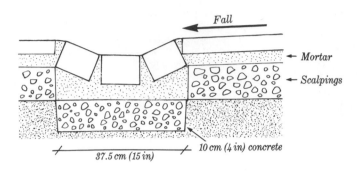

Fig. 5.16 Brick drainage channel.

Precast concrete

This is the material of the commonly used path edging which is useful for straight runs but its unit length makes it impractical for tight curves. Both round and flat top edges are available, although the latter is more suitable to set flush with paving or grass. The unit may also be laid flat to give a broad mowing edge which may also be achieved by using the more decorative, precast concrete slabs. This would provide a visual link with any adjacent patio areas of the same material (Fig. 5.17).

Fig. 5.17 Precast concrete edging.

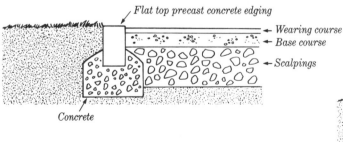

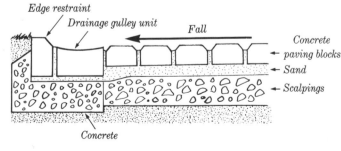

Fig. 5.18 Block paving edge restraint with drainage gulley unit.

Concrete paving blocks

These units, as well as clay pavers, are used to retain flexible drive surfaces of the same material and are mortar bedded on to concrete footings and haunced up (i.e. supported at the front and back by concrete). Special curved bricks are available or standard bricks may be used, laid flat or sometimes on edge, although their built-in spacers could make this second method unsightly as there would then be small ridges on the top face of the edging (Fig. 5.18).

Granite

This is the most common type of natural stone for trim as it is extremely durable and is available in blocks of a manageable size. It may be used to retain flexible surfaces such as tarmac or shingle, as well as creating drainage channels (Fig. 5.19).

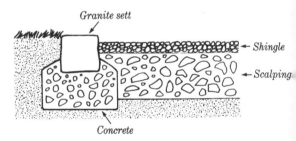

Fig. 5.19 Granite sett edge restraint.

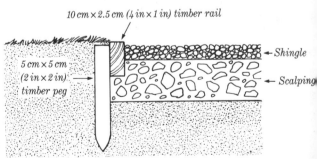

Fig. 5.20 Timber path edging.

Timber

Timber path edgings normally in 10 cm × 2.5 cm (4 in × 1 in) treated soft wood are fixed to driven timber pegs to retain paths of shingle or bark chippings. Straight runs of edging are practical, but shallow curves may be achieved by making closely spaced saw cuts on one face of the timber (Fig. 5.20).

OTHER HARD LANDSCAPE CONSIDERATIONS

Manholes

Manhole covers are a nuisance in paving areas as they are invariably in eye-catching positions and set at awkward angles. In some cases, it may be possible to lift and rebed the cover if only a slight adjustment of angle is needed so that it aligns with the direction of proposed paving units. Recessed manhole covers are manufactured to accept paving slabs so that a continuity of surface finish is achieved; deeply recessed manhole covers are also available to receive paving blocks and so provide an uninterrupted surface to flexible drives. Shrubs may be planted to grow out and over manhole covers, or loose cobbles may be used to disguise them.

Raised beds

Raised beds are literally beds that are raised above ground level and retained at the sides; they are often free-standing but may equally be combined with steps and seating areas to create interesting features. The raised bed makes maintenance easier and also adds visual interest by introducing the extra dimension of height. Raised beds which create a division between lawn and patio should be avoided if they impede on sitting space and interrupt movement around the garden. If they are to be constructed, they should be bold and not so narrow that only a single row of annuals can be planted.

Most materials can be used for construction to tie in with paving or other walling; brick is the usual choice for its obvious links with other types of construction but timber may also be used, especially railway sleepers which form a simple and pleasing construction. Rock is useful for creating a low scree bed which, when backfilled with well drained top soil and a dressing of grit, will provide an ideal setting for alpine plants.

STEPS

Steps may form a functional role in the garden but may also be a feature in their own right. Like pathways, steps must be seen to lead somewhere and should be designed to fulfil their proposed functions; when quick access is needed from point A to point B, for example from the kitchen to the washing line, the steps should be direct rather than meandering to avoid walking halfway around the garden with a basket full of washing. When time and space allow for a leisurely walk however, the steps may then zig-zag up a slope rather than taking the shortest line and should be as wide as possible to enhance the relaxed pace. Broad steps may even be used on fairly flat sites to introduce a small change of level and add interest to the floor pattern (Fig. 5.21).

Steps should never look awesome but should be attractive and inviting, often helped by planting within the steps or by positioning plant containers on wide flights of steps.

When planning steps, first calculate the height of the bank and then divide this height into sensible step heights; this will determine the number of steps needed. Divide that number into the horizontal distance from the top of the bank to calculate the depth of each step tread; the height of a step should normally be no less than 7.5 cm (3 in) and no more than 15 cm (6 in), with a tread being no less than 45 cm (1 ft 6 in) (Fig. 5.22). There should always be a slight fall on the step in order to remove surface water and so remove the danger of ice being formed. If possible, steps should be wide enough to let two people pass and on long flights of steps, landings must always be allowed for after no more than 13 steps, with the landing itself being no less than 1 m (3¼ ft) wide. Steps are often cut into banks

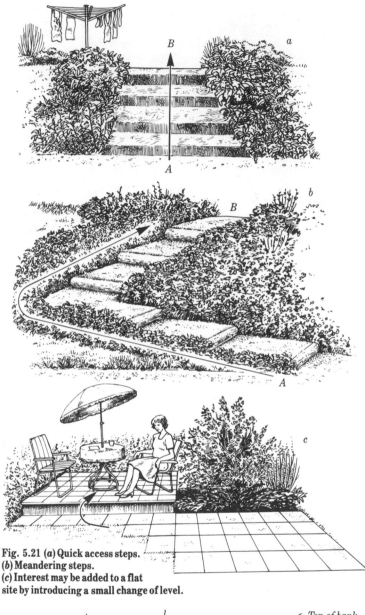

**Fig. 5.21 (a) Quick access steps.
(b) Meandering steps.
(c) Interest may be added to a flat
site by introducing a small change of level.**

Fig. 5.22 Calculating the number of steps.

and therefore retaining walls much be constructed at each side and mowing edges should be provided to assist maintenance where steps are set into grass. A paving slab set at the top and bottom of a flight of steps which run on to grass is useful in order to avoid a worn muddy patch being formed.

Choice of materials

Brick and precast concrete slab

The lowest brick riser should be set on a concrete footing and backfilled with scalpings before bedding a concrete paving slab on mortar to form the first tread. The next brick riser is set behind the slab and so the construction continues up the bank; it is not a good idea to set the risers on to the previous tread as any movement in a slab would disturb the step above, and also individual slabs which may become damaged would be impossible to remove. A series of pegs set adjacent to the steps will show the proposed finished height of each step and so form an invaluable guide during construction. It is normal for the slab tread to overhang the brick riser by approximately 1 cm (⅜ in) to create an interesting shadow effect, but the overhang should never be more than 2.5 cm (1 in) as it would form a dangerous trip.

Natural stone

This may be in the form of squared flags or crazy paving, which should be laid in the same manner as above, either on bricks or stone risers. Particular care should be taken to allow a good fall on each tread as stone can be treacherous when it's wet.

Brick

Brick steps are usually constructed with brick on edge forming both the riser and first half of the tread. This may be completed with either a second brick on edge or brick laid flat. The overall effect of brick steps is very crisp and smart and may be softened, if you wish, by the use of specially shaped bricks for the leading edge (Fig. 5.23).

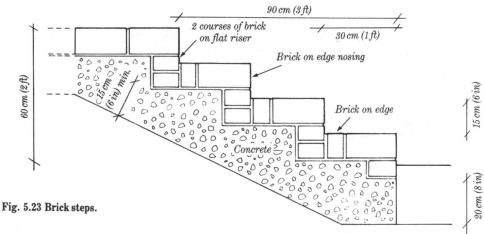

Fig. 5.23 Brick steps.

90 cm (3 ft)

2 courses of brick on flat riser

30 cm (1 ft)

Brick on edge nosing

60 cm (2 ft)

15 cm (6 in) min.

Brick on edge

Concrete

15 cm (6 in)

20 cm (8 in)

Rock

Sections of rock may form informal flights of steps through rock gardens and planted slopes but will also look good when used in association with timber decking. The rules applying to tread width and height of risers may be disregarded here as rocks will be of such varied dimensions that a degree of stretching may be required when walking up or down them. No detailed construction is necessary for rock steps as their strength lies in the mass of the material.

Timber

Timber is one of the most versatile materials for steps as it can be used as sawn timber with decking or for a more woodland effect by the use of railway sleepers, telegraph poles or machine-rounded logs to form the risers. These should be pegged at the front to prevent any movement. Treads may be shingle, bark chippings or timber blocks which are available as cubes. Log slices will also make one the simplest and most effective flights of steps for woodland areas.

Combinations of materials

Many interesting effects can be achieved, as with paving, by a simple combination of different materials. This may simply be a contrast in brick colour between the tread and the riser but more usually two different materials will be used. Timber is often used to

good effect in woodland settings as already indicated but, when combined with bricks or granite sets to form the treads, the overall appearance will be far crisper and so the steps will look good when set close to the house or adjacent to paved areas.

RAMPS

Ramps with a maximum gradient of 1:10 with a non-slip surface are essential when access is required for wheelchairs, push chairs and lawn mowers. Allowance should always be made to shed surface water across the width of the ramp. Ramps will look better if they are designed to zig-zag up the face of a slope rather than cut into it, which will require long retaining walls to be built.

Ramped steps

Ramped steps may be used to connect two points in a shorter distance than by building a continuous ramp of the same gradient. The ramped section of this construction should still not exceed 1:10 and the steps, which should be clearly seen, must not exceed 10 cm (4 in), so that push chairs may be easily bumped up the ramp (Fig. 5.24).

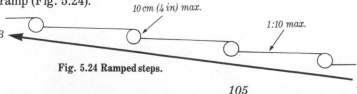

10 cm (4 in) max.

1:10 max.

B

A

Fig. 5.24 Ramped steps.

CHAPTER 6

FEATURES

Once a sound structure of walling and paving has been planned for the garden then the embellishments such as water features, rock gardens or statues may be considered. These features will provide strong points of interest and, although they will become the focal points of the garden, they should never be positioned before the overall structure has been planned or a weak design will be the inevitable result.

The features of a garden are often the luxury items which may be expensive but are not essential and may therefore be added at a later date when the budget allows; however, if at all possible, try to co-ordinate the work so that any heavy machinery used for digging wall footings or paving foundations also excavates areas for ponds or water courses whilst still on site to save it being brought in at a later stage over an established lawn or patio.

Cable runs for lighting and electric pumps should also be considered at an early stage and even if the expensive cable itself is not bought a plastic pipe containing a length of nylon cord may be laid so that in time the cord may be tied to the proposed cable which can then be pulled through the pipe. The beauty of planning ahead, and hence the necessity of an initial layout plan, is that the prime position for a feature may be found and given a temporary cover of grass or other cost effective surfacing, until such a time as the scheme is finalized. Without early planning, gardens tend to develop in a piecemeal fashion, where features are often denied their optimum positions.

WATER

Water forms one of the strongest elements in a garden and should be used with care to create subtle understatements and designs which are not pretentious and do not detract from or dominate any other area in the garden. It is unfortunate that water features are much maligned as dirty, muddy holes which are hard to look after, as they can be extremely attractive, with the minimum of maintenance.

Water may be used in most gardens to provide a point of interest or to complement a particular theme; rock gardens always associate well with moving water but may be unsuitable for small town gardens where a bubbling millstone would be more practical. Japanese style gardens often benefit from the addition of water, usually crossed at some point by a simple bridge or stepping stones. Do not forget the value of humour in the garden, for example the illusion of the sea splashing onto rocks in a coastal garden can be simple to create and will be a source of endless pleasure and amusement.

Pools

Careful thought should be given to the siting of pools and if the pool is to be a focal point then ensure that it is clearly visible rather than tucking it away at the bottom of the garden. An open, sunny position is preferable so avoid siting pools directly under trees where there would be too much shade and where fallen leaves could build up a toxicity in the water which could be harmful to fish. However, some light foliage trees may be tolerated and they provide interesting reflections, too. If the pool is to incorporate a pump and lighting, then make sure it is close to a supply of electricity.

Formal pools
Geometrically-shaped pools associate well with the regular lines of architecture and for this reason are often sited on the terrace or at some

close proximity to the house. The pools can be planned to fit in with the ground pattern of the paving and edged in a material to match, or they may be raised for added interest and safety, in which case the side walls may reflect a walling material used elsewhere in the garden and thus provide continuity in design. Although the success of formal pools often lies in the reflective quality of a still mirror surface, some movement may be introduced to good effect by the use of gentle fountains. Just as the sides of the pool must be in proportion to its surrounding area, so must the fountain be in proportion to the pool; a large fountain should not be used for a small pool as it will not only look wrong but also the jet of water is likely to get caught by the wind and soon empty the pool!

CONSTRUCTION OF A FORMAL POOL

Concrete blocks are a useful material for constructing formal pools that are both below and raised above ground level. Their main advantage is that reinforcing rods may be passed through them to connect the concrete floor pad and so provide an extremely strong structure. Bricks may also be used to construct solid walls or to form cladding to the concrete blocks, at the same time visually linking with brick in other areas of the garden.

A 10 cm (4 in) concrete floor pad must be laid first, slightly larger than the overall dimensions of the pool, on to and around the edge of which the walls of concrete block or brick should be constructed. The walls will be constructed (as described in Chapter 4), building up the courses until the correct height has been reached. It is not necessary to build sloping walls to allow for the pressure of ice as long as the walls are properly constructed; if necessary a plastic football may be left in the pool during winter, to take up any pressure from expanding ice. A concrete block, or brick, box will not be watertight and will therefore need to be sealed or lined in order to retain water; pools of this type are often given two

skins of render made up from one part cement to six parts sharp sand and containing both a plasticizer and water sealant. A better key for the render will be provided if the brick joints are raked out and the walls are first treated with a resin bonding agent.

The pool walls should be finished off with a coping, commonly brick on edge or maybe a precast concrete paving slab; if the pool is to finish flush with ground level then it is a good idea to have a contrast between the coping and the surrounding paving as it not only defines the pool edge and is therefore far safer, but it also creates the illusion of a larger pool. The coping should overhang the pool by approximately 5 cm (2 in), to form a shadow line which will obscure any change in water level and also any scum line which may develop. Overflow pipes to remove surplus water after heavy rain could also be set in the mortar joint under the coping, as could any cables for proposed pumps or underwater lighting.

Once the pool has been constructed, a period of about one month should elapse before it can safely be stocked with fish or plants. During this time the pool must be filled and emptied three times to remove the harmful lime which will have come out from the concrete and mortar. This process may be speeded up by painting a sealant on to the pool sides which will neutralize the lime and may also give a darker and more suitable colour to the walls.

Butyl rubber or heavy duty PVC liners are available which will give a completely watertight finish to the pool without the need for additives or sealants; they also have the advantage of being black, which will mask the bottom of the pool and improve the reflective quality of the surface. If liners are to be used for formal pools then it can be useful to have them made to measure so that they fit snugly into the corners without unsightly folds. Fitted liners are available from specialist manufacturers and when ordering, do not forget to allow enough overlaps to fit under the coping (Fig. 6.1). An inner lining of fibre matting or polystyrene should be set under the butyl

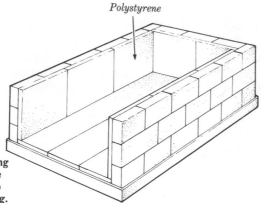

Polystyrene

Fig. 6.1 An inner lining of polystyrene or fibre matting is essential to protect the butyl lining.

along the sides and bottom of the pool to prevent the liner being punctured by any sharp pieces of aggregate in the walling.

Informal pools

Informal pools are usually designed to simulate natural water features and will therefore look best if they are larger and sited further from the house than their more formal counterparts. Try not to position the pool directly underneath large trees as falling leaves will rot and build up toxins in the water which will be harmful to fish; this will be worse in small ponds as the rate of toxic build up will be quicker. If such a position cannot be avoided, then cover the pool with netting during autumn to catch the bulk of the leaves.

Informal pools associate well with rocky outcrops and ground modelling and also with native planting, bog gardens and pebble beaches.

To achieve this type of pool it must be in proportion to the surrounding landscape and have a simple flowing outline as tiny pools with a serpentine edge will look contrived. The profile of the pool must also be carefully considered so that shelves for aquatic plants are provided and the pool is deep enough to support fish – a depth of 60 cm (2 ft) is essential so that fish can escape freezing winter conditions. This is also about the right depth for deep water plants, whereas marginal plants should be supported on a 30 cm (1 ft) shelf around the pool which finishes approximately 23 cm (9 in) below the surface of the water.

There are various methods of constructing informal pools, including the ancient art of puddling clay. Here, a fine quality, plastic textured clay must be used which is spread and moulded over the contoured pool sides and base before being trampled by feet (either human or animal) to give a watertight 'basin'. This is not a totally realiable method of creating a pond as the clay may shrink and crack in extremely hot weather and thereby lose its ability to hold water. The method also relies on availability of the right type of clay, so it may be advisable to consider more up-to-date methods.

Concrete is a possibility, involving considerable excavation to allow the right depth of base construction; the concrete will also have to be rendered (as described on page 107) to provide a watertight surface. There is still the possibility that if used in heavy clay soils, which tend to shrink, the concrete may develop hairline cracks and subsequently leak.

Rigid fibreglass pools with built-in planting shelves come in all shapes and sizes but never manage to look convincing. One of their drawbacks is the steep side wall terminating in a rigid lip which is hard to conceal in a subtle, soft manner and so tends to be paved over, therefore detracting from the proposed natural effect. Their main advantage is that they are easy to install; a hole is dug to approximately the same size and contours as the pool, excavating an extra 2–4 cm (¾–1½ in) all around for bedding sand. The pool is then positioned and checked for level in both directions, and sand packed in tightly behind it. When the correct level is achieved, the coping stones may be laid and the pool construction will be complete.

Flexible liners in butyl rubber or thick PVC are the most satisfactory solution to the construction of natural or informal pools as they can be laid to fit any desired contour and comply with any proposed outline. Ground shrinkage can be tolerated as the liner will not crack and the edges can be tucked away neatly and masked with soft landscaping. The use of black butyl will also hide the bottom of the pool and allow good surface reflection of the surrounding landscape.

CONSTRUCTING AN INFORMAL POOL

The shape of the pool is marked out on the ground and a datum peg driven in to establish the correct finished level; this level should be transferred to other pegs, positioned around the outside of the pool, which should be referred to constantly during excavation. It is very important that the pool is prepared to the same level all around the perimeter to avoid the unsightly appearance of uneven amounts of liner showing above the water level. Once you have excavated the pool to the correct profile, (remembering to separate any useful topsoil from the subsoil), the pool sides and base should be dressed with a covering of sand or weak mortar mix to protect the liner from being punctured; fibre matting may also be used as a quicker, and probably more satisfactory, alternative. The dimension of a liner is calculated as follows:

Length = overall length of pool + twice the depth + approximately 45 cm (18 in) for overlap.

Width = overall width of pool + twice the depth + approximately 45 cm (18 in) for overlap.

Fig. 6.2 Constructing an informal pool.
(*a*) **Mark out the shape of the pool.**
(*b*) **The pool sides must be checked for level.**
(*c*) **The pool is excavated to the finished profile.**
(*d*) **Filling the pool.**
(*e*) **Excess liner is trimmed off.**
(*f*) **The pool edge is masked by beach pebbles and planting.**

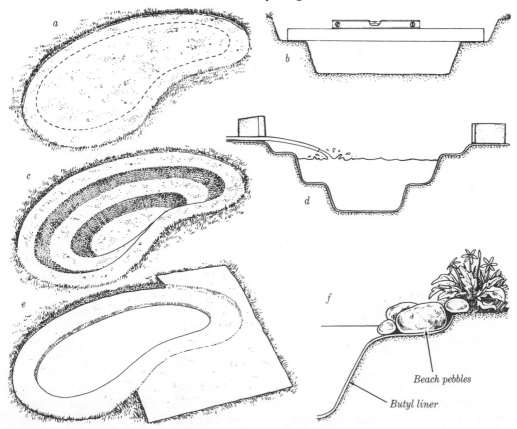

Beach pebbles

Butyl liner

The liner is laid over the hole, pulled taut and held in position with bricks or stones. Water is then allowed to run from a hose pipe on to the liner, which will gradually stretch into the shape of the hole. When the pool is full, the excess liner can be trimmed off and the overlap tucked down into the ground to be masked by turf, planting or beach pebbles (Fig. 6.2).

Moving water

Moving water brings life to gardens of all sizes and styles, formal or informal. The sight and sound of moving water is a source of constant fascination, whether in the form of a gentle fountain or fast-flowing water over a pebble-lined stream. Moving water also serves a practical purpose by helping to aerate pools, although a balanced plant life is also required for a clear, healthy pool. Lastly, the splash of moving water will help the establishment of moisture-loving plants adjacent to the water's edge and so enhance the whole picture.

Waterfalls

Waterfalls should always be constructed to a scale that suits the site and in a style and from a material that blends with the character of the garden. Waterfalls are often associated with rocky outcrops and racing mountain torrents; however, more peaceful effects can be achieved when small, formal features are constructed. Raised pools of different heights, in brick or railway sleepers, lined with butyl rubber, may be linked together by simple overflows. There is no need for a big overflow which would require a large pump and create too much turbulence for the desired, peaceful effect. On the other hand, it is important that a clear, uninterrupted flow of water is created from one pool to another to avoid water trickling around the outfall and down the face of the pool wall; a slate or tile should be set into an opening in the upper pool and well bedded in mortar with additional water sealant. A fine groove should be cut on the underside of the tile just back from the leading edge, to act as a

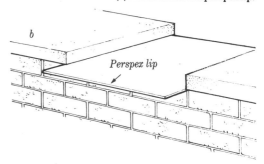

Fig. 6.3 (*a*) A formal waterfall.
(*b*) Introduction of a perspex lip.

drip groove and ensure that the sheet of water is thrown clear and does not dribble backwards. As an alternative to brick or tile, a sheet of clear, smooth perspex may be used to good effect as it is practically invisible when the water is flowing over it, although it may eventually turn green with algae (Fig. 6.3).

Great care must be taken when constructing waterfalls which are designed to imitate natural features as, although illusions can be created in gardens, the idea of integrating mountain waterfalls with flat suburban gardens is somewhat far-fetched.

No great height is necessary to form a waterfall but, even so, a change of level will obviously be needed and should be created with sympathetic ground modelling and shrub planting to avoid an artificial hummock that is so commonly seen. The flow pressure itself should be considered as there is no need for a large crashing fall when a gentle trickle would be more in keeping, and just as effective. If possible, take a look at natural waterfalls before starting your own construction; see how the rocks lie and how deep plunge pools cut in below the waterfall. Notice how stones are often strewn in the pool bottom and how the rocks seem to rise out of the water rather than perch around the edge of the pool.

The waterfall may be constructed to be visible from the house, or from a seating area nearby. As with any other water features, try to avoid siting it directly underneath tree canopies, not only because of the problems associated with leaf fall but also because of the shadows cast, which would lessen the visual impact of sunlight glinting on the water. From a practical point of view try to ensure that the site is accessible as you will need to get heavy rocks, and possibly machinery, to the area. Bear in mind also that the cost of excavating trenches and running power cables will increase with distance from the house, and that there may also be a voltage drop in extremely long cable runs. Use the natural fall of the ground for the backdrop of the waterfall if at all possible, otherwise the ground will have to be built up artificially; any mounded areas should be graded out as naturally as possible and softened with shrub planting. 'Outlier' rocks positioned in planted areas away from the waterfall will also help the illusion of a natural, rocky outcrop.

WATERFALL CONSTRUCTION (NATURAL ROCK AND BUTYL LINER) (Fig. 6.4)

A waterfall may simply form a link between a top header pool and the bottom main pool and so, in this case, it may be possible to use one piece of liner for the whole construction. The liner should be extended under the waterfall rock at the side of the pool and be used to create the header pool so that the whole

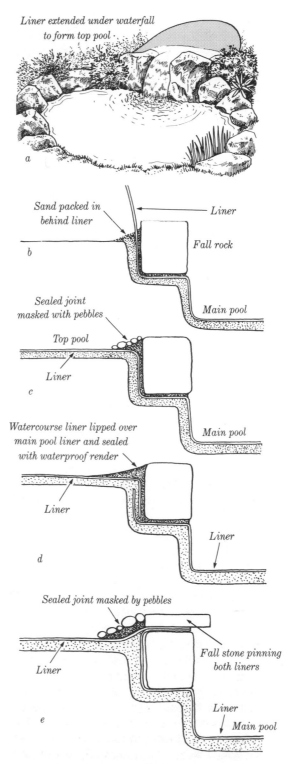

Fig. 6.4 (*a*) One liner may be used for both the main pool and the top pool.
(*b*) Sand must be packed tightly behind the liner.
(*c*) The joint between the liner and rock must be sealed with waterproof mortar.
(*d*) When two sheets of liner are used it is essential that the top liner overlaps the bottom liner.
(*e*) The overlapping liners may be pinned underneath the fall stone and sealed with waterproof mortar.

Liner extended under waterfall to form top pool

a

Sand packed in behind liner — *Liner*

Fall rock

b

Main pool

Sealed joint masked with pebbles

Top pool

Liner

c

Main pool

Watercourse liner lipped over main pool liner and sealed with waterproof render

Liner

d

Main pool

Liner

Sealed joint masked by pebbles

Liner

Fall stone pinning both liners

e

Liner

Main pool

feature is held within one impervious membrane. If a watercourse or series of waterfalls is to be created, then it is easier to use a separate sheet of liner which must be lipped over the main pool liner to avoid the possibility of water leaking out of the system. A concrete pad (minimum 10 cm/4 in) must always be constructed to support waterfalls and should be reinforced for large constructions involving a great weight of rock. If the waterfall is to be raked back into an area of mounded soil, it is imperative that the rocks are supported by a continuous stepped bed of concrete; fabric sheeting should be laid over the concrete to protect the liner, on to which the rocks will be built up using mortar to bed them in place. To prevent water from seeping down behind the waterfall rocks, a strong, fatty mortar containing a waterproof resin should be used to form a sealed joint; this mortar may later be masked by loose pebbles. A fall rock (the rock over which the water falls) should be laid and bedded into the surrounding rocks using the same strong mortar and set level across its width to create an even sheet of water.

A submersible pump must be positioned in the main pool and hidden by rocks, from which a flexible pipe will feed into the top pool and again be masked by rocks. Surface pumps, that are necessary for large waterfalls, must be set at water level in a dry housing which should be camouflaged by planting.

Streams

Streams used to connect a water source with a finished pool are very often a mimic of naturally occurring mountain streams, with boulder-strewn beds occasionally interrupted by low water falls. Streams can also be used to connect pools in a formal garden where they will tend to be in the form of long narrow channels; the water channels may run down beside steps in a series of low waterfalls known as a water staircase, or a cascade when used on a much grander scale. Careful observation of natural watercourses will be invaluable when designing an informal stream. Note how the

water cuts into soft banks, leaving pebble beaches on the inside of the meander. Study the different types of waterfalls that are created along its course and how these falls cut deep pools in the stream bed. Rocks tend to rise out of the water at the edge of streams which are softened by turf or water-loving plants.

STREAM CONSTRUCTION (NATURAL ROCK AND BUTYL LINER)

Natural streams are constructed as a series of low waterfalls and shallow pools which ideally are all built within one large liner so that all water is kept within the system. If different sections of liner are used, as in the case of long watercourses, it is important that liners overlap to prevent water being lost.

The shape of the stream should be excavated to the correct contours, making sure that the stream is level across its width, building in steps in the right positions for the low waterfalls. The area should then be screeded with a weak mortar mix, or covered with fibre matting to protect the liner, prior to bedding the rocks. If any large waterfalls are to be constructed, they will need to be supported by concrete pad foundations.

It is important that the individual pools within the watercourse always retain water. This is achieved by ensuring that the top of each fall stone is higher than the bottom of the previous one; it is not essential that each individual stream bed is level but if this is the case, then deeper pools will be created that will give more scope for planting (Fig. 6.5). The natural appearance of the watercourse will also be enhanced by creating varying stream widths, to give different rates of flow along its length. The low waterfalls are built up, bedding rocks on mortar and sealing the fallstones at the rear and at each side with a strong mix containing waterproof sealant. When the watercourse is completed, pebbles may be strewn across the stream bed for natural effect, taking care not to damage the liner. The edges of the stream

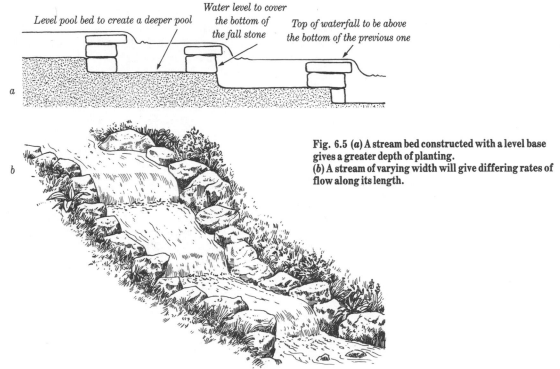

Fig. 6.5 (*a*) A stream bed constructed with a level base
gives a greater depth of planting.
(*b*) A stream of varying width will give differing rates of
flow along its length.

should be softened with planting or masked
with rocks, tucking the excess liner into the
soil and covering it over.

Fountains

Fountains often provide the focal point in
formal pools which are set close to the house,
and are particularly attractive when positioned to catch the sunlight. Simple fountains
are the most pleasing, either linked to well
designed vases or statues, or when rising
straight from the surface of the water. Bubble
fountains, which give a frothy head of water,
look particularly good especially when splashing through beach pebbles and when surrounded by a backdrop of good foliage plants.
Other effects will be achieved by the use of
different fountain heads: a delicate spray of
water will be provided by a fountain with many
fine jets whereas a bell type fountain head will
produce a smooth umbrella of water.

Ideally, fountains should be sited in sheltered positions to avoid being disturbed by the
breeze. In addition, although large geysers

should normally be reserved for municipal
parks, do ensure that no matter how tall the
fountain is, the surrounding pool is large
enough to catch any windblown spray or the
water system will soon be emptied. For this
reason high fountains should be set in the
middle of a pool, or in the case of a wall
mounted jet, the water should be directed
towards the centre of the pool (Fig. 6.6).

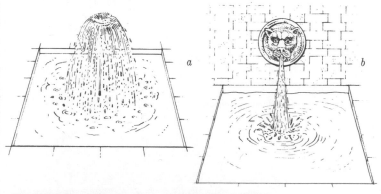

Fig. 6.6 (*a*) Fountains should be set in the middle of the pool.
(*b*) A wall mounted jet should be directed to the centre of the pool.

113

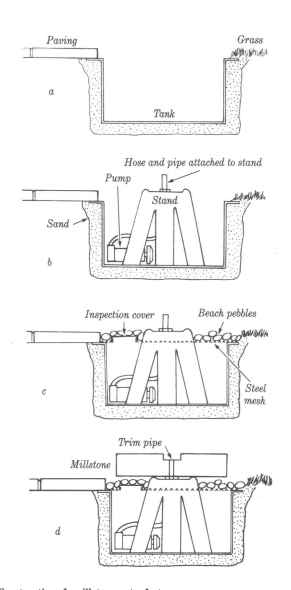

Fig. 6.7 Construction of a millstone water feature.
(*a*) A fibre glass tank is set into the ground.
(*b*) A stand and submersible pump are positioned in the tank.
(*c*) The tank is then covered with a steel mesh to hold the beach pebbles.
(*d*) The millstone is set onto the stand.

CONSTRUCTION OF A MILLSTONE WATER FEATURE

Millstone water features may be constructed using old millstones or, more commonly, replicas in either natural stone of fibreglass.

Drilled stone boulders may also be used for a similar effect.

Water is pumped up from a small tank emerging as a bubble fountain in the centre of the millstone before spilling over the edge into the surrounding pebbles and back into the hidden reservoir. A backdrop of planting around the pebbles will enhance the whole feature. The advantage with this type of construction is that it is attractive, takes up very little room and is one of the safest types of water feature available, making it particulalrly useful in small family gardens. The feature, which requires little or no maintenance, is available in kit form and may be installed as a do-it-yourself operation (Fig. 6.7).

A hole is dug into which a 1 m (3¼ ft) fibreglass tank is sunk and bedded on to sand so that the top of the tank finishes approximately 6.5 cm (2.½ in) below ground level. A stand is positioned in the middle of the tank, through which a hose is passed and fixed at one end to the submersible pump set on the bottom of the tank. The tank is then covered with a steel mesh, ensuring that the integral inspection cover is over the pump position to enable easy maintenance. A fine netting is subsequently laid over the mesh and dressed with 5–7 cm (2–3 in) beach pebbles prior to positioning the millstone on the sand. The pipe from the submersible pump is passed through the stand into the millstone where it is trimmed back to the base of the recess in the stone and sealed with silicone sealant. Once the pump has been wired in and the tank filled with water, the feature is ready for use. The water catchment area of the feature may be increased by the addition of an optional piece of butyl rubber liner which is taped to the inside of the fibreglass tank.

Paddling pools

Paddling pools are the simplest and cheapest form of water feature, available with either rigid or inflatable side walls. Their great advantage is that they do not require a fixed position and can easily be stored away when not in use; if a more permanent structure is required then a shallow splash pool can be constructed, using a non-slip material such as exposed aggregate concrete to surface the floor.

Swimming pools

Where paddling pools may be at the bottom end of the scale for water features, swimming pools are right at the top. These often involve complex installation techniques and high cost, as well as being perhaps the most difficult type of feature to design into the garden. The difficulty of blending swimming pools into gardens is due to their size, shape and often unsightly appearance for many months of the year, all of which may result in a dominant feature out of harmony with the surrounding landscape. However, swimming pools that are designed sympathetically may provide breathtaking results.

CHOICE OF SWIMMING POOLS

There is a whole range of swimming pool styles and types of construction available, so consider carefully all your requirements and your budget before making a choice. If serious swimming is a priority, then a large rectangular-shaped pool would be ideal whereas free form shapes lend themselves to a more leisurely swim. Small above-ground pools will be adequate for a cool splash in summer while covered or indoor pools will provide swimming facilities throughout the year (Fig. 6.8).

Swimming pools may be constructed as either 'in ground' or 'above ground', with the most unobtrusive type being the 'in ground' pool whose finished height is at ground level. This type of pool will involve the most excavation and subsequently be the most expensive. 'In ground' pools normally have finished water level at 15 cm (6 in) below the surrounding coping stone or paving but as an alternative pools known as 'deck level' may be constructed, in which the finished water height is at the same level as the surrounding paving.

This attractive type of pool, which is easy to climb into, requires perimeter overflow channels to cope with the splash, but unfortunately the volume of splashed water tends to wash dirt from the surrounding paving back into the pool.

Swimming pools that are set half in and half out of the ground involve less excavation and are therefore a cheaper solution than totally 'in ground' pools; they are particularly useful for areas with high water tables but also provide added interest to flat sites and a degree of protection from debris which may blow in from the surrounding garden. 'Above ground' pools are the cheapest type as they are quick to assemble and do not involve expensive

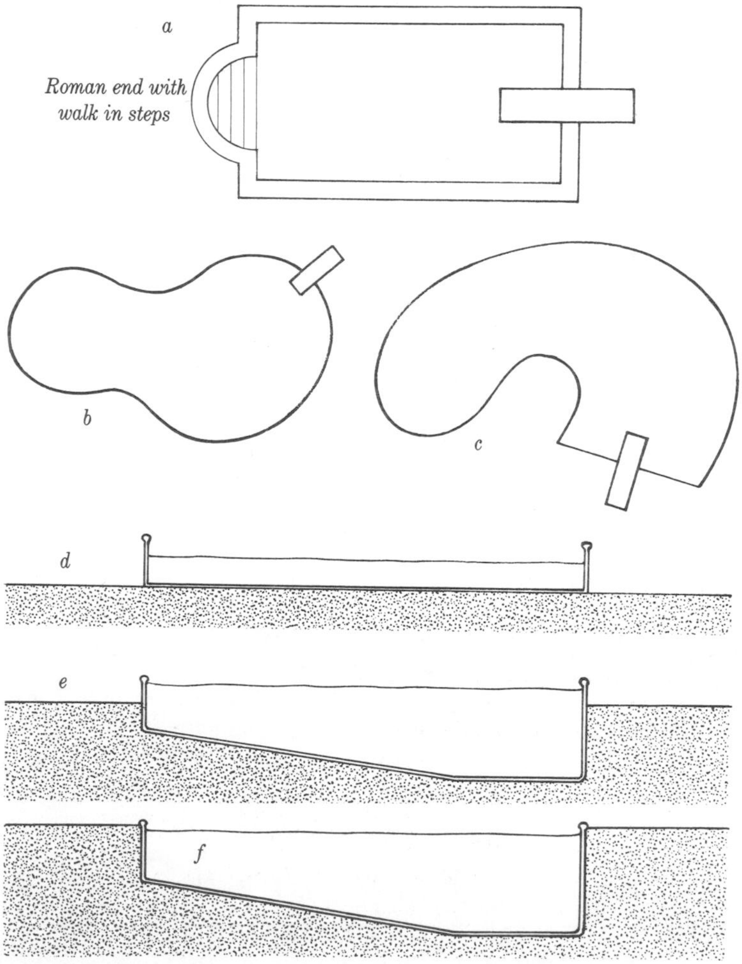

Fig. 6.8 Swimming pool shapes.
(*a*) Rectangular with Roman end.
(*b*) Curved.
(*c*) Freeform.

Swimming pool levels.
(*d*) Above ground.
(*e*) Half in — half out.
(*f*) In ground.

a

Roman end with walk in steps

b

c

d

e

f

excavation. People are far less likely to fall into them, and they may be dismantled and moved with relative ease. This type of pool needs to have well designed ground shaping and planting to blend it into the garden which may be helped by setting the pool into the ground slightly, provided that the surrounding soil is well drained and supported. There is also a choice of materials for swimming pool construction, influenced by both type and shape of the pool. 'Above ground' pools are constructed from liners supported by either steel, reinforced plastic or timber sides. 'In ground' pools may be in kit form, comprising a liner with side panels of either steel or reinforced plastic. An alternative is a pool constructed from reinforced concrete blocks which must be rendered and given a finish with marble chippings known as 'Marblite.' At the top of the range are the pools with reinforced walls made from sprayed concrete known as 'gunite.' This method is used for large pools of free form shape which are often finished in attractive mosaic tiles.

There are other considerations when planning a swimming pool, namely whether facility should be made for diving; 2.5 m (8¼ ft) depth of water is required for diving off a deckboard and should be increased to 3 m (10 ft) when diving off a spring board. The additional excavation in providing a suitable depth for diving will obviously mean an increase in cost. Step construction should also be planned for, which may simply be in the form of a bolt-on ladder type, although the more expensive walk in steps are more attractive and practical, especially for young children.

Swimming pool installations may be carried out as a do-it-yourself operation if you are extremely capable and ambitious, although it is probably more sensible to employ the services of a professional contractor. He should carry out a thorough survey, assessing soil condition, service runs and access for machinery as well as providing advice on the most suitable shape and type of construction for your garden. Open pools for private use do not normally require planning permission but it is always worth checking with your local authority. The style of your pool will not only depend upon the type of intended use but will also be influenced by the character of both house and garden; architectural details, such as archways, may be mirrored by the semi-circular 'Roman end' of a pool. Look for ground patterns in adjacent paving or in the shapes of lawns and planted areas to provide a link with the outline of your pool. Paving surrounds should ideally have a non-slip surface in brick or textured slabs which should be laid to fall away from the pool; coping stones give a neat and definite outline although certain paving styles, taken up to the pool edge and omitting the coping stone, can look very good. Kidney-shaped pools may be used effectively to wrap around the contours of the ground which may be modelled using excavated spoil rather than piled up in an obvious mound. The added dimension of height should not be ignored when planning a swimming pool as a large expanse of water set flush into a flat area of lawn can look uninspired. Consider pergolas to add interest and cast semi shade or to form a partially covered walkway to the changing rooms or house. Raised beds may be constructed to provide a degree of protection from cool breezes and to combine with a barbeque, seating and garden lighting to form the perfect area for entertainment. The ideal location for the pool will be in a position that catches the most sun, although some shade from light foliage trees or a pergola is useful on hot days. Some form of enclosure should be provided to give comfortable swimming conditions; this may take the form of ground modelling; planting, fencing or a combination of more than one method. It is a normal safety precaution for any pathway leading to a pool to be directed towards the shallow end and so consequently that end of the pool is normally nearest the house. If the ideal location is at some distance from the house then consider the extra cost in running services to that position and allow for pool-side changing facilities.

ROCK GARDENS

Groups of rock and areas of loose stone may be used with good effect to imitate rocky outcrops seen in both mountain and coastal settings as well as to represent dry river beds and pebble beaches. If rock gardens are well constructed they look superb but if they are not they can resemble currant buns and the effect is awful. Simple, bold rock beds may also be effective if well constructed but all too often they are built to look like graves. It is important that, to be really effective, these two rock features should mimic nature as failure to do so will result in the all too common appearances described above. Earth mounding should be well contoured and faired into adjacent planted areas, not raised up as a contrived and artificial hummock. Rocks should appear to grow out of the ground and not look as if they have been dropped on to it from a great height.

Rock gardens do not need to be mountains but they should have a sense of solidity; even small rock outcrops should evoke a feeling of permanence as though they overlay a great mass of rock below. Unless you actually live on a mountainside or on hilly and undulating ground, your rock garden will be an illusion of the real thing. This illusion can be created, like many other garden features, with imaginative design and careful planning. The finished effect will be more convincing if a source of indigenous rock can be utilized which may provide a visual link with adjacent buildings and stone walls and give a feeling of continuity. If there is no local stone available then you will have to choose the type of rock which you feel would be most in keeping with the style of your garden; sandstone and limestone which are both sedimentary rocks are the most suitable for rock gardens and are therefore widely available through garden centres and stone merchants. Sandstone is particularly useful as, not only can it be linked to areas of sandstone paving and walling, but its mellow colour blends so well with many other artificial types of paving. Most sandstones and lime-stones have the advantage of obvious bedding plane lines which makes it easier, when constructing a rock garden, to produce a convincing, natural line of strata.

Metamorphic rocks such as slate are extremely durable, often hard and angular in appearance and available in many colours; they too have an obvious bedding plane line which is helpful when building, but generally the rock is more difficult to handle and harder to use in the construction of a natural looking outcrop. Granite is an extremely heavy and hardwearing igneous rock which is again difficult to use in a convincing manner; sources of granite are more limited than the other types of rock and so it is more costly and not so widely available.

Most of the rockery stone that has been described is available from garden centres, quarries or stone merchants; however, many garden centres will, unfortunately, only stock pieces of stone that are convenient to handle but are too small for the creation of realistic rocky outcrops. A few large rocks will always look better than a collection of small pieces, although it is important when constructing a rock garden to use a good mix of sizes, including some small chippings of the same material to create the effect of scree at the base of an outcrop.

Tall cliff faces of rock can be built by stacking large rocks up to create a sheer wall of stone, softened only by occasional plants growing in crevices. When used in association with a large waterfall this feature can be stunning, although a big garden would be necessary for it to be really effective. It is more ususal for groups of rock to be constructed in outcrops with soil and planting between them to give the appearance of rock pushing up through the ground. The rocks are also set to an angled slant in bands which follow the line of the bedding plane and so imitate natural strata lines which may have been tilted by a fault; all rocks shold be set to the same line and angle with the exception of a few rocks laid loose at the bottom of the outcrop as though they have

Fig. 6.9 Rock garden.

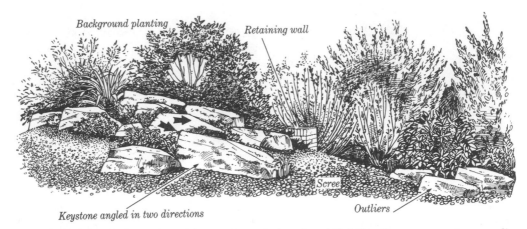

Background planting   Retaining wall

Scree

Keystone angled in two directions   Outliers

sheared off through the action of freeze-thaw. Additional small groups of rock or individual pieces known as 'outliers', set apart from the main outcrop in adjacent beds, will help the illusion of a large mass of rock below the surface. The picture may be further enhanced by introducing areas of loose scree around the base of an outcrop; small chippings may be used here to resemble the scree which is rock that has again been shattered by the action of freeze-thaw. These areas are naturally well drained and provide ideal conditions for many alpine plants which thrive in the thin gritty soil, pushing their roots down into rock crevices.

This natural habitat can be recreated by incorporating sharp sand with the soil before planting the alpines and dresssing with stone chippings to retain moisture; the chippings may also be used to dress any pathways around the rock garden to complete the picture (Fig. 6.9). Water features obviously associate well with rock gardens and therefore natural pools may be constructed at the base of rocks surrounded by moisture-loving plants to represent low lying, wet areas. Waterfalls and streams may also be built but great care must be taken to create a natural effect.

Rock garden construction

Rock gardens should be planned to be in sunny, well drained sites and ideally set against naturally sloping ground. If height has to be intro-

duced artificially then any soil mounding should be carefully blended into the garden using shrub planting where necessary to mask the edges of the mound. If there is not room to grade out the soil in all directions, the rear of the mound may be supported by a retaining wall, often in concrete blocks, which must again be well disguised to maintain the effect. The natural appearance will also be enhanced by setting the rock garden against a backdrop of trees and shrubs, but the illusion will be spoilt if the feature is set adjacent to the house or against a garden wall. Although individual rock positions cannot be planned until the stone has been delivered, a base plan should be prepared indicating the main outcrops and hollows for planting, as well as any outlier positions. The site must be thoroughly prepared, removing any perennial weeds as this job can prove a real chore when the rock garden has been planted. Good access should be allowed to get the stones as close to the site as possible; this may involve laying tracks so that lorries or dumper trucks can get across grassed areas with minimal damage. The type of equipment used for the construction will depend on the scale of the job but if excavators can be used they will make light work of handling the rock, otherwise a block and tackle may be rigged up and sack barrows as well as plank rollers can all be used to move the stone; no matter how the rock is moved it will always be easier and safer with at least two people.

The first stone to be laid, known as the

'keystone' will set the pattern for the remainder of the rock garden so it is important to get this stone aligned properly. The soil underneath the keystone should be loosened so that the rock can be bedded down to the correct position; it must be angled in two directions as previously described and held firm by rammed earth. The lines of rock are then built, using hardcore where necessary to make up any areas of very soft ground. Be sure to create gentle slopes between the bands of rock and at the extremities of the feature, otherwise the soil may be eroded. Rocks can also be laid to link the lines together in a series of informal steps, which will give access through the area and allow easy maintenance. Pathways may also be laid using chippings of the parent rock, as previously described, to represent scree. Any outliers laid in surrounding beds will look more convincing if they too are set to follow the alignment of the keystone.

Rock and stone features

The inherent qualities of rock make it suitable for use either as an individual piece or as an element in a clump to form a purely ornamental feature, as opposed to a rock garden which seeks to mimic nature. Rock boulders are often seen today set in planting around office developments, but they look equally effective when used on a small garden scale, perhaps with an overhanging maple to suggest an oriental theme, or when set around an eye-catching plant or garden light.

Loose beach pebbles may also be used for simplicity and to good effect, especially when dressed around plants, large rocks or other garden ornaments; the pebbles are available in bags normally weighing 50 kg (1 cwt) which cover approximately 5 m² (5.98 yd²) and may be purchased in a range of sizes and colours.

BARBECUES

Barbecueing has become extremely popular in recent years, evident by the huge array of portable barbecues and cooking utensils that are now available. There is a lot to be said for the portable barbecue which can be moved around to prevent changeable winds blowing unwelcome smoke across your guests. This type of barbecue can also be packed away when not in use, which may be for many months of the year; some types can even be folded away like a suitcase and are ideal for taking on holiday whereas other gas burning types are more complex, even having rotisseries on which to cook the Sunday roast.

If you do develop an interest in outdoor cooking you will find it extremely rewarding to cook on a barbecue which you have built yourself, but do take care to construct a simple unobtrusive feature rather than an elaborate eyesore. Choosing the right place for a built-in barbecue is often difficult but earlier trials with a portable type may help you find the most convenient and sheltered position. The barbecue may also be sited so that you face the guests when cooking rather than have your back turned towards them; and if possible position the barbecue so that the main view from the house is not on to an unsightly, smoke blackened hole. It was once popular to construct free-standing barbecues like miniature temples with huge chimneys and Spanish tiles, but do try to avoid such elaborate structures as the most pleasing results will always be achieved when simplicity and restraint are employed. Barbecues are normally built so that you stand up to do the cooking but low level structures which may be linked to adjacent sitting areas will be less obtrusive and easier to plan into the garden.

The construction of a barbecue is usually from simple brickwork on a concrete base and will incorporate flat, mild steel bars set into the brick joints to support both the grill and the charcoal tray; using the same type of bricks that have been laid elsewhere in the garden will obviously provide a good visual link. Barbecues should be easy to clean out and cover when not in use and they may also have integral work surfaces, cupboards and other storage areas. Do-it-yourself barbecue kits are now available containing all the necessary iron work which needs only to be supported on dry laid bricks.

PERGOLAS, OVERHEAD BEAMS AND ARBOURS

These three features are closely related and may even be of the same construction; the only difference between them is their position within the garden. Pergola is the general name which could be applied to all three features, although technically a pergola is a long and free-standing overhead structure which often spans a pathway. Overhead beams are pergolas that are attached to a house wall on one side and are therefore not free standing, while arbours, which may again be of the same construction, tend to be built over sitting areas at some distance from the house.

The main purpose of these structures is to provide a welcome area of semi-shade over walkways and patios that is particularly useful when dining outside on hot summer days. The additional cover of climbing plants will not only be attractive but will also increase the privacy and, therefore, be of great value in gardens that are overlooked. Pergolas built over pathways and draped with climbing plants form relaxing walkways; this may be towards an attractive garden seat or to a further opening, thus adding an element of intrigue to the garden.

Pergolas always look good as an intermediary between house and garden when used to link the vertical house walls with the horizontal plane of the patio. In this setting, pergolas are effective in framing views of the garden, particularly when framing the view from a large patio window, but you need to ensure that the pergola posts do not interrupt the view. Arbours, which are commonly used in larger gardens, often form secret sitting areas and look particularly good when covered with fragrant climbing plants. The design of a pergola should, as always, relate to the style of

the house and the garden; this is most relevant when the pergola is used to link these two elements. Remember that a pergola is a vehicle for plants and they should be the focal point, not necessarily the structure itself. It is important that a pergola is sturdy without looking oppressive and that all the elements of construction are in proportion to each other; all too often pergolas are constructed from large, heavy posts with flimsy horizontal rails which will always look unbalanced.

The degree of shade created by a pergola will not only be affected by the density of climbing plants but also by the spacing of the horizontal rails; the usual spacing of rails is approximately 45–60 cm (18 in–2 ft) with the wider spacing obviously letting in more light.

The pergola posts should be positioned so that the span of the cross beam between them is never more than 3 m (10 ft), and therefore large pergolas may often be built up on a grid pattern of 3 × 3 m (10 × 10 ft) squares. It may also be possible to position the posts so that they fit into a ground pattern in the paving, but be careful that these post positions do not make sitting areas too cramped. It is also important that the posts are not in the middle of pathways or in any other potentially dangerous positions. The height to the underside of the cross member must be approximately 2.1 m (7 ft) to allow for hanging climbers and still give sufficient headroom. Bear in mind that if the patio steps up under the pergola, then the pergola must also step up accordingly to maintain the correct clearance height. Pergolas that are any higher than 2.1 m (7 ft) need extremely thick posts to maintain a sturdy construction and do, therefore, begin to lose their domestic scale.

Choice of material

Pergola cross beams are normally made of wood and supported by brick, timber or metal uprights but occasionally natural or reconstituted stone may be used to blend with a period or style of property.

Timber

Timber is the most common material used for the vertical and horizontal sections of a pergola; the timber is normally soft-wood which should be treated with preservative, or painted in which case prepared soft-wood must be used. Pergolas are sometimes constructed from cedar wood which ages to a mellow, grey colour and is protected by its own natural oils. As an alternative, hard-wood forms a more durable material than soft-wood for pergola construction, although it is more difficult to work with and its initial cost is often prohibitive.

Always inspect timber carefully before purchasing and discard any banana-shaped pieces as well as those that are badly cracked or have an excessive number of knots. Rustic timber pergolas, normally constructed from larch poles, can be fine if used in an informal setting but unfortunately the bark soon falls off the poles making them look tatty and also the timber rots through very quickly. It is, therefore, often necessary to support the posts with concrete spurs and so spoil the rustic effect or leave the posts unsupported resulting in a leaning structure held up by climbers.

Brick

In large gardens pergola uprights are traditionally constructed as brick piers as they are needed to support sturdy timber cross members. The piers should be a minimum of one and a half bricks square (32.5 cm (13 in)) and be constructed around a central reinforcing rod. It is possible to build one brick square piers to support lightweight pergolas although crisp, semi engineering type bricks would have to be used as it is almost impossible to build true and vertical 21.5 (9 in) piers around a reinforcing rod using more decorative facing bricks.

Metal

Metal scaffold poles can be used to form the vertical supports for pergolas and look especially good when painted black; they may either be fixed half way into the overhead timber beam or alternatively a dowel of wood can be set into the top of the pole which is secured to the beam by a double ended screw. The timber cross beams are braced together with a steel rod to give a stable construction (Fig. 6.10). Metal is also used for creating tunnel walkways or simple arches which may be covered

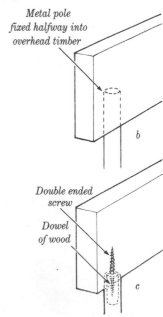

Metal pole fixed halfway into overhead timber

b

Double ended screw

Dowel of wood

c

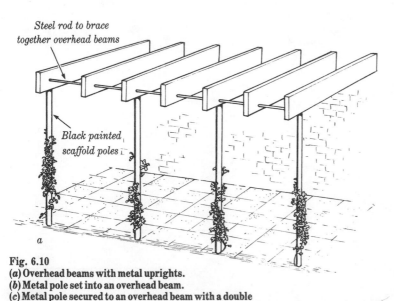

Steel rod to brace together overhead beams

Black painted scaffold poles

a

Fig. 6.10
(*a*) Overhead beams with metal uprights.
(*b*) Metal pole set into an overhead beam.
(*c*) Metal pole secured to an overhead beam with a double ended screw.

with fruit trees or fragrant climbers. These structures were often built from wrought iron and constructed on a grand scale to frame views and create scented walkways; today a cheaper alternative is tubular steel, often nylon coated for durability, which forms a very strong and easy to assemble framework for heavy climbers. Metal may also be used in the form of strained steel wire as an overhead support for climbing plants which looks very good when used adjacent to the house. The wire is trained between eye bolts secured to the side walls to give a light and effective medium for climbers.

Pergola construction – timber

The jointing of posts should be carefully planned to avoid wasting wood and should be carried out at ground level before the posts are set upright. The posts, which are normally 10 or 12.5 cm (4 or 5 in) square are positioned at suitable spacings, as previously described, and set into concrete; the concrete must be rammed firm and chamfered at the top to allow drainage away from the post which must, in turn, be checked for vertical in both directions using a spirit level. Metal shoes are available to support the posts and eliminate the problem of rot at ground level; the shoes may either be set

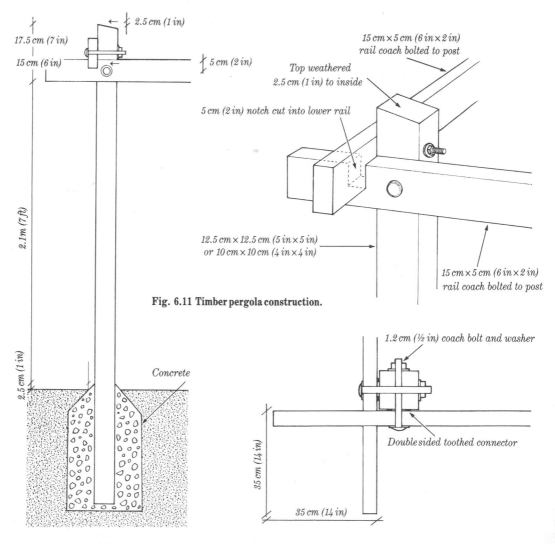

Fig. 6.11 Timber pergola construction.

into concrete or bolted on to a paved surface. The cross beams, which should already be notched out to receive the rafters, are bolted to the uprights using rustproofed coach bolts. The beams are usually 15×5 cm (6×2 in) in section and may either be set alongside the face of the post or set flush into a jointed post. The coach bolts can be recessed into the timber using washers to prevent them being pulled through when tightened with a spanner; galvanized toothed connectors set between the faces of the timber make an even stronger joint (Fig. 6.11). The rafters, which are again 15×5 cm (6×2 in) are set into the beams by approximately 5 cm (2 in) thus leaving 10 cm (4 in) proud of the beam. It is possible to notch the rafters over the beam for the same effect although they may tend to twist and pop off when not held tight into a joint. A smart appearance that looks good with modern buildings is created when both rafter and cross beam are jointed to half their depth so that their tops finish flush when the two pieces are jointed together. The rafters can either be cross nailed into the beam with galvanized nails or alternatively rustproof screws may be used for a stronger fixing. Normally rafters are set level along the top of a pergola although occasionally they may slope down from a house wall so that the front supporting posts do not need to be excessively high. When overhead beams are fixed to a house wall they are either let into a notched supporting timber that has been bolted to the wall or they sit in joist hangers which are fixed to the house with galvanized screws. The rafters, which look good extending beyond the cross beam by approximately 30 cm (1 ft) may be left square or be given a shaped end for a softer effect. Although the timber should have been treated before assembling, any cut ends that were subsequently made during construction must be rubbed down and treated with non toxic preservative. Plant supporting wires are then fixed along the underside of the rafters and held taut by vine eyes screwed into the timber.

There are many elaborate variations to pergola construction but remember that the strength of a pergola is extremely important so try to avoid too many cuts in a post, which would weaken the structure, and, as always, keep the design simple for the best result.

GARDEN BUILDINGS

The manufacture of garden buildings is a huge industry that produces a wide range of structures which cater for both utility and relaxation. Sheds, dustbin stores, workshops and greenhouses therefore may be grouped together in a designated utility area and are often screened by trellis work or shrubs. Buildings that are designed for relaxation, which include summerhouses, conservatories and gazebos, tend to be more decorative and are therefore often positioned to form a focal point.

Buildings are usually large structures which are difficult to fit into a garden unless initially planned for, so always consider their position in the early design stages even if they are not to be built straight away. Utility buildings, such as greenhouses, sheds and compost areas, should if at all possible be grouped together to avoid these different stuctures being dotted all over the garden; adequate provision should also be made for adjacent service paths which should be wide enough for wheel barrows and lawn mowers, especially outside shed doorways where more space is needed for turning. Position the buildings so that shed doors, for example, open against planting areas not across pathways where you need to walk. Bin areas, which are never the most attractive feature, may be enclosed in simple structures and if possible positioned in the shade; it may also be useful to grow fragrant plants nearby to mask any unpleasant smells.

Garden buildings, especially those that are used as focal points, should relate to the character of both the garden and the house, and are often linked visually to the latter by the style of the windows, the pitch of the roof or some other architectural detail.

Sheds

Sheds tend to be multi-purpose storage rooms for housing garden tools, lawn mowers, wheel barrows and pedal cars but unfortunately they often become unwanted focal points. Careful planning of storage space in the garage, which admittedly can be barely big enough for the car, may eliminate the need for a shed altogether. However, if it is absolutely necessary to have a shed, it should be carefully sited and screened with shrubs or trellis, positiong any shed with an apex roof sideways on to avoid the uncomfortable view of a gable end which can be difficult to disguise. Sheds are often tucked away under trees or in awkward corners of the garden which is fine as long as good access is provided; although sheds are usually positioned at the bottom of the garden, consider siting them behind a garage

or at a half way point in long, sloping gardens to shorten the walk with heavy garden equipment.

Although shed suppliers may offer a cheap assembly service, sheds can be put up by two people as a fairly easy do-it-yourself operation (Fig. 6.12). A suitable base must first be constructed which may be in the form of timber bearers as a support for simple structures; the ground should be roughly levelled prior to laying the 7.5 × 7.5 cm (3 × 3 in) timber bearers level to each other and along their length and set to run at 90° to the floor joists. A strip of damp-proof membrane may be run along each bearer before positioning the floor which can then be tacked temporarily to the bearers to prevent any movement during construction. Larger sheds that require a more solid base may be set on paving slabs, possibly reusing durable but dull looking slabs lifted from an old

Fig. 6.12 Timber shed construction.

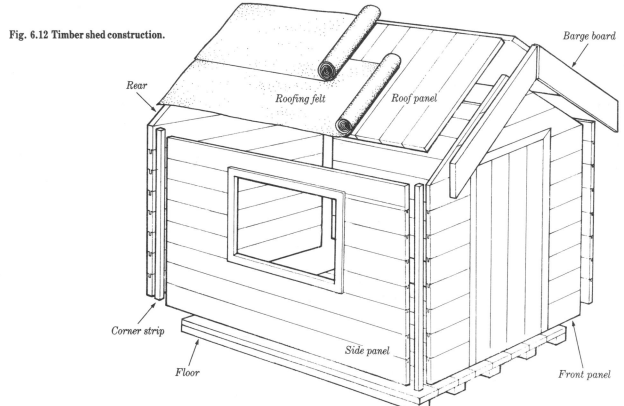

path or patio. Very large structures that need a strong, long-lasting base should be set on an area of 10–15 cm (4–6 in) of concrete over a layer of compacted hard core. The whole shed is supplied in self assembly kit form with side and roof panels which simply bolt together; do not tighten the bolts completely until the whole building has been assembled as minor adjustments may be needed during the course of construction. The roof is finished in felt, available either in rolls or in strips of decorative tiles, which should be secured with felt tacks. Once the shed has been assembled, it must be treated with a suitable non-toxic preservative.

Greenhouses

Greenhouses will often look good in their own right if they are treated properly as a working unit with plants growing in them rather than if used as a storage shed. A greenhouse full of plants will look far more interesting than the side wall of a shed and will, therefore, not require such dense screening which would cut out too much light anyway. Managing a greenhouse requires a commitment which can be quite a tie especially watering during the summer; going away on holiday during this period can prove disastrous and leaving next doors' children to do the job may be far from satisfactory. In this case, if you intend to develop a serious interest in greenhouse gardening, it would be more beneficial to invest in automatic vents and an irrigation system.

Greenhouses are available in all manner of shapes and sizes with the most usual type having a span roof and sides where the lower part is enclosed or where glass extends to the floor; this choice is dependent on the type of material you wish to grow. If you are not an enthusiastic grower, it may be that the appearance of the building is the most important factor in which case greenhouses with cedar wood frames are particularly useful as they blend into the garden more easily that those with aluminium frames (Fig. 6.13).

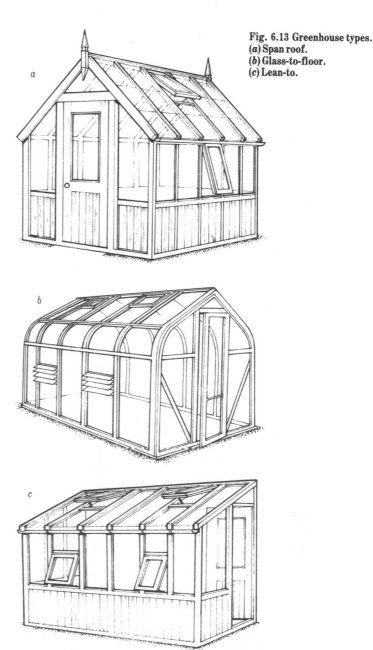

Fig. 6.13 Greenhouse types.
(a) Span roof.
(b) Glass-to-floor.
(c) Lean-to.

Suppliers of greenhouses may provide a cheap assembly service or you could carry out the construction yourself with the help of the instruction manual and an assitant. The base may either be concrete slabs or more usually two courses of brickwork on to which the greenhouse frame will sit and lip over the edge of the bricks. As with shed construction, do not over tighten all the fixing bolts of the greenhouse until it is assembled and try to choose a calm day before attempting to fit the glass. A particular compass axis for the ridge is not so relevant as ensuring that the greenhouse has an open sunny site away from the shade of trees and overhanging branches.

A hedge or other windbreak should be provided if the greenhouse is to be in an exposed position and also site the building as close as possible to the house for convenience and to save cost on the installation of services.

Summerhouses

Summerhouses are decorative buildings which are again available in a wide range of styles. They are often no more than glorified sheds embellished with verandahs, shutters and window boxes and used for storing garden furniture that will not fit anywhere else. These chalet style buildings come in self assembly kit form and are bolted together in the same manner as sheds. The more useful summerhouses are those that can be used as an extra room which are often in tasteful designs and therefore quite rightly command a position as a focal point within the garden.

Gazebos

This type of building often has two or more open sides and is positioned so that different areas of interest within the garden may be viewed. They are normally used for large landscapes although on a smaller scale they can still be decorative and used to form a focal point. Gazebos are available in kit form with side panels of trellis for climbing plants or they may be purpose built in a variety of styles including Victorian and oriental.

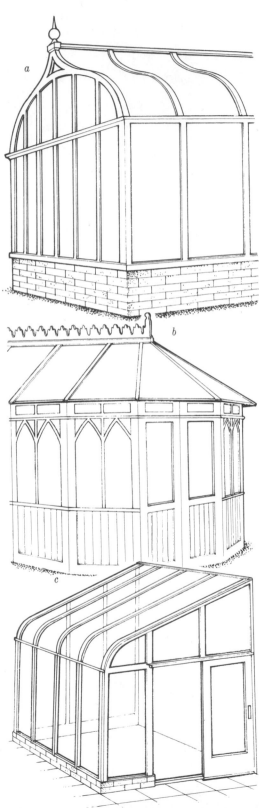

Fig. 6.14 Conservatory styles.
(*a*) and (*b*) Traditional styles.
(*c*) Modern style with curved eaves.

Conservatories

Conservatories were originally developed as buildings in which to grow ornamental and exotic plants but later developed as a place for grand tea parties. The conservatory today combines the two functions of growing plants and entertaining in an extra room which is often far cheaper to construct than a conventional house extension. A single glazed conservatory would be too cold for use in winter whereas as a double glazed room could be used all the year round.

Emphasis may be put on the conservatory as a plant room with occasional seating in which case the floor may be tiled in terracotta with plants set into beds or the room may be treated as a house extension which could be furnished, carpeted and decorated with house plants.

The style of conservatory may be Victorian or modern which could be a simple rectangle or have curved eaves; as always try to choose a style that complements your house. The cheapest conservatory is the single glazed do-it-yourself building with the double glazed made-to-measure version being the most expensive.

Obtaining planning approval is not normally a problem although bear in mind that any existing extensions will be considered before approval is granted as you will only be allowed to increase your house size from the original by a limited amount (Fig. 6.14). Solid foundations will be necessary including a damp proof course membrane which will link to the damp proof course of the house. A solid floor of hardcore, concrete and mortar screed should also be laid prior to tiling, allowing a duct under the floor to any airbrick in the house wall. As a safety precaution it would be wise to use laminated glass for the conservatory or toughened glass may be used which can also be covered

with plastic safety film to hold the glass together should it be cracked.

Conservatory construction involves many aspects which although you could handle yourself are often best left to a reputable company.

PLAY AREAS

If you do have young children it is important that their requirements are considered when designing the garden which can still be attractive and cater for your needs as well as theirs without looking like the local recreation ground. Keep your children safe by ensuring that all fences and gates are secure but never banish them from certain areas or restrict them to others as they will soon lose interest in the garden or in playing outside altogether which would be sad in either case. Some parents have been known to ban their children from playing on the lawn which is ridiculous and as bad as municipal parks which display 'Keep off the grass' signs. Gardens are an

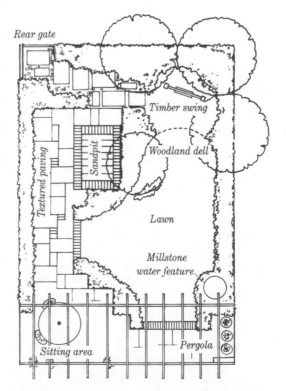

Fig. 6.15 'The Chenies Young Family Garden', a medal winner at The Chelsea Flower Show in 1989, was designed specifically for a young family to live and relax in.

extension of the house and should be for the whole family to enjoy; they are a source of great imaginative play and therefore children should be considered in every element of the design.

Paved areas should not be so small that all the space is taken up in garden furniture, leaving no room for children's play. Larger areas of paving will be more useful especially if extended around the garden to provide a track for bikes and other wheeled toys. The paving material should be non-slip with a textured surface to give a good grip; riven slabs should be avoided as they would trip up little feet in full flight every time. Gentle ramps, where necessary, are more suitable in paved areas than low steps which may form a trip and interrupt the bike track.

A well laid lawn, no matter how small, is essential in a children's garden but it should be laid with a hard wearing turf made up of tough grasses such as dwarf rye; it should also be set flush with adjacent paving to give good movement from one area to another (Fig. 6.15).

The addition of a simple sandpit will be the source of endless enjoyment and imaginative play; the sandpit need only be small but it will attract neighbouring children like bees around a honey pot — more than once I counted seven youngsters playing in a sandpit that I constructed for my children which only measured 1.35 m × 90 cm (4½ ft × 3 ft). A sandpit that is set flush with the surrounding paving is particularly useful as when it is covered it can be ridden across with bikes or used as an extra sitting area. Plan the size of the sandpit to fit paving units so that no slab cutting is required around its perimeter and so that it may be paved in at a later date or turned into a pool when the children are older. The depth of the pit must allow for 25–30 cm (10–12 in) of silver sand (not builder's sand which would stain) laid over a drainage membrane (e.g. the plastic mesh used for windbreaks) which in turn is laid over 25 cm (10 in) of reject stone to act as a soakaway. The sandpit must always be

covered over when not in use to prevent cats using it at night. The lid can be constructed from slatted timber boards (15 × 2.5 cm (6 × 1 in)) with planed edges which are fixed to a framework of 5 × 5 cm (2 × 2 in) timber battens and should be made in two halves so that it may be easily removed. The lid will look good if set into a border trim of bricks laid on edge which will also form an ideal dry seat for children to sit on. A raised sandpit may be constructed from either brick or timber but in each case adequate drainage must be provided as well as air gaps in the lid to keep the sand fresh and dry; the sandpit may again be converted into a raised bed or pool when the children are older (Fig. 6.16).

A swing is almost as essential in a children's garden as a sandpit but care should be taken to site the swing away from sitting areas and in a position which will allow room for a full swing and for someone to do the pushing. The swing should be sited over a soft surface which is normally grass, however if it is to be combined with other play equipment, an area of bark chippings would be more practical to prevent a mud bath being created. A sturdy timber swing looks good and will blend with the garden or alternatively a rope swing may be constructed by passing a rope through a timber seat and attaching it to a suitable tree branch but always check this for strength and safety. Swings in kit form available from shops are fine if you do not mind the bright colours and accept that they will never blend into background planting.

Water features must be planned carefully if they are to be used in children's gardens as even shallow depths of water are potentially dangerous. However, water does provide a constant source of fascination for children and if it can be incorporated it will provide an additional element to their play which should nonetheless be supervised at all times. A paddling pool is the simplest water feature which will give hours of enjoyment on a hot summers day; the pool may either be prefabricated or built with a non slip surface incorpor-

Rock should always be set to a 'bedding plane' to
simulate natural strata.

Above:
Posts and ropes can form a delightful screen and are ideal for climbing roses.

Opposite:
Pergolas should always have adequate headroom and provide the ideal frame for climbing plants.

Right:
Timber slats are fixed to low walling to form a useful corner seat.

An arbour can be built from many materials and here
trellis panels are topped with a wrought-iron dome.

This ground level sand pit, when covered, can be ridden across with bikes or used as an extra sitting area.

xviii

Opposite above:
Ornamental planting at Givergny with an amazing diversity of plants and colours.

A narrow border in the shade of a high wall where the bold leaves of hostas contrast with the more delicate leaves of the overhanging acer.

Opposite below:
A subtle combination of planting will provide colour and interest throughout the year as well as keeping maintenance to a sensible minimum.

A harmony of complementary colours: yellow achillea and hemerocallis with the lilac blue of *Salvia uliginosa*.

Water and planting always associate well as do different
leaf shapes and textures. The acer and ligularia are a
particularly fine combination.

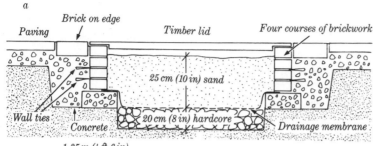

Fig. 6.16 Design for an in-ground sandpit.
(a) Construction detail.
(b) Plan view showing brick on edge trim.

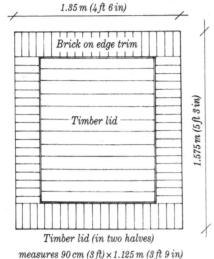

Timber lid (in two halves)
measures 90 cm (3 ft) × 1.125 m (3 ft 9 in)

ating a simple drain. Water bubbling through rocks or a millstone forms one of the safest water features, but should be kept away from the sandpit to avoid a quagmire being formed. Small ponds which will attract wildlife and provide hours of interest can be constructed in the garden when the children are no longer toddlers.

These days there are countless play structures on the market which cater for all the physical elements of climbing, swinging, sliding and balancing as well as providing quiet areas for sitting and reading. However, these items tend to be quite bulky and expensive, geared more to recreation grounds and less viable for individual families. It is often more satisfactory to construct your own play equipment but do carry out regular maintenance to ensure there are no splinters and that all bolts are tightened up. Seats and balancing bars may be easily constructed from logs and planks, while tree houses are great if you are lucky enough to own a suitable, mature tree.

Children also love little buildings which may be a house one minute and a shop the next but you do not need to buy an expensive purpose built article as a blanket laid over a couple of garden chairs will be just as effective and far more interesting.

It is important to keep an eye on toddlers when they are playing but older children like secret corners to hide in so consider this when designing the garden; a simple group of well positioned shrubs will be all that is needed. A low wall or seat in the garden will form an ideal table top for outdoor painting but do ensure that water based paints are used which can be washed off paving to avoid a multi-coloured patio.

Apart from safety, the main consideration in a children's garden must be simplicity; nothing should be too fussy or elaborate so bear in mind before you rush out to buy some expensive play equipment that children will probably have more fun and use more imagination playing with a few large cardboard boxes!

LIGHTING AND POWER

Electricity is the main source of power in the garden; it has already been shown that it is used to run submersible and surface pumps as well as automatic watering systems for greenhouses. Electricity is also used for many power tools including lawn mowers, concrete mixers and hedge trimmers but it also has a decorative function when used for garden lighting. Electrical installation is best left to a professional electrician which will not cost a fortune on a simple scheme especially if you prepare the trenches and lay the cable yourself. Employing an expert will not only give you peace of mind but also a professional will be familiar with all the latest wiring regulations. Some garden lighting systems are stepped down to a lower voltage from the mains supply through a transformer for safety while other lighting systems, as well as large submersible and surface pumps, run directly off the mains supply and should, therefore, be wired into a residual current circuit breaker (R.C.C.B.) which will cut off the power if the cable is damaged in any way. Special safety plugs may also be purchased for use with power tools, such as electric hedge trimmers. Armoured cable should always be used for electric installations in the garden; this is an extremely heavy cable which carries the electric wires in a protective armoured sheath. The cable may be attached to the house wall using special clips and should be set at a depth of 60 cm (2 ft) under the ground to prevent it being dug up or damaged. Proper waterproof connections must be made at all outlets for lights or pumps and outdoor sockets, which have screw on caps to keep out small fingers, may also be wired in; these sockets are particularly useful in large gardens to avoid long cable runs from the house.

The electrical layout of the garden should be planned out at the early stages of the design to prevent either expensive paving being lifted at a later date or to avoid ugly wiring around the outside of the paved area if the slabs are to remain intact. It is also useful if you indicate any cable runs on your garden plan not only for your benefit but for subsequent owners too.

Lighting

This is an aspect of garden construction which is sadly underused as even the most ordinary gardens take on a magical appearance at night when illuminated with subtle lighting. When garden lighting is installed it not only provides an interesting view but it extends the room beyond the window rather than cutting it off.

One reason for lighting being underused is that many people feel that it is complicated and therefore expensive, however, with professional help, it can be simple and cheap to put in as has already been indicated; there are even specialist garden lighting companies who will design and install the whole system for you. The other reason that lighting is seldom installed is due to the staggering array of appallingly designed garden lights on the market.

Garden lighting may be functional or decorative but in each case should be well planned. If it is necessary to have floodlights on a house for security then it is more considerate if they are only switched on by hidden beams or sensors rather than blasting away continually as though in a prison camp. Porch lights should be sited to one side of the porch not directly overhead, to avoid insects buzzing around visitors who are waiting at the door.

Lights are essential for safety to illuminate steps and paths and to indicate the direction from the drive to the front door. Steps may be lit by recessed lights set into the brickwork of the side wall or by simple bulkhead lights which are available quite cheaply. Bollard lights look good when used next to drives or to illuminate pathways, they provide a pool of light where it is needed and may incorporate opaque glass to avoid glare. Choose the sturdy type of bollard, not the flimsy plastic type and set rocks or foliage plants around the base for good effect.

Spotlights are often used to shine down and illuminate working areas such as barbecues but they may also be used for more decorative purposes by shining up into a tree canopy or to provide a subdued glow through shrub planting. When spotlights are used to highlight a focal point such as a statue it is best to mask the source of light so as not to detract from the main point of interest; equally in daylight it is a good idea to disguise the light fitting with planting unless it has some ornamental value. Spotlights that are set at ground level should be left with enough cable so that they may be moved around until the most effective position is found. Interesting effects can be achieved by illuminating plants against a wall to provide a delicate tracery of shadows or when lights are used in association with water but try to avoid the fairy grotto coloured lights which can look pretty grim.

Many garden lights have now been developed which incorporate a transformer to provide a low voltage system; some of these lights are very flimsy and with no particular design value whereas others blend well with the landscape and look superb.

Lighting technology has now advanced with the use of fibre optic lighting which relies on a single light source being fed along strands of glass fibre. The light may be taken to a single point at the end of the strand and therefore used to illuminate a feature, or if the strand is purposely interrupted along its length then light will shine from those points to produce an interesting effect. A colour wheel may be positioned in front of the light source to create a shimmering light along the strands which looks particularly good when used to illuminate a water feature. The advantage of fibre optic lighting in the garden is that there is no electric current running through the strands of light so they are quite safe to lay among shrubs or even in water. This type of lighting may be used for safety by running light strands around a paving edge or for decorative effect when draped through waterfalls to illuminate the cascades of water.

FURNISHINGS

Garden seating

Seating is an important element which fulfils both a practical and aesthetic role in the garden but all too often is left as an after thought; this is fine if areas are built which allow space for seating so that time can be spent shopping around for the right pieces at a later date. It is wise, however, to plan sitting areas at the early design stage so that the possibilities of built-in seating can be explored.

Fixed seating (built-in and permanent seating)

Seating may be fixed either because it has been built in, for example around a tree, or because it is so heavy that once a position has been found for it then that is where it will stay. It is important that both these types of fixed seating look good in their own right as they will very often be used as a focal point within the garden.

Built-in seating A tree seat may be a particularly prominent feature in a garden and can either be a graceful, circular structure; which is a difficult do-it-yourself construction or a rather simpler rectangular design. In the case of the former it would make sense to purchase one of the superb manufactured pieces that are available on the market. However, there are other types of built-in seating which are far easier to construct yourself which may be considered when planning the garden. Low walls at a height of 45 cm (18 in) that surround a patio are ideal for sitting on especially if the brickwork is 21.5 cm (9 in) wide or if it forms a raised bed in which an area of the planting can be replaced by paving slabs, bricks or timber slats to create an integral seat.

All areas of the garden may be considered to provide informal seating especially where changes of level occur as broad steps will often make perfect seats; a few cushions set on to timber steps or a strategically placed stone in a rock garden will both form simple, pleasing places to sit.

The great advantage of built-in seating is that it saves space and does not have to be tidied away to make use of a paved area; if well planned it will form an integral part of the garden and will be both simple and economical in construction.

Permanent seating Other points of interest will be formed by seats that are too heavy to move around; the positioning of these seats should be carefully thought out as, not only will they be attractive structures, but you will not want to move them again. Permanent seating must obviously be in harmony, as well as in scale and proportion, with both the architecture of the house and the style of the garden. Although the function of this type of seating is not purely ornamental, it should have sufficient qualities to make it an attractive feature; a stone bench or graceful timber seat would fulfil that role whereas a stacking plastic chair clearly would not.

Seating will often look better with a backdrop of shrubs or a well clipped hedge, or set under a pergola or well formed tree; this type of position feels more secure and inviting than a bench set out in open ground. A seat may be positioned to one side of a paved walk to offer a moment's rest or the far end of the garden on a circular walk looking back at a water feature or another point of interest.

CHOOSING FIXED SEATING

Built-in seating Any type of construction can be used for built-in seating as has already been described. Low brick walls with seats of timber, concrete slabs or natural stone are all effectcive perhaps with cushions being used for the latter two. Wood can be used to provide a good link in the garden either by the construction of a simple plank bench or for a more refined tree seat.

Permanent seating Stone benches, either in natural or reconstituted stone, make excellent features but it is important that they are set on level sites or at best they will wobble and at worst the stone may crack. Simplicity itself can be achieved by a slab of slate set on a couple of rocks or bricks to form a low bench. Pieces of natural stone grouped together can also make a simple seating arrangement and similarly logs may be used as seats in an informal woodland setting. Timber seats in natural or painted wood look equally good, as do picnic tables which are either round or more usually rectangular with integral bench seats, but in either case are so heavy that they tend to be found a permanent siting.

Portable furniture
Furniture that can be moved around serves a more functional than ornamental purpose; it may be used for al-fresco dining, general relaxing or pool side sunbathing. That does not mean to say that functional furniture should not look good as well; on the contrary, these furnishings add the finishing touches to a garden and can enhance good design or, on occasion, seriously detract from it. There has never been a wider choice of furniture on the market so there is no excuse for not finding a piece to suit your garden.

CHOICE OF MATERIALS
Wood The natural qualities of wood look right in any garden setting but, as good quality furniture will be quite sturdy, and will therefore not get moved around too often nor stacked in a garage over winter, it is extremely important that furniture made from durable hard wood be selected. This tends to be tropical hard wood whose natural oils act as a built-in preservative so always check that the timber originated from managed plantations. Less durable soft woods can be used if given regular treatment with non-toxic preservatives or micro-porous paint which allow the wood to breathe.

There is a wide selection of timber furniture available, ranging from solid seats, tables and garden benches of great character to the simple, practical and extremely comfortable deck chair. Deck chairs can be used in almost any type of garden and if an area of timber decking is constructed then there is no other type of seating that could possibly look as good. The canvas chosen for the deck chair could be in pastel colours for a country garden or bold stripes for a modern town garden; the design could even be chosen to link with the interior decoration of the house. Avoid flimsy, collapsible timber furniture which needs constant maintenance and must also be stored. If you construct your own furniture then ensure that rust proof bolts and hinges are used and that the structure is solid as there is nothing worse than sitting in a chair meant for relaxation which wobbles or at worst collapses.

Metal The vogue for Victorian style gardens has caused the re-emergence of cast iron seats and tables with intricate patterns into the market; steel and aluminium furniture are also available, in simpler designs, which are more suited to modern gardens. Both of these types will require regular maintenance which will be reduced if the metal is combined with plastic; this combination of materials is often used for folding chairs but beware of possible in-built weaknesses in the folding joint which could prove disastrous when relaxing with a cup of tea. Plastic coated metal chairs will reduce maintenance to a minimum and simply require wiping over with a cloth.

Plastic Plastic or more technically lacquered resin is used to manufacture moulded furniture which looks good with almost all properties. The advantage of this type of furniture is that it is sturdy and can be stacked if necessary as well as being maintenance free. To make the seats more comfortable in hot weather cushions may be used which are available in a variety of colours and patterns; the brightly coloured stripes produce a Mediterranean poolside feel whereas the many muted floral patterns are more suited to country gardens.

Umbrellas and awnings

Garden umbrellas are often part of a combined table and chairs set and are essential to take the glare from the white table and provide more comfortable shady conditions when dining in hot sun. These umbrellas fit through a central hole in the table and are supported in a hollow base which may be filled with water or sand for stability; the spike on the bottom of the umbrella also allows it to be free standing as it may be stuck into the lawn. Other free standing umbrellas are available that look good, including those with huge canvasses supported by timber struts and a timber pole, as

well as the more delicate oriental style parasols.

Awnings are available which are similar to those used outside shops and their purpose is to provide shade for sitting areas adjacent to the house and also prevent furniture and carpets being faded by the sun without having to draw curtains. They do a similar job to that of a well clothed pergola next to the house but have an advantage in that they can be retracted to allow light back into a room. Fabrics may again be chosen to match interiors or other garden furnishings but unless they are plastic coated they will eventually fade.

Pots and containers

Plant containers may be pots, wall pots, urns and vases, troughs and barrels or anything else that can be given drainage holes and in which plants will grow. Pots are usually added as an embellishment to a garden to be planted up for instant colour and, therefore, do not necessarily have to be included at the formative design stage. However, a well designed pot or urn, even without plants, can provide a strong focal point especially when framed by strong foliage or viewed through an archway. Containers themselves can also be used as a frame; as tubs with clipped bay trees or box bushes are often seen framing a doorway or flight of steps. Pots look good when grouped to soften the straight edge of a terrace or used to give direction by barring access from one area and encouraging you to walk along a different route.

The most effective display of plant containers is when simple designs and bold groups of pots are used so avoid the fussy decoration of pots dotted all around the garden. Ensure that the containers have adequate drainage holes and that the pots are deep enough so as not to dry out too quickly. Use pieces of terracotta at the bottom of the pots to prevent the drainage holes clogging up with compost and make sure that the pots are frost proof if you intend to leave them out all year.

Choice of materials

A wide choice of both materials and designs are available so ensure that both these elements are in keeping with the style of the house and garden; brightly coloured plastic pots for example would look incongruous in a country cottage garden. Try not to create a mixed group of pots from different materials unless those pots are to be obscured by abundant planting, as the effect can often be messy.

RECONSTITUTED STONE

Garden centres stock many pots manufactured from this material which range from excellent to frankly awful. The style of these containers often imitates carved natural stone at a fraction of the price and tends to complement classical architecture rather than modern housing. It is a heavy material, not to be moved around too many times and is often seen as a large urn set against a backdrop of yew or other hedging to create a focal point in a country garden.

CONCRETE

Concrete pots are also very heavy and are stark in appearance; they look best in settings which reflect their straight-lined architectural shapes.

STONEWARE

Stoneware pots are made from a coarse clay, fired at high temperatures which give rise to wonderful colours and a more durable product than terracotta; metal oxides may be mixed with this material to give an attractive metallic finish.

SINKS

Old sinks can be treated with a mixture of cement and peat coated on to the outside to create the convincing appearance of an old stone trough. These look particularly good when planted up with alpines and dressed with gravel and small stones; choose the position carefully for this container as you will not wish to move it twice.

TERRACOTTA

The warm, natural colour of terracotta, which blends so well with planting, makes it one of the most useful materials for all styles of gardens. Pots come in all shapes and sizes, some ornate and fussy but normally the simple designs will look best. Pots will often be available with saucers that match to avoid dirt rings being left on the patio when the pots are moved. Be careful when buying terracotta pots as some are not frost proof and may shatter if left out all year.

WOOD

Wooden containers are usually manufactured from durable hard wood and like other timber products you should first check the source of the raw materials. There are normally two styles of wooden planter which evoke two different themes. The Versailles tub is a square planter constructed from vertical slats set into a framework with small timber balls at each corner; the planters are often supplied with a liner and are usually planted up with clipped shrubs for a formal setting which reflects their place of origin. Timber half barrels may be either reused old barrels or newly manufactured ones which should both be maintained by treating the wood with preservative and painting the hoops to prevent rust. The tubs should be kept moist at all times to stop the hoops falling off and as an alternative to timber preservative they may be painted; normally the wood will be white and the hoops black. This treatment should be discreet and tubs kept to a minimum to avoid looking like a pub garden requiring only painted waggon wheels for the finishing touch.

PLASTIC

Plastic, fibre glass and other similar products are widely manufactured, having the distinct advantage of being lightweight; this enables large pots to be constructed which are still easy to move around. Pots in this material may also be left out all year without danger of frost damage. The best designs again follow simple clean lines but it should be said that despite their advantages in the garden, plastic pots still look best inside with the interior landscape of an office or reception area, unless in the most contemporary setting when they can make a real contribution.

Window boxes

Window boxes can be the source of great floral displays all year round in towns and cities and may form the only areas for city dwellers to grow plants other than house plants. It is unfortunate that a lot of modern architecture does not allow wide enough sills to support window boxes which should measure approximately 21.5 cm wide by 21.5 cm (9 in × 9 in) deep to avoid the compost drying out too quickly. Window boxes are in extremely exposed positions and so not only do the plants require regular maintenance but so do the containers, especially if made from wood.

Containers should again be chosen to complement the style of the house but may also be colour co-ordinated with other paintwork, for example the front door. Window boxes should have sufficient drainage holes and be raised slightly off the sill to ensure adequate drainage. If possible, secure boxes to the window frame with hooks and wire to avoid dislodging them, as safety is obviously of vital importance.

Hanging baskets

Well planted hanging baskets will provide a terrific show of colour for street frontages, adjacent to terraces or in porches. The open wire type (preferably plastic coated for durability) are the most useful as plants can grow through the mesh and cover it completely in time; the alternative is the plastic bowl with is impossible to conceal and looks no better than hanging up a plastic flowerpot. Planting up a hanging basket is best done with the basket supported over a bucket to hold it still and catch the surplus compost; the basket should

Fig. 6.17 Planting a hanging basket.

(a) **Positon the basket over a bucket and fill with moss.**

(b) **Fill with compost as you plant up.**

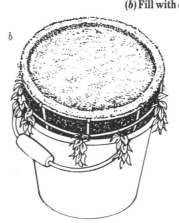

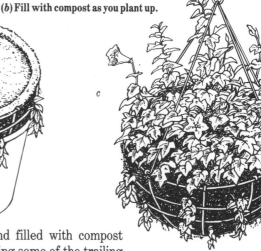

(c) **The completed basket.**

be lined with moss and filled with compost prior to planting, pushing some of the trailing plants through the moss so that in time the basket will be completely obscured (Fig. 6.17).

The baskets may hang from a purpose made bracket which in turn is fixed to the house wall with long rust proof screws; a timber batten may first be secured if the wall is at all uneven or pebble dashed, before fixing the bracket to the timber with wood screws. Alternatively the basket may hang from a long galvanized threaded hook which is screwed into an overhead pergola beam or into the porch; special 'S' shaped hooks are available which link the basket ring to the fixing hook and make removal of the basket a lot easier. Hanging baskets can be quite heavy so ensure that all fixings are secure, that baskets never hang above pathways and are always above head height.

Statues and ornamentation

Some gardens are specifically designed to demonstrate the sculpture of an artist or group of artists, this, however, is not normally the case and statues and other ornaments will be used in moderation as focal points or incidental points of interest around the garden. Ornaments should not be overused but be placed in a subtle manner, for example behind a plant group to create an element of surprise when found from a passing path or to the rear corner of a garden to create a diagonal viewpoint.

Almost anything can be called an ornament if used as a point of interest. It has already been shown how a well positioned rock or group of pots may be used for such a purpose. Garden ornaments tend to be personal, often having a sentimental value as some people will carry little figures and pieces of sculpture with them from garden to garden whenever they move. Individual ornaments should be well designed and complement the style of the garden; as they will often be an after thought their exact location may not have been predetermined and so time should be spent moving the object around until it looks just right. Avoid the tacky classical imitations in concrete or plastic that are available from garden centres as they will always look out of place in modern gardens. Some good terracotta and reconstituted stone pieces are available off the shelf and are worth hunting for and there are also some good bargains to be had from dealers in antique garden ornaments. Sculptors will produce pieces in bronze, stone and wood as well as in brick and terracotta and are all worth investigating although a one off piece or one of a limited edition may cost you a fortune. If this is out of the question, then do not succumb to the garden centre 'nasty'; a well positioned rock or group of pots will be far more effective.

CHAPTER 7

MAINTENANCE

Good initial design and subsequent construction of the major hard landscaping elements, i.e. walls, fences and paving should require little maintenance; however, it is inevitable that some minor tasks will need to be carried out from time to time in order to keep those elements in good condition.

Walls

Well constructed walls need little upkeep apart from replacing the occasional coping brick that may have been dislodged, in which case the brick should be rebedded using a galvanized steel cramp to help hold it in position. The most usual maintenance task for walls is repointing mortar joints either on old walls where soft lime mortar was used and subsequently pulled out by climbers or on modern walls where the strength of mortar mix was far too weak and has therefore deteriorated over a period of time. The old, loose mortar should be raked out to a depth of 1.2 cm (½ in) and the joints brushed clean prior to repointing with a 1:6 mortar mix which tones as closely as possible with any of the remaining original mortar. It is often helpful to use a plasterer's hawk, which is a small flat board on a handle, to hold the mortar up so that it may be pushed off and into the joint; the joints should then be finished in a style to match those in the rest of the wall.

Fences

Fences and other timber constructions, including pergolas and arbours, will need to be treated with a non-toxic preservative, never creosote, every couple of years; shrubs and climbers should be covered with sheeting and held away from the fence with string to avoid possible damage from the preservative.

Protect adjacent areas of paving from splashes with polythene sheets and protect yourself from splashes by wearing gloves, a mask and overalls. Preservative, which must be used in dry weather on dry fences, can be applied with a sprayer and although it is a far quicker method than using a brush should only be used when absolutely necessary on long fence runs as the fine spray will blow everywhere making it an extremely unpleasant job.

The most common problem with fences is timber rot which occurs at the bottom of a fence panel if in contact with the ground or a fence post at ground level. Gravel boards, set under fence panels or close board fencing, will minimize the problems as they are easier and far cheaper to replace than a panel or a section of feather edge boarding; the rotten gravel board may simply be levered off and a new one tacked into position with galvanized nails.

Repairing a rotten fence post is a much more awkward job as it will be necessary to fix on a concrete spur from around the old post. First excavate the rotten timber and remove the old supporting concrete; this is a hard and tedious job made easier by hiring a concrete breaker especially if you have more than one post to repair. Once the hole has been excavated to its original depth, the rotten post should be cut back to sound wood and the concrete spur set in position.

Concrete spurs are either 7.5 cm (3 in) or 10 cm (4 in) wide and selected to suit the width of the post; they are usually 90 cm (3 ft) long allowing 60 cm (2 ft) in the ground and 30 cm (1 ft) to be bolted to the post above ground level. The spur should be positioned against the posts so that its lower bolt hole is approximately 5 cm (2 in) above the bottom of the cut off post; the bolt holes should be marked through on to the post which can then be

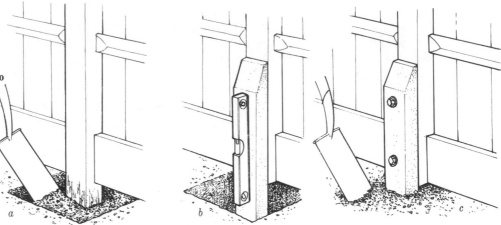

Fig. 7.1 Fitting a concrete fence spur.
(*a*) Remove the old supporting concrete.
(*b*) Cut the fence post back to sound timber and set in the spur.
(*c*) Bolt on the spur and backfill with concrete.

drilled and fixed to the spur with coach bolts. The fence post must be held to vertical and concrete should be set around the spur to hold it in position; it is, of course, essential to strut the post until the concrete has gone hard.

If more than one spur is to be used on a fence run, ensure that they are all set to the same finished height otherwise the appearance is unsightly (Fig. 7.1). If the post has been pushed off vertical due to high winds but is otherwise undamaged and therefore does not require a fence spur, it may be possible simply to lever that post back to its original position, set concrete around it and provide a temporary strut to prevent movement.

Gates

Gates can have several problems which require maintenance; they may sag or bind against the shutting post or the latch may not fit properly. These problems are a result of many factors including gates being left to swing or children taking rides on them, both of which will cause unnecessary strain on the hinges and the hanging post. Timber gates will also be affected by the weather causing them to contract and swell leading to subsequent problems.

If the hanging post has been pulled off vertical by excessive swinging or by a particularly heavy gate, it should be pulled back and held with a temporary brace while new concrete is placed around it and allowed to harden; if the post is a long way off vertical then it may have to be dug out and reset. The above problem will cause the gate to sag and foul on the shutting post.

Sagging may also be a result of weak hinges which should be replaced, redrilling the holes if necessary and using longer screws; the hinges should also be oiled regularly. It may also be that the gate is binding on the shutting post because it has swollen; if the gate opened easily in dry weather and not in wet weather then that is the reason and this can be remedied by planing a little off either the gate or the post. The gate may not latch properly because it has shrunk or dropped, in which case it may be necessary to reposition either the hinges or the latch or even change the latch to one with a longer reach.

Like fences, gates should be treated regularly with preservative.

Paving

Properly laid paving requires little maintenance, however, if an edging brick or slab has settled then it must simply be lifted and re-bedded; a slab or brick in the middle of a patio is more difficult to replace as it must be broken out with a hammer and bolster in order to remove it before cleaning out all the old mortar. The new slab is set flush with the surrounding paving using a straight edge prior to repointing with mortar that matches the adjacent paving joints.

Paving, especially natural stone, may need to be cleaned down every now and again especially when laid in shaded areas under trees; clean the paved area with a stiff broom and weak solution of cleaning fluid before hosing down.

Tools

An infinite number of tools are required to carry out hard landscaping operations which, if all bought at the outset would cost a huge amount so tool kits are something that people tend to build up and add to over a period of years. It always makes sense to buy professional tools from good manufacturers as these will last a lifetime whereas cheap tools can often be used only once before throwing them away. Hardware shops sometimes have sales where bargains can be picked up so it is worth looking around but if there are certain tools that you only need for a limited time then consider hiring them.

Hire shops are essential when expensive equipment is required only for a short time but on large projects it is worth doing your sums as it may well be cheaper to buy (albeit second hand) rather than to hire. When hiring equipment always check the hire charge and period of cover as well as any delivery charges. You will be charged for any repairs so check them over and point out any existing defects before hiring. It would also be in your own interest to make sure that all safety features such as switches and guards are functioning correctly. Ensure, too, that all hire equipment is returned in a clean condition or you may incur a cleaning charge.

Looking after tools and equipment

If treated properly, good tools will last a lifetime and will always be a lot easier to work with as there is nothing worse than trying to lay bricks with a mortar encrusted trowel or using a cement mixer that is solid with old concrete. Tools should always be cleaned and dried, oiled if possible and stored in a dry place to avoid the possibility of rust.

Plan the storage of tools, be it in the shed or garage, so that tools are fixed up on the wall and not left in a jumbled pile on the floor which can be infuriating when looking for something and all too easy to trip over. Any equipment that has been used for mortar or concrete should be cleaned thoroughly, removing all the muck before washing and scrubbing clean. Saws, chisels and planes should have covers to avoid blunting and be kept in a box for safety. Tools will last a lot longer if they are used correctly to do the job for which they were designed so never, for example, use a spirit level to ram concrete around a fence post.

GROUND WORKS

WHEELBARROW Builder's type with a pneumatic tyre, not a flimsy garden type with a narrow wheel which is only suitable for carrying leaves.

FORK A strong heavy fork not a small border fork.

SPADE A strong heavy spade, not with a thin pressed steel blade that bends in the softest of ground.

MATTOCK This is an invaluable tool similar to a pickaxe but with a flat not a pointed blade – useful for cleaning trenches and paved areas where a fork would disturb too much ground.

SHOVEL You could not do without this tool as it is used for loading barrows, mixing concrete and mortar and for backfilling around posts.

SLEDGEHAMMER This is useful for breaking up old concrete and bricks to make hardcore; it may well be hired.

PICK AXE This is essential for making in-roads into hard ground when digging out for paving.

IRON BAR A long heavy bar is useful for breaking out old concrete and as a lever for rockwork as well as adjusting leaning fence and gate posts back to vertical.

Tool kit

It has already been stated that there is a huge range of tools available to carry out hard landscape operations and so set out below is a typical tool list of a professional landscape contractor made up of both hand and powered equipment and obviously including tools which may be used for soft landscaping as well. Other contractors may have variations on this list but it does show the wide range of tools necessary and, although much of the equipment can be hired, a keen amateur would begin to build up a fair collection of the listed items. The tools can be categorized into ground works (G), paving and walling (P), fencing and woodwork (F) as well as equipment which may often be hired (H); obviously some of the equipment, for example a spirit level, will fall under more than one category. A brief description of some of the tools has been given where it was felt necessary.

TOOL LIST

GENERAL TOOLS
P Brooms
P Bucket
G Garden fork
G Heavy fork
G Spade
F Grafter spade
G Mattock
G Shovel
F Double handers (H)
G Sledge hammer (H)
G Pick axe (H)
G Iron bar (H)
P Straight edge
G Wheelbarrow
P Rammer (H)
F Drivall (H)

SMALL TOOLS
P Club hammer
P 30 m (100 ft) tape
F Pliers
P Cold chisels
P Bolster
P Pointing trowel
F Adjustable spanner
P Line & pins
F Saw file
P Float
F Junior hacksaw & blades
F Small set square
F Surform
P Spirit levels (long & short)
Nail box
Tool box

POWER TOOLS
P Mixer (electric & petrol) (H)
P Vibrating plate compactor (H)
G Electric concrete breaker (H)
P Slab cutter (H)
F Circular saw (H)
G 7.5 cm (3 in) sludge pump (H)
F Electric drill (H)

F Claw hammer
P 3 m (10 ft) tape
F Brace & wood drills
F Wood chisels
P Brick trowel
P Brush & dust pan
F Pincers
F Garden lines
F Screwdrivers
F Hacksaw & blades
P Large set square
F Hand drill & bits
F Panel saw
P Goggles, face mask & gloves
First Aid box

BROOMS A stiff broom with a large head is essential for cleaning up areas after work and can be bought with replaceable heads which obviously wear out before the handle. A soft broom will be needed to brush sand over block paving and to clean off any newly laid paving.

PAVING AND WALLING

BUCKET This should be the heavy duty plastic type and apart from carrying water will be used as a gauge for cement and sand used in pointing mixes.

SPIRIT LEVEL A 90 cm (3 ft) long level is best but a 60 cm (2 ft) level is also useful. Choose a level with the bubble on the top edge for convenience when paving. A small boat level is also useful for more intricate work.

STRAIGHT EDGE A length of 7.5×5 cm (3×2 in) planed timber between 2 and 3 m (6½ and 10 ft) long will be useful for setting pegs and laying paving.

RAMMER This has a long metal handle and heavy metal foot necessary for compacting small areas of hard core prior to paving

CLUB HAMMER Often known as a lump hammer, it has a short handle and a 1–2 kg (2.2–4.4 lb) head and is used with a bolster for cutting bricks and a cold chisel for breaking out concrete.

TAPES A 30 m (100 ft) cloth tape is used for setting out any garden construction while a 3 m (10 ft) retractable steel tape will be used for more detailed work.

COLD CHISEL This chisel is available in different lengths and weights and is used for cutting out concrete and old mortar.

BOLSTER This is a chisel with a broad flat head used for cutting bricks; alternatively a brick layers' hammer may be used having one end of its hammer head like a curved chisel.

BRICK TROWEL The largest trowels, approximately 25 cm (10 in) are better than the narrow ones and are used for spreading mortar when paving as well as for brick laying. Small round ended pointing trowels are excellent for finishing joints in natural stone paving.

BUILDERS' LINE AND PINS Nylon cord is used as it will not rot and when pulled taut will not sag either. The cord is attached to steel pins which stick into the mortar of the wall or alternatively a mason's block may be used which is an 'L' shaped piece of wood attached to both ends of the line and fixed on to the corner of the brickwork.

FLOAT This is a flat steel blade used for creating a smooth finish to concrete surfaces; a wooden float will give a more textured appearance.

FENCING AND WOODWORK

GRAFTER SPADE This spade has a narrow curved blade it is used for digging post holes.

DOUBLE HANDERS Also known as 'spoons' having two long handles with spoon shaped blades; they are excellent for digging deep tight post holes where it would often be more difficult with a spade.

DRIVALL This is a two-handled steel tube which is open at one end to fit over a round post. The drivall is rammed up and down to knock the post in and is more easily used by two people.

PANEL SAW This is a general purpose saw for all woodworking. A short 25–30 cm (10–12 in) tenon saw may be used for cutting joints; if a lot of cutting has to be done then a power or skills saw, which can be hired, will make it an easier job.

CLAW HAMMER General purpose use.

PLIERS General purpose use.

TIN SNIPS General purpose use.

PINCERS General purpose use.

WOOD CHISELS 0.6, 1.2, 2 cm (¼, ½, ¾ in) chisels are sufficient for woodworking joints

and should be used with a wooden mallet not a hammer.

DRILL A two speed or variable speed electric drill with hammer action together with a selection of high speed twist drill bits for wood and masonry is an essential part of the tool kit.

ADJUSTABLE SPANNER For general use including tightening bolts in timberwork.

SCREWDRIVERS A selection of flat head and phillips types of various lengths.

HACKSAW Large and junior hacksaws are needed for cutting metal.

SET SQUARE A large set square in the ratio of 3:4:5 will be needed for setting out paving and walling but a small set square is also useful for timber work.

SURFORM This is a general purpose tool for smoothing down timber; a plane may well be used for finer work.

HIRED EQUIPMENT

MIXER Useful for all jobs using concrete or mortar; electric mixers are usually hired out as there is less to go wrong and they are less messy than petrol mixers as well as being more neighbour friendly.

VIBRATING PLATE COMPACTOR To use for compacting scalpings or lean mix concrete and for compacting block paving when a rubber sole plate should also be fitted.

CONCRETE BREAKER An electric concrete breaker is essential for breaking out concrete around old posts and for breaking up existing pads of concrete paving.

SLAB CUTTER A fibre disc slab cutter is an excellent tool for cutting both paving slabs and brick pavers. It is normally a two-stroke petrol machine and so is very noisy; always wear a dust mask and goggles as well as ear defenders if a lot of cutting is to be done, also consider your neighbours and the inconvenience that the resulting noise and dust may cause.

PART III

CHAPTER 8

AN INTRODUCTION TO PLANTING

Introduction

Plants are used to soften and clothe the garden framework of paths, paved areas, walls, fences and structures. They can also provide the framework, hedges replacing walls and fences, lawns replacing paving and trees giving height.

In many gardens plants are used simply for their ornamental value i.e for the colour of their flowers or perhaps foliage, the result being a very empty garden in winter and early spring. The ideal is a combination of hard and soft landscaping designed to provide a garden of interest and beauty throughout the year.

The gardener versus the non-gardener

Before embarking on the planting the garden owner needs to decide on how important the actual plants are within the context of his or her garden. The majority of garden owners are not gardeners i.e. they do not include gardening as one of their leisure time activities. For them plants may be a necessity in terms of clothing their outside room but are otherwise a chore and a nuisance. In a small garden it may be a better solution to maximize the paved areas so as to eliminate lawns that need mowing and to reduce planting to ground cover and trees, neither of which require much maintenance.

However there are many garden owners who are gardeners and who enjoy gardening, at least in part, perhaps mowing grass, growing vegetables, or weeding borders. For them the secret is to decide which particular aspect of gardening they enjoy and which they dislike, and then to include plenty of the former and little if any of the latter. An example is the keen lawn mower but loather of weeding who should have plenty of grass areas but few beds and borders. A third group are the keen plantsmen or women who really enjoy plants and want to grow as wide a range as possible—for them gardening is a real pleasure and they need to plan as many and as varied planting areas as possible. The only restriction will be the size of garden and perhaps the limitations of their soil.

The secret of low maintenance

One of the secrets of low maintenance is to create a garden in which the chore of garden maintenance becomes the pleasure of pursuing the hobby of gardening—so that the time spent in the garden is considered time well spent. To reach this objective you would need to be honest about which aspects of gardening you enjoy and which you dislike.

Start by making a list of the plants that you like and the types of garden activity you enjoy. You could use the checklist shown in Table 8.1, ticking those you like and crossing those you dislike.

Plan your planting to include all those things you enjoy and few, if any, of those you don't.

Do not be misled by apparently good intentions; for instance if you dislike growing vegetables then exclude them—just because you think you should grow vegetables is not a reason for putting them in your garden. Similarly, just because the last owner of the house had a large rockery does not mean you have to keep it.

Styles of planting

Just as there are styles in garden design so there is a range of different planting styles. These range from the very formal parterres and knot gardens of the seventeenth and eighteenth centuries to the freedom of the cottage garden. Three basic styles predominate today: the formal, informal and natural.

Formal planting

This is a style of planting in which all the plants are controlled to rows or blocks, frequently clipped, and all kept within the rigid confines of formal beds or borders. An example would be a neat rose bed enclosed by an edging of clipped *Santolina chamaecyparissus* (cotton lavender).

Informal planting

This has plants in drifts or clumps, often spreading out over the edges of the bed with perhaps some hardy annuals e.g. *Nigella damascena* (love-in-the-mist) allowed to seed themselves where they will. An extreme form of this is the cottage garden which, at its best, is a muddle of dozens of different plants growing happily together.

Natural planting

This type of garden is trying to copy nature with an expanse of a single plant punctuated with odd specimens of other plants. Examples include a mass of ivy beneath woodland trees, or bluebells below birch trees, or even a mass of daffodils amidst a few species roses. This style can be extremely effective but needs a relatively large garden to look at its best. It

TABLE 8.1 PLANTING CHECKLIST			
Decide which plants and types of planting you particularly like and tick those boxes; then put a cross in the box of those plants you dislike			
Trees	☐	Fruit trees	☐
Avenues	☐	Hedges	☐
Conifers	☐	Shrubs	☐
Roses—bedding	☐	Shrub roses	☐
Rhododendrons	☐	Bamboos/grasses	☐
Heathers	☐	Climbers	☐
Ferns	☐	Herbs	☐
Mixed borders	☐	Herbaceous border	☐
Alpines/rock plants	☐	Scented plants	☐
Water lilies	☐	Marsh plants	☐
Annuals	☐	Bulbs	☐

also needs careful planning and planting.

The problem, in selecting the style of planting to adopt, is frequently the opposing wishes of different members of the household. The usual problem is that one member, the mower of the lawns, favours a formal approach, and another member, the planter and weeder of beds, favours the informal. One answer is to allow beds to 'overflow' where they are edged with paving, and to be confined next to lawns.

Generally, the more formal styles of planting should be kept next to the formal elements of the garden—the house and terrace, and the more informal away from the house.

SOILS ASPECT AND DRAINAGE

Soils

Before proceeding further, it is necessary to check the soil in your garden, to understand

143

which plants you will be able to grow. Firstly you need to know the depth of topsoil present; secondly the texture of your soil, finally the pH or level of the soil's acidity.

Topsoil

This is the fertile and living part of the soil, the layer in which organic matter is present, as well as the soil bacteria which break down plant material such as dead roots and leaves into compost and then humus, which provides a source of plant nutrients.

Topsoil can vary in depth from a few centimetres or inches to a metre or several feet. You can check the depth of your topsoil by digging a small pit, 60 cm (2 ft) is enough, and looking at the cut surfaces of the exposed soil. The topsoil shows up as a darker layer at the top in which plant roots are visible; below this is the duller unstructured subsoil. The depth can be measured with a tape measure.

In a garden it may be worth digging several pits in different parts of the garden to find out where the soil is deepest or where there may be

problems. In digging down you may find your spade hits a hard brown layer which is difficult to break through. This is called a 'hard pan' and is often present in poorly drained soils, the pan stopping the free drainage of water through the soil. It will be necessary to break up this hard pan before starting planting.

The deepest topsoil is needed for vegetables and border plants, a minimum of 30 cm (1 ft) is essential, whereas grass will grow on a depth of 75 mm (3 in) of topsoil, and trees will grow on very thin topsoil areas provided that a generous pit is dug for each tree and back-filled with additional topsoil after planting.

If you find that your topsoil is very thin it is possible to buy in additional topsoil, but do make sure that you buy from a reputable source and that the topsoil is similar in texture and pH to the soil already present.

Soil texture

The texture of the soil is the relative proportion of clay, silt and sand particles present in the soil. A high proportion of clay particles gives a clay soil, a high proportion of silt gives a silty soil, a high proportion of sand gives a sandy soil and a mixture of the three gives a loamy soil. There are a variety of types of soil between the extremes depending on the balance of clay, silt and sand.

Sand	— 90% sand:10% silt and clay
Loamy sand	— 75% sand:25% silt and clay
Sandy loam	— 60% sand:40% silt and clay
Loam	— 50% sand:50% silt and clay
Clay loam	— 40% sand:60% silt and clay
Sandy clay	— 30% sand:70% silt and clay
Clay	— 55% sand and silt:45% clay
Silty loam	— this contains a higher proportion of silt than sand and clay

To decide on your soil texture first look at your soil both in wet and dry weather; if it is sticky to walk on when wet, with clods of earth sticking to your shoes, and then rock hard when dry, it is almost certainly a clay or sandy clay soil. Whereas if the soil drains quickly,

---

TABLE 8.2 TEST FOR SOIL TEXTURE

1. Take a small amount of soil in your hand, removing any stones or bits of root etc.

2. Wet the soil and then work it down, by kneading it with the fingers of your other hand, until it forms a smooth paste.

3. Now feel the soil layer and decide if it feels *gritty*, *silky* or *sticky*.

4. If it feels both gritty and sticky then it is a LOAM

5. If it feel predominantly *gritty*, try to roll the soil up to form a ball:
   a. if it is impossible to form a ball it is SAND.
   b. if it will form a ball but it falls apart easily it is a LOAMY SAND.
   c. if it readily forms a ball that sticks together then it is a SANDY LOAM

6. If it feels predominantly *silky* or slippery it is a SILTY LOAM.

7. It if is predominantly *sticky*, roll the soil into a ball and then roll it out to form a worm:
   a. if the worm breaks up when rolled then the soil is a LOAM.
   b. if the worm forms easily then rub the surface of the soil with your finger:
      i. if the surface remains rough the soil is a CLAY LOAM.
      ii. if the surface becomes shiny when rubbed but is also gritty then the soil is a SANDY CLAY.
      iii. if the surface becomes shiny and the soil is not gritty then the soil is CLAY.

even after heavy rain, and is always easy to dig then it is almost certainly a sand or sandy loam. To check the precise soil texture it is quite easy to carry out a simple test — see Table 8.2.

The type of soil will decide which plants will grow most happily in your garden and the secret of successful planting is to choose plants that will not only survive in your garden but actually thrive.

There is no ideal soil for plants, for every type of soil from thin chalk to deep acid loam there are a range of plants to grow. The answer is to make the best of the soil you have and to use plants that will like it.

Soil pH

The soil pH is a measure of the acidity or alkalinity of the soil. The pH can be measured for any liquid and ranges from pH 0.0 extremely acid to pH 14.0 extremely alkaline. Half way between these extremes is pH 7.0, the point at which liquid is neither acid nor alkaline but neutral. Soils are neither very acid nor very alkaline and usually are found in the range pH 4.5 — pH 8.5. You can test the pH of your soil by buying a test kit at your local garden centre. Most of the kits available consist of a small tube in which a sample of top soil is added to a coloured liquid. The liquid changes colour depending on the pH of the soil, you then match up the resulting liquid with a chart included in the kit. Most liquids are a khaki colour when neutral, changing through yellow, orange to red for acid soils, and through green to greeny-blue for alkaline soils. The soil pH may vary in different parts of the garden so it may be necessary to do several tests to get an overall idea of your garden's acidity or alkalinity.

Having carried out a pH test or tests the question most gardeners want an answer to is 'how acid does the soil need to be to grow azaleas and rhododendrons?' The answer is not an exact pH figure but rather that the soil needs to be lime-free, and although pH readings of below 5.5 should be lime-free this is

not always true. A far more accurate guide is to look around adjacent gardens and if azaleas are flourishing then try some yourself even if your pH reading is above 6.0. If, however, no other garden in the area is growing azaleas, then even with a pH 5.5 you may not be successful. If you are lucky enough to have a deep acid loam then do please restrict your planting to the large range of acid-loving plants (see list of ericaceous plants in the appendix) and don't try to have masses of lime-loving plants such as thyme and lavender.

Use of organic matter

Making the best of what you have usually means ensuring that there is plenty of organic matter in your soil and replenishing it at frequent intervals. Every soil, except perhaps a woodland soil rich in leaf-mould, benefits from the addition of organic matter. It helps sandy soils to hold water and nutrients; in clay soils it helps to break down the 'clods'; and in thin chalk soils it helps build up the top soil layer and temper the alkalinity of the chalk. It doesn't matter which form of organic matter you use, manure, garden compost, peat or leaf-mould, as long as you use one of them and replenish it at regular intervals.

Aspect

This is the direction which a planted area faces, north, south, east or west. In your site analysis you will have noted the overall aspect of the garden but each planted area will be affected by any vertical elements within the garden such as walls, fences or buildings whether already present or planned. The aspect will affect the amount of sun that reaches the plants and often the amount of rain, particularly in beds beneath high walls (Fig. 8.1).

North-facing areas

These areas are frequently in full shade throughout the day and may retain moisture, particularly where the soil is a clay loam, and

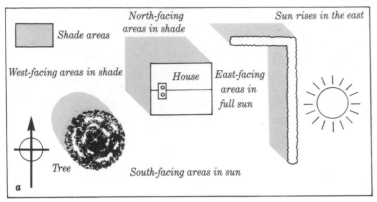

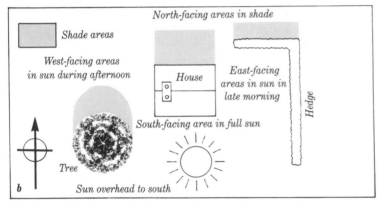

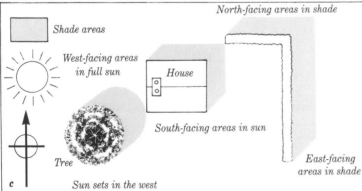

Fig. 8.1 The effect of different aspects.
(a) Morning.
(b) Mid-day.
(c) Evening.

hostas and astilbes. (See list of plants for shade in the appendix). Plants that thrive in the shade often have large leaves to absorb as much light as possible and usually look very attractive when planted together. Many of them have white or yellow flowers which help to brighten dark corners.

East-facing areas

East-facing areas are the hardest to plant successfully, particularly those beneath house walls because these areas are exposed to three adverse conditions. Firstly, as the sun rises in the east, these beds receive the sun early in the morning and if overnight frost is still affecting the leaves or buds, the sun's rays will be magnified by the frost and will burn the plant tissues, causing brown patches on the leaves and blackened buds. Secondly, most of our wet winds come from the west which means that the wall behind the east-facing bed shelters it from the rain, and in extreme examples these areas receive no rain at all (Fig. 8.2). Finally, east winds, when we get them, which is usually in the winter, are cold winds blasting all plants in their path.

To combat these three problems plants for east-facing areas need to be very tough and tolerant. *Parthenocissus quinquefolia* is one of the few good climbers for an east-facing wall with *Bergenia cordifolia* and *Alchemilla mollis* planted below. In some gardens you may be able to avoid planting these areas altogether.

South-facing areas

South-facing areas receive, if not the most, then certainly the hottest sun. Luckily plants from Australasia and the Mediterranean love sun-baked areas and there is usually no problem in finding enough plants that love hot, dry conditions to fill even the largest south-facing border. Avoid using plants that require more moist conditions in these areas, as they tend to look dried out and unhappy (see list for plants for dry, sunny positions in the appendix).

Plants which like hot, dry, sunny places

therefore will be colder and wetter than other parts of the garden. They may also be subject to cold north winds although these are infrequent. Luckily there are many plants that thrive under such conditions, a high proportion of which naturally grow in woodland areas, including ivy, periwinkles, epimediums, ferns and, if the soil remains fairly moist, then

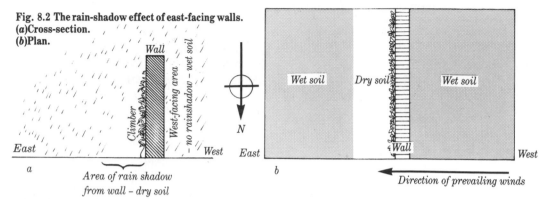

Fig. 8.2 The rain-shadow effect of east-facing walls.
(*a*)Cross-section.
(*b*)Plan.

Area of rain shadow from wall – dry soil

Direction of prevailing winds

often have small grey leaves which are, in fact, green leaves covered in white hairs. These hairs trap the moisture produced by the plant, holding it against the leaf to keep the surface cool and to prevent the plant from wilting. The small leaves of many grey-leaved plants are also, by virtue of their size, less likely to wilt. It makes logical sense to plant grey-leaved plants together in the sunny beds for which they are adapted, and not to try to mix them with the large green leaves of plants found in shady areas.

West-facing areas

These are much the easiest areas to plant, the sun reaching them in the afternoon when all danger of frost-burn is over. Wet westerly winds ensure adquate moisture and the walls or fences behind protect them from the cold north and east winds of winter. Almost any plant will thrive in these conditions except those requiring hot, dry soils or deep shade.

Many houses are not set square to the compass but rather at an angle, so that the beds are south-east or north-west. In such cases the choice of plants will depend on which aspect has the most influence, the hot dry sun or the cold winds or both! A bed with a south-west aspect is perhaps the easiest to plant almost any plant surviving in this position. The north-west areas usually get some sun in the late afternoon but need to be planted with shade tolerant plants; any grey-leaved plants will tend to get leggy and look miserable. North-east aspects are very difficult, needing tough shade-tolerant plants that can endure dry, cold conditions.

Drainage

Having selected plants for soil and aspect they also have to be selected for the level of moisture in the soil i.e whether the soil is wet or dry. This may vary in different parts of the garden depending on changes of level; the lower parts of a garden are generally more moist than higher levels and any hollows tend to collect water and to remain damper than the rest of the garden.

Whether your garden is wet, damp, well-drained or dry there are a range of suitable plants to grow. Very damp, boggy areas can be planted with some of the lovely poolside plants like *Caltha palustris*, *Rodgersia pinnata* and *Trollius europaeus*. If your soil is also slightly acid then the candelabra primulas such as *Primula japonica* will flourish.

The problem area is one where soil is cold and wet in winter and then dries out completely in summer, so that the plants either rot in winter or die from drought in summer. Plants selected will need to be tolerant of both these extremes.

Very dry areas due to thin chalk soils or well-drained sand can be helped by adding well-composted organic matter which will increase the water retention, or by irrigation. They should be planted with plants that enjoy dry conditions, such as lavenders, cistus, thymes and genistas.

Fig. 8.3 Frost pockets.
(*a*) Cold air flows downhill and collects in hollows at the base of the slope, forming a frost pocket.
(*b*) If a barrier is planted on the slope, the cold air is trapped uphill.

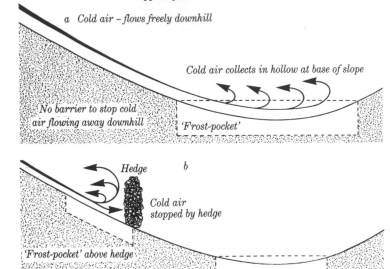

a   Cold air – flows freely downhill

Cold air collects in hollow at base of slope

No barrier to stop cold air flowing away downhill

'Frost-pocket'

Hedge *b*

Cold air stopped by hedge

'Frost-pocket' above hedge

Frost-pocket at base of slope may be reduced by hedge holding frost up-slope

Fig. 8.4 The effect of barriers on wind speed.
a

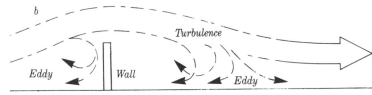

(*a*) Where there is no barrier the wind speed remains constant.

b

Turbulence

Eddy *Wall* *Eddy*

(*b*) A solid barrier e.g. a brick wall, will cause turbulence on both sides of the barrier.

c

Tree belt

Reduced wind flow

(*c*) A tree belt or hedge will allow the wind to dissipate its speed gradually, so a minimum of turbulence is caused and the reduced wind speed is felt for up to 10 times the height of the barrier.

Checking the microclimate

Frost pockets

Frost occurs when the temperature falls below 0°C (32°F). Plants are affected by water being unavailable to the roots and by the rupturing of sensitive cell walls. Frost hardy plants are less sensitive to cell rupturing but may be affected if the frost is very severe or prolonged. In a garden there will be areas which are more protected from the frost than others i.e. in front of a south-facing wall or beneath trees and these areas should be chosen for more frost sensitive plants. Problem areas to check for in any new garden are potential frost pockets (Fig. 8.3). These are areas more prone to early and late frosts and tend to have more prolonged frosts. They are found in hollows and on slopes where there is a downhill barrier. Frost always drains downhill but remains at the lowest position or where a barrier prevents free drainage.

Avoid planting fruit or frost tender plants in potential frost pockets. Fruit trees are particularly sensitive as late frost will damage the blossom and prevent pollination to produce fruit. Similarly any early flowering shrubs such as magnolias will suffer from frost-burnt flowers. It may be possible to temper the frost pocket effect by removing barriers on a sloping area and allowing the frost to drain away.

Prevailing winds

These should also be marked on your site analysis with a note as to whether wind protection is needed and in which areas. In a badly wind-swept garden, shelter belts may be needed before attempting any other planting. The most effective shelter belt is made up of rows of trees and shrubs which act to break the force of the wind without creating any side-effect of turbulence (Fig. 8.4).

In smaller gardens adequate wind protection may be given by trellis work covered with climbers, or, where the wind is very severe, by a plastic netting wind-screen. These are very effective but rather ugly; netting screened by trellis may be a good alternative.

Sheltered areas

Now look for the really sheltered areas in the garden — those with least wind and the warmest. These are potential sites for tender plants, and for sitting areas. If you want to grow plants that are really too tender for your garden then it may be necessary to create sheltered areas where they do not already exist.

The right plant in the right place

One way of checking whether an unknown plant will grow in a specific area in your garden is to check up on where and how it grows in its natural habitat. This should help you to understand the conditions which are necessary for the plant to flourish.

It may help you to understand by looking at two examples; Mediterranean plants grow on exposed thin soils on limestone and are baked by the summer sun; planting these plants in acid, clay soils in deep shade almost certainly will prove to be unsatisfactory!

Plants native to the high Alps are adapted to thin soils on free-draining rocky slopes, short hot summers and very cold winters; the intensity of the cold is reduced by the plants hibernating throughout the winter under a protective blanket of snow. Although the soil is well drained, there is usually plenty of moisture in summer from thawing snow from higher slopes. Such conditions are almost impossible to recreate in most gardens and the successful cultivation of these alpines requires special scree beds or alpine houses.

The successful cultivation of plants is based on understanding the plant's requirements and then providing them, and if you can't provide the correct requirements, then avoid growing that particular plant.

It is very easy, with a little plant knowledge, to despise common plants which are easy to find and simple to grow such as *Viburnum tinus*, *Buddleia davidii* or *Vinca major*. The reason that everybody grows these plants is because they flourish in most soils and in most gardens and give pleasure year after year with almost no effort on our part. The plants that are readily available and cheapest to buy are usually those which are easiest to grow.

PLANT NOMENCLATURE

A frequent annoyance to novice gardeners is the use of unpronounceable Latin names for plants, when it should be possible to give each plant a sensible common name. The problem is that for the majority of our plants there is no common name and it would be a mammoth task to rename them all. There is also the major advantage of Latin names in that the nomenclature is international: throughout the world *Viburnum tinus* is known as *Viburnum tinus* and not as laurustinus or any other of the local names.

The reason that we have Latin names is that the first person to write down and list the names of plants was a Roman doctor, Dioscorides. He actually wrote in Greek but his writings were quickly translated into Latin, the written language of the period. Dioscorides used several words to describe the plant and these descriptions were copied, and added to, by later writers. These included the botanical writers of the Renaissance, some of whom gave a local name to the plant as well, which was frequently a direct translation of the original Latin. Gerrard in his Herbal of 1596 refers to plants by Latin descriptions such as *Narcissus juncifolius montanus minimus* or the lesser flowered, rush-leaved mountain narcissus. The nomenclature of plants was finally resolved in 1754 by Linnaeus, a Swedish botanist, who devised the binomial system of classification that is still used today.

This system gives two names to each plant, firstly the generic name and secondly the specific name. In many cases he used the first two words of the original Latin name e.g. *Narcissus juncifolius*. As the Linnaean system of nomenclature has been accepted as the standard for all plant nomenclature, so we have to accept Latin names for our plants.

Families, genera and species

Linnaeus also gave a classification to plants which allows any new plant discovered to be added in the appropriate position. This classification was based on flower structure, plants with the same basic structure being grouped first into families e.g. *Rosaceae* and then into genera (plural of genus). A genus is a group of plants with very similar flower structures, frequently easier to see when the plant produces fruit — all *Acer* have winged fruits, all *Rosa* have hips, all *Malus* have apples.

Species within a genus differ from each other by having a variety of vegetative characteristics, or by different growth habits, e.g. *Rosa moyesii* has long thorny branches, bright red flowers and flask-shaped hips; *Rosa rugosa* has shorter prickly branches with rough leaves and flattened rounded hips. Plants of the same species are capable of inter-breeding and producing new plants which are similar to the parent. Generally plants of separate species are incapable of breeding. When this does happen, either in the wild or in the nursery, the result is a hybrid which usually displays some of the characteristics of each parent e.g. *Rosa × paulii*, the result of a cross between *Rosa arvensis* and *Rosa rugosa*.

The generic name is always written with a capital letter for the initial letter, and the specific name i.e. the name of the species, is written with lower case letters e.g. *Rosa moyesii*. Hybrids are written with an ' × ' before the specific name e.g. *Rosa × paulii*.

Varieties — wild and cultivated

Unfortunately plant names are not always that simple, and frequently they have three or even four names! A third is added when a variety of a species is found, either in the wild or in the garden, which is not sufficiently different to be another species. In the wild the difference may be larger flowers, smaller growth habit or narrower leaves. This difference, if it is displayed by the offspring of the plant, is known as a natural variety or subspecies and is written with a lower case letter e.g. *Rosa pimpinellifolia altaica*, which is a stronger growing, larger flowered form of *Rosa pimpinellifolia*. If the change is not seen in the seedling plants and can only survive if vegetatively propagated, then the different plant is known as a cultivated variety or cultivar and is written with capital initial letters inside single inverted commas e.g. *Weigela florida* 'Variegata', the variegated form of *Weigela florida*. Variegated leaves frequently appear on plants but will not survive if left uncultivated as the green shoots are always stronger and will take over. Variegations are also not carried by the seeds of the plant so propagation has to be vegetatively by cuttings. Cuttings are taken from the variegated shoot and when rooted are grown on as new plants. If the variegation on the new plant is found in all new leaves and does not revert to green then it is permitted for them to be marketed as a new cultivar.

Usually cultivar names are in English or the language of the country in which they are developed rather than in Latin. In some cases nurserymen have crossed two species and then recrossed with a third or even more species, giving rise to cultivars belonging to no clearly defined species. These cultivars cannot breed true from seed and are written without a specific name, just the generic and the cultivar names e.g. *Rosa* 'Peace'.

Bi-generic hybrids

Just occasionally nurserymen have managed to cross two genera to produce a bi-generic hybrid which is written with a ' × ' before the generic name, the generic name usually being a combination of part of each of the parent names. An example is the cross between *Cupressus macrocarpa* and *Chamaecyparis nootkatensis* which was named × *Cupressocyparis leylandii*. These bi-generic hybrids are unable to produce viable seed and must be propagated vegetatively by cuttings.

Summary and example of plant nomenclature

Family	— *Rosaceae* — names usually end in -aceae
Genus	— *Rosa*
Species	— *moyesii*
Wild variety	— *Rosa moyesii fargesii*
Cultivar	— *Rosa moyesii* 'Geranium'
Hybrid	— *Rosa* × *alba*
Bi-generic hybrid	— × *Cupressocyparis leylandii*

ACQUIRING NEW PLANTS

Traditionally, gardeners didn't go to garden centres to buy plants; instead they took divisions from friends' plants, or collected seeds, or took cuttings. Taking your own cuttings is still much the cheapest method of acquiring new plants, and the most rewarding, but it does take longer for the plants to make a display. It is also the only way of acquiring some new varieties that are, as yet, not available in the trade.

Propagating plants

Dividing plants

This method is used for multiplying herbaceous plants. It is best to lift the whole plant and then divide it with two forks. Plant half the plant back into its original site and then take the rest to its new home. Make sure to remove all traces of perennial weed that may be infesting the division. The most satisfactory method is to wash all the roots in water, removing any dead tissue and weed roots as you go.

Collecting seed

Seed should be collected during the summer and early autumn on a warm, dry day. When the seed is nearly ripe, place a small paper bag over the seed head so that all seed drops into your bag. If the seed is already ripe, collect the seed into brown paper bags or envelopes, one plant to each bag or envelope. Label clearly and store the bags or envelopes in a dry drawer until spring.

Some plants need pre-germination treatment such as freezing or stratifying. Seeds needing freezing can be placed in polythene bags in the freezer for several weeks before sowing.

A few seeds are only viable immediately they ripen such as angelica. These need to be allowed to drop and germinate by the parent plant. When the seedlings are large enough to handle they should be lifted and planted in their new position.

Most seed is best sown into pots or trays to germinate and then the seedlings planted out into a bed or border, rather than sowing the seed direct onto the soil.

Cuttings

The right time to take cuttings is usually when you find yourself standing next to a plant you haven't got and the owner says 'do take a cutting'. Preferably the plant has some good green 'growy' shoots on it at the time. In summer take green cuttings and place in a propagator; in autumn and winter take hardwood cuttings and place outside in a nursery bed or in a frame.

Buying plants

The answer to buying plants is to go to a reputable nursery or garden centre with a list of the plants you need and then not to be seduced into buying lots of other plants because they look attractive. If you can't resist 'spur of the moment' purchases then the safest approach is to send away for plants by post using your prepared list!

If you are buying in person and selecting your own plants, then avoid choosing plants in full flower. They may look much more attractive than a plant with just a mass of leaves but they will not transplant nearly as well. Whilst the flowering plant is having a rest from

TABLE 8.3 SIZES OF TREES			
Description	Circumference of stem*	Height from ground level	Clear stem height from ground to lowest branch
Feathered	4–6 cm (1½–2 in)	0.90–2.40 m (3–8 ft)	no clear stem
Half standard	not given	1.80–2.10 m (6–7 ft)	1.20–1.50 m (4–5 ft)
Light standard	6–8 cm (2–3 in)	2.50–2.75 m (8–9 ft)	1.50–1.80 m (5–6 ft)
Standard	8–10 cm (3–4 in)	2.75–3.00 m (9–10 ft)	1.80 m minimum (6 ft)
Heavy standard	12–14 cm (5–5½ in)	3.50–4.25 m (12–14 ft)	1.80 m minimum (6 ft)

*Circumference is measured at 1 m (3¼ ft) from ground level.

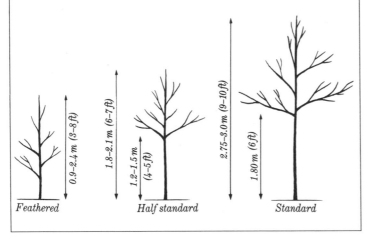

Feathered Half standard Standard

grown plants available which, although more expensive, give an immediate impact. These may well be worth investing in for a few choice positions.

SIZES OF PLANTS

Trees

Trees come in a range of sizes based on the overall height of the tree, the height of clear stem and the girth measurement at 1 m (3¼ ft) from ground level (Table 8.3).

The most satisfactory size for most gardens is the standard as this already has a good clear stem and branching head, will transplant well, and only requires a single stake for support. In large gardens, where substantial quantities of trees are needed, it might be sensible to consider buying the smaller feathered trees, these are much cheaper to buy, require little staking, if any, and grow away very quickly. They will however make less impact in the first few years.

Larger size trees may require more substantial staking or even guying, and tend to spend their first few years, after planting, recovering from being moved rather than making new growth; so, unless a larger tree is absolutely essential, it makes sense not to bother with anything larger than the heavy standard.

Shrubs

Almost all shrubs are now container grown i.e. they have spent all their life in pots rather than in the open ground. The result is that all the shrub's roots are contained within the pot so that there is little disturbance when they are planted out. Shrubs can be bought by size of container or height of shrub. Container sizes are measured in litres and the smallest shrubs are usually in a minimum size of 1 litre with many shrubs starting at 2 litres. These sizes are perfectly satisfactory if you are patient and prepared to wait for shrubs to grow.

growing after flowering, the green leafy plant will be busy putting new roots down into the soil and getting on with the job of growing.

Check for potential new growth at the base of the plant, looking for new buds or shoots, and avoid any plants that are leggy or look starved. Avoid buying herbaceous plants in the middle of winter when all that can be seen are a few dead leaves and a pretty label. It is far safer to wait until the new growth appears in the spring when you can be sure you have a living plant in the pot.

There are now larger sizes of container-

However, some of the slower growing evergreens are probably best bought in 5-litre pots to give more impact.

Conifers

Most of the conifers are also container grown although some of the larger varieties are field grown and root-balled. The conifers are grown in open ground for the first few years and when they have grown into a substantial bush are lifted complete with their root-ball which is then wrapped in hessian. Root-balled plants are usually very strong plants and well worth buying where the conifers are important or impact is needed. Small conifers are available in 2-litre containers but the larger conifers are best purchased in 5-litre pots.

Herbaceous plants

These are available in a range of different containers and a variety of sizes. It is much cheaper to buy the smaller sizes as 9 cm (3½ in) pots, particularly for front of border plants such as *Alchemilla mollis* and *Nepeta faassenii*; however, some of the larger border plants such as paeonies which do not produce flowers until the plant has reached a mature size, are a better buy in 2-litre pots, so that you won't have to wait nearly so long before they flower.

CHAPTER 9

PLANTING DESIGN AND PLANTING PLANS

PLANTING DESIGN

Planting design is the selection and placing of suitable plants within the overall design of a garden so that the plants chosen create the desired visual effect, the individual species blending together to form an integrated picture. Plants should be chosen for their shape, habit and texture as much as for their colour, and for their long term survival rather than instant appeal. To understand how to design with plants it is important to segregate the different ways in which plants can be used in the garden. Plants can be used to create the vertical structure of the design e.g. using trees, or the horizontal pattern of the plan e.g. using grass. Altogether there are five ways in which plants can be used in the garden:

1. Structural — to create the vertical lines and shapes of the design.

2. Focal points — to create pictures within the garden

3. Ground cover — to create the horizontal pattern and cover.

4. Ornamental — to decorate the garden and to give added interest.

5. Functional — planting for use rather than to contribute to the design e.g. vegetables.

The most important use of plants, in terms of garden design, is for structural planting and it may be helpful to explain this in more detail.

Structural planting

Structural planting is the use of plants to form the vertical structure of the garden. A garden which does not use plants for at least part of its structure is flat and dull for most of the year, whereas a garden with a clear structure of hedges, blocks of shrubs and lines of trees is never dull and can look particularly attractive when covered in frost in the depths of winter. Plants may be used structurally to create the lines of the design whereby eyesores may be screened, views framed, boundaries disguised, vistas enhanced, and vertical pattern and division created. In selecting plants for structural planting it is essential that they are chosen first for the soil, aspect and drainage of your garden so that they will grow well. They will almost certainly be trees or shrubs to give height, and they should also be evergreen where possible so that the planting is effective all year round. Structural planting can be further sub-divided into four different uses:

1. To provide a screen.
2. To provide a background.
3. To delineate areas.
4. To re-inforce vistas.

1. To provide a screen
Screens may be needed for a variety of reasons: to give shelter from winds; to hide views; to give privacy.

As soon as the site analysis of your garden is complete it should be obvious where such screens may be needed i.e. to protect the garden from the prevailing winds, to screen the garage of the house next door, or to give privacy to the terrace to allow sun-bathing!

The materials used for these screens will depend on the height needed, the space available and the cost. Walls and fences will give instant screening effect but are limited in the overall height and can be expensive to erect. Using plant screens may well be a more attractive alternative, although it may take longer for the screen to be fully effective.

2. To provide a background

This is the use of plants to provide a green background for the more decorative features in your garden. These features may include statues, summerhouses, seats, flower beds or borders, all of which are enhanced by being set against a plain backdrop, just as a flower arrangement usually looks best against a black velvet cloth. The nearest to black velvet in the garden is a mature yew hedge but other fine-leaved evergreens are almost as effective. The alternative to plants as a background would be stone or brick walls but these would be an expensive indulgence simply to provide a background to your herbaceous border (Fig. 9.1).

3. To delineate areas

Once you have some idea of the different features you wish to include in your garden you will need to provide separate areas for different activities e.g. the rose garden will want to be separated from the rock and water garden. Plants as hedges or informal groups of shrubs can be used to delineate the various areas. They may also be used to re-inforce the shape of the spaces created e.g. a circular hedge around a circular lawn.

Although walls, fences and trellis can be used for delineation of areas, planting is much softer in its impact and in some cases as well as delineating an area the planting may also be acting as a background to a feature (Fig. 9.2).

4. To re-inforce vistas

Within the design there should always be vistas created, however limited their extent. A vista may be a path leading a few yards to a rose-arch, or an extension of the lawn leading to a gate. Plants can be used to make these vistas more visually important. Usually such planting is in the form of an avenue but it may also be parallel hedges or scattered groups of shrubs (Fig. 9.3).

Use of evergreen trees and shrubs for structural planting

Where plants are used for structural planting they will have more impact if they are evergreen rather than deciduous in that they retain their leaves in winter. Conifers are particularly useful where height is required as in Britain there are few evergreen trees and those that do exist grow extremely slowly e.g. *Quercus ilex*. Where less height is needed there are a great many good evergreen shrubs that can be used, and a list of them can be found in the appendix. The structural planting outlined above is the first planting to be included on your overall plan and needs to be marked in at an early stage as it will help in the creation of your design.

Focal point planting

Having worked out your design you have probably marked in where focal points will be needed to create pictures within your garden. These focal points might be features such as

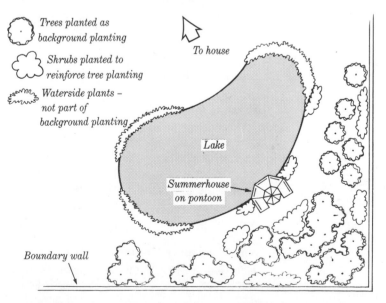

Fig. 9.1 Plan to show use of planting as a background. Part of the plan of a large informal garden where trees have been planted beyond a new lake to provide a green background to a summerhouse and pontoon.

Trees planted as background planting

Shrubs planted to reinforce tree planting

Waterside plants – not part of background planting

To house

Lake

Summerhouse on pontoon

Boundary wall

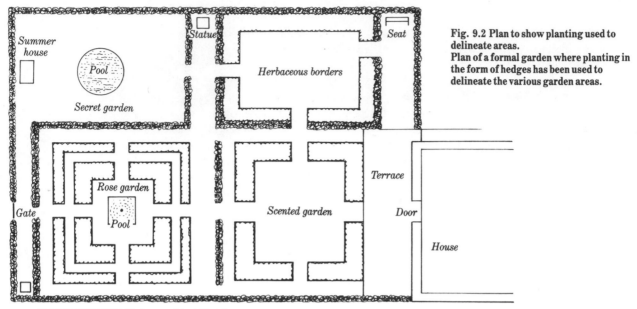

Fig. 9.2 Plan to show planting used to delineate areas.
Plan of a formal garden where planting in the form of hedges has been used to delineate the various garden areas.

seats, statues, containers, or sundials but they can also be plants.

Plants used as focal points must be capable of standing out strongly from their surroundings, otherwise they will hardly be seen as focal points! They must also be placed at the end of a vista which will help to draw the eye to the focal point.

To stand out, the plant or plants must display strong shape or habit, or be much larger than the surrounding plants, or have brightly coloured foliage. Flowers, however large or brightly coloured, are only effective for a very limited time and a focal point has to work throughout the year.

Existing focal points

There may be an existing tree in the garden that will provide an effective focal point due to its size or position. If this is the case, then make sure that a vista is cleared to lead to the tree. If the tree is not sufficiently interesting by itself then placing a seat or a statue beneath it will enhance its visual appeal.

Selecting plants for focal points

The shapes that stand out amongst other plants are those that are strongly archi-

Fig. 9.3 Plan to show plants used to re-inforce a vista.

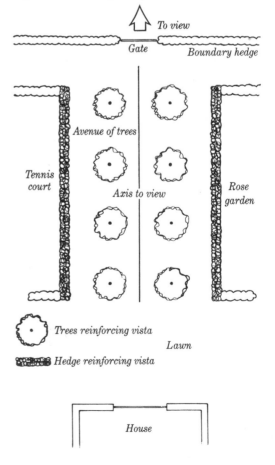

tectural, either fastigiate, conical or spiky. If placed other than as focal points they tend to stick out like 'sore thumbs'. A weeping or horizontal habit will also stand out and, again, such plants make good focal points (Fig. 9.4).

Major focal points could be trees displaying these shapes or habits but minor focal points i.e. at the bend in a path, can be shrubs e.g. *Viburnum plicatum* 'Mariesii' which has a pronounced horizontal habit.

Trees with coloured foliage will become focal points when in leaf but will recede into the background in winter unless they are evergreen — e.g. *Thuja plicata* 'Zebrina' — or much larger than the surrounding plants, or have a weeping habit or fastigiate shape. So *Fagus sylvatica* 'Dawyck Purple' being both fastigiate and purple leaved is always a focal point, whereas *Fagus sylvatica purpurea* (copper beech) is only a focal point in summer, or when it has grown large enough to stand out by virtue of its size.

Ground cover planting

Having placed the structural and focal point planting on your garden plan, you now need to cover the ground. It is important to realize that all areas must be covered either by hard materials such as paving, or by planting such as grass. Any part of the garden not so covered will very quickly become overrun with weeds. The ground covering should be used to create horizontal patterns which can be formal, informal or even abstract.

Ground cover planting should complement the hard materials chosen and as with all other types of planting must first be selected for the soil, aspect and drainage of each area. Grass grows particularly well in the climate and soils of Britain, so it is often the easiest and cheapest ground cover to establish. When well-maintained it creates a superb, smooth carpet which sets off the rest of the garden.

In other countries, where the climate is less suitable for grass, other ground cover plants predominate e.g. ivy where there is more

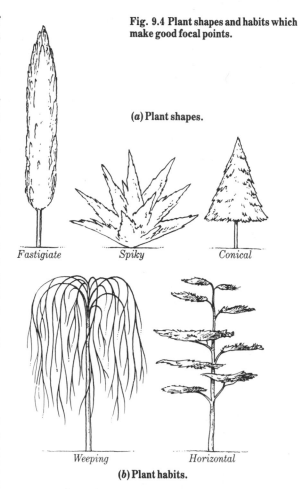

Fig. 9.4 Plant shapes and habits which make good focal points.

(a) **Plant shapes.**

Fastigiate   Spiky   Conical

Weeping   Horizontal

(b) **Plant habits.**

shade, or moss in parts of Scandinavia where the climate is colder and wetter.

Covering the ground

The usual approach to covering the ground is to use hard materials such as paving, bricks or gravel around the house to provide a good surface for use in all weathers and then to use lawn grass next to the paving as a 'soft' extension to the terrace. Further into the garden the lawn may become longer grass and areas not suited to grass growth e.g. under trees or on steep banks, can be planted with ground cover plants.

Where beds and borders are used it is important to decide what sort of plants will be planted e.g. plants for scent, and how weeds will be controlled e.g. with mulch or by hand-weeding.

Creating patterns and shape

When using ground cover planting to create horizontal patterns and shapes, first decide whether a formal or informal approach is most suitable. Formal ground patterns are based on straight lines or circles and should be close to the other formal elements in the garden e.g. the terrace. The classic examples of formal ground cover are the great parterres at the Palace of Versailles in France where formal patterns of clipped box create a vast formal carpet on which the palace appears to sit. A less formal example would be a rectangular lawn leading from the terrace of the house with the straight lines of recent mowing enhancing the formality.

Informal shapes are based on curves, these curves varying in their radii so that they flow through the garden rather than form circles. Grass can be informal if the lawn is informal in shape and mowing is done with a machine that does not leave the neat lines of the cylinder mower. Curved beds of ground cover plants complement curved lawns, with plantings in drifts rather than rows.

Ground cover does not need to be low. Any planting whose purpose is to cover the ground can be included e.g. banks of *Juniperus × media* 'Pfitzerana', beds of *Rosa rugosa* and, as can be seen in parts of Holland, large expanses of *Quercus coccinea* kept cut at 1.2 m (4 ft) high.

Ornamental planting

Ornamental planting is the use of plants to decorate and add interest to the overall design, the plants usually being planted in beds and borders. It also includes planting to enhance a particular garden feature e.g. climbers on a pergola, or marginal plants around a pool.

Unfortunately, this is how many people see the use of all the plants in their garden, simply as the decoration of the design which has to be created through the use of hard materials alone. Plants are only used for the filling-in of the beds created, or to decorate the walls of the house, with perhaps an odd tree to provide spring blossom.

But as can be seen, ornamental planting is only one part of the planting of a garden, often the least part, and in fact is not necessarily essential to creating a satisfactory and attractive garden. Many very lovely gardens e.g. the gardens at Dartington Hall in Devon, have little or no ornamental planting.

If you are a non-gardener, then plan your garden using structural and focal point plants to create the design, and ground cover plants to form the base, and don't bother with ornamental planting at all. Beds and borders require maintenance, possibly skilled, and on a regular basis.

However, this does not apply to the gardener and plantsman or plantswoman who will want some ornamental planting to grow plants they enjoy, the gardener so that he or she can practise their gardening skills, and the plantsman to be able to grow the widest possible range of plants.

Selecting ornamental planting

In the early stages of planning your garden, you should decide which plants you wish to find space for in your plan and make a list (Table 9.1). Then in preparing your plan areas can be created for each group of plants listed e.g. a herb garden for herbs, rose beds for roses, herbaceous borders for colour. Every planted area shown on the plan should have a clear reason for its existence i.e. to grow a certain type of plant, for colour in a particular season, or perhaps to provide fragrance.

Ornamental plants are chosen for their flowers, their foliage, or, in some cases for their fruit or winter stem colour. They should also be selected for their suitability for soil, aspect and drainage as with the other types of planting, although it is possible, if you wish to grow a particular group of plants which are not suitable for your garden, to change the soil for a single bed or small area.

Functional planting

These are plants that do not necessarily form part of the garden design and may in fact detract from it but are needed by the members of the household.

They include vegetables, fruit—particularly soft fruit in fruit cages—herbs when not in herb gardens, and flowers for cutting and drying. They might also include plants for dyeing and even nettles grown for caterpillars!

Functional plants can be placed in an ornamental setting e.g. vegetables planted in an ornamental 'potager', in which case they are considered ornamental planting, as are herbs in a herb garden. Fruit trees in an orchard become part of the structural planting as do nut bushes when planted as an 'allee'.

Where functional plants are within the more normal setting of a vegetable garden they may well need screening from the rest of the garden. The positioning of the vegetable garden, with its need for deep soil and full sun, should be considered right at the outset when looking at the functional use of the garden. Any necessary screening then becomes part of the structural planting of the garden.

Using plants in planting design

These then are the five ways in which plants can be used in the garden, although sometimes the divisions between one type of planting and another can become blurred. In a small garden part of the structural planting may also be ornamental, an avenue of flowering cherries giving structure all the year round but adding greatly to the decorative value of the garden in the spring. Equally a large tree might be considered functional in providing shade for a sitting area, but at the same time may be an important focal point. The background to a border may well be selected for its summer foliage colour which will complement the

colours seen in the flowers of the border e.g. *Berberis thunbergii* 'Rose Glow' planted as the background of a purple, pink and grey border.

In a small garden ground cover planting may need to be ornamental as there may be no room for beds and borders. The variegated leaves and purple flowers of hostas, and the bold leaves and pink flowers of bergenias can be considered ornamental whilst acting as highly effective ground cover.

TABLE 9.1 CHECKLIST FOR ORNAMENTAL PLANTING

For each bed or border decide which season of interest and which colour scheme is most appropriate.

SEASON OF INTEREST

Spring — bulbs	☐	Autumn colour	☐
— bedding	☐	Winter — flowers	☐
Summer — roses	☐	— foliage	☐
— bedding	☐		
— mixed borders	☐		

COLOUR

Foliage colours		*Flower colours*	
Grey leaves	☐	Pinks and blues	☐
Purple leaves	☐	Bright reds	☐
Gold leaves	☐	Yellows and purples	☐
Variegated green/white	☐	Yellows and creams	☐
Bright green	☐	Blues and creams	☐
Dark greens	☐	Oranges	☐
Lime greens	☐	Crimson and pinks	☐

PLANTING PLANS

Now you need to get started on putting some planting ideas down on paper. What is needed is an indication of where structural planting such as shelter belts are needed, where the lines of hedges and blocks of planting should be positioned, and where focal point plants will be placed in order to create the overall design. This is known as an outline planting plan.

Outline plans

Start with any sketch proposals that you have drawn for your new garden and put in areas of proposed planting, starting with the structural planting.

Place shelter belts and screens first, and then boundary hedges where required. If you are dividing up your garden then decide how the divisions are to be created e.g. hedges or trellis with climbers, and then mark these down. Mark down the main vistas of the design and then note any focal points needed and whether these should be trees or shrubs. If the vista needs enhancing consider an avenue or parallel hedges and put them in. Decide on areas suitable for vegetables and fruit and mark these down on the plan.

Grass and ground cover areas go in next and then finally the ornamental planting i.e. the beds and borders. At this stage it is useful to note the type of planting for each planted area e.g. roses, herbs or annuals.

Symbols for outline planting plans

At this stage very simple symbols are used, some of which are shown in Fig. 9.5. They are best drawn in pencil to begin with as you may need to erase your ideas quite frequently. When your ideas are definite the plan can be drawn over using ink or felt pens (Fig. 9.6). It is possible to get rubber stamps of tree symbols which are great fun to use but unfortunately can't be removed when stamped in the wrong position!

Detailed planting plans

Having completed your design you will need to prepare planting plans for each area of planting. These will show exactly where each

Fig. 9.5 Symbols for outline planting plans.

(*a*) Tree symbols.

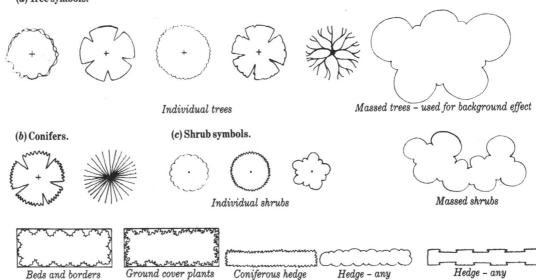

Individual trees

Massed trees – used for background effect

(*b*) Conifers.　　(*c*) Shrub symbols.

Individual shrubs

Massed shrubs

Beds and borders　　*Ground cover plants*　　*Coniferous hedge*　　*Hedge – any*　　*Hedge – any*

Informal ground cover planting at East Lambrook Manor.

A lovely example of a herb garden which is both ornamental and functional.

Marginal plants *Eriophorum angustifolium* and
Zantedeschia aethiopica planted in shallow water at the
edge of a pond.

A beautifully filled urn at Erdigg planted as a flower arrangement of pink, grey and cream.

Below: Simple but very attractive planting of roses at Tintinhull.

Wherever a garden is in the world the same planting design rules apply. Yellow and purple foliage is always an excellent combination, the latter providing a perfect ground cover.

Many alpines are well suited to a rock or scree garden and
you can provide an endless wealth of flower and foliage.

Opposite:
Planting in colour ranges is always effective and shades
of blue and pink form a delightful harmony.

A superb combination of architectural foliage including
grasses, hellebores and phormium.

plant is to be planted. When complete they can also be used to draw up a list of plants to be planted which can be used as a 'shopping list' for your garden. Each bed or border to be planted needs to be drawn up on a piece of paper at a large enough scale to show each plant clearly. 1:50 is the best scale for general planting with 1:20 used for very closely planted areas e.g. herb gardens or alpine beds. The nearest appropriate scales if you are measuring in imperial measurements are 1 in = 4 ft for 1:50 and 1 in = 2 ft for 1:20. Draw the outline of each bed and border marking clearly any fences or hedges adjacent to the border (Fig. 9.7). Next mark North to remind you whether the bed is in sun or shade.

Use of circles in planting plans

In planting plans each plant is represented by a circle, the planting position being indicated by the centre of the circle and marked with a dot or cross. The diameter of the circle is selected according to the planting distance of the plant i.e. plants spaced 45 cm (18 in) apart are drawn to scale with a circle of 45 cm (18 in) diameter. Groups of plants of the same species or variety are drawn as a group of linked circles (Fig. 9.8).

It often helps to make sure that the plan is drawn at a large enough scale to be able to write all the plant names on the plan even if the plants are to be planted very closely together.

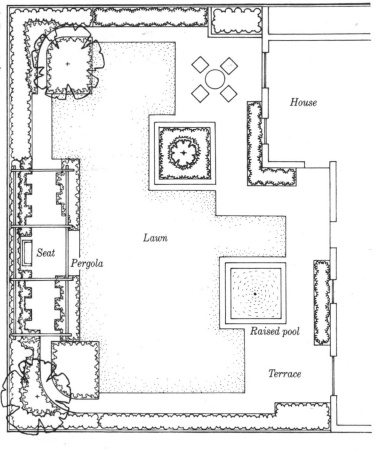

Fig. 9.6 Outline planting plan.
Design for a small urban garden showing use of symbols to indicate types of planting to be used.

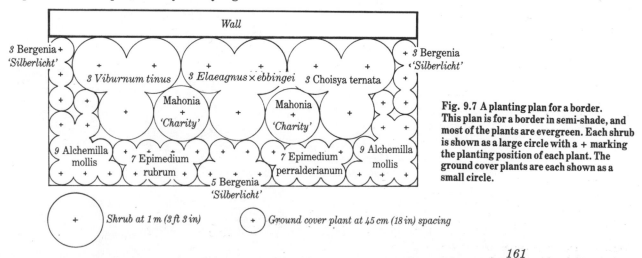

Fig. 9.7 A planting plan for a border.
This plan is for a border in semi-shade, and most of the plants are evergreen. Each shrub is shown as a large circle with a + marking the planting position of each plant. The ground cover plants are each shown as a small circle.

Fig. 9.8 Circles for planting plans.
All plants are drawn as a circle with a + to indicate
the planting position of each plant. Groups of several
plants of the same species can be drawn as linked circles
and, for further clarification, the centres of the circles
can be linked with straight lines.

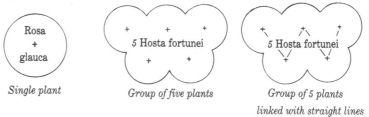

Single plant   *Group of five plants*   *Group of 5 plants*
linked with straight lines

Spacing of plants

This is one of the hardest parts of all garden planning as so many of the reference books and catalogues disagree on both the spacing and ultimate spread of specific plants. Rather than have every plant circle with a different diameter it is far easier to use a few standard spacings. Plants vary in their response to different soils and localities, and the same plant may grow twice as well in one garden as in another; but having spaced your plants out regularly it will then be quite possible to move plants that outgrow their alloted space and fill in with extra plants where plants turn out to be slow growers.

The spacings given in Table 9.2 will fill a bed or border within three years from planting in most areas; in particularly cold areas it may take four or five years. At the end of this period a certain amount of thinning may be necessary. Using wider spacings in the first instance will means lots of empty space in the first few years. Closer spacing will give an 'instant' garden but will create a 'jungle' before long.

Use of detailed planting plans

Detailed planting plans are not just for beds and borders but can be used for any planted area e.g. shrubs in grass, hedges or ground cover areas. In each case use circles to indicate plant spacings and always add the correct plant name.

TABLE 9.2 PLANT SPACINGS		
TYPE OF PLANT	**PLANT SPACING**	**PLANTS PER m² (yd²)**
Tree — large	8.0 m (26 ft)	—
Tree — medium	5.0 m (17 ft)	—
Tree — small	3.0 m (10 ft)	—
Shrub — vigorous	1.5 m (5 ft)	—
Shrub — medium	1.0 m (3 ft)	1
Shrub — small	60 cm (2 ft)	3
Roses — shrub	1.0 m (3 ft)	1
Rose — bedding	60 cm (2 ft)	3
Herbaceous — large	60 cm (2 ft)	3
Herbaceous — medium	45 cm (18 in)	5
Herbaceous — small	30 cm (12 in)	10 (9)
Ground cover plants	45 cm (18 in)	5
Heathers	30 cm (12 in)	10 (9)
Climbers — vigorous	3.0 m (10 ft)	—
Climbers — medium	2.0 m (6 ft)	—

CHAPTER 10

TREES AND SHRUBS

PART I

DESIGNING WITH TREES AND SHRUBS

Trees, shrubs and conifers give year round height and structure to a garden. They all have woody tissue and may be deciduous or evergreen. Trees have a single stem and are capable of growing to heights in excess of 20 m (66 ft), whereas shrubs are multi-stemmed and are rarely capable of growth above 6 m (20 ft). Conifers have needles instead of leaves and cones instead of flowers and fruit. Conifers range in size from completely horizontal to *Sequoia sempervirens* (Californian redwood), which can reach 100 m (330 ft).

When designing with trees and shrubs it is important to understand the materials we are using in design terms. We need to look at plants in terms of their shape, habit, texture and colour.

The shape or form of a plant is the outline shape seen as a silhouette and is most clearly seen in summer in deciduous plants but is equally apparent all the year round in evergreens.

A plant's habit is the direction in which the branches grow and is most clearly seen in winter in deciduous trees and shrubs. The habit of many conifers is hidden by the fine foliage.

The texture of a plant usually refers to the pattern created by the leaves but interesting textures are also found in some stems and trunks and in some flowers.

Colour in plants usually means flower colour, but much more important in most planting design is foliage colour, not only when strongly defined as in purple foliage but also the more subtle differences between the various tones of greens found in different plants. Colour will be discussed in Chapter 13.

Shapes of trees and shrubs

The shape of a tree or shrub is only important if it is clearly discernible. There are ten different and distinct shapes that can be seen in trees, shrubs and conifers (Fig. 10.1).

Round

Round or spherical plants are those where the foliage forms a ball of equal height and width with the base curving in. It is a formal shape and round trees make very good avenue trees and minor focal points. Plants can be clipped to this shape, and spheres of clipped box and yew are often used within formal planting schemes.

Dome

The dome shape can be seen in many plants, becoming a hummock in many low ground cover plants. Domes have rounded tops with the width of the foliage being greater than the height. It is a lovely shape to use as it associates well with all other shapes frequently softening their impact.

Bell

The third of the rounded shapes is the bell seen in many of our larger native trees such as the oak and the beech. The height is greater than the width and the base of the foliage spreads outwards. Bell shaped trees are good for screens and shelter belts.

Oval

The oval shape is seen in conifers and trees more frequently than in shrubs. The height is considerably greater than the width and the base of the shape turns inwards. This shape is more formal than the bell and can be used for formal avenues, or placed at either side of a formal vista.

Fig. 10.1 Shapes found in plants.

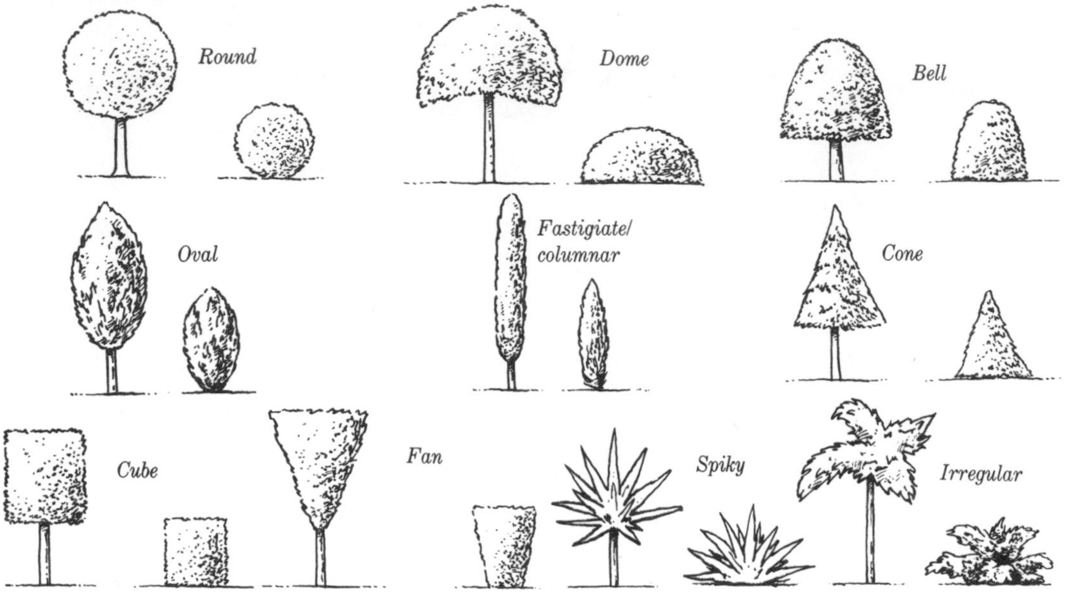

Fastigiate/Columnar

When the height is at least five times the width the shape becomes fastigiate or columnar. This is a very extreme shape and if wrongly placed becomes a visual eyesore. Fastigiate plants can be used as focal points, when placed with great care.

Cone

Two other formal shapes are the cone and the cube, the first is found in many young trees and, more strongly defined, in conifers. Cones can be softened by planting with dome or bell shaped plants or can be used on their own as focal points. Small cones are often used in formal planting schemes.

Cube

Cubes and oblongs are always artificial shapes created by man. They are found in clipped hedges and in pleached trees. They are always formal and if used as hedges, will add a formality to the area in which they are planted.

Fan

Fans are inverted cones and seen in a great many trees and shrubs but few conifers. It is a useful shape for a tree in a small garden as it

allows plenty of space for planting underneath. A pair of fan shaped trees make an attractive arch.

Spiky

Spiky shapes are rarely found in British gardens and when seen are apt to look uncomfortable. They are best used in isolation where they can be very dramatic e.g. *Phormium tenax* planted in gravel beside a paved area. In hotter climates the spiky shape is very common and planting in those areas would use a range of spiky shapes together.

Irregular

The final shape is tabular or irregular. Very many trees and shrubs exhibit no definite shape but very few are specifically irregular, an example would be a mature *Pinus sylvestris* (Scots pine) or *Cedrus libani* (cedar of Lebanon). It is a fine shape seen against buildings and makes a good focal point.

Habits of trees and shrubs

The habit of a plant should not be confused with the shape; it is quite different and in fact trees with the same habit can display a range of different shapes (Fig. 10.2).

There are five habits that are important in the effect they have on planting design and these are illustrated in Fig. 10.3:

Weeping

A weeping habit is only found in trees, as the effect is caused by the branches of the tree all drooping down from the main trunk. This is a lovely habit particularly when seen in a tree with a round shape. Weeping trees make good focal points particularly if placed by water e.g. *Salix chrysocoma* (weeping willow) beside a pond.

Pendulous

A pendulous habit can be seen in a few conifers and several trees. The main branches grow upwards but then droop at the ends. It is less dramatic than a weeping habit but equally attractive. Where shrubs have branches with drooping ends they are usually termed arching rather then pendulous. Pendulous trees can look marvellous when placed next to buildings as they will soften their harsh lines. They also make very good focal points.

Tortuous

A tortuous habit is where the branches are twisted, this occurs in several plants as they age but is found in a few plants whilst still young. These are mostly cultivars which have been selected for this habit. It is difficult to place tortuous plants as they tend to 'quarrel' with others plants. It is a very informal habit and most effective when used with rocks and water.

Fig. 10.2 The range of shapes found in trees with a weeping habit.

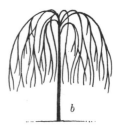

(a) Round e.g. *Prunus subhirtella* 'Pendula'.

(b) Dome e.g. *Betula pendula* 'Youngii'.

(c) Bell e.g. *Salix × chrysocoma*.

(d) Oval e.g. *Salix caprea* 'Kilmarnock'.

Vertical

A great many plants have a vertical habit but it is not usually important in design terms as it is rarely visible in summer when leaves hide the branches. In plants used for winter stem colour this habit becomes very apparent and most effective.

Horizontal

The last habit to be important in design terms is a horizontal habit where the branches leave the main stem at right angles. It is found in a few trees, shrubs and conifers and is always obvious. Plants with a horizontal habit should be used as focal points.

Fig. 10.3 Habits of trees.

Weeping

Pendulous

Tortuous

Vertical

Horizontal

TREES

Trees provide the vertical element in planting, giving instant height when planted. They can be planted singly, in small groups, in blocks, in lines, or in avenues. A single tree will have a quite different effect than a group even if the group consists of all the same species. In a single tree the shape will be most important in summer and the habit in winter, whereas with a group the canopy effect of massed foliage will hide the individual shape of the trees, although the habit may still be discernible. Texture is not usually important unless the tree has very large leaves creating a very bold effect.

Use of trees in the garden

Trees can be used for structural planting; as focal points; for their ornamental value; and functionally, for fruit, or for shade, or as a support for a hammock, a swing or even a tree house! An existing tree is more useful for the last four functions than a newly planted specimen, but if there are no existing trees in your garden it is very sensible to plan for the future when planting trees.

Trees take from 20 to 100 years to reach maturity so it is worth taking care in both the choice and positioning of new trees for your garden. It is possible to move trees once planted but it is far better to plant them in the correct position in the first place.

Existing trees, however badly sited or unsightly, should not be removed unless dead, badly diseased or dangerous. A mature tree is irreplaceable for at least the next 20 years and even an ugly or misshapen tree can often be pruned to create a more interesting shape or be clothed by planting a rambling rose at its base. Start by considering existing specimen trees as potential focal points and design the garden around them if at all possible. If the existing trees are grouped together and generally are uninteresting e.g. a group of sycamores, then one answer would be to clear the lower branches to create more light and plant underneath the trees with taller-growing evergreen shrubs to create background planting. Another idea would be to plant beneath the sycamores with ground cover plants to create an interesting woodland area.

Structural planting of trees

In larger gardens some of the structural planting will be trees as well as shrubs, particularly where the garden is exposed to strong winds. Trees should be selected for the soil and ability to grow fast and well. Often it will be better to use native trees rather than the ornamental species.

NATIVE TREES

Native trees are those which have been growing in a country or area since prehistoric times. They are well adapted to the soils and climate of the area and freely produce seed which then germinates to produce new trees. Since man first started to travel he has 'introduced' trees from other areas. Occasionally these trees adapt to the soil and climate so that they seed themselves and become 'naturalized'. In Britain, naturalized trees include the sycamore and sweet chestnut. Other 'introduced' trees are incapable of survival and reproduction outside the protection of the garden and are called 'ornamental' trees.

TREE BELTS AND SCREENS

Tree belts are only suitable for planting in larger gardens where they are used for wind protection. Native trees should be used and species selected which are tolerant of winds and have a bell shape with fairly dense foliage. *Crataegus monogyna* is one of the best. Tree belts are even more effective with an underplanting of native shrubs. Trees in tree belts should be planted a maximum of 3 m (10 ft) apart, preferably in three rows (Fig. 10.4).

The choice of trees for screening depends on the feature to be screened. There are no fast-growing evergreen broad-leaved trees in Britain so a tall screen will either need to be conifers or deciduous trees with very close growing branches. *Carpinus betulus* (hornbeam) makes a good screen where there is room.

WOODLAND PLANTING

Woodland planting can be natural or ornamental, it can be large scale or merely a small clump of trees. In smaller gardens woodland gardens are usually only created where there are already existing trees providing a shady canopy.

In larger country gardens, it can be very rewarding to plant new woodland for the future. There are several uses for woodland, as a habitat for wildlife, as an arboretum, or to create an area for shade-loving plants. To encourage wildlife, the trees chosen must be native trees and of as wide a range as possible of species suitable to the soil and drainage. The woodland will also want to have an understorey of native shrubs and a ground cover of wild woodland plants. Trees can be planted in the form of an arboretum, which is a collection of trees. Trees included can be ornamental as well as native and naturalized, but should be planted in groups of one genus in each area i.e. plant all the *Sorbus species* in the same area. Arboretum planting can be made interesting by creating vistas through the planting and planting trees along the vistas as avenues. Open woodland can be planted as a garden feature to give an area in which the gardener or plantsman can grow a range of plants that like shade and protection. The trees can be ornamental and should be chosen for their ornamental and seasonal interest as well as different degrees of shade. Birch trees will provide very light shade and beech trees very heavy shade.

AVENUES

An avenue consists of two rows of trees planted parallel to each other. They are usually planted along a path or drive and thereby make the roadway more important. When planted along the drive to a house they add a feeling of

Fig. 10.4 Plan to show arrangement of trees in a treebelt.

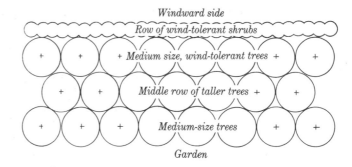

Windward side

Row of wind-tolerant shrubs

+ + + *Medium size, wind-tolerant trees* + +

+ + *Middle row of taller trees* + +

+ + + *Medium-size trees* + +

Garden

(*a*)Plan — Trees are 3 m (10 ft) apart in three parallel rows, with an outer row of shrubs at 1 m (3ft) apart.

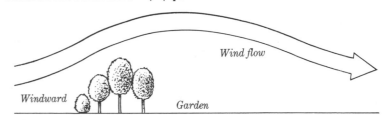

Wind flow

Windward   *Garden*

(*b*) Cross section — The trees break the force of the wind and also push the flow upwards so that the full force of the wind is not felt within the garden for up to 10 times the height of the trees.

expectancy as the visitor approaches the house. In choosing trees for an avenue to a house, be careful to keep the ultimate size of the trees in the scale of the house e.g. an avenue of apple trees would be more in scale with a cottage and an avenue of horse chestnuts more in scale with a manor house than vice versa. The size of the trees should also relate to the width of the roadway or path and the space available (Table 10.1).

Avenues are most effective when planted with all trees of the same species, however, where greater variety is desired then trees can be planted in pairs with every pair different. When using more than one species make sure that all trees used reach the same ultimate height and have at least one feature in common e.g. shape, habit or autumn leaf colour.

The planting distance shown in the chart refers both to the space between trees on one

167

side of the vista or drive, and to the distance between trees across the drive i.e. the trees are planted in a square.

If the avenue is at the side of a road or drive then avoid using trees with large leaves, particularly those with leaves that are slow to disintegrate after leaf-fall. The leaves left lying on the road in autumn may cause vehicles to skid. Other trees to avoid beside roads are those with greedy roots e.g. poplars and willows, that may cause damage to the road surface.

Trees as focal points
Large existing trees make the most effective focal points in a new garden but don't be put off if you have to start with newly planted trees as many of them grow surprisingly quickly.

TABLE 10.1 TREES FOR AVENUES

SIZE OF TREES	ULTIMATE HEIGHT	PLANTING DISTANCE
Small trees:		
Crataegus oxyacantha	6 m (20 ft)	4 m (13 ft)
Crataegus prunifolia	8 m (26 ft)	5 m (16 ft)
Malus hupehensis	6 m (20 ft)	5 m (16 ft)
Prunus 'Tai-Haku'	8 m (26 ft)	6 m (20 ft)
Prunus 'Ukon'	8 m (26 ft)	6 m (20 ft)
Pyrus calleryana 'Chanticleer'	8 m (26 ft)	5 m (16 ft)
Sorbus hupehensis	10 m (33 ft)	6 m (20 ft)
Sorbus 'Embley'	10 m (33 ft)	5 m (16 ft)
Sorbus 'Joseph Rock'	10 m (33 ft)	5 m (16 ft)
Medium trees:		
Carpinus betulus 'Fastigiata'	16 m (53 ft)	8 m (26 ft)
Fraxinus ornus	16 m (53 ft)	8 m (26 ft)
Malus tschonoskii	12 m (40 ft)	5 m (16 ft)
Prunus avium 'Plena'	15 m (50 ft)	8 m (26 ft)
Sorbus aria 'Lutescens'	12 m (40 ft)	8 m (26 ft)
Large trees:		
Acer cappadocicum	20 m (66 ft)	12 m (40 ft)
Acer platanoides	20 m (66 ft)	12 m (40 ft)
Aesculus × carnea 'Briotii'	15 m (50 ft)	10 m (33 ft)
Aesculus hippocastanum	25 m (83 ft)	12 m (40 ft)
Fagus sylvatica	25 m (83 ft)	12 m (40 ft)
Platanus orientalis	20 m (66 ft)	12 m (40 ft)
Tilia tomentosa	24 m (80 ft)	12 m (40 ft)

Select trees for year round effect, and the right scale for your garden. A small garden is not the right setting for either a cedar of Lebanon or a copper beech. Choose trees for shape or habit, suitable shapes are cones or ovals, suitable habits weeping, pendulous or hroizontal. Fastigiate trees should be used with care as they tend to look awkward, however a group of fastigiate trees planted together can be very attractive.

Coloured-leaved trees will act as focal points in summer but lose their impact in winter unless combined with an interesting shape.

FRAMING VIEWS
If the focal point is a view out of the garden then trees can be planted either side of the view to act as a frame. Select trees which complement the view e.g. apples trees framing the fields of an adjacent farm, birch trees framing distant mountains, or rowan trees framing a view of woodlands.

Ornamental value of trees
In small gardens trees must be chosen not only for their use in providing structure, focal points or shade but also for their ornamental value. The ornamental value of trees may be the beauty of their flowers, the colour of the foliage in summer or autumn, the richness of their fruit, or the winter colour of their stems. Preferably every tree chosen should have at least two seasons of interest e.g. *Amelanchier lamarckii* which is a small tree with delicate white flowers in spring, attractive leaves in summer and bright orange and red autumn colour. Trees can also be used simply for their ornamental effect and planted within beds and borders to give added height. Usually trees are chosen for their coloured foliage which should harmonize with the other colours in the border e.g. *Pyrus salicifolia* with grey leaves planted at the back of a grey border.

GROUPING TREES FOR EFFECT
A single tree may not be interesting enough on its own whereas a group of trees might give

sufficient impact. A group consists of a minimum of three trees and may well be five or seven. It is always easier to group odd numbers of plants together. Trees can either be grouped with all trees of the same species or be in mixed groups. Trees within a mixed group must have at least one feature in common e.g. all trees for autumn colour, or all similar shape, or all of the same genus.

An attractive group for a small garden would be:

Prunus subhirtella 'Autumnalis' for winter flowers;

Prunus sargentii for early spring flowers and autumn colour;

Prunus 'Shimidsu' for its late flowers and dome shape.

For a larger garden a dramatic grouping would be:

Acer platanoides 'Crimson King' with purple leaves;

Acer cappadocicum 'Aureum' with bright yellow leaves;

Acer griseum with its marvellous bark in winter and orange and red autumn colour.

TREES FOR WINTER INTEREST

In many gardens winter is not considered part of the garden calendar, the garden being left sleeping until the spring. This means that if you want to go into your garden on a crisp, sunny winter's day there is nothing to look at and enjoy. There are several trees that can be used to give colour and interest in winter and several of them are listed in the appendix. Trees chosen for their winter interest need to be placed so that they can be viewed from the house, and stem colours are best when seen with the sun shining on them and in the case of the coloured branches of *Salix alba* 'Chermesina' against a backdrop of blue sky! White birch stems need to be grouped together and a clear space left in front of the group so that all the stems can be seen clearly with perhaps just an underplanting of snowdrops to add to the overall winter effect. There is only one tree

particularly noted for its winter flowers, *Prunus subhirtella* 'Autumnalis' (winter-flowering cherry). Room should be found for a specimen in all but the smallest garden. *Parrotia persica* has attractive, though small, red and brown flowers in winter and although normally planted for its marvellous autumn colour is worth considering placing in the winter garden.

TREES FOR SPRING INTEREST

Ornamental trees come into their own in the spring, with apple and cherry followed by hawthorn blossom. It is possible to have blossom from the earliest spring days through to midsummer when the flowers will have to compete with the first flush of roses. Plant spring flowering trees with spring bulbs to maximize the overall effect. Avoid the very strong pink coloured cherries e.g. *Prunus* 'Kanzan' particularly when the trees are to be planted with yellow daffodils. Try restricting your trees to white or creamy blossom using *Malus hupehensis* and *Prunus avium* 'Plena' or the beautiful *Prunus* 'Ukon'. There are some trees whose spring foliage is particularly attractive. Amongst these is *Acer pseudoplatanus* 'Brilliantissimum' with glorious shrimp pink young foliage. Another good tree is *Populus × candicans* 'Aurora' with foliage splashed pink and white and a delicious 'balsam' scent as the leaves unfurl. This tree is best kept pruned hard in late winter as the young wood always produces the brightest coloured leaves. It will also keep this potentially untidy tree under control.

TREES FOR SUMMER INTEREST

Having stated that spring is the best time for flowering trees there are several trees that flower in summer and others whose foliage colour is best at this season. However, summer is the season in which many of the other plants in the garden are at their best so it may be more sensible to let the trees provide shade and structure and enjoy the colour and impact of the border plants and roses. If you need a tree with summer interest as a focal point or for an otherwise dull area then consider using *Paulownia tomentosa* which has strange fox-glove-like flowers in early summer and large furry leaves.

TREES FOR AUTUMN INTEREST

There are so many lovely trees for autumn colour that it seems surprising that so many gardens don't appear to have given any thought or space to these plants. Many of the trees have another feature or period of interest so it should be possible to include at least one tree for autumn within even the smallest garden.

Place trees, shrubs and other plants for autumn interest together for maximum impact. A group of these plants might include *Sorbus* 'Joseph Rock', a small tree with both yellow berries and orange-red autumn colour, with *Rhus typhina* 'Laciniata', the cutleaf form of the familiar sumach, with *Cerato-stigma willmotianum*, a low-growing shrub with wonderful leaf colour plus gentian blue flowers in autumn. Blue flowers and berries are a marvellous complement to the reds and gold of autumn leaves.

Softer autumn colour schemes are possible if you select trees and shrubs with leaves which turn gold and yellow in the autumn; with this colour scheme the soft lavenders and purples of michaelmas daisies provide a very satisfying colour combination.

Planting trees

Trees are planted to last for a great many years so they deserve to be planted with care and attention to detail. First of all decide on the size of tree, feathered, half standard or standard. In a small garden is makes sense to plant standard trees as these are already well grown. Plant all deciduous trees in early winter if at all possible. Before starting to plant your trees you will need the following:

A stake — preferably rounded in cross section with a diameter of 100 mm (4 in) with one end pointed and *not* longer than 1.75 m (5 ft 9 in). It doesn't need to be treated with preservative as by the time it starts to rot it will no longer be needed.

Two tree ties — plastic or rubber with a spacer; an old pair of tights will *not* do! Nor will bits of string or rose ties.

Some compost and bonemeal — to improve the soil and encourage rooting. Bonemeal is an organic form of phosphate which dissolves slowly in the soil to provide nutrients for the developing roots for the first few years. Each tree will need at least a large bucket of compost and a handful (25 g or 1 oz) of bone-meal.

A rabbit guard — if rabbits are a problem, the spiral type of guard is relatively cheap and effective.

You will also need an implement for digging the tree pit and a tool for driving in the stake.

The procedure for planting a tree is as follows (Fig. 10.5):

1. Dig the hole large enough to be able to spread out the tree roots easily and with enough room at the base of the hole for the compost. Don't dig the hole in very frosty weather as ice can form in the hole before planting. The ice will be covered by the soil during planting and will remain unthawed until the spring.

2. Make sure that the bottom of the hole is broken up by forking before planting, this will ensure that the tree has proper drainage.

3. Place the stake in the hole and drive it in firmly so that at least 45 cm (1½ ft) of the stake has been driven into the ground. Check that the stake is absolutely rock solid and does not move at all when pushed.

4. Compost mixed with the excavated soil and the bonemeal should be placed in the bottom of the hole.

5. The tree should be placed on the leeward

side of the stake i.e. so that the stake is between the tree and the prevailing wind. The tree needs to be held at the right level, i.e. the same level as it was planted in the nursery which should be just above the junction of roots and stem, whilst the hole is filled in, and the soil firmed down.

6. Check the stake is not rubbing any part of the tree and if the stake is above the lowest branch of the tree, remove the top of the stake by careful sawing.

7. Tree ties should be placed at the bottom and top of the stake, making sure that the buckle is against the stake and not the tree. After fixing, the top tie should be nailed to the stake to prevent it slipping down.

8. If the branches of the tree look lop-sided the tree can be pruned to a form a better shape.

9. Finally water the tree well and fix the rabbit guard if used.

To assist the young tree to grow fast in its first few years it is sensible to mulch the base of the tree after planting to stop weeds, to keep up the soil temperature and to prevent surface evaporation of water. Proprietary tree mats are available, or you can cut a circle of black polythene and lay it around the tree digging the sides into the soil. An alternative is to use a bark mulch at least 75 mm (3 in) thick. Taking time to plant your trees properly will result in the trees getting established quickly and growing away strongly. All that will be needed afterwards is watering in dry periods in the first summer, checking and loosening the tie every six months and removing the stake at the end of the third winter after planting.

Trees and the law

There are two aspects of the law which relate to trees: Tree preservation orders, and the legal obligations of landowners relating to trees on their land.

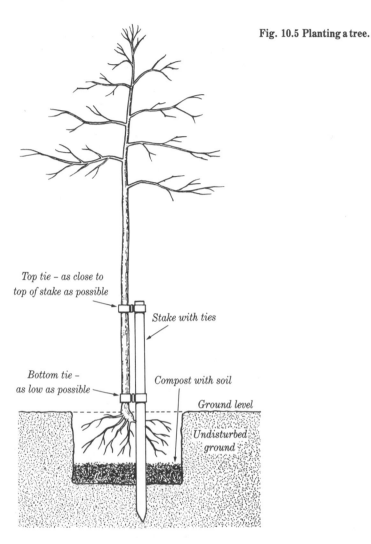

Fig. 10.5 Planting a tree.

Top tie – as close to top of stake as possible

Stake with ties

Bottom tie – as low as possible

Compost with soil

Ground level

Undisturbed ground

Tree preservation orders *(T.P.O.s)*
These are placed on trees by the local planning authority to protect trees in the interests of amenity. This amenity should normally be capable of enjoyment by the general public. An order may cover a single tree or trees, a group of trees or woodlands, but not hedges or shrubs.

The order makes it an offence wilfully to damage or destroy or to fell, top, lop or uproot a tree or trees specified in the order, without the planning authority's consent.

The only trees which cannot be covered by a

T.P.O. are cultivated fruit trees in an orchard or garden. You can check if there are any T.P.O.s on your existing trees by looking in the local land charges registry which can be seen at your local planning offices or town hall. If there are any orders then you will need to take advice from the planning authority before doing any tree work. If the tree concerned is dead, dying or dangerous you may remove it only after telling the authority, giving them at least five days' notice.

Legal obligations of landowners relating to trees

A landowner is responsible for the trees on his land and any damage they may cause. Problems usually occur with trees at or near a boundary with a neighbour. The law in Britain states:

1. The tree's owner may go on to his neighbour's land to pick fruit where the fruiting branch overhangs the neighbour's land.

2. The neighbour may cut off the branches hanging over his land *but* he must return the branch to the owner.

3. The neighbour may not do anything that might result in the death of the tree e.g. he can't pour weedkiller over the roots; although he is allowed to remove roots that appear on his land.

4. The owner is responsible for any damage caused by the roots of his tree e.g. roots damaging drains, but it has to be proved which roots from which tree are responsible for the damage.

5. The owner is responsible for any damage caused by the branches of his tree whether on, or off, his property.

6. Only the owner, not his tenant, can remove trees on his land only provided that they are not subject to T.P.O.s.

All these matters will depend upon the interpretation of the law and therefore always consult a solicitor before taking the law into your own hands.

CHAPTER 11

TREES AND SHRUBS
PART II

CONIFERS

Conifers are considered simpler plants than the flowering trees and shrubs. They have no recognizable flowers as such, carry their seeds in cones, and have needle-like leaves. They do however have certain advantages over broad-leaved trees. They have little leaf fall, and what there is can be left to lie where it falls as a mulch; their roots are not as invasive nor their branches as wide-spreading as broadleaves, and they include species which are more tolerant of extremes of cold and exposure.

Most are evergreen and among them can be found some of the strongest of plant shapes. They range from giants that grow to over 100 m (330 ft) to dwarfs that stop growing at 60 cm (2 ft) and others that remain completely prostrate.

Conifers, more than any other group of plants, are capable of producing 'sports', mutations of colour or habit which have given rise to literally hundreds of cultivated varieties whose nomenclature can become almost incomprehensible and certainly impossible to remember e.g. *Juniperus* x *media* 'Plumosa Albo-variegata' and *Chamaecyparis pisifera* 'Plumosa Aurea Nana' both horrendously long names for two relatively small plants. The second roughly translated means the dwarf form of the golden form of the feathery foliage form of the sawara cypress. Its almost as bad as the plant names in use before Linnaeus. I am sure that the cypress known as 'Boulevard' is as popular as it is because everyone can remember its name!

Soils, aspect and drainage

Garden conifers are not generally fussy about soils, except for some of the larger pines and spruces which need lime-free soils. For thin chalky soils it is safer to stick to *Juniperus* and *Taxus* species and varieties as both of these genera grow well in these conditions. As a general rule gold foliage conifers should be planted in full sun and preferably sheltered from very cold winds. The grey and blue foliage forms will tolerate light shade but are seen at their best in sunlight. For shady areas the following species and their cultivars can be used:

Chamaecyparis obtusa
Chamaecyparis pisifera
Cryptomeria japonica
Juniperus × *media*
Juniperus sabina
Taxus baccata

For deep shade only the *Taxus* will be suitable and even then may grow rather untidily. There are conifers for every level of soil moisture, from extremely dry to permanently wet, but the majority of conifers prefer good drainage if possible. Conifers for wet soils include:

Cryptomeria japonica
Metasequoia glyptostroboides
Taxodium distichum (swamp cypress). This will grow right in water as its name suggests.
Thuja occidentalis
Thuja plicata

The value of conifers in planting design

Many gardeners only see conifers as dwarf plants for use in the rock garden. Unfortunately this is the least valuable of their uses and the most easily overdone. They are far more useful as structural plants, their fine foliage remaining unchanged throughout the seasons and providing a marvellous background. Their strong shapes make them excellent focal points when placed sympathetically, and the low-growing junipers make very attractive ground cover for difficult banks.

Structural use

Many conifers tolerate much greater extremes of climate than the broadleaved trees and shrubs. They are very useful where shelter belts are needed in more northerly areas exposed to cold north and east winds. *Pinus nigra* will grow on the thinnest soils, is tolerant of strong cold winds and maritime conditions. *Chamaecyparis lawsoniana* and *Thuja plicata* are also tolerant of high winds but may look too ornamental for many shelter belts.

NATIVE CONIFERS

There are only three conifers which are native to the British Isles:

Juniperus communis (juniper) — found on chalk soils and being distinctive in having what appear to be berries instead of cones. Forms a low spreading bush.

Pinus sylvestris (Scots pine) — usually found on poor soils but capable of growing almost anywhere. A tall graceful tree with distinctive reddish bark. It needs to be planted as small as possible and takes time to get started. Its typical umbrella shape only develops with age.

Taxus baccata (yew) — found on chalk soils but will grow in all soils even very acid sands. A medium-sized tree retaining a shrub-like habit and producing red berry-like cones. Poisonous in all parts.

All of these three are excellent plants in the right place but not particularly good where native plants are needed in the garden. None of them make good hedgerow plants or are particularly effective in shelter belts although the Scots pine is worth including in suitable areas.

CONIFERS FOR SCREENS

Conifers are very useful for creating tall evergreen screens. The best are *Chamaecy-paris lawsoniana* for dry soils. *Thuja plicata* for wetter conditions and ×*Cupressocyparis leylandii* when really fast growth is required. These will all eventually make screens up to 20 m (66 ft) high, a point to be remembered when planting 1.2 m (4 ft) high plants against a boundary fence in a small suburban garden! They can be kept trimmed at a lower height, which is fine as long as you can reach the top of the screen to cut it. ×*Cupressocyparis leylandii* is the fastest growing but will also need more pruning to keep at the required height.

When planting screens the conifers should be spaced at 1.5 m (5 ft) apart. If a thicker screen is required then plant two rows of plants rather than one.

CONIFERS FOR BACKGROUND PLANTING

Conifers are the best plants for producing a dark matt background for flower beds or garden features. They can be planted as a screen, hedge or in groups. In a small garden a coniferous hedge which doubles as a space division and as a background will be the most sensible use of the space available. In larger gardens groups of conifers can be used, selecting the individual plants for conical or cylindrical habit. Foliage colour should be selected to complement the foreground feature, dark green being the best for most statues and seats, but a golden background could be planted behind a winter border, and a grey-blue background behind a summer flowering rose border.

CONIFERS FOR HEDGING

Some of the finest hedges are coniferous, they combine evergreen dense foliage with a relatively fast rate of growth. Unfortunately all too often gardeners are seduced into planting leyland cypress as a hedge, being assured by the nursery that it is the fastest growing hedging plant. It certainly is fast growing — a 1.5 m (5 ft) hedge only taking three to four years from planting — but it then continues to grow at the same rate and is really

TABLE 11.1 CONIFERS FOR HEDGING	
NAME	**PLANTING DISTANCES**
Chamaecyparis lawsoniana	75 cm (2 ft 6 in)
× *Cupressocyparis leylandii*	90 cm (3 ft)
Taxus baccata	60 cm (2 ft)
Tsuga canadensis	60 cm (2 ft)
Tsuga heterophylla	60 cm (2 ft)
Thuja plicata	75 cm (2 ft 6 in)
Thuja occidentalis	75 cm (2 ft 6 in)

much better used as a screen rather than a hedge. The other two conifers suggested for screens, *Chamaecyparis lawsoniana* and *Thuja plicata* will also make good hedges, but again are better used as a screen.

For more ornamental hedges the coloured foliage varieties of the above species can be used but planting distances should then be reduced e.g. × *Cupressocyparis leylandii* 'Castlewellan' should be planted at 60 cm (2 ft), not 90 cm (3 ft) for the species.

Taxus baccata (yew) is the best hedging plant of all making a dense dark green, almost black, hedge which is tolerant of almost all soils and aspects except badly drained sites. It has a reputation for being slow growing but yew is capable of growing 30–45 cm (12–18 in) a year providing it is given a good start. Before planting the ground should be well dug adding well-rotted manure and bonemeal to the base of the planting trench. A top dressing of fertilizer should be applied in the spring after planting and the new plants kept well watered throughout the first two or three growing seasons. Yews should be planted in late autumn or late spring and trimmed in late summer. If planting is left until the spring then additional care needs to be taken in the first summer to ensure that the new plants have enough water.

TOPIARY

Topiary is the art of clipping evergreen shrubs and conifers into elaborate shapes. First popular in Roman times, and found in gardens of sixteenth, seventeenth and nineteenth centuries, and now enjoying a revival together with formal gardening. The best plants to use are yew and box. Many of the more complicated shapes are created by using a wire mesh shape placed over a young shoot, and as the shoot develops the leaves are clipped against the wire. Simpler shapes can be cut in existing growth but require a good eye and a steady hand.

Specimen conifers for use as focal points

Conifers tend to form conical, oval or cylindrical shapes, with many conifers starting out conical and then narrowing to form cylinders as they age. A few have a clearly defined habit and these make particularly strong focal points. The cedars are particularly good where there is room; unfortunately there is a tendency among gardeners to underestimate their ultimate size and, all too often, *Cedrus atlantica* 'Glauca' is seen planted within 5 m (16 ft) of a small house usually in the middle of the front lawn. Cedars grow to 36 m high which is 100 ft! It is not a tree for the average front garden.

A group of *Calocedrus decurrens* (incense cedars) make a very dramatic focal point for a large garden but will take time to show their full potential. Plant five to nine plants together 2 m (6 ft) apart and wait!

Medium-sized gardens should have room for one of the weeping conifers e.g. *Chamaecyparis nootkatensis* 'Pendula' with wonderful down sweeping branches and hanging fronds of foliage. It takes time and training to get going but it can eventually grow to 25 m (80 ft), so it needs room.

A better specimen for a small garden is one of the golden cypresses, perhaps *Chamaecyparis lawsoniana* 'Lanei' which ultimately makes a golden cone 10 m (33 ft) high. An alternative would be one of the blue spruces e.g. *Picea pungens* 'Moerheimii' which has a horizontal habit, a cone shape and lovely silvery blue colour. It takes time to get established but is worth the wait.

TABLE 11.2 CONIFERS FOR GROUND COVER		
NAME	ULTIMATE HEIGHT	PLANTING DISTANCE
Juniperus communis depressa	30 cm (12 in)	60 cm (2 ft)
Juniperus communis 'Hornibrookii'	25 cm (10 in)	60 cm (2 ft)
Juniperus communis 'Repanda'	30 cm (12 in)	60 cm (2 ft)
Juniperus conferta	25 cm (10 in)	60 cm (2 ft)
Juniperus horizontalis	15 cm (6 in)	75 cm (2 ft 6 in)
Juniperus horizontalis 'Bar Harbour'	15 cm (6 in)	75 cm (2 ft 6 in)
Juniperus procumbens	15 cm (6 in)	60 cm (2 ft)
Juniperus × *media* 'Pfitzerana'	1.5 m (5 ft)	1.0 m (3 ft)
Juniperus sabina tamariscifolia	60 cm (2 ft)	1.0 m (3 ft)
Juniperus 'Grey Owl'	60 cm (2 ft)	1.0 m (3 ft)

Conifers for ground cover

There are a large number of semi-prostrate or prostrate conifers which make excellent ground cover. Most of them are junipers and are ideal for chalk soils and dry areas. They make neat level growth and once established cover the ground beneath completely. The fine texture of the needles and irregular shape of many of the plants complement paving and other hard materials and they are particularly useful filling in the odd corners next to buildings. The prostrate forms of *Juniperus horizontalis* are especially effective covering steep banks which are impossible to mow. The effect of the juniper is similar to that of a fine-leaved grass but without the need for regular cutting. If taller ground cover is needed, *Juniperus* × *media* 'Pfitzerana' is probably the best, growing well in sun or shade and in any soil. There is a gold-leaved version but the green form is really the best.

Ornamental value of conifers

Conifers provide a range of evergreen foliage colour, with many of the plants subtly changing colour with the seasons. They are particularly valuable in winter but can be used to add interest throughout the year.

WINTER COLOUR

Conifers come into their own in the winter when there is little other colour in the garden.

One of the best ways to use conifers for winter enjoyment is to plant them with the winter flowering heathers, *Erica carnea* and *Erica* × *darleyensis*. This combination is suitable for most gardens as these particular heathers are lime tolerant and grow well on all but the thinnest chalk soils. Plant the heathers in large groups of one variety and use the conifers singly if large-growing varieties and in groups of three with smaller forms. The best conifers to use are the taller-spreading junipers listed above. With pink and white-flowering heathers, the blue-grey foliage of a *Juniperus* × *media* 'Hetzii' looks marvellous. The blue-grey foliage varieties are usually the best to use but if the warmth of gold foliage is desired then try planting *Erica carnea* 'Foxhollow', *Erica* × *darleyensis* 'J.H. Brummage' with *Chamaecyparis pisifera* 'Filifera Aurea' and *Juniperus* × *media* 'Old Gold'.

CONIFERS FOR AUTUMN COLOUR

There are four conifers which lose their leaves in the autumn and all exhibit beautiful autumn colours before leaf fall.

Gingko biloba (maidenhair tree) has extraordinary fan shaped leaves that turn to butter yellow.

Larix decidua (larch) has tufts of bright green needles which turn yellow.

Metasequoia glyptostroboides (dawn redwood) has bright green leaves turning to bronze and then gold; it is very similar to:

Taxodium distichum (swamp cypress) whose leaves turn rusty orange.

All the above deserve a place in the larger garden.

USING DWARF CONIFERS

There are now hundreds of dwarf forms of conifers, with new varieties being listed each year, all needing to be found a place in the garden. The advantages of dwarf conifers is that they are easy to grow, they are inter-esting for twelve months of the year, and they come in a range of shapes and colours. This last

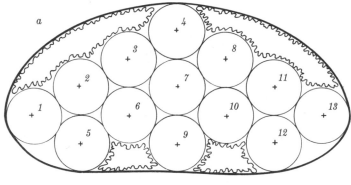

Fig. 11.1 Planting plan for dwarf conifers.
(*a*) Plan
1. *Juniperus* 'Green Carpet'. 2. *Juniperus squamata* 'Meyeri'. 3. *Thuja occidentalis* 'Smaragd'. 4. *Picea glauca* 'Albertiana Conica'. 5. *Juniperus horizontalis* 'Glauca'. 6. *Pinus mugo* 'Gnom'. 7. *Cryptomeria japonica* 'Vilmoriniana'. 8. *Juniperus chinensis* 'Pyramidalis'. 9. *Juniperus horizontalis* 'Banff'. 10. *Picea pungens* 'Globosa'. 11. *Juniperus recurva* 'Embley Park'. 12. *Juniperus procumbens* 'Nana'. 13. *Juniperus* 'Blue Carpet'.
The conifers selected are all green or silvery blue in colour. The gaps at the front of the bed could be planted with winter flowering heathers, selecting varieties with pink flowers for maximum impact.

(*b*) Elevation.

advantage becomes a disadvantage when a single specimen of each shape and colour is selected and then planted together in one bed.

Dwarf conifers add their own scale to any area in which they are planted. For this reason they look 'out of scale' planted among border plants and large shrubs. Plant them on their own, or with heathers as suggested above, or with some of the lower growing and smaller leaved herbaceous plants and shrubs. If planted on their own use the horizontal forms to create a base on which to build up a composition of shapes with the tallest cylindrical and cone shaped plants in the middle, and then the lower dome shapes around them (Fig 11.1). Check the 10-year or ultimate height of the conifers before starting to plant. Many conifers listed as dwarf will ultimately grow to 7–10 m (20–30 ft) high.

Planting conifers

Conifers are best planted in the autumn or spring rather than the middle of winter. Dig a hole rather larger than the root ball and dig some garden compost or well-rotted manure into the soil at the bottom of the hole. Plant the conifer so that the soil reaches the same level as the soil in the container or just above the top roots. If the conifer is a large specimen it may need a stake. This should be driven firmly into the base of the hole before planting. The stake should be just tall enough to leave 30 cm (12 in) above ground when the hole is filled. Use a rubber or plastic tree tie with spacer to fix the conifer to the stake.

Conifers planted into grass need to have the base of the conifer kept clear of grass or weeds after planting. Leave a 30 cm (1 ft) circle of clear soil around the base of the foliage of the conifer i.e. if the conifer base has a spread of 60 cm (2 ft), the total diameter of the clear soil will be 1.2 m (4 ft). This can then be covered with a mulch of composted bark. In cold or exposed gardens most newly planted conifers will benefit from being given a wind shelter for the first winter to prevent wind scorch, and to alleviate the worst effects of frost.

SHRUBS

Shrubs are woody plants with several stems. They can be deciduous or evergreen and range in height from completely prostrate up to

6–8 m (20–25 ft). Some shrubs can be trained to form small trees by removing all the stems except one e.g. *Cotoneaster frigidus*. Some shrubs are very specific as to the soil and aspect needed e.g. *Kalmia latifolia*, which needs lime-free moist soil and full sun. Other shrubs seem to thrive whatever the conditions e.g. *Cotoneaster horizontalis*, which grows on any soil and in sun or shade, which is probably why it is so popular.

Use of shrubs in the garden

Shrubs can be found and used in all areas of the garden except as aquatics or marginal plants in ponds, although some species of salix would survive even there. Shrubs can be planted together in shrubberies or the shrub border, or mixed with other plants, with trees in woodland, or with herbaceous plants in ground cover areas or the mixed border. They can form hedges, or provide focal points, and in the fruit garden we find shrubs providing us with gooseberries, raspberries and black and red currants.

A useful group of shrubs are those which grow very rapidly, reaching full size in two or three years. These give an instant look of maturity to the new garden, a real bonus as you wait for the slower plants to mature. Being fast growing, they are greedy, so repay with regular feeding, and you must be prepared to prune them vigorously once they reach full height.

Fast growing shrubs include:

Abutilon vitifolium
Buddleia davidii
Ceanothus — most
Cistus — all
Fuchsia magellanica
Hebe — all taller varieties
Lavatera olbia
Philadelphus — most
Phlomis fruticosa
Ribes sanguineum
Salix — most
Senecio greyi

Shrubs for structural planting

Shrubs provide most of the structural planting for the small garden, the most useful shrubs being those which are evergreen as these provide a strong green structure throughout the year. All shrubs used for structural planting must be chosen for the soil, aspect and drainage of the garden or area, and then for the specific requirements for each type of structural planting.

NATIVE SHRUBS

There are relatively few native shrubs of the British Isles and few of these are evergreen. The most important native shrubs are those which are found in hedgerows providing habitats and food for wildlife. In gardens these same hedgerow plants can be used for shelter belts and for boundary hedges where appropriate. The following are native shrubs for hedgerow planting:

Cornus sanguinea (dogwood)
Corylus avellana (hazel)
Euonymus europaeus (spindle) poisonous
Rhamnus cathartica (buckthorn)
Rosa canina (dog rose)
Rosa eglanteria (sweetbriar)
Sambucus nigra (elder)
Salix caprea (goat willow)
Salix cinerea (grey willow)
Viburnum lantana (wayfaring tree)
Viburnum opulus (guelder rose)

Evergreen hedgerow shrubs:

Buxus sempervirens (box)
Ilex aquifolium (holly)
Ligustrum vulgare (privet)
Ulex europaeus (gorse)

Several of Britain's native trees are also found as part of hedgerows, becoming shrubby when regularly trimmed:

Acer campestre (field maple)
Crataegus monogyna (hawthorn)
Prunus spinosa (sloe)
Sorbus terminalis (wild service)

THE VALUE OF EVERGREEN SHRUBS

Evergreen shrubs are the most useful plants for the garden, providing a green structure throughout the year. Where background planting is required then select evergreen shrubs with small leaves, as large shiny-leaved shrubs e.g. *Prunus laurocerasus*, will tend to stand out from the rest of the planting

A list of evergreen plants for structural planting can be found in the appendix. Evergreen shrubs suitable for hedging are listed with the hedging plants in this chapter.

SHRUBS FOR SHELTER BELTS

Shelter belts of trees are often more effective with an underplanting of shrubs, to give additional shelter at the lower levels where the tree trunks are not covered by foliage. The most suitable shrubs are native species which will survive and grow in any conditions and all those on the hedgerow list above would be suitable.

Unfortunately there are very few British evergreens amongst either trees or shrubs, so some of the tougher ornamental evergreens may need to be included. Suitable shrubs would be:

Berberis darwinii
Cotoneaster salicifolius
Elaeagnus pungens
Mahonia aquifolium
Pernettya mucronata — only for acid soils
Prunus lusitanica

Where shelter is needed in coastal areas the shrubs should be tolerant of salt winds. Suitable shrubs include:

Cytisus — most
Elaeagnus × *ebbingei*
Escallonia macrantha
Fuchsia magellanica
Hippophoe rhamnoides
Olearia macrodonta
Spartium junceum
Tamarix — all
Ulex europaeus

When planting shrubs for shelter, plant in large clumps, five, seven or even nine of one species. Avoid coloured or variegated leaves, as shelter belts are not intended to be ornamental but purely structural and functional. Amongst the deciduous shrubs the most valuable are those which come into leaf early and then hold their leaves on well into the autumn. The British hawthorn is one of the best in this respect, with the new leaves in spring appearing first amongst the hedgerow plants.

Hedges

A hedge is a row of shrubs planted in a line, closely enough to form a uniform texture. They can be planted in single or double rows. They are used for a variety of purposes from keeping stock out (cats) or children in, for privacy, for division and for creating pattern and line. The choice of plants for each hedge will depend on its intended use.

BOUNDARY HEDGES

Hedges, along with walls and fences, are used to define boundaries of properties. When hedges are used for boundaries they may need to be:

1. Stockproof — at least against cats and dogs but possibly cows or even deer. For cats and dogs thorny hedges are a deterrent if thick enough, for farm animals and deer a fence plus hedge may be necessary.

2. High — for privacy, hedges should be above eye level i.e. above 1.5 m (5 ft). For shelter, hedges should be as high as possible.

3. Tough — boundary hedges may need to compete with traffic fumes if adjacent to a road.

4. Preferably evergreen — so that the boundary is clothed throughout the year.

5. Fast growing — to give quick cover

The choice will also depend on the position of the garden, whether in the town or country.

The most suitable boundary hedge in the country will be a hedge of native shrubs, either just hawthorn or a mixture of the native hedgerow shrubs already listed. Buy small plants and plant in two rows 45 cm (18 in) apart in the rows and 25 cm (10 in) between rows.

In less rural areas *Fagus sylvatica* (beech) or *Carpinus betulus* (hornbeam) make excellent boundary hedges which can be kept clipped and tidy. Plant as for the field hedge above.

Gardens in seaside areas should use hedging plants that are tolerant of salt winds e.g. *Olearia macrodonta* or *Escallonia macrantha*.

In the centre of towns, evergreen hedges give more privacy. *Ligustrum ovalifolium* (privet) and *Prunus laurocerasus* (cherry laurel) are good choices, both being resistant to pollution.

INTERNAL HEDGES

Hedges within gardens can be high or low, flowering or foliage, and formal or informal. The choice will depend on the style of the garden and the position and function of the hedge within the garden. Formal hedges are usually non-flowering hedges which are kept clipped to form a neat rectangular barrier, they can be high to give privacy or low to create pattern. The best plant for tall formal hedges is yew, which is discussed under conifers. The best plant for low formal hedges is *Buxus sempervirens* (box). This has several varieties but the best for very low hedges i.e. under 30 cm (12 in), is *Buxus sempervirens* 'Suffruticosa' and for taller hedges up to 1.2 m (4 ft) the species *Buxus sempervirens*.

Flowering hedges are usually only clipped to keep them within bounds. They are suitable for informal areas where they can be used for division. If they form a background to a border then the hedging plant should be selected to harmonize with the colour scheme of the border e.g. *Prunus × cistena* behind a purple, pink and grey border, or, *Berberis × stenophylla* behind a yellow and gold border. It is usually more satisfactory to use one plant in a hedge rather than a mixture, a uniform

texture being part of the attraction. If a more ornamental hedge is wanted then you could plant a 'tapestry' hedge as at Hidcote in England, mixing green and purple beech or beech and holly, but then keep other planting in front of the hedge as simple as possible (Table 11.3).

TABLE 11.3
LIST OF HEDGING PLANTS

Dwarf hedges	PLANTING DISTANCE
Buxus sempervirens 'Suffruticosa'	15 cm (6 in)
Lavandula spica 'Hidcote'	30 cm (12 in)
Santolina chamaecyparissus	25 cm (10 in)
Teucrium chamaedrys	25 cm (10 in)
Taller formal hedges:	
Buxus sempervirens	45 cm (18 in)
Carpinus betulus	45 cm (18 in)
Fagus sylvatica	45 cm (18 in)
Ilex aquifolium	45 cm (18 in)
Ligustrum ovalifolium	30–45 (12–18 in)
Lonicera nitida	30 cm (12 cm)
Prunus laurocerasus	75 cm (2 ft 6 in)
Prunus lusitanica	75 cm (2 ft 6 in)
Flowering hedges:	
Berberis darwinii	60 cm (2 ft)
Berberis × stenophylla	60 cm (2 ft)
Cotoneaster 'Cornubia'	60 cm (2 ft)
Escallonia macrantha	75 cm (2 ft 6 in)
Prunus 'Cistena'	60 cm (2 ft)
Pyracantha rogersiana	60 cm (2 ft)
Rosa glauca	90 cm (3 ft)
Rosa rugosa	90 cm (3 ft)
Viburnum tinus	60 cm (2 ft)

PLANTING HEDGES

Before planting a hedge peg out the proposed line of the hedge and dig out a trench at least 45 cm (1 ft 6 in) deep. Place a layer of well rotted manure or garden compost, plus bonemeal, in the bottom of the trench and then set up a line along the centre of the trench. Space out the plants at exact planting distances and then plant the hedge, backfilling the trench as you go. To ensure good establishment of the plants keep the base of the plants clear of weeds and water frequently in the first summer after planting.

Shrubs for avenues

Avenues do not have to be planted with trees, Both conifers and shrubs can be used to create the same effect. Where the path is narrow or the distance to be covered by the avenue is limited then shrubs are more suitable than trees. The same principles for spacing should be adopted as for trees i.e. the space between shrubs on the same side should be equal to the space between shrubs across the path. Shrubs selected should have a strong shape or habit or be suitable for clipping into formal shapes.

Do not mix shrubs in avenues except where using shrub roses which can be planted in pairs of different varieties.

Suitable avenue shrubs include:

Buxus sempervirens	— can be clipped to any shape
Choisya ternata	— forms neat round shape
Lonicera nitida	— can be clipped
Prunus lusitanica	— can be pruned as standards

Standard roses can also be used for avenues, particularly when the avenue leads into or out of the rose garden.

Shrubs as focal points

Shrubs for focal points need to have a very strong shape or habit or to be of a much larger size than the neighbouring plants. They need to be planted on their own in grass, or if planted in a border must be positioned towards the front to give maximum impact. If a single shrub does not have sufficient impact then plant a group of them. Shrubs for use as focal points are listed in the appendix.

Shrubs for ground cover

There are a range of shrubs suitable for use as ground cover particularly for difficult areas such as steep unmaintainable slopes or beneath trees. *Hedera helix* (ivy) and *Vinca minor* (periwinkle), being fast growing, evergreen, and suitable for all soils and situations, provide an excellent alternative to grass particularly in shade. Deciduous shrubs are not so effective for ground cover as weeds tend to germinate in spring before the leaves of the shrubs appear, these weeds can then be difficult to eradicate.

The ornamental value of shrubs

Shrubs have a long season of interest and can be used for ornamental planting, on their own, in shrub borders, or in combination with herbaceous plants in the mixed border. Shrubs provide foliage colour, autumn fruit and leaf colour, and winter flowers, as well as spring and summer flowers. Some of the most valuable shrubs have both foliage and flower colour e.g. *Philadelphus coronarius* 'Aureus' which has golden foliage and white scented flowers, and *Weigela florida* 'Variegata' with variegated leaves and masses of pink flowers. Both of these will thrive in almost any garden.

SHRUBS FOR WINTER INTEREST

In winter shrubs can provide both foliage and flower colour. Foliage colour is provided by the coloured and variegated forms of evergreen shrubs, lists of which can be found in the appendix. Many of the winter flowers are scented which provides an added bonus and the best of these shrubs should be included in every garden.

A list of winter flowering shrubs can be found in the appendix with notes on those that are scented. Plant scented winter shrubs near to the house where they can be easily reached and appreciated on cold winter days.

Another group of shrubs that give winter colour are those with coloured stems e.g. *Cornus alba*. As with coloured stemmed trees they are best viewed with the winter sun shining on the stems and with a backdrop of the sky, an expanse of water, or dark green foliage.

SHRUBS FOR THE SPRING GARDEN

The majority of our shrubs flower in spring including several whose flowers appear before the foliage e.g. *Chaenomeles japonica*. Unfortunately some of our commonest spring flowering shrubs have the most lurid colours such as the bright yellow of many forsythias and the harsh pink of *Ribes sanguineum*, (flowering currant), which are so frequently seen planted together and shrieking at each other. Equally strident is the orange of *Berberis darwinii* flowers and the orange yellow flowers of *Berberis thunbergii atropurpurea*, which definitely clash with the emerging red purple leaves. These plants, however, are some of the easiest to grow and are often the first heralds of spring so grow them in your garden but separate the *Forsythia* from the *Ribes* placing the first with other yellow and cream flowers and yellow variegated plants e.g. *Ligustrum ovalifolium* 'Aureum', (golden privet), and *Ribes* with the pink flowered *Chaenomeles speciosa* 'Moerloosii'. Gardens with acid soil have the full range of *Azaleas* and *Rhododendrons* to choose from in spring. Again, be selective with the colours chosen for each area and avoid clashing colours. Often it is stated that nature doesn't display clashing colours but nature didn't produce the vividly coloured hybrids offered by today's nurseries!

SHRUBS FOR THE SUMMER BORDER

The best of the summer-flowering shrubs are the roses, although they are usually considered in a class of their own and are discussed in chapter 14 as ornamental plants. Other shrubs for summer interest are those with coloured foliage which can be used to reinforce colour schemes in the mixed border. Gold-leaved shrubs with gold and blue plantings and purple leaves with purple, grey and pink colour schemes. Many of the grey-leaved Mediterranean and Australasian shrubs flower in summer and these can be planted in dry sunny beds with the grey-leaved herbaceous plants, again being selected for specific colour schemes.

SHRUBS IN AUTUMN

In autumn shrubs provide both fruit and foliage colour and even a few flowers. Hydrangeas, fuchsias, hebes, hibiscus and buddleias flower well into the autumn and are worth planting in the mixed border for autumn interest. Berrying shrubs are best planted together in the more informal areas of the garden, perhaps being planted with berrying trees, and with plants selected for autumn leaf colour. The reds and oranges of autumn leaves are so vivid that they can be planted at a distance from the house and will still be seen, particularly when massed together. A list of plants for autumn colour is given in the appendix.

Planting shrubs

All shrubs can be bought container grown which allows them to be planted throughout the year. However, it is still better to plant deciduous shrubs in early winter and evergreen shrubs in late autumn. This allows the shrub roots to start growing immediately before the mid-winter frosts reduce the soil temperature. Then as soon as soil temperatures begin to rise in the spring, the roots again grow and by the time the dry days of summer arrive the new plant is capable of surviving with the minimum of additional water.

CHAPTER 12

LAWNS AND GROUND COVER

LAWNS AND THE NEED FOR GROUND COVER

Grass areas can be lawns or longer grass, a perfect green sward or a cultivated meadow dotted with buttercups and daisies. Lawns are areas of grass that are regularly mown to create a tight green sward. They make the ideal carpet for most parts of our gardens and will survive, if planted with the right species of grass, being walked over and played on. Britain has a near perfect climate for lawn grasses. These are evergreen, low-growing grasses which grow well despite being cut as low as 15 mm (½ in) at regular intervals. They need an equable climate with moist summers and moderate winters and a deep well-drained soil in full sun. There are other species of grasses that will grow and form a green surface in almost all parts of the world, except desert areas, but many of these grasses are very coarse and the resulting turf is rough and may well die back in winter from the extreme cold or in summer from drought.

Designing lawns

Most garden owners will want to include at least one lawn area in the garden, unless the garden is very small or in total shade. The usual area selected for a lawn is the part of the garden which is closest to the house, perhaps separated from the house by a paved sitting area.

First decide on the shape of the lawn, as this will dictate the shape for the whole of this part of the garden. Always create shapes with grass or other flat areas such as water or paving and not with beds and borders. Beds and borders should follow and reinforce the shape created by the grass.

The shape can be formal or informal but should be kept as simple as possible, firstly as simple shapes are most attractive to look at, and secondly, simple shapes are much easier to mow. Formal shapes include squares, rectangles, circles and ovals. Informal shapes are irregularly curved i.e. each part of the curve is an arc with a different radius, but the curves should flow around the shape rather than form 'wiggles'. No part of an informally shaped lawn should be a straight line (Fig. 12.1).

It is important to decide on the use and type of lawn required. A lawn can be a perfect green sward of an even green colour with no irregularities marring its surface, with the stripes of the cylinder mower emphasizing its orderliness. This is how many gardeners will visualize their grass area, but the perfect lawn is ornamental rather than practical; any regular use destroys its perfection, and it requires an enormous effort in mowing,

Fig. 12.1 Shapes for lawns.

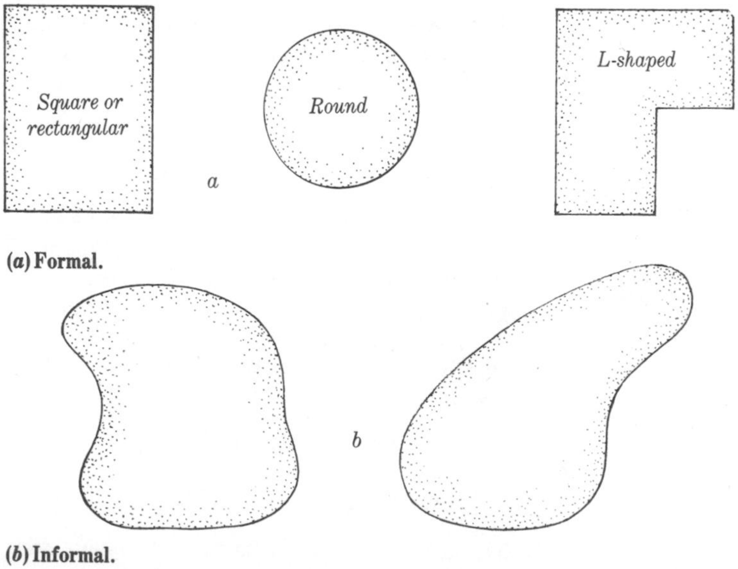

Square or rectangular

Round

L-shaped

a

(*a*) Formal.

b

(*b*) Informal.

feeding, raking, spiking, weed-killing and rolling to keep it in top condition. For some gardeners, the most enjoyable part of gardening is lawn maintenance so, provided there are paved paths for access and no children requiring play areas (or these can be provided elsewhere in the garden), a 'bowling-green' lawn is perfectly feasible. For gardens with children and/or dogs, or where less effort or labour is available, a utilitarian lawn is more practical. The mixture of grasses used will vary from the perfect lawn, as it will need to include species that will stand up to constant wear from running feet, but will not form such a close green sward. If a cylinder mower is used then the resulting stripes will at least give the impression of a quality lawn!

In larger gardens, it would be possible to have a 'bowling-green' lawn nearest to the house to be looked at, and admired, from the windows; and a more utilitarian lawn to be used further away from the house or to one side.

Grass areas which are underplanted with bulbs, or are to be cultivated for wild flowers, are not lawns and are discussed later in this chapter.

Grasses found in lawns

There are a large number of grass species that will survive regular mowing and can be found in lawns. Only those that form a dense green sward and are evergreen are useful lawn grasses, the others can be considered weeds. There are a range of grass seed mixtures available and the choice of mixture to be used will depend on the type of lawn required and the soil, aspect and drainage of the area to be grassed.

Luxury lawns — with little or no wear. Can be mown to 5 mm (¼ in) high.

80% Chewings fescue — *Festuca rubra commutata*
20% browntop bent — *Agrostis tenuis*

These two grasses make the best lawns and suit all well-drained soils in full sun. This is the most expensive mixture and must be kept tightly mown.

Croquet lawns — luxury lawn with occasional wear. Can be mown to 12 mm high.

40% Chewings fescue
40% creeping red fescue — *Festuca rubra rubra*
20% browntop bent — *Agrostis tenuis*

The creeping red fescue is tougher than the other two grasses but will not tolerate very close mowing.

Utility lawn — for regular use, will not tolerate mowing below 15 mm (⅝ in).

50% creeping red fescue
10% browntop bent
40% perennial ryegrass — *Lolium perenne*

The addition of perennial rye grass allows this mixture to stand up to children's games, using the lawn as a path or for hanging out laundry. The sward is coarser and will require mowing more frequently in spring and summer. It will, however, withstand being neglected or left unmown for a period. Make sure that the variety of perennial ryegrass used in the mixture is one of the new dwarf, fine-leaved varieties.

Grass for very hard wear — football pitch.

20% creeping red fescue
80% perennial ryegrass

Lawns in shade.

40% creeping red fescue
10% browntop bent
30% rough-stalked meadow grass — *Poa trivialis*
20% wood meadow grass — *Poa nemoralis*

Lawns will not survive in deep shade under trees, but the above mixture can be used for areas with some shade.

Lawns in moist areas — for good quality lawns on heavy soils. Minimum cut 15 mm (⅝ in) high.

10% browntop bent
40% chewings fescue
40% creeping red fescue
10% timothy — *Phleum pratense*

Timothy is an excellent grass for heavy, wet soils but it is quite coarse and will not survive close mowing.

Lawns for low maintenance — or where mowing is difficult e.g. banks. The following mixture is available in dwarf-growing varieties. Minimum cut 20 mm (⅞ in) high.

15% browntop
55% creeping red fescue
15% hard fescue — *Festuca longifolia*
15% smooth-stalked meadow grass — *Poa pratensis*

These mixtures can be found in grass seed catalogues but often trade names will be used for the grasses. Look for the English and botanical names which are given next to the trade name.

Other grasses which may be included are:

Velvet bent — *Agrostis canina canina* — good in damp and shady areas, but tends to tear during mowing. Sometimes used in a mixture with browntop for special areas e.g. golf greens.

Sheeps fescue — *Festuca ovina* — this can be used instead of chewings fescue but seed is scarce.

Crested dog's-tail — *Cynosurus cristatus* — often found in mixtures for utility lawns as it is extremely hardwearing and resistant to drought. The only problem is that it produces hard stalks which resist mowing.

Seed versus turf

The easiest way to establish a grass area is to dig the area, then level it and leave it! The grass seeds in the air will quickly settle and germinate, together with various weeds. Mowing and rolling the resulting green cover will give you a lawn, of sorts, within a season. However, most garden owners prefer not to wait and see what happens but either to sow one of the grass seed mixtures given above or to lay turf.

The advantages of sowing grass seed is that it is cheaper and you can choose a mixture of grasses which are suitable to your conditions and the type of lawn you require. It is possible to purchase the seed in advance and then sow when the weather is right. The disadvantages of seed are the need for a more thorough preparation of the area to be seeded, and the longer period (9–12 months) before the lawn will survive hard wear.

Turf is available as standard (meadow) or seeded turf. Standard turf is lifted from the field in which it has been growing and is transported to the garden. The advantages are a mature-looking lawn almost immediately, and the site for the new lawn does not need to be so thoroughly prepared. Turf is also laid in autumn and winter when there is less other work to do in the garden. The disadvantages of standard turf are the cost and the lack of uniformity in the turf offered for sale, much of which contains a high proportion of coarse grasses. Turf must also be laid immediately it arrives, as it deteriorates quickly after lifting.

Seeded turf is produced by sowing one of the grass seed mixtures on prepared beds, allowing it to germinate and grow into a dense sward and then lifting the resulting turf and relaying in the garden. It is sold under various trade names 'Rolawn' being one of the better known brands. The advantages are those for standard turf plus being able to select a particular grass mixture. Being recently sown the turves are much thinner and therefore lighter to handle and lay, and it comes in standard size rolls. The disadvantages are higher cost than standard turf, with luxury quality very expensive indeed. A level, well prepared surface is essential and the turves need to be laid immediately they arrive. The final choice will depend on the money available, the size of area to be grassed, how soon the grass will be used and the time of year.

Sowing a lawn

Areas to be grassed should be cleared of all vegetation and rubbish and then levelled. If perennial weeds are present these must be killed by using an appropriate herbicide before levelling. Lawns should not be completely flat as this will allow rain water to lie on the surface after a downpour. A minimum gradient of 1:100 is essential for drainage and is almost imperceptible to the eye, and all bumps and hollows should be evened out. At this stage drainage should be incorporated if necessary. A depth of 15 mm (6 in) of topsoil is needed and this may need to be brought in and spread before digging or rotovating the area. During digging all large stones and roots of perennial weeds should be removed. If a rotavator is to be used it is even more important to make certain all perennial weeds have been killed before starting work.

The next step is to consolidate the soil by treading or rolling; treading i.e. walking over the area with short overlapping steps with your weight on your heels, is preferable but time consuming. Soft spots can be felt when treading and then filled. After treading or rolling, the surface needs to be brought to a fine tilth by raking. This process of treading and raking may need to be repeated several times before a firm, even surface is produced.

The above preparations are needed whether seed or turf is to be used.

A week before seed sowing, apply a general fertilizer e.g. Growmore at 60 g/m^2 (2 oz/yd^2) and lightly rake into the surface. A final levelling may be needed using the back of a rake or a board. Sow seed in late summer — early autumn, when the soil is still warm and watering should not be necessary. Spring sowing is often successful but watering may be more of a problem.

Seed should be sown at a rate of 45 g/m^2 (1½ oz/yd^2), dividing the seed into two equal parts. The first part should be sown across the lawn area, the second part sown up and down the lawn. For a more even spread it may be better to divide into four parts, two spread across and two spread up and down. Seed can be sown by hand or using a distributor (this can be hired from your local garden centre).

After sowing, lightly rake the seed into the surface. Germination should take between 7–21 days, depending on the temperature of the soil. Watering may be necessary after germination if there has been no rain.

When the grass is 5–7 cms (2–3 in) high it should be lightly rolled using the back roller of a cylinder mower which will encourage the seedlings to produce more shoots. When the grass has recovered from the rolling it should be cut using a rotary mower or a cylinder mower, with the front roller removed. Only the tips of the grass or the top 1 cm (½ in) should be removed.

Further mowing should be carried out when necessary, gradually lowering the cutting blades of the mower during successive mowings until the final height is reached.

Laying turf

Follow the preparation of grass areas as above and apply 60 gm per m^2 (2 oz/yd^2) Growmore or other general ferlilizer a week before turfing. Mark the area to be turfed using a garden line.

The best time for laying turf is mid to late autumn but it can be laid right through the winter provided that the soil is not frozen or water-logged. Turf laid in late spring may need watering right through the first summer to prevent shrinkage.

When the turves arrive, lay them out flat and water well unless they are quite damp already. Lay the first row of turves along the garden line making sure they are level and even; any hollows must be filled before laying the turf. Tamp the row of turves firmly into position using a tamper. Do not beat them down with the back of a spade! Lay the second row of turves so that the joints are staggered and avoid using a small piece of turf at the edge by

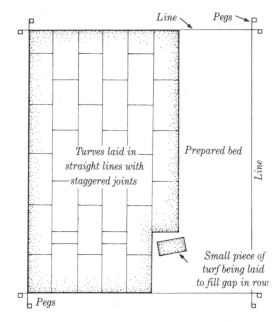

Fig. 12.2 Laying turf.

laying a full size turf against the edge and filling between this and the rest of the row with a small piece of turf cut to fit (Fig. 12.2). Avoid walking on newly laid turf, use planks if you need to have access across the turf. After the turf is laid, brush a top dressing as described below, into the surface to fill all the cracks and to help the turves to knit together. Top dressing mixture:

4 parts coarse sand
2 parts loam
1 part peat

Standing on planks trim the edges of the turved area with a sharp spade or edging iron to the exact shape required. For the curves use a garden hose or rope as a guide.

When the grass begins to grow trim the tips of the grass with the lawn mower adjusted to a high setting. Gradually lower the blades as the seasons progress.

Maintenance of lawns

Lawns must be regularly mown to maintain a smooth usable green surface. Regular mowing will also help control weeds and, if kept to the correct level for the grass mixture used, will ensure that the sward stays true to type.

For easy maintenance all grass areas must be readily accessible to the mower to be used. Unless a light-weight electrical mower is to be used, then all areas must have access without steps or steep slopes. One large area of grass is easier to mow than several small areas and avoid island beds in lawns as these can create awkward corners. Where a ride-on mower is to be used then all curves and corners must be designed with wider arcs than the turning circle of the mower. Where grass paths are planned make sure that the path widths are either the width of the mower to be used or multiples of the width. This will avoid parts of the path having to be mown twice.

Types of mower

There are a range of mowers available for the gardener, from lightweight electrical machines which can be lifted by hand, to ride-on machines which can be adapted to a variety of other uses. The right choice of mower for a garden is the machine which is large enough to mow all the grass to the standard required in the time available and is at a price within the family budget.

For high quality lawns a cylinder mower is essential to give a clean low cut, and to leave the lawn with stripes which are usually desired. Cylinder mowers come in a range of widths and can be hand-driven, electrical, or petrol driven and can be equipped with a seat or can be incorporated into a ride-on mower. For large areas a series of cylinder mowers, called gang mowers can be drawn behind a tractor. The advantages of cylinder mowers is the fineness and cleanness of the cut, the disadvantages are that the larger machines are very expensive and there is a limit to the length of grass that can be cut.

The alternatives are rotary and hover mowers.

Rotary mowers cut grass with a scythe-like

action with a blade or blades rotating horizontally at high speed; wheels support the machine above the grass. Rotary mowers can be electrical or petrol driven and can be pushed by hand, hand controlled, or ride-on. They are an excellent general purpose mower where there are long and short grass areas in the garden, as they are capable of tackling both, but the finished cut is not suitable for the finest quality lawns.

Hover mowers have the same action as the rotary mower but are supported by an air cushion. They can be electrical or petrol driven and can be hand controlled or ride-on. They are easier to use in awkward corners and on slopes, or if the ground is wet, but are less good in long grass than rotary mowers and do not produce as good a cut as cylinder machines. They are only available in the narrower widths and they must be used with extra care to avoid accidents.

Too often gardens are planned with a front lawn requiring a cylinder mower, with grass slopes requiring a hover mower and a long grass area with bulbs requiring a rotary mower. This may be inevitable and acceptable in a larger garden but should be avoided by careful planning in the small garden.

Lawn edges

Another potential problem with grass areas are the edges which, if adjacent to beds and borders, will require regular trimming. This can be avoided by separating the lawn from the border with a row of paving or bricks. This edging will emphasize the shape of the lawn, and will act as a mowing strip to support the wheels of the mower and ensure that all the grass can be cut.

Make sure that all hard materials laid adjacent to grass are set below its level, to allow the mower to cut the grass without damaging the blade on the hard surface. Where grass is laid beneath a wall a mowing strip will be needed to allow the mower to reach all the grass. An elecrical strimmer can be used to tidy up grass beneath a wall if there is no mowing strip.

Alternatives to grass for lawns

There is no real alternative to grass where a green cover is wanted that can be walked over and played on, unless you are prepared to use artificial grass. This is made from polypropylene and comes in rolls, and a good quality make is expensive. The colour needs to be checked in daylight to ensure that it is a good dark green, many of the cheaper makes are an ugly mossy green which inevitably looks drab and artificial. Synthetic turf is laid on a concrete base and should be fixed down with the appropriate adhesive. It is already in use for playing surfaces and although most gardeners would find the idea abhorrent, could be used in the garden in areas where grass will not survive and a hardwearing surface is required. Synthetic turf is softer and more resilient than paving, and for balconies, poolsides and conservatories, could be considered a sensible alternative.

Plants that have been used instead of lawns include chamomile, thyme and pearlwort. None of them are suitable for large areas but all can be used for odd corners where a fine texture is needed and grass would be impossible to mow.

Traditionally, chamomile lawns were found in the formal gardens of the fifteenth and sixteenth centuries. Grass would have been difficult to cut, a scythe being the only tool available, so chamomile with its rosettes of fine-scented leaves and its ability to survive a certain amount of walking or sitting on, was a good alternative. Today the work involved in weeding and rolling a chamomile lawn means that only the real enthusiast will want to try. The plant to use is *Anthemis nobile* 'Treneague' a non-flowering form of lawn chamomile. As there are no flowers, seed is not available and small rosettes have to be acquired and planted. Rosettes should be planted 15 cm (6 in) apart in weed-free, fertile, well-drained soil in a sunny position. After planting, the lawn should be rolled or trodden to firm the rosettes onto the soil. Alternative uses of chamomile are to fill in gaps in paved surfaces or to make 'chamomile seats'.

Thyme 'lawns' can be found in several gardens including Sissinghurst in Kent, England. The creeping thymes, varieties of *Thymus drucei* and *Thymus serpyllum*, make fine-leaved green mats but these will not survive being walked over so are lawns for looking at rather than use. Whilst very attractive in summer when the thymes are flowering, they tend to look rather dull for the rest of the year. Like chamomile, thyme can be used to fill in gaps in paving on terraces or to make a scented seat (Fig. 12.3). Thymes need a dry well-drained soil in full sun and should be planted 225 mm (9 in) apart. The third plant as a potential lawn plant is pearlwort, *Sagina pilifera*, which forms a fine-textured spongy carpet with tiny white flowers. It needs well-drained soil wirh adequate moisture and partial shade. It is useful as a grass substitute for odd corners but planted in a bed may become a weed.

OTHER USES FOR GRASS

Grass is usually seen in a garden planted and maintained as a lawn but it can be used as a green cover for other areas, being planted in combination with bulbs and/or wild flowers and being irregularly mown. It can be used purely functionally as a surface for a tennis court, football field, cricket pitch, or other specific games area. Grass species can also be selected for their ornamental value and planted in a bed or border.

Rough grass areas with bulbs

One of the most attractive features of gardens in spring is drifts of daffodils in grass. Much less attractive are dotted groups of daffodils in lawns, where the clumps of grey green leaves break the smooth expanse of grass. Suitable

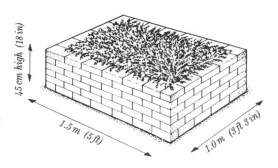

Fig. 12.3 A thyme seat.
Thyme plants are planted in a soil-filled seat using creeping varieties spaced at 25 cm (10 in) apart.

grass areas to plant with bulbs are alongside the drive, on grass banks, and in grass areas away from the house or beneath trees. Grass planted with bulbs must be left uncut until the bulb leaves have died down in the late spring or early summer. Cutting the grass before the leaves are dead will prevent the developing bulb making enough growth to flower the following year.

The problem with leaving the grass is that by the time the area can be cut, the grass is too high to be cut with a mower and has to be scythed off, and the cut grass then has to be removed by raking. In gardens with deep clay loams where grass growth is very vigorous and late cutting is a real problem, bulbs should be selected for early flowers so that the bulb leaves are dying down by late spring before the grass has really started to grow.

Areas to be treated as long grass with bulbs should be sown with grass in the first year using a meadow seed mixture. In the following autumn bulbs can be planted in the sward, the bulbs being scattered by hand and being planted where they fall. Bulbs chosen should be those that readily naturalize in grass and are suitable for the site. Plant deeply, at least twice the depth of the bulb.

Suitable bulbs for planting in grass

Anemone blanda
Chionodoxa luciliae

Crocus 'Dutch Yellow'
Eranthis hyemalis
Fritillaria meleagris
Galanthus nivalis
Narcissus bulbocodium
Narcissus pseudo-narcissus
Narcissus poeticus
Scilla sibirica

Plant bulbs in drifts of one variety and for added interest plant overlapping drifts of varieties which flower at different periods. Avoid brightly coloured, large-flowered, modern varieties and use species rather than cultivars where possible. Plant at a rate of 10 bulbs/m² (10/yd²), or 5/m² (5/yd²) if planting a very large area.

When planting alongside the drive, leave a mown grass strip at least 1 m (3¼ ft) wide next to the drive. This will provide a visual distinction between the formal lines of the roadway and the informality, and untidiness, of the long grass. The mown line of grass between lawn and long grass areas should be used as part of the design following the curves formed by the edge of lawn and beds. Gently curving paths can be mown in the longer grass to give access to the area. Old orchards or stands of birch trees can look very dramatic when underplanted with bulbs. Use early daffodils beneath apple trees and drifts of blue *Anemone blanda*, and *Scilla sibirica* beneath birch for maximum impact.

Wild flowers in grass

Recently there has been an upsurge of interest in planting wild flowers in all parts of the garden but particularly in grass to create wild flower meadows. Unfortunately Britain is not the best country for this type of garden, grass dominating other plants on our well fertilized lowland soils, and successfully competing with almost all other plants with the exception of yarrow, *Achillea millefolium*, and creeping buttercup, *Ranunculus repens*. Ideally you start with a piece of unfertilized meadowland and allow the wild plants present to flower, delaying the mowing until they have finished flowering and set seed. Additional wild flower plants can then be added selecting those particularly suited to your soil and area. Most of us don't have a piece of meadow however, and it will be much harder to start from scratch. If your soil is rich and well-fertilized, don't try to grow a wild flower meadow. Plant early spring bulbs instead, and satisfy your desire for native plants by planting wild roses and honeysuckle with the bulbs. If your soil is very thin and impoverished it will be easier to grow wild flowers, particularly on thin chalky soils where grass tends to be very sparse. There are a large number of attractive plants which are native to chalk downs, including several wild orchids.

Don't try to establish wild flowers by sowing seed on the soil. Sow suitable seeds in seed trays and allow them to germinate, prick out seedlings into pots and then plant out into the meadow when the plants are strong and vigorous. All wild flowers in grass areas need to be perennials i.e. plants that come up year after year. Annuals which set seed will not survive after the first year, their seeds finding too much competition with the established plants.

Ornamental use of grasses

There are a range of grass species which are very attractive and can add interest and colour to our ornamental borders. A few grasses are large and dramatic enough to be used as focal points e.g. *Cortaderia selloana* (pampas grass). The most useful of the ornamental grasses are those that are evergreen and perennial

Ornamental grasses:

Acorus gramineus
Agropyron magellanicum
Cortaderia selloana E
Deschampsia caespitosa
Festuca glauca E

Glyceria maxima 'Variegata'
Hakonechloa macra 'Albo-aurea'
Helictotrichon sempervirens E
Holcus mollis 'Variegata' E
Milium effusum 'Aureum'
Miscanthus sinensis
Molinia caerulea E
Pennisetum alopecuroides
Phalaris arundinacea 'Picta' E
Spartina pectinata 'Aureo-marginata'
Stipa gigantea E
Stipa pennata

E = Evergreen

Grasses look particularly effective when planted with each other, or with other linear leaves e.g. *Iris sibirica, Hemerocallis flava, Liriope muscari*. They are also attractive planted in gravel where their domed shape and arching habit can be fully appreciated.

GROUND COVER PLANTS

Ground cover is a relatively modern term for the use of clump forming plants planted closely together to form a weed-eliminating blanket. It came into the gardening vernacular after the Second World War and became fashionable in the 1960s, when many gardeners planted large areas of their gardens with 'ground cover' plants thinking that it meant an end to all weeding. Many plants were introduced from the USA as exciting new 'ground cover' plants and planted in great numbers, often quite unsuccessfully, with little thought being given to the soil and aspect requirements of the new plants or how to establish them. The untidy remnants of such plantings were then used to decry ground cover planting as of no practical use or ornamental value.

This is a great pity as when the plants are chosen carefully, and planted properly, ground cover planting can provide some of the most satisfying and attractive examples of planting for our gardens, and once established, can need little if any maintenance.

The historical perspective

Until the middle of last century, gardens were the preserve of the wealthy who had the ability to employ and pay labour to look after their gardens. There was labour to scythe lawns, rake gravel and tend beds and borders; and ground cover as such was not included except to fill the knots of knot gardens or in the form of Victorian bedding. The informal 'landscape garden' of Capability Brown and Humphry Repton was based on large expanses of grass and water; both might be considered 'ground coverers', but not in the same context as ground cover planting.

In the latter part of the nineteenth century, the idea of the 'informal garden' was promoted with great success by William Robinson and other writer/gardeners. The use of shrubs and herbaceous plants planted in clumps in natural settings could be seen as a form of ground cover but there were still large numbers of gardeners to look after the plants, importance being placed on the large range of plants to be grown and not on the ability of the plants to eliminate weeds.

After the Second World War the cost of labour rose to the point where very few householders could afford to employ a gardener and welcomed any idea that would reduce the work needed to maintain their gardens. Minimum maintenance meant either increased use of paving and hard landscaping materials or using plants that would look after themselves i.e. ground cover plants.

Nature as an example

Nature naturally covers any bare soil with a layer of plants. As soon as an area is stripped of vegetation, airborne seeds settle on the soil and germinate, and those plants which find the soil and aspect of the particular site suitable will grow and flourish. The seedlings which find the soil conditions unsuitable will quickly die out, being unable to compete with their more vigorous neighbours. These first plants are colonizers which will spread over the area until all the space is occupied. The next group of plants to arrive will be plants who need the cover of other plants to germinate and develop. These plants are usually shrubs and small trees and again the soil conditions will determine which species survive and grow and which are unable to compete. The plants will eventually begin to crowd out the original colonizers.

Finally the dominant plants will begin to appear. In Britain these include large trees such as the oak and beech which will grow up and eventually shade the entire area, only allowing a few of the colonizers and their successors to survive. At this 'climax vegetation' stage the soil beneath the trees may be bare, particularly under mature beech trees, but it only needs the beech tree to die for the whole cycle to start again.

When planting ground cover in the garden it can be useful to look at nature's example and to use plants which are particularly well suited to the soil, aspect and drainage of the particular area to be covered. The plants need to be planted closely together and in large groups of the same species. Britain's natural vegetation is woodland — grassland only surviving by being mown or grazed — so most native ground-covering plants are those found under trees. These woodland floors are frequently covered with a carpet of a single species e.g. wood anemones, bluebells, or ivy. In more open areas this ground cover may be higher with expanses of brambles or nettles! Where several plants grow together, one species tends to dominate in any one area, a second species taking over as the amount of shade or soil type changes. Other less dominant plants form isolated clumps within the mass of the main plants, e.g. clusters of foxgloves arising out of a sea of ivy. We can copy this when planting beneath trees, selecting one or two plants to form the carpet of planting and then choosing some taller plants to place as isolated clumps within the carpet. The results can be highly effective and natural-looking.

Using ground cover plants

Ground cover planting can be used for areas where grass would have been planted but is impractical either because the conditions are unsuitable for grass growth e.g. shady areas beneath trees, boggy sites, or because the area is difficult to mow e.g. steep banks and odd corners. In these cases plants chosen as an alternative to grass should have the same effect as mown grass i.e. creating a smooth green carpet. This is usually most easily achieved when the planting is of a single species.

Small gardens can be designed for low maintenance by eliminating grass and using paving and gravel as surfaces to be walked on. Evergreen ground cover is then used to soften the harshness of the hard surfaces. The majority of the plants chosen should be evergreen and many of them might be selected for foliage or flower colour to add colour and seasonal interest.

Larger gardens could be planted with all the herbaceous plants and smaller shrubs selected for their ability to look after themselves and cover the ground. There is such a large choice of attractive plants that come into this category that it would still be possible to have a very attractive garden but with the advantage of minimum maintenance once the plants were established.

Ground cover planting is not necessarily synonymous with low maintenance, for instance when it is used to create formal carpets e.g. parterres, it will need a lot of attention and labour.

Formal ground cover

Formal ground cover is the use of low growing plants to create a formal pattern which covers the ground. It has been used for centuries, each period and country developing its own style. The English in Tudor times had knot gardens, the French in the sixteenth century developed the parterre, and the Victorians in Britain had their elaborate bedding schemes.

This seat is framed by a subtle combination of roses, alchemilla, marguerites and climbing plants.

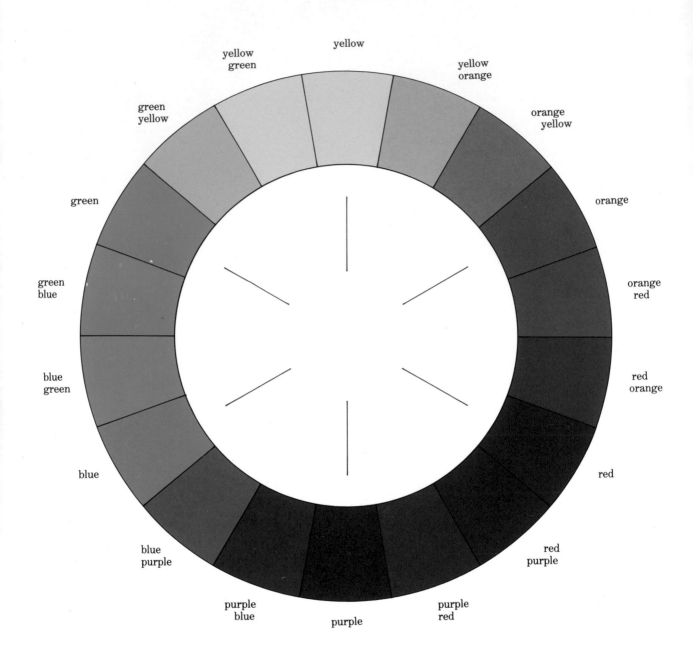

The spectrum, to show arrangement of primary,
secondary and intermediate colours.

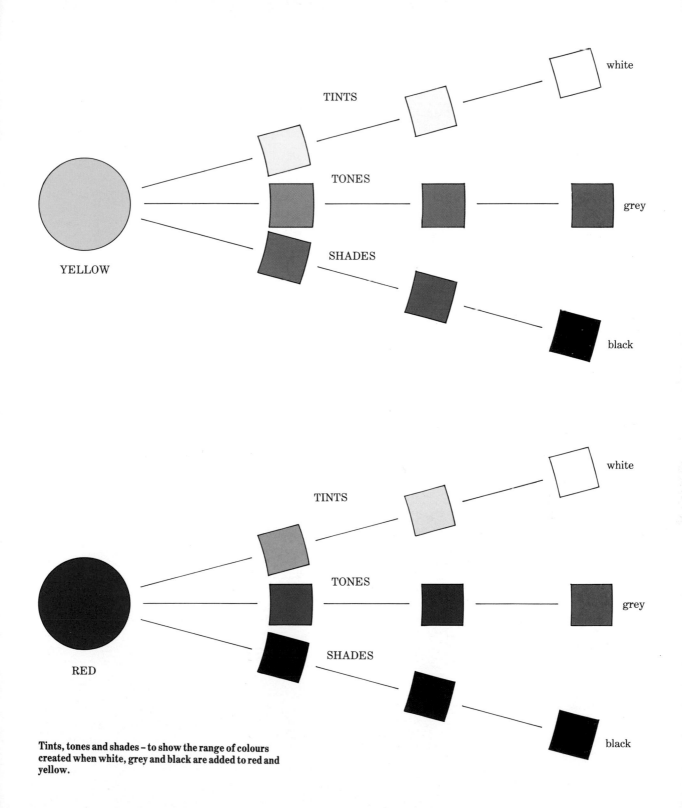

TINTS

white

TONES

grey

YELLOW

SHADES

black

TINTS

white

TONES

grey

RED

SHADES

black

Tints, tones and shades – to show the range of colours
created when white, grey and black are added to red and
yellow.

Harmony of adjacent colours – groups of colours that form natural colour harmonies.

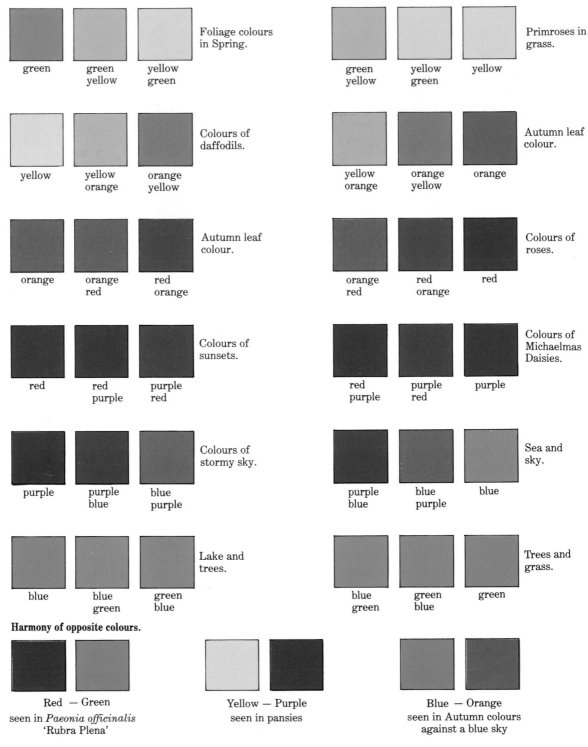

green	green yellow	yellow green	Foliage colours in Spring.

green yellow	yellow green	yellow	Primroses in grass.

yellow	yellow orange	orange yellow	Colours of daffodils.

yellow orange	orange yellow	orange	Autumn leaf colour.

orange	orange red	red orange	Autumn leaf colour.

orange red	red orange	red	Colours of roses.

red	red purple	purple red	Colours of sunsets.

red purple	purple red	purple	Colours of Michaelmas Daisies.

purple	purple blue	blue purple	Colours of stormy sky.

purple blue	blue purple	blue	Sea and sky.

blue	blue green	green blue	Lake and trees.

blue green	green blue	green	Trees and grass.

Harmony of opposite colours.

Red — Green
seen in *Paeonia officinalis*
'Rubra Plena'

Yellow — Purple
seen in pansies

Blue — Orange
seen in Autumn colours
against a blue sky

xxxii

KNOTS AND PARTERRES

Knots or knot gardens were a feature of the gardens of the fifteenth and sixteenth centuries. A series of intertwining hedges were laid out to form a pattern set out in a square (Fig. 12.4). Different hedging plants were used together and the spaces between the hedges could be left 'open' with just a base of gravel, or planted to form a 'closed' knot. Knot gardens can form very attractive features when planted within the formal area of the garden e.g. on the terrace or as a centrepiece to the rose garden. It is expensive to buy the plants and it needs care to get the hedges established, but once grown it will give pleasure all year round. Select a pattern and mark it out on the ground and then plant hedging plants at 15 cm (6 in) apart. It is easier to maintain open knots as the space between the hedges can be covered with gravel and kept weed free (Fig. 12.5).

Suitable hedging plants for knots include:

Buxus sempervirens 'Suffruticosa'
Santolina chamaecyparissus
Santolina virens
Teucrium chamaedrys

These plants make the neatest hedges, tolerating being clipped regularly to 25–30 cm (10–12 in) high. A less formal knot could be planted with:

Hebe albicans
Hyssopus officinalis
Lavandula spica 'Hidcote'
Thymus vulgaris

Parterres are far more elaborate than knots, with the hedging plants (usually just dwarf box), being used to create swirling patterns which frequently covered large areas. Usually the hedges are planted in gravel, but occasionally they are planted in beds within lawns and the spaces within the parterre planted with flowers. Parterres require a large space to be effective and are not as appropriate as knots for the gardens of today.

Fig. 12.4 Patterns for knot gardens.

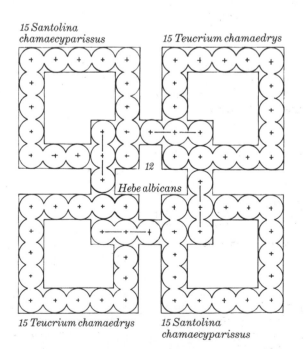

Fig. 12.5 Planting plan for a knot garden.
Plant hedging plants at 15 cm (6in) apart on lines as shown on plan. The centre of the knots can be left empty or filled with bedding plants.

15 *Santolina chamaecyparissus*

15 *Teucrium chamaedrys*

12
Hebe albicans

15 *Teucrium chamaedrys*

15 *Santolina chamaecyparissus*

MAZES

Another old idea currently enjoying a revival is the maze. These are complicated patterns designed to be walked round which can be created at ground level with grass, or raised using hedges. Turf mazes were cut out of the grass to be seen as a pattern, and to make a long walk within a very restricted area — possibly a good idea for utilizing the limited space in most modern gardens. However they require a lot of work to keep the edges clipped and the grass growing well. Used regularly, the grass would tend to become very worn.

Hedged mazes were designed to be explored by the visitor, the object being to reach the centre, any number of blind alleyways being included to increase the time taken in the maze. Hedges were high enough to block the view out so that the secret of the maze could only be solved by walking through it. Hedged mazes can be amusing to design but will take some years before they reach maturity, and will then need to be cut regularly. The best plants to use are holly or yew both of which will only need cutting once a year. Beech can also be used but will not be so effective in winter.

ANNUAL BEDDING AS GROUND COVER

Summer bedding plants can be used as ground cover when planted in beds on their own. Providing that the soil is clean before planting and plants are spaced at a maximum of 225 mm (9 in) apart, then the annuals will quickly cover the space in the bed, forming a solid mass of leaves and then flowers. Annual weeds can't compete and provided adequate water is given, the bed should have a complete cover throughout the summer. In the autumn the plants are all removed, including the few weeds that have struggled to survive. The cleared bed can then either be left fallow for the winter or planted with winter bedding such as wallflowers and pansies. Whilst growth in the autumn may not be sufficient to give a complete ground cover, few weeds germinate or grow in the winter and should not be a problem.

Informal ground cover

Ground cover plants can be used in beds on their own or to edge shrub borders to emphasize the line of the border and to cover up the bases of the shrubs. Where ground cover is planted on its own, plant in drifts of one species with at least nine plants in each drift. Where the ground cover area needs to be more ornamental use variegated or coloured-leaved plants and select some of the plants which have attractive flowers.

Natural ground cover

In the larger rural garden with views out to the surrounding countryside, areas for ground cover planting may need to look more natural. The plants to use should be those found in the surrounding area or garden forms of these. In moorland areas, for example, ground cover could be heathers; in chalk downland, junipers and thymes.

Selection of ground cover plants

Ground cover plants should first be selected for the soil, aspect and drainage of the area of the garden in which they are to grow. They must be capable of flourishing in that particular area in order to make good strong growth and quickly cover the space allocated to them , as well as to provide competition for potential weeds.

The best ground cover plants are evergreen, clumpforming or spreading plants with good foliage. Flowers are not particularly important unless the ground cover is also intended as ornamental planting.

Deciduous plants can be successful ground cover plants provided growth is very rapid in the spring e.g. *Alchemilla mollis*, or the dead leaves in autumn provide a mulch throughout the winter until the new growth appears in spring e.g. *Polygonum affine*, or the resulting foliage is so dense as to eliminate any weeds that have germinated e.g. *Hosta sieboldiana*. Lists of both evergreen and deciduous ground cover plants are given in the appendix.

Ground cover plants for banks

The best plants for steep banks are those which are low growing and whose branches tend to root as they grow. These spreading roots help to hold the bank and prevent any soil erosion after heavy rain. Banks are usually better drained than other areas so the plants used must be tolerant of dry conditions.

Plants for steep banks:

Hedera helix
Hypericum calycinum
Lamium galeobdolon 'Variegatum'
Rubus tricolor
Vinca minor

Most of the above plants prefer light shade rather than full sun. *Hypericum* may be a problem as it has recently become susceptible to the disease, hypericum rust. For banks in full sun, suitable plants to use are:

Helianthemum nummularium
Juniperus horizontalis
Parthenocissus henryana
Thymus vulgaris

Ground cover for planting under trees

Plants beneath trees have to compete with the tree roots for water and food and to tolerate shade from the tree's canopy. Some trees are so greedy and create so much shade that no plants will survive beneath them e.g. *Fagus sylvatica*.

Plants for planting under trees:

Asperula odorata
Aucuba japonica
Cyclamen neapolitanum
Hedera helix
Lamiun galeobdolon 'Variegatum'
Mahonia aquifolium
Sarcococca humilis
Vinca minor
Waldsteinia ternata

Ground cover plants for areas in the shade of buildings

High buildings create shade on their north facing sides but do not compete for moisture or food. Any of the plants which tolerate shade can be used providing that they are selected for the soil type and drainage. Large or shiny-leaved plants look particularly effective against building materials and some of the best to use are:

Bergenia cordifolia
Choisya ternata
Euonymus japonicus
×*Fatshedera lizei*
Helleborus corsicus
Hosta sieboldiana
Prunus laurocerasus 'Otto Luykens'
Skimmia japonica
Symphytum grandiflorum
Viburnum davidii

All the above grow well in most soils, though *Skimmia japonica* and *Prunus laurocerasus* will suffer on thin chalky soils.

Ground cover for dry sunny areas

Very dry sunny areas can be difficult to cover effectively as most plants that grow in dry soils have small leaves and will not cover the ground completely. Select plants with larger leaves protected by hairs — grey-leaved plants. Some of the best and most attractive include:

Cistus×*corbariensis*
Nepeta×*faassenii*
Salvia officinalis
Senecio greyi
Stachys olympica

Ground cover plants for large areas

In large gardens there may be extended areas that need ground cover planting to reduce maintenance, particularly outlying areas away from the house. There are vigorous ground cover plants which will cover large areas quickly and need no further maintenance except the occasional cutting back to keep under control. These plants include:

Alchemilla mollis
Euonymus fortunei radicans
Hedera colchica
Gaultheria shallon — acid soils only
Geranium macrorrhizum
Lonicera pileata
Rosa rugosa
Rubus odoratus
Symphoricarpus rivularis
Symphytum × uplandicum
Tellima grandiflora
Vinca major

Planting and establishment of ground cover

Before planting ground cover plants the area must be cleared of all weeds. Care must be taken to ensure that all perennial weeds are killed or removed completely. Ground cover plants are not 'weed killers' and cannot compete with existing weeds.

Planting distances
The following spacings will give a good cover after two or more years. If faster cover is needed then spacing should be less generous, but some thinning may be necessary.
Heathers — 30 cm (12 in)
Herbaceous plants and small shrubs — 45 cm (18 in)
Medium shrubs — 60 cm (2 ft)
Large shrubs, Climbers and Conifers — 90 cm (3 ft)
Adjacent rows should be staggered so that the second row of plants are placed in the space between the two plants on front.

Weeding and aftercare
Ground cover areas can be mulched with bark to stop weeds growing between the plants but only if plants are chosen that will not want to root as they spread. Hoeing and hand weeding is more effective for most ground cover for the first year or two, until the adjacent plants grow into each other and inhibit further weed growth. This initial weeding is vital if a good

dense weed-free mat is to be created. Adequate water will also be needed whilst the plants are getting established, particularly in the first summer after planting. Once the ground cover has grown the surface of the soil is protected by the foliage and water loss from evaporation is reduced so that further watering should not be necessary even in the driest summers. Once established ground cover plantings should survive for years with the minimum of maintenance, just a quick check for weeds in spring and perhaps the removal of dead leaves.

Maintenance and control of ground cover
Any plant that flourishes and grows well to the extent that it prevents weeds growing can readily become a weed itself once it grows out beyond its designated area. The definition of a weed is a plant in the wrong place so it isn't very difficult to label *Hypericum calycinum* as useful ground cover when seen on a clay bank and a weed when it spreads into the adjacent rock garden! To avoid this particular situation the rock garden should be separated from the bank of *Hypericum* by a path or flight of steps.

Ground cover planted next to lawns is no problem as once it starts encroaching on the lawn regular mowing should control further growth. In fact the trimmed edge of ground cover plants can be very attractive used to reinforce and enhance the shape of the lawn.

Avoid planting ground cover areas directly adjacent to ornamental beds and borders, by always leaving a path between. Grass paths are mown and so will control the ground cover as with lawn edges. Paved paths will act as a boundary to ground cover provided that they are properly constructed. Loose paving laid on sand is no barrier to the roots of most ground cover plants which will take a positive delight in lifting and rearranging your path and applying a chemical weedkiller to the path may result in the death of your ground cover as well. Gravel paths can be an effective deterrent as any stray roots can be quickly spotted and removed.

A further problem with ground cover near beds and borders is the spread of seed from the flowers of ground cover plants. These germinate readily in the spaces between border plants or roses. *Alchemilla mollis* is particularly prolific in this respect. There is no real answer except to hoe out the seedlings as they appear. Ground cover next to shrubs is not normally a problem as the ground cover will probably spread over the ground beneath the shrubs until the shade and competition from the shrubs becomes too great.

FERNS AND THEIR USE IN THE GARDEN

Ferns are quite different from most of our garden plants having no flowers at all, reproduction being by spores which are borne on the back of the fronds or leaves. Despite the lack of flowers they include some very valuable garden plants.

Ferns are just beginning to come back into fashion, having been all but excluded from our gardens since the beginning of the century. The Victorians were great growers of ferns, building elaborate ferneries in which to grow them. Books of the period list up to 2000 varieties of ferns which could be grown! A few years ago you would be lucky to find ten. Now many more are being listed by nurseries, along with their requirements for soils and drainage. Not all ferns need the damp shady places that would seem their natural habitat.

Ferns provide us with a marvellous range of light green colours which act as a foil for many of the darker greens found in the flowering plants. They include a variety of leaf shape, habit and texture, many of which are seen only in ferns. The upright 'shuttlecock' shape of many ferns is quite unique, as is the curled habit of the unfolding fronds in spring.

There are ferns for almost every soil and position, from ferns that like to grow with their feet in the water to ferns for acid soils in shade or limy soils in full sun. Many of them are excellent for ground cover as even the deciduous ferns tend to retain their dead fronds to cover the plant in winter, only disappearing when the new fronds appear in early spring. A list of ferns can be found in the appendix.

CHAPTER 13

COLOUR IN THE GARDEN

COLOUR IN THE GARDEN

Many gardeners think of colour in their gardens simply in terms of flower colour, completely ignoring foliage colour to the extent that they will say that their garden has no colour in it when the flowers have finished flowering. There are always colours present, in any garden at any time of the year. These may be just the deep brown of bare soil, the lighter brown of the stems and branches of shrubs and trees, the red brick of buildings and the yellow of stone walls, but even in the middle of winter there will almost certainly be some green. The green may be the very dark green of conifers, the lighter green of some of our evergreen shrubs or the dull green of grass.

As the spring approaches, the greens become more noticeable, the new grass being bright green and new leaves in a range of greens from the lime green of beech leaves to the apple green of *Rosa rugosa*, to the dull metallic green of some of the *Elaeagnus*. We simply do not have a large enough vocabulary to describe adequately all the greens found in the average garden!

Beautiful gardens can be created using green as the only colour and omitting flower colour completely. These gardens can be very relaxing as there are no bright colours to distract and demand your attention. But unless very well designed and planted they can be boring, and most gardeners will want to include some colours and some flowers in their gardens.

Many gardens are planted with no thought to colour harmony, beds and borders being full of every possible colour combination. A mass of colour but no subtlety, with bright orange dotted amongst a drift of mauve and red, with blobs of lemon and perhaps a single spike of deep purple. All this makes a bold splash of colour, vibrant and exciting, but utterly unharmonious.

Very rarely will people get dressed and go out without giving some thought to the colours of the clothes they wear. The combination of red skirt, lemon yellow blouse, mauve and green jacket and blue hat would seem excessively bright and only possible if the various shades were very carefully matched. Why then do gardeners continue to jumble all the colours together in their gardens!

A visit to the gardens at Hidcote Manor in Gloucestershire or Sissinghurst Castle in Kent will show just how effective it is to use colour harmonies in planting. In both of these gardens each separate area has a colour scheme, which is followed in both foliage and flower colour and creates a distinct character for each 'room' of the garden. These gardens are infinitely more rewarding to visit than gardens without colour schemes.

To understand the ways in which colours can be used and how different colours influence each other, it is helpful to look at the spectrum.

The spectrum

The spectrum is the range of colours produced when light passes through a prism and is usually shown as a wheel in which the colours of the rainbow are formed into a circle so that red, for example, is next to red-purple. The colours included in the spectrum are pure colours or hues in that they contain no white or black (see Colour Plate, p. *xxx*).

Primary and secondary colours
The spectrum consists of three primary colours, red, yellow and blue. These three

colours contain no pigment of each other. Equal quantities of pigment from any two of the primary colours are found in the secondary colours, orange, green and purple. Orange contains equal portions of red and yellow, green equal portions of yellow and blue, and purple equal portions of blue and red. In the spectrum these six colours are arranged so that red, blue and yellow are spaced at a third of the circle apart and the secondary colours are spaced equally apart between the primary colours. So that the order is red, orange, yellow, green, blue, purple, red.

Intermediate colours

Between each primary colour and its neighbouring secondary colour there are intermediate colours, these contain varying portions of the primary colours. Usually twelve intermediate colours are included which are:

Red-orange — 5 parts red:1 part yellow
Orange-red — 4 parts red:2 parts yellow
Orange-yellow — 2 parts red:4 parts yellow
Yellow-orange — 1 part red:5 parts yellow
Yellow-green — 1 part blue:5 parts yellow
Green-yellow — 2 parts blue:4 parts yellow
Green-blue — 4 parts blue:2 parts yellow
Blue-green — 5 parts blue:1 part yellow
Blue-purple — 5 parts blue:1 part red
Purple-blue — 4 parts blue:2 parts red
Purple-red — 2 parts blue:4 parts red
Red-purple — 1 part blue:5 parts red

There are alternative names which are used for some of these colours: scarlet is red-orange, lime is yellow-green, and mauve is purple-red.

Tints, tones and shades

To create the full range of colours that are found in nature, black, grey and white can be added to the spectral hues. Colours formed when white is added are called tints; colours formed when grey is added are called tones; and colours formed when black is added are called shades. The colour pink is a tint of red, olive is a tone of green and brown a shade of orange (see Colour Plate, p. *xxxi*).

Depending on the proportion of hue to white, grey or black, tints, tones and shades will vary in colour.

When all the tints, tones and shades of all the primary, secondary, and intermediate colours are put together there is a seemingly endless range of colours from which to choose.

Artists through the ages have studied colours and their interaction and have put forward various theories and rules for colour harmonies. At its simplest these state that colours next to each other in the spectrum harmonize, as do colours that are diametrically opposite each other. The first is known as the 'Harmony of adjacent colours' and the second as the 'Harmony of opposite colours' (also known as complementary colours). Other harmonies include the 'Harmony of tints, tones and shades'.

The harmony of adjacent colours

The first rule of colour harmony states that any two or three colours that are adjacent to each other in the spectrum form a natural colour harmony. Such harmonies are readily found in nature, the dark blue green of distant hills against the blue of the sky, the scarlet and orange of leaves in autumn and the red and red-purple of the sky at sunset are all examples of adjacent colour harmonies. These colour harmonies can be deeply satisfying, particularly where the two colours are seen as large expanses of each colour as in the examples given above (see Colour Plate, p. *xxxii*). In the garden adjacent colour harmonies need to relate to the colour that is nearly always present i.e. green. This may be the true green of grass in summer or it may be the blue-green of conifers, or the yellow-green of new leaves in spring. The adjacent colours for the grass would be the other greens, whereas the adjacent colours for the conifers would include blue, and the adjacent colours for spring growth would include yellow. This may help to explain why some of the loveliest garden pictures are created with a sweep of lawn leading to distant trees, and why so many of our flowers which look attractive in shade are blue (foliage in shade being a blue-green rather than bright green) and why so many of the prettiest spring flowers e.g. daffodils and primroses, are yellow.

Using adjacent colour harmonies

These are the simplest and often the most effective colour harmonies to use in the garden provided they are used in mass and not as dots of colour. The following combinations work well:

yellow-green and yellow — use gold and gold-variegated foliage with yellow flowers. Particularly effective to brighten borders shaded by buildings and where winter colour is needed.

yellow and yellow-orange — this can be used in bedding schemes, the flowers covering up the green of leaves. Try using wallflowers in winter and marigolds in summer.

orange and orange-red — these are the colours of autumn and can be used to combine chrysanthemums and dahlias with the autumn colours of shrubs.

red and red-purple — used with plum and grey foliage this can be a very dramatic colour scheme next to grey paving

blue and blue-purple — the colours found in delphiniums and campanulas, these colours can be very effective when seen with dark green or grey foliage.

blue and green — the colours of bluebells, of trees and sky, grass and water. Effective as a mass of blue flowers in grass or a a blue flower border, but as it may tend to lack impact add some cream-coloured flowers for lightness.

Really dramatic use of adjacent colours is when the two or three hues are used as adjacent masses, not diluted by using a variety of tints and shades.

The harmony of opposite colours

If two colours lying opposite each other in the spectrum are placed together they harmonize. This is known as the harmony of opposite colours, or sometimes called complementary contrast. Red is opposite and complementary to green, yellow is opposite and complementary to purple and blue is opposite and complementary to orange.

Every colour in the spectrum, including all the tints, tones and shades, has an opposite or complementary colour. These pairs of colours are in use all the time in the design of dress fabrics, wallpapers and other furnishings, designers having recognized their decorative value and impact.

In the garden it is sufficient to look at the three primary colours and their opposites: red/green, yellow/purple and blue/orange. These are very exciting harmonies to use but to work have to be used in isolation away from other colours (see Colour Plate p. *xxxii*).

Red and green as complementary colours

The red colour of this harmony is not the scarlet of many hybrid tea roses, but the true red found in the red paeony *Paeonia officinalis* and in *Rosa gallica officinalis*, the green being the green of their leaves. This is a very exciting colour harmony to work with and can be used for a border or a whole garden area. The red borders at Hidcote in England are an example of the effective use of this colour harmony.

There are plenty of red flowers that can be used, but they should be the full hue, not a tint of red. Although the purists would insist on pure red and pure green, an equally exciting planting is with bright red flowers and a range of greens including green-blue and green-yellow.

It is a colour scheme for the summer and for full sun or light shade. It would work very well in some warmer climates e.g. Australia where many of the native plants have red flowers which offer fascinating opportunities for the plantsman.

Yellow and purple as complementary colours

These are the colours seen together in the flowers of pansies. When the full hues of yellow and purple are placed together it is intensely dramatic. Less dramatic but more relaxing are the tints of yellow and purple planted together e.g. golden marjoram and lavender. Both approaches can be used with effect in the garden but is most effective when green is reduced to a minor colour or preferably absent.

Green can be eliminated by using all gold foliage plants and introducing spots of purple flowers e.g. *Viola cornuta* 'Prince Henry' and *Berberis thunbergii* 'Aurea'. Some gold-leaved plants help by having purple flowers e.g. gold marjoram and golden sage. At Hidcote 'Mrs Winthrop's' garden is planted in gold and purple colours and is very attractive apart

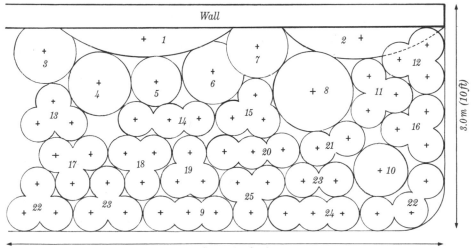

Fig. 13.1 Plan of yellow and purple border.

List of plants

Climbers	1	*Solanum crispum* 'Glasnevin'	— purple flowers
	2	Rose 'Golden Showers'	— yellow flowers
Shrubs	3	*Cytisus battandieri*	— yellow flowers
	4	*Physocarpus opulifolius* 'Dart's Gold'	— gold foliage
	5	*Perovskia atriplicifolia*	— pale lavender flowers
	6	Rose 'Graham Thomas'	— gold flowers
	7	*Abutilon × suntense* 'Jermyns'	— dark mauve flowers
	8	*Philadelphus coronarius* 'Aureus'	— gold foliage
	9	*Helianthemum* 'Wisley Primrose'	— pale yellow flowers
	10	*Salvia officinalis* 'Purpurascens'	— purple foliage
Herbaceous Plants	11	*Campanula glomerata*	— purple flowers
	12	*Alchemilla mollis*	— pale yellow flowers
	13	*Campanula lactiflora* 'Prichard's Variety'	— violet blue flowers
	14	*Delphinium* 'Black Knight'	— blue purple flowers
	15	*Achillea* 'Coronation Gold'	— yellow flowers
	16	*Nepeta × faassenii*	— pale lavender flowrs
	17	*Achillea* 'Moonshine'	— pale yellow flowers
	18	*Coreopsis verticillata*	— yellow flowers
	19	*Aster × frikartii* 'Monch'	— pale purple flowers
	20	*Salvia superba* 'East Friesland'	— deep purple flowers
	21	*Agapanthus* 'Bressingham Blue'	— deep blue flowers
	22	*Origanum vulgare* 'Aureum'	— gold foliage/mauve flowers
	23	*Campanula glomerata* 'Purple Pixie'	— purple flowers
	24	*Erigeron* 'Darkest of All'	— purple flowers
	25	*Oenothera glaber*	— deep yellow flowers

from the plum-coloured *Phormium tenax* in the centre which spoil the harmony. The purple of this harmony needs to be a true purple even a blue-purple and not purple-red.

The less dramatic use of the purple/yellow harmony is in a pale yellow/lavender colour border. There are a great many grey-leaved plants with lavender coloured flowers, and an equal number with yellow flowers. Providing the border is in a dry sunny position a very beautiful planting can be created. For additional impact some gold foliage plants can be included and even some green foliage if these plants are placed at the back of the border where the leaves will have little impact (Fig. 13.1). The gold foliage border with occasional purple flowers can be of interest all year round as there are several evergreen gold foliage plants e.g. *Choisya ternata* 'Sundance' and *Ligustrum ovalifolium* 'Aureum', which can be used together with purple-flowered pansies for winter flowering. This range of plants will also tolerate light shade as well as full sun.

Blue and orange as complementary colours

Many people find it difficult to visualize these two colours as complementing each other until they look at autumn beech leaves against a blue sky, or study *Ceratostigma willmotianum*, whose bright blue flowers appear in late summer just as its leaves turn orange and scarlet. In the garden an orange and blue-flowered border is not very easy to plan as most orange flowers have bright green leaves which destroy the blue/orange harmony. The only planting that seems to work using these colours is the orange of autumn leaves and the blue flowers of michaelmas daisies. Most of the other blue flowers do not flower in the autumn and are over before the leaves change colour.

The harmony of tints, tones and shades

The tints, tones and shades of any one hue harmonize i.e. reds, pinks, carmines and dusky rose look attractive together. This colour harmony can be stunning when used in the garden, as long as green is either excluded or made part of the harmony.

So the harmony of tints, tones and shades can be used for green, for red as this is the complementary colour to green, and for yellow and blue as adjacent colours of yellow-green and blue-green.

The tints, tones and shades of green are often used in ground cover planting and for planting near water. They are seen in the flowers and foliage of many of the hellebores.

The tints, tones and shades of red can be used very effectively in rose gardens, particularly when the old-fashioned roses are planted together.

There are plenty of plants whose flowers or foliage are tints of yellow i.e. pale yellow, but far less which are tones or shades. The euphorbias are an exception, displaying flowers and foliage in a range of yellow tones. This is a good colour harmony for the spring garden, to use with daffodils and primroses.

The blue border, as mentioned in the section on adjacent colours (see page 200) could be planted with tints and tones of blue. The problem with many of the blues is that they tend to disappear into their background and make little impact, so the bright blues or the very pale blues are most valuable.

The use of white in the garden

Pure white is not a colour as such and needs to be used very carefully in the garden. It reflects light and instantly becomes a focal point and so if used as small patches of planting along a border can be intensely distracting to the extent that it completely ruins the balance of the planting. Avoid using white flowers or green and white variegated foliage in colour borders. If very pale colours are needed to lighten the border use the off-white colours of buff, cream and very pale pink.

The white garden

There has been a vogue recently for 'white' gardens where the entire garden area is planted with white flowers. There is a very beautiful white garden at Sissinghurst in Kent which has been endlessly copied, not always successfully. White flowers and grey foliage are just dull, particularly when planted in beds edged with grey yorkstone paving. White needs rich green foliage to be seen to its best advantage and this is why the Sissinghurst garden is so attractive; both the boundary of the garden and each bed are hedged with dark evergreen plants. White also looks more dramatic in shade where it positively glows, whereas in full sunlight amidst a background of grey it hardly shows up at all.

A gloomy basement or small urban back garden can be made into an exciting living space by the use of white flowering plants and white and green variegated leaves. The white flowers and foliage will need plenty of green background to have real impact e.g. cover walls or fences with ivy; and planting needs to be planned for all year round interest. Use annuals, biennials and bulbs as well as shrubs and herbaceous plants to provide pure white flowers throughout the year.

The following varieties could be used:

Winter — white universal pansies
  — snowdrops
Spring — crocus — 'Jeanne d'Arc'
  — daffodil — 'Mount Hood'
  — narcissus — 'Thalia'
  — tulip — 'Diana' and 'Schoonord'
Summer — white petunias
  — white impatiens
  — white *Nicotiana affinis*
Autumn — *Colchicum autumnale* 'Album
    Plenum'.

Add to these white-flowering pelargoniums which will flower until the first frosts. For background planting use *Viburnum tinus* and *Choisya ternata*, and as additional wall cover, *Clematis* 'Marie Boisselot' and 'Huldine'. If there is room, include one or two hydrangeas; 'Madame Emile Moulliere' and 'Sister Teresa' are both white flowered. All the above plants will grow in town gardens with some shade. A list of white and green variegated plants can be found in the appendix.

Seasonal use of colour

Another problem with trying to use colour effectively in the garden is the change brought about by the different seasons. Throughout the year the quality and intensity of daylight varies from the very light intensity of winter to the glaring light of a midsummer's day. The different light quality of the seasons will affect how colours appear and how they influence other colours.

Winter colour

In winter, daylight is very cold with very low light intensity particularly on a cloudy day. The background colours in this season are the dark green of evergreen shrubs, the near black-green of conifers, the dark brown and grey of trunks and bare branches of deciduous trees and shrubs, and the rich brown of bare soil.

Against this background the very palest colour will glow e.g. the blossom of *Prunus subhirtella* 'Autumnalis' or the first snowdrops. Strong, vibrant colours e.g. the vivid pink of almond blossom, *Prunus dulcis*, are outstanding and do not have to compete with green, as the first leaves are still to appear and the dormant grass in winter is a dull matt colour. The same vivid pink is to be found in *Prunus* 'Kanzan' in mid spring, but by then it shrieks out against the lime green of new spring foliage and the bright yellow of many spring flowers.

Spring colour

The spring sunlight is much warmer and stronger so that the late snowdrops tend to appear 'washed-out', the new leaves appear lime-green along bare branches and the grass 'greens up' as it starts growing again. Spring flowers and blossom are pale colours, primrose, pink and cream. At ground level new bright green foliage appears along with yellow, white and occasional blue flowers. It is easier to copy these spring colours in planting spring borders than to try and compete.

Summer colour

In summer the sun shines for more hours per day and with a much stronger intensity. On very sunny days even bright colours tend to look faded and pale colours quite insipid. In the southern Mediterranean or Australia the sunlight is much more intense and only the very brightest colours show up at all. In the garden the dominant colour is bright green, of both grass and foliage, and there is a full range of flower colour available for use. Red borders look wonderful as do yellow/purple beds or yellow/lavender. The traditional English border of pink, blue and grey looks lovely on a cloudy day but in intense sunlight can look disappointingly flat. Luckily most of the British summers are more cloudy than bright and this particular colour combination is amongst the most attractive in our gardens.

Autumn colour

Autumn light is a very warm yellow light gradually losing its warmth and intensity as the season progresses. The foliage of most deciduous plants looks less green as it prepares to fall, and with many trees and shrubs changes to the yellow, orange and scarlet colours associated with autumn. Planting for autumn should be based on these colours, with blue used as an alternative colour if additional impact is needed.

Summary of the use of colour in the garden

It may be helpful to summarize the use of colour and to outline some simple rules.

1. Keep colours simple. If in doubt stick to green

2. Select a colour scheme for each area of the garden and a main season of interest.

3. Don't compete with nature. Follow seasonal colour schemes.

4. Experiment with colour. Start with the colour combinations mentioned here first but do try others. Use two colours in combination first, then try adding a third.

CHAPTER 14

ORNAMENTAL PLANTING

ORNAMENTAL PLANTING

Ornamental planting is the use of plants to add colour and interest to the garden, and is usually planted in beds and borders. For many garden owners this is the main reason for having a garden allowing them to indulge in an enjoyable leisure activity. Where garden owners are not gardeners, due to lack of interest or time, ornamental planting should be kept to a minimum as this is the type of planting that needs regular maintenance. There can still be colour and interest by using flowering trees as focal points, and selecting ground cover plants with coloured foliage and flowers.

Beds and borders can be almost any shape or size within reason and can be planted with annuals, biennials, bulbs, herbaceous plants, shrubs, and roses in any combination. The number and size and contents of beds and borders will depend on the size of the garden, the specific interests of the owners, the style of garden chosen, and the amount of time available for gardening. Early in the planning of a garden it is necessary to decide which types of beds and borders are to be included in the garden and the colour schemes to be used.

Beds and borders

Beds are planted areas which can be viewed from all sides. When placed in isolation in the middle of grass they are referred to as 'Island' beds.

Borders are planted areas which have a barrier e.g. a wall or hedge, on one side so they can only be viewed from the sides and front.

Beds and borders can be formal or informal; formal borders being rectangular, round or square. Informal beds and borders have curving shapes and are irregular in outline. The choice of formal or informal beds and borders will depend on the style of that part of the garden and the plants to be grown in the beds or border, roses and herbs usually being more attractive in formal beds and shrubs in informal borders, but there are no hard and fast rules.

The herbaceous border

Traditionally borders were herbaceous borders; that is only herbaceous plants were used and then only those which were deciduous i.e. losing their leaves and dying back to the rootstock in winter. Large country gardens often had pairs of herbaceous borders flanking wide grass paths and frequently backed by tall hedges designed to protect the plants from the wind and to provide a green background. These borders were designed to be at their peak from mid-summer to the autumn, and to provide a succession of colour for about four months of the year.

First promoted by Gertrude Jekyll at the turn of the century they became a feature found in nearly every country garden until the Second World War. Then lack of labour led to many borders being dug up and when peace arrived the high cost of labour meant that many were never replanted, shrub borders and mixed borders being planted instead.

Herbaceous borders have their disadvantages. Firstly they are completely bare in winter and they are only at their best for a relatively short period; secondly, they need regular maintenance to keep them free of weeds and to stake the taller plants; and thirdly, every few years many of the plants need lifting and dividing to prevent them from going bare in the centre. On the scale of the great herbaceous borders of the past, many of which measured 6 m (20 ft) wide and 20 m (66 ft) long, they are not usually a practical proposition for today's gardens. However, scaled down in size, and planted with plants that do not require staking or dividing they can still be a viable choice for the keen gardener. Some gardeners actually like the idea of putting a border 'to bed' for the winter and providing that there are other planted areas for winter interest within the garden and that the herbaceous border can be placed so that it is not visible from the house, then go ahead and have one. The advantages of a herbaceous border include the regular routine of maintenance, weeding and forking in spring, hoeing through the summer, and cutting down and cleaning in the autumn. Provided this is done properly, perennial weeds will be contained and will not become a problem.

Fig. 14.1 Plan of bed and border to show layout and heights of plants.

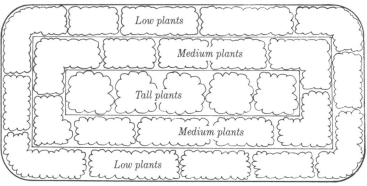

Low plants

Medium plants

Tall plants

Medium plants

Low plants

(a) Bed — can be viewed from all sides.

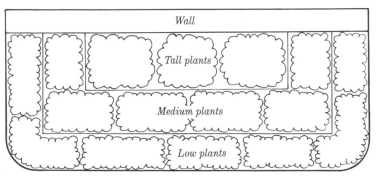

Wall

Tall plants

Medium plants

Low plants

(*b*)Border — can be viewed from front and sides only.

The mixed border

The alternative to the herbaceous border is the mixed border. This was devised in an attempt to try and have interest and colour throughout the year. Shrubs are used to give structure and either flowers in winter or flowers in spring or foliage colour in summer or autumn colour or berries. Bulbs are added for early spring colour and annuals may be used to fill in gaps with splashes of extra colour in summer. At their best mixed borders can be very attractive but too often they suffer from trying to be interesting every moment of the year. The result of this is that there is no period when the border looks really beautiful, whereas the herbaceous border could look fantastic in the few months of its glory, even if it was uninteresting for the rest of the year. The answer is to plan mixed borders to have a period for maximum interest, with a minimum of interest at other seasons. Most gardens have at least four planted areas so one area can be planned for spring interest, one for summer, one for autumn and one for winter. There will then be one really attractive feature to look at throughout the year.

Size of beds and borders

Beds and borders need to be in scale with both the size of the garden and the size of the house. A small cottage garden looks best with several small beds, whereas the same size area in a large country garden might be more in scale if left as a single planted area.

To have impact a bed or border should be wide enough for several rows of different size plants. A border should be wide enough for a minimum of a row of low plants at the front, a row of medium plants in the middle and a row of tall plants at the back. A bed should be wide enough for a row of low plants around the outside, a row of medium plants inside this, and a central row of tall plants (Fig. 14.1) The maximum height for foliage and flowers planted in a bed or border will depend on the width. In a border the maximum height should not exceed the width of the border, and in a bed

Fig. 14.2 Heights of plants in relation to width of bed or border.

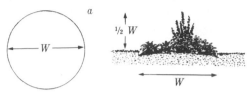

(a) Bed
W = width of bed. Tallest plant should not be higher than
½ W.

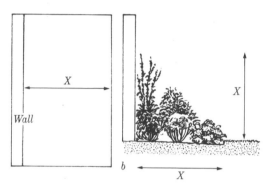

(b) Border
X = width of border. Tallest plant should not be taller than X.

should not exceed half the width. Taller plants will tend to look out of scale and dominate the planting (Fig. 14.2). The length of a bed or border should also be considered, normally the length being longer than the width in borders, and the same in beds unless they are square or circular.

There is a supposedly perfect dimension for a rectangle, the 'golden' rectangle (see page 24) whose proportions are 16 units length to 10 units width. These are useful proportions to adopt for beds whether formal or informal and whatever the scale, i.e. 16 m (53 ft) × 10 m (33 ft) would be a very large bed, and 8 m (26 ft 6 in) × 5 m (16 ft 6 in) would be a medium sized bed and 4 m (13 ft) × 2.5 m (8 ft 3 in) would be just about right for a bed for a small garden. Borders based on the 'golden' rectangle tend to look out of proportion and need greater length. The length of a border needs to be at least three if not four or five times the width,

depending on whether the border is to be viewed from the end looking along the border or from the front, and whether the border runs across the garden or down its length.

Positioning of beds and borders

The obvious answer to where you should place beds and borders in the garden is the sunniest, warmest, most sheltered corner where the soil is deep, fertile and well-drained. This may be the ideal but fortunately it is not always absolutely necessary.

Many border plants need sun for most of the day and if you are planning a colour border using grey foliage it must be sited in full sun. However a border planted for foliage effect may well be more effective in shade, particularly when including large-leaved plants.

A warm site will obviously speed growth and reduce problems of frost damage, but unless you wish to plant the more tender plants, it isn't strictly necessary. However, shelter from wind is; very few border plants look their best when constantly battered by strong winds, and staking plants is both time consuming and unsightly.

A good, deep fertile soil is needed for roses and some of the more colourful border plants e.g. phlox, paeonies, campanulas, lupins, lilies and delphiniums. But shallower poorer soils can still be perfectly satisfactory for herbs and grey foliage plants, including catmint, pinks, sage and mullein. The answer is to appreciate the soil that you have and choose plants that will thrive and grow in it.

Selection of plants

Before planning the planting of a bed or border it is necessary to make a list of plants to be included. The following points need to be considered in the selection of possible plants:

Checklist for planting

1. Type of soil
   acid ☐ neutral ☐ alkaline ☐ chalky ☐
   peat ☐
   sand ☐ clay ☐ loam ☐

2. Aspect
   shade ☐ semi-shade ☐ full sun ☐
3. Drainage
   boggy ☐ damp ☐ well-drained ☐ dry ☐
4. Season
   winter ☐ spring ☐ summer ☐ autumn ☐
5. Colour scheme
   select appropriate scheme
6. Type of plantings
   herbaceous ☐ shrubs ☐ roses ☐
   annuals ☐ bulbs ☐ mixed conifers ☐
   heathers ☐ alpines ☐ climbers ☐
   bog plants ☐
7. Other considerations
   scent ☐ coloured foliage ☐
   low maintenance ☐
8. Maximum height of plants
   in scale with width of border

Having filled in the above checklist for each bed or border, you then need to compile a list of plants that comply with all the details on your checklist. A good selection of plant books and nursery catalogues will be needed to help you to make up your plant list and to include sufficient plants to allow plenty of choice. As you compile the list, separate plants into low growing, medium and tall plants as this will help in the actual planning of the border. There are now computer programmes available for use on the home computer that, given a list of criteria e.g. clay soil, summer flowering, blue flowers, 60 cm (2 ft) high; will produce a list of plants which fulfill these requirements. This certainly can save time but you will still need to know the plants concerned, or be able to look them up in a book, to decide whether you want to include them in your border.

Planning the bed or border

The next step is to plan your bed or border on paper using the techniques discussed in Chapter 9. First draw an accurate plan of the bed or border and then start selecting and spacing plants. Beds and borders are planned differently so look at them each separately.

Planning the border

Before starting on planting the border, it is important to decide whether the border needs a path between the back of the border and the barrier behind. If this is a brick or stone wall a path is unnecessary, but a fence which needs regular treatment with a non-toxic preservative will almost certainly require a path, as will a hedge which needs cutting and will compete with the back row of border plants for food and water. Where the barrier is a fence only a narrow path needs to be left which can be trodden earth rather than paving or grass; it just needs to be wide enough to allow access, during winter when plants are dormant, to be able to treat the fence without treading on, or splashing preservative on, the back row of plants. The width of path between a border and backing hedge will depend on how much growth the hedge makes between cuts. There needs to be room for this growth plus the hedge-cutter plus some elbow-room! The minimum width of path is 60 cm (2 ft) and it may well need to be 90 cm (3 ft). Narrow paths are best paved and wider paths grassed, but the mower must have sufficient width to be able to cut the grass path before the hedge is cut. Having decided on the necessity, or not, of a path the planning of the border can begin. If there is a wall at the back decide on whether this is to be clad with climbers as these need to be selected and positioned first. This is due to the fact that the spread of a climber across a back wall will occupy a larger area visually than a clump of plants in the border. Select climbers according to the aspect of the wall and the colour scheme you have chosen and space them out along the wall allowing a minimum of 2 m (6½ ft) between climbers and placing them 30 cm (1 ft) in from the face of the wall. Now divide up the rest of the border into low, medium and tall plants checking the space available and allowing 45 cm (1 ft 6 in) for each row of low and medium plants and 60 cm (2 ft) for each row of tall plants. Remember to take low and medium plants around each end of the border. Now select the plants for the front of the border. These need to be selected for foliage as wall as flowers, the leaves being visible throughout the season; they need to cover completely their allotted space so flowering ground cover plants may be the best to use.

Front of border plants should be planted with at least five plants to a group and can either be planted in a row or in two staggered rows. All borders look more attractive when plants are repeated down the length, so in planning the front row select a few plants for each colour and then repeat each of them along the border, repetition should be irregular rather than regular i.e. if you use six different plants A, B, C, D, E, and F, then place them as:

A B C D E F A C E F B D A E B D E C
and not
A B C D E F A B C D E F A B C D E F.

The middle row or rows of plants should be selected for their flower colour; foliage is not so important as once the front row has grown up the leaves of the middle row will be covered. Plant in groups of three or five plants depending on ultimate size and repeat this along the border. Where plants are used that have a large number of cultivars, repetition can be with different cultivars within the same colour range e.g. in a pink and blue border paeonies might be repeated using the cultivars 'Sarah Bernhardt', 'Glory of Somerset', 'Claire Dubois' and 'Cornelia Shaylor' all of which are pink flowering paeonies and all incidentally very fragrant.

Back row plants need to be selected specifically on the shape and habit of their flowers, tall spikes of delphiniums or the flat plates of *Achillea* 'Coronation Gold'. Foliage is not very important as it may hardly be visible at all. Plant in three plants to a group and repeat shapes, as well as colours and plants, along the border.

In a short border place the strongest shapes in the centre, and in a long border space out, and repeat, the strong shapes along the length of the border.

Planning a bed

The same rules apply as for planning a border but there is no necessity to consider paths or climbers. The front row plants encircle the bed and should be planted in groups of five plants, chosen for foliage as well as flowers, and repeated around the bed. Plants of medium height are placed behind the low plants and chosen firstly for their flower colour and then to a certain extent for their foliage. Plant three or five to a group and repeat plant. The centre of the bed is filled with tall plants selected for flower shape and habit, usually the tallest and most dramatic in the centre, only repeated if there is room. Centre position plants should be planted in three to a group unless the bed is very small when they can be planted singly.

Plans for beds and borders

The herbaceous border (Fig. 14.3)

Now to look in detail at the planting of different types of border. The traditional herbaceous border is planted as outlined above. Overleaf is the plan for a border planted with herbaceous plants selected for low maintenance in that all the plants in the front row and many of the plants in the middle and back row are ground cover plants which will reduce the amount of weeding.

The mixed border (Fig. 14.4)

The mixed border is planted with shrubs as well as herbaceous plants. It may also have shrubs used as wall shrubs to reinforce the planting against the back wall. The wall shrubs need to be selected and positioned at the same time as the climbers. Space the climbers at 3 m (10 ft) apart and the wall shrubs alternating with the climbers so that wall shrubs are 1.5 m (5 ft) from the adjacent climber. Shrubs are usually planted singly and should be spaced out in the middle and back rows leaving room for a group of herbaceous plants between each shrub. Front row plants are usually herbaceous ground cover plants but may include low spreading shrubs e.g. *Helianthemum*

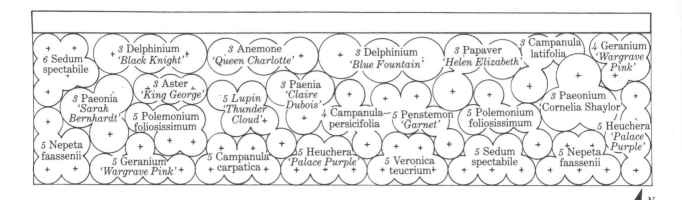

Fig. 14.3 Plan for a herbaceous border.
Colour scheme — pink, crimson and blue.

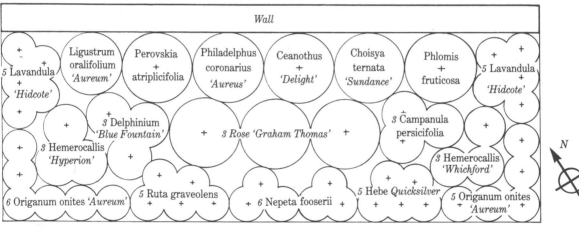

Fig. 14.4 Plan for a mixed border.
Colour scheme — blue and yellow.

'Wisley Primrose'. The predominantly summer flowering mixed border below is designed for a warm, dry, sunny position against a grey stone wall.

The shady bed (Fig. 14.5)

Beds and borders in shade can be herbaceous or mixed, and plants selected for foliage interest or flowers. This border has foliage interest and winter and spring flowers.

A bed for annual planting (Fig. 14.6)

Annuals and biennials are used in ornamental planting to give colour impact. The colours can be very strong and need to be chosen and harmonized with care. For summer and early autumn colour, annuals and half-hardy perennials are planted out in prepared beds. Annuals should be spaced 20–25 cm (8 in–10 in) apart and half-hardy perennials at 30 cm (12 in) apart. Planting can be formally arranged in regular blocks of colour or informally planted in drifts of plants. The smaller plants are placed in the outer rows, medium-height plants in the middle rows and tall plants in the centre. An architectural plant such as a *Phormium tenax* or a standard fuchsia can be placed in the centre to give impact.

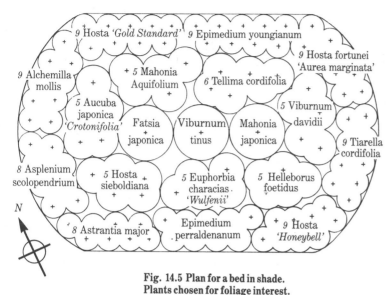

Fig. 14.5 Plan for a bed in shade.
Plants chosen for foliage interest.

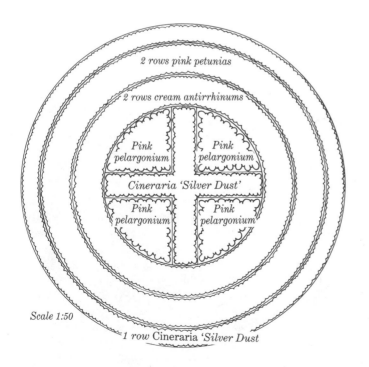

Fig. 14.6 Plan for a circular bed of annuals.
Colour scheme — pink, cream and grey.

ROSES IN THE GARDEN

All the many roses grown in gardens belong to a single genus *Rosa*. They are all shrubs but they are so numerous and diverse that they are usually considered as a separate group of plants. For centuries, roses have been celebrated as supremely decorative flowers, so they are included under ornamental planting rather than with the other shrubs in this book. Roses can be separated, by their habit and their use in the garden, into three main groups: the shrub roses, the bedding roses, and the climbing and rambling roses. All have been developed from the 150 species of wild roses found growing throughout the northern hemisphere. Breeding of new roses is possible because, unlike most other plants, many of the *Rosa* species are capable of crossing with other *Rosa* species and producing viable seed and thus new hybrids. Crossing and re-crossing of roses by breeders through the centuries has led to the thousands of cultivars that are available today. There are still however several *Rosa* species which have been found impossible to use for breeding e.g. the purple-leaved *Rosa glauca*; if the secret of crossing this particular rose could be found imagine the hybrids possible, all displaying the soft purple foliage of this species.

Shrub roses

Shrub roses include all those roses which are neither bedding roses nor climbers and ramblers. They include several distinct groups of roses which are:

1. Species roses.
2. Old-fashioned roses.
3. Victorian roses.
4. Modern shrub roses.

1. Species roses

These are the original wild roses many of which make excellent garden plants. They have single flowers which flower in summer and many have ornamental hips in autumn.

211

They usually have an attractive shape and arching habit which makes them very effective when planted on their own in grass so that the shape can be seen. They fit well into the more informal areas of the garden particularly areas for wild-life (bumble-bees visit roses for pollen, and birds take the hips) and for autumn colour.

2. Old-fashioned roses

These are the roses which have been planted in gardens since Roman times. They include five groups of roses, the red gallicas, the white albas, the damasks, the centifolias, and the moss roses. They are all summer flowering with the exception of the autumn damask; they include no yellow roses, the colour range being true red, pink, and all tones of red to deepest crimson, and white; and all are richly scented. These roses have recently staged a come-back having been in decline since the arrival of the bourbon rose in 1817. Their garden value is in their scent and in the range of deep red colours of the gallicas and centifolias which are not found in any other roses, e.g. 'Cardinal Richelieu' which is a dark red-purple rose, and 'Robert le Diable' which is a mixture of cerise, purple and slate-grey. The alba roses are particularly useful in that they will tolerate some shade, they also have the most beautiful grey green foliage.

3. Victorian roses

These are the roses which were the fashion in Victorian times and include the China roses, the Bourbon roses, and the hybrid perpetual roses. They are all repeat flowering, have large double flowers, but are still limited to red, pink and white, and not all are scented. The original China roses were introduced from China at the end of the eighteenth century, and a chance crossing of 'Parson's Pink China' and the autumn damask rose on the island of Bourbon in 1817 produced a new breed of roses — the Bourbon roses. Further crossing produced the hybrid perpetual rose in 1837. These three groups of roses were then crossed and recrossed throughout the nineteenth century to produce a large number of new roses. The China roses are very pretty roses which flower constantly through the summer, they have scented flowers on long stalks which tend to have slightly pointed petals. The new young leaves are red, a characteristic that has been passed on to many of the bedding roses. They are very attractive planted in beds on their own or mixed in a border. The Bourbon roses include some of the loveliest flowers in the garden. They have beautifully rounded blooms with a strong scent and delicate pink colours. They flower continuously through the summer and look best when planted in borders with paeonies and phlox in the same colour range, and contrasted with the blues of campanulas and delphiniums. The hybrid perpetuals tend to be rather leggy roses often with little fragrance and with some quite extraordinary coloured flowers e.g. the white and crimson stripes of 'Ferdinand Pichard'. They are however very tough and can be useful at the back of a border. Some of the smaller varieties e.g. 'Mrs John Laing' can be included with the Bourbon roses in the planting described above.

4. Modern shrub roses

This section includes some of the most useful roses for the garden. It includes the Rugosa roses, the hybrid Musks, the English roses and many others which fall into no specific category such as 'Nevada' and 'Fruhlings-gold'.

Rosa rugosa which has given rise to a range of useful sports and hybrids has suckering prickly stems, rough apple green leaves and long pointed buds. They flower continuously all summer and most of the varieties have large rounded hips which appear from mid-summer onwards. They are some of the toughest, easiest roses to grow and form thick inpenetrable hedges as well as being suitable planted as specimens in grass.

The hybrid musk roses are almost as tough as the rugosa roses although quite different in appearance. They were bred by the Rev. J. Pemberton between the wars using the multiflowered *Rosa moschata* (musk rose) in the breeding. They are all tall graceful roses with scented, delicate-coloured flowers in trusses and disease-resistant, shiny foliage. They flower profusely in mid-summer and then intermittently until the first frosts. Although too large for small borders reaching an average of 1.8 m (6 ft) × 1.8 m (6 ft) in growth, they provide a mass of flower colour in a large mixed or shrub border or can be equally effective planted in large beds on their own. They can also be trained along fences as wall shrubs.

The English roses are a new group of roses bred and introduced by David Austin. They combine the fragrance and graceful growth of shrub roses with the recurrent flowers and colour range of bedding roses. They need far less attention than bedding roses and are attractive planted in rose beds or in the mixed border. They are the answer for the gardener who wants to have beds of roses which flower all summer without the problems of pruning, feeding and continuous spraying.

Bedding roses

Bedding roses are the modern large-flowered roses usually seen in rose beds. There are two types, the hybrid tea with large flowers often of a perfect conical shape, and the floribunda which has smaller flowers borne in large trusses. They were first introduced in 1867 when a hybrid perpetual rose was crossed with a tea rose to produce the first hybrid tea. The gardeners of the time found the large flowers and continuous flowering of the hybrid tea much more exciting than the other roses of the period, particularly when finally it was found possible to breed yellow flowered varieties. This occurred in 1898 and opened up the way to a whole range of new colours including orange and multi-coloured roses. The modern floribunda rose was first introduced in 1924 and has since given rise to the smaller patio and miniature roses.

The problem with bedding roses is that to ensure strong growth and good flowering they must be pruned hard each year, nearly all the previous year's growth being removed. Additional food in the form of manure or fertilizer is then needed to replace the lost growth. They are also susceptible to a wide range of diseases and the attention of insects such as greenfly and rose sawfly, and will need a regular programme of spraying to maintain top quality blooms. To give these roses the attention they need it is usually more practical to plant them on their own in rose beds than to try and incorporate them in a mixed border.

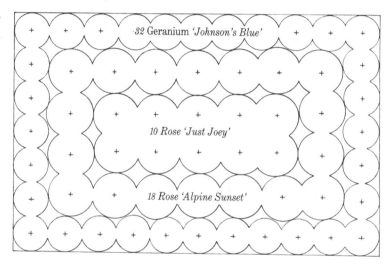

Fig. 14.7 Plan for a rose bed.
Colour scheme — blue and buff.

Planning rose beds (Fig. 14.7)

Bedding roses look best when planted in rows in formally shaped beds with several beds creating a formal pattern. They should be positioned with other formal elements in the garden e.g. by the terrace, or can form a separate area — the rose garden. The beds tend to look dull in winter when just the pruned stumps of the roses are visible, but it is not advisable to try to underplant the roses for winter interest as this is the period when you will want to be able to walk over the bed to prune the roses and then to cover the surface with manure. In the summer when the roses are in full bloom they will cover the whole surface of the bed so underplanting would not be visible. However, it is worth edging rose beds with suitable plants as these will not interfere with the maintenance and can serve to give definition to the pattern created by the rose beds. Dwarf box is the most suitable for very formal settings, and lavender, *Bergenia cordifolia* or *Alchemilla mollis* for less formal gardens. Plant bedding roses 60 cm (2 ft) apart and refrain from mixing colours. A bed of a single rose variety looks much more attractive than a bed with every rose a different size and colour. For more variety use low floribunda roses in one colour around the edge of the bed and fill the centre with taller hybrid teas of another colour which harmonizes with the colour of the floribunda roses.

Climbing and rambling roses

Roses include some species which are naturally climbers and these are usually called rambling roses or ramblers, and include such giants as *Rosa filipes* 'Kiftsgate' which is capable of reaching 12 m (40 ft) or more in height. These ramblers do not require pruning and are excellent plants for covering pergolas and arches and for climbing into trees. They are usually scented, once-flowering and the flowers are often small but carried in large trusses.

Climbing roses are garden roses which have developed or been bred to produce long shoots., They have larger flowers than the ramblers and many are repeat flowering but are often awkward in habit and many require pruning to keep them flowering. They do not grow as tall as the ramblers, few growing more than 5 m (16 ft 6 in) high. They are excellent planted to grow up pillars or walls where they can be easily reached for pruning and spraying if necessary.

There are several excellent climbing roses which will grow on a north-facing wall including.

Rose 'Madame Alfred Carrière'
Rose 'Zephyrine Drouhin'

CLIMBERS AND WALL SHRUBS

Climbers and wall shrubs are used to clothe walls, fences and other vertical structures in the garden. Climbers are plants that produce long leading shoots and need the support of a structure or another plant to stay upright. Wall shrubs are shrubs which are quite capable of growing without support, but may grow more strongly with the protection of a wall, or shrubs that may be easily trained to cover a vertical surface.

Climbers

All climbers if not given support will grow flat along the ground as they do not have the ability to support their own weight and growth. In the wild they rely on the support of neighbouring trees or shrubs, which they climb or clamber over to reach the sun. Depending on the type of vegetation found in the native locality of a climber, the climbers have developed a variety of ingenious ways of hanging on to the surrounding plants. Climbers native to woodland areas produce suckers to grip onto the smooth trunks of trees e.g. virginia creeper and ivy. Other climbers produce tendrils which twine around adjacent shrub branches so that the climber can haul itself upwards e.g. *Clematis montana* and *Vitis coignetiae*. In some climbers the whole stem twines as in honeysuckle and wisteria, slowly throttling their host plant in the process. The laziest climbers are the rambling roses which droop their long stems over adjacent plants and hope that the downward pointing thorns will act as crampons and prevent the shoot from slipping down. Climbers can be annual and herbaceous as well as woody plants. Annual climbers include the sweet pea and nasturtium, and herbaceous climbers, e.g. the hop, with its incredible ability to climb to 6–8 m (20–26 ft) each year!

The use of climbing plants

Climbers are very useful plants in any garden as there are a large variety of ways in which they can be deployed. Structurally, they can provide fast and effective screens both for hiding ugly views or to provide a green background for other garden features; they can also be used to cover up unsightly buildings or structures. They can be used as focal points if the climber is attractive for an extended period and if given a suitable support e.g. an arbour.

Climbers can also be used as ground cover plants provided they are given the correct soil, aspect and drainage so that they flourish. *Hedera helix* (ivy) is the climber most frequently used as ground cover but *Parthenocissus quinquefolia* (virginia creeper), *Hydrangea petiolaris* and *Clematis montana* can be equally as effective when given the right conditions.

For ornamental use climbers give vertical colour and interest. They can be planted against the wall at the back of a border, the climbers being chosen for their foliage and flower colour to harmonise with the other plants in the border.

Climbers can also be used to enhance another feature e.g. an ornamental arch or pergola; or to decorate the walls of buildings. The climbers chosen should complement the structure both in colour and texture, e.g. the yellow flowers of *Clematis orientalis* look lovely against the grey and yellow of many stone walls but not so attractive against red brick; and the pendulous flowers of *Wisteria sinensis* can be used to complement the curving dome of a gazebo.

Climbing plants can be used as an ornamental feature in their own right when given the support of a pergola. Climbers for pergolas need to grow tall to reach the top of the pergola post and to cover the cross beam. Pendulous flowers are very suitable as they will hang down below the cross beams and be seen, whereas more upright flowers will stay up out of sight. Pergolas planted with all the same plant can be very dramatic e.g. *Wisteria sinensis* 'Alba' when in full flower looks wonderful on its own; but in a small garden it is more attractive to vary the climbers to give flowers throughout the year.

The following list of climbers will give flowers and colour through the seasons and many of them are scented:

Clematis cirrhosa balearica — winter flowers
Clematis alpina — spring flowers
Clematis montana 'Elizabeth' – scented spring flowers
Wisteria floribunda — scented spring flowers
Jasminum officinale — scented summer flowers
Clematis flammula — scented late summer flowers
Lonicera japonica 'Halliana' — scented late summer flowers
Clematis tangutica — summer flowers and autumn fruit
Vitis coignetiae — autumn leaf colour

Climbers can also be planted to climb through existing trees so that the flowers of the climbing plant appear through the trees branches creating an appearance of blossom. Where the tree already has blossom of its own e.g. apple trees, then the climber should be chosen to flower in a different season, a summer flowering rose or late honeysuckle.

Climbers should be planted at least 30 cm (12 in) out from the base of the tree and planted in a large planting pit with plenty of organic matter and fertilizer. The climber will need plenty of water for the first few years after planting as it will be competing with the tree for moisture.

Supporting climbers

Climbing plants may be adapted for climbing trees and shrubs but in nature there are no brick walls or fences so they cannot be expected to cope with these man-made features unless they have a system for self-clinging e.g. the adventitious roots of ivy which can climb virtually anything including a sheet of glass. All other climbers will need some help in the form of trellis or wires which they can cling onto with their tendrils or twine round.

Horizontal lines of galvanized wire are the best, and least visible, support for most climbers on walls and fences. The wires should be spaced 45 cm (1 ft 6 in) apart and fixed firmly to the wall with vine eyes and strainers.

Vertically placed wires or netting are more suitable for encouraging climbers up pillars and pergola posts, and for supporting some of the less rampant climbers.

Trellis should be used as a decorative feature in its own right, or fixed to a wall which is un-attractive and needs an instant cover.

Climbing roses will also need to be tied onto the wire or trellis as their thorns have no real ability to cling. Rambling roses placed to climb apple trees will need to be trained up wires around the tree trunk until they grow tall enough to spread out into the tree's branches and use them for support.

Wall shrubs

Wall shrubs include all shrubs which for one reason or another are planted against walls or fences. Some are rather lax in growth and tend to be untidy when planted without support e.g. *Jasminum nudiflorum* and *Cytisus battandieri*. Some evergreen shrubs need protection from cold winds which blacken their leaves e.g. *Garrya elliptica* and *Camellia japonica*, which will grow against a north or west wall where there is protection from cold east winds. Many wall shrubs are plants that need the protection of a sheltered south-facing wall to survive cold winters, and if they are planted away from the wall would be unlikely to survive e.g. *Grevillea sulphurea* and *Fremontodendron californicum*.

Shrubs may also be planted against walls and fences where cover is needed, particularly evergreen cover, and where climbers such as

ivy might damage the wall with its adventitious roots. Suitable evergreen shrubs include *Cotoneaster franchetii* and *Pyracantha rogersiana* and both these shrubs can be trained to lie flat against the wall.

FRAGRANCE IN THE GARDEN

The sense of smell is one of the strongest senses; a sudden whiff of a long forgotten fragrance is often able to bring back memories of childhood places and people. Yet it is often neglected in the garden, beds and borders are planned and planted without thinking of the many marvellous scents and fragrances which might be included.

There are lots of sources of scent in the garden already — newly mown grass; the soil after rain; even the smell of smoke from autumn bonfires can be included. But scent in a garden usually refers to the smell of roses or lily of the valley, the scent that is most noticeable when flowers are fully open. This scent is released by the nectaries — small organs at the base of the petals — and is produced to attract insects to pollinate the flowers. The scent is usually only produced when the flower is ready for pollination i.e. when the flower is fully open, and when the insects needed for pollination are about. Flowers that are pollinated by moths give off their scent in the evening rather than during the day e.g. *Oenothera biennis* (evening primrose) and *Nicotiana affinis* (tobacco plant).

There is another type of fragrance produced by plants and this is found in essential oils within the cells of the plant, the oils being found in all parts of the plant including the roots, or they may be in just the leaves, or the stems and leaves. These plants are called aromatic plants and include many of the herbs. The essential oils are usually only released when the cell walls are broken, by treading on the plant or by breaking a leaf off the stem. In some aromatic plants the oils are given off as the temperature rises so can be smelled when walking past the plant on a hot day e.g.

rosemary. Many aromatic plants are ever-green so their elusive fragrance is present all year round e.g. sage, lavender and thyme. Other aromas are seasonal, balsam poplars only give off their heady scent when new leaves are opening. Some plants have both aromatic leaves and scented flowers e.g. *Choisya ternata* and *Myrtus communis*.

Planting for fragrance

Fragrance in a garden is only effective if it can be smelled! Scented plants at the back of a large border will be completely wasted unless they are one of the few plants which are so free with their fragrance that they scent all the air around them e.g. *Clethra alnifolia*, which gives off its almond scent so freely it will scent a whole garden. Low-growing scented flowers planted at ground level lose their appeal if you have to kneel down on the wet lawn to appreciate their fragrance e.g. pinks. Position such plants in beds on the top of low walls where they can be reached more easily.

Scented climbers are very effective because they produce their flowers at 'nose level', whether planted on a pergola to walk through, on an arbour with a seat beneath to sit on, or on the walls of the house next to an open window through which the scent can drift.

Plan for scent throughout the year; start with the scented winter flowers such as *Mahonia japonica*, *Viburnum farreri* and *Daphne odora*. Plant these in beds around the house where they can be appreciated on a cold winters day as you rush from the back door to the car, they will also be easy to reach for cutting to bring indoors.

Spring scents abound from the rich scent of hyacinths to the rather odd scent of *Ribes sanguineum* (flowering currant). This smells like cats to some people but pleasantly fruity to others, but is instantly recognized and the first whiff of it on a crisp morning heralds the end of winter and the beginning of spring. Separate the best of the spring scents from each other so that each can be appreciated: place the lilac away from the *Ribes* and the hyacinths in a separate bed to the wallflowers, each scent can then be enjoyed in isolation. Just as colours are more effective when only one or two are used together, so separate out different scents. There are lemon scents, floral scents, musky scents, honey scents and even peppermint scents found amongst plants and they certainly don't want all to be planted together.

Summer scent is found in roses, jasmine, honeysuckle and lilies, and also day lilies and paeonies. Their scents can be purposely planned for, or ignored. Most of these plants have floral scents which will harmonize when planted together. Plan for scent by selecting varieties of roses, paeonies, phlox, lilies and day lilies which are strongly fragrant and edge your border with pinks and aromatic plants such as lavender and catmint.

Autumn scent is provided by the late roses and *Ligustrum ovalifolium* and *Elaeagnus × ebbingei*, the latter plant having hidden flowers with an amazing 'gardenia' scent. *Lonicera japonica* 'Halliana' (Japanese honeysuckle) produces its richly scented flowers well into the autumn to give scent for arbours and pergolas. Many of the annual flowers are also scented and some of the best keep on flowering until killed by the first frosts including *Nicotiana affinis* (tobacco plant) which flowers right on until early winter.

Lists of both aromatic plants and plants with scented flowers can be found in the appendix.

CHAPTER 15

ROCKS, WATER AND THE WILD GARDEN

The rock garden

Whether the rock garden is existing or about to be constructed, it is important to make sure that the soil and drainage are suitable for the plants you wish to grow. These might be dwarf conifers, heathers, rock-plants or alpines. The term 'rock-plant' is used to include a range of low-growing shrubs, herbaceous plants and bulbs that are suitable for planting among rocks. They include plants that need acid soil and those that like lime, they include plants for sun and plants for shade; some rock-plants remain tiny, and others will cover the whole rockery if they are allowed to!

The choice of plants will depend on firstly the soil, aspect and drainage of the rock garden and then on personal preference and the amount of time available for maintenance. A large rockery planted with large drifts of heathers will need very little maintenance, whereas a rockery full of precious alpines will take several hours per week. If maintenance is a limiting factor, then choose plants that are happy in the soil and the amount of drainage in the rockery, and which are fairly vigorous. Plant in groups of three or five plants of the same species and make sure that all pockets of soil are planted.

Vigorous, low growing plants include:

Alyssum saxatile
Armeria caespitosa
Aubrieta 'Dr Mules'
Campanula carpatica
Dryas octopetala
Erigeron 'Dignity'
Euphorbia epithymoides
Geranium dalmaticum
Helianthemum nummularium
Polygonum vaccinifolium

Prunella webbiana
Saxifraga 'Pixie'
Sedum spurium
Viola cornuta

The next range of plants that might be chosen for the rock garden are the plants that are called 'alpines' in many nurseries, but are merely low-growing plants that tend to form hummocks like the true alpines. These are usually native plants of the lower slopes of mountains and are tolerant of temperate soils and weather conditions. They need more attention than the vigorous plants as they need to be kept free from the competition of weeds or neighbouring plants.

These plants include:

Aethionema 'Warley Rose'
Dianthus 'Oakington'
Erinus alpinus
Gentiana acaulis
Leontopodium alpinum
Lewisia cotyledon
Phlox douglasii
Pulsatilla vulgaris
Saponaria ocymoides

Dwarf bulbs can be planted with both the above groups of plants to give colour and interest in the early spring.

When planting rock gardens it is important to remember to keep the planting in scale with the size of rocks and the size of the rock garden. Very large boulders look far more natural in gardens if the plants beside them are of the same scale. Clumps of ferns, day lilies, or *Acanthus mollis* will look far better than isolated mounds of thrift.

Perennial weeds are the major problem in maintaining rockeries, given the chance, and the room, they will spread their roots under the rocks where they will be impossible to eradicate without completely dismantling the rockery. The answer is to make sure that you start with weed-free soil and that you immediately remove any weeds that subsequently appear.

Alpines

The true alpine plants come from the high alps where the plants are subjected to nine months of freezing winter weather followed by three months of scorching sun. The plants are adapted to these conditions by being very low growing so that they are covered by a blanket of snow during the winter, and by producing masses of flowers to make the most of the brief summer. There is very little soil, as much of the terrain consists of crags and shattered rocks, the plants managing to survive in tiny pockets of soil between the rocks. The plants have plenty of moisture at root level due to continuously melting snow from higher levels which percolates down through the rocks, however, they also have excellent drainage at root level due to the very stony sub-soil. These conditions are virtually impossible to produce in the average lowland garden with mild wet winters and not enough snow to cover plants for any length of time. So the gardener who wants to grow alpines needs to create special beds for them, mimicking the alpine conditions of good drainage on the surface and continuous moisture beneath. To grow alpines from the high alps, an alpine house will be necessary, this will give protection from excessive winter rain. The alpine house is an unheated greenhouse with plenty of ventilation; the alpines are grown in individual shallow clay pots on benches, each plant being given the exact soil mixture and drainage that it prefers.

The scree bed

Scree beds are an alternative method of creating the right conditions so that alpines can be grown successfully. They are raised beds which are constructed to give plenty of drainage material underneath a top layer of soil. The soil is then covered with a layer of stone chippings — the scree; this gives a very freely drained bed. A series of perforated pipes are laid at or just below the soil surface so that additional water can be given as and when required.

A false scree bed can be created by covering the surface soil of the rock garden with stone chippings, this will keep the stems of the plants well-drained but sub-surface drainage and irrigation are missing. Small scree beds can be made in stone troughs and are an attractive method of growing a few special alpine plants (Fig. 15.1).

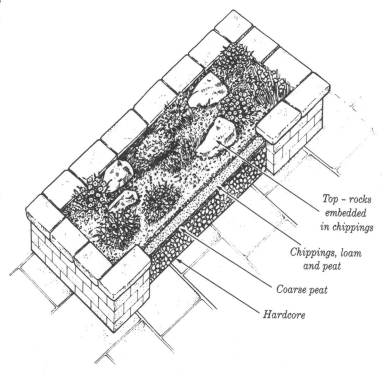

Top – rocks embedded in chippings

Chippings, loam and peat

Coarse peat

Hardcore

Fig. 15.1 Diagram of a raised scree bed.
The bed is shown with the centre front removed to show the layers of material used to make up a scree bed. The bed is constructed of brick walls with a stone coping. The overall height is 45 cm (18 in) with the following layers:-

top	— dressing of chippings	
	— chippings, peat and loam	15 cm (6 in) deep
middle	— coarse peat	7.5 cm (3 in) deep
bottom	— hardcore	22.5 cm (9 in) deep

THE WATER GARDEN

Water in the garden can be formal or informal, man-made or natural, moving or still. Whatever form it takes the gardener will probably want to plant within or around it, and it may also need to be planted in order to ensure that the water stays clear.

Any still pool of water eventually becomes colonized by plants—algae. These are very simple plant organisms which rapidly grow and divide given water and warmth. In the space of a few days in the spring, they can turn a pool of clear water into a pea-green 'soup' or alternatively cover it with blanket weed. Like all plants the algae need food and sunlight to survive, the food will be present as dissolved mineral salts in the water, and the sunlight will be there during the day unless the pool is completely covered.

There are several ways to control algal growth, including the use of chemicals or filters, but the most satisfactory method in the garden pond is to try and create a healthy balance in the water using plants that will compete with the algae for mineral salts or will cover the pool with their leaves so depriving the algae of sunlight.

Planting the pond

To create a healthy balanced pond with clear water and attractive planting, there are several types of plants that must be included; these are submerged oxygenating plants, floating aquatics, deep water aquatics, and marginal plants.

Oxygenating plants

Oxygenating plants live and grow within the water utilizing the dissolved mineral salts. They are capable of photosynthesizing whilst submerged and the by-product of this reaction, oxygen, is released into the water; on a hot summer's day streams of oxygen bubbles can be seen rising from the oxygenating plants to the surface of the pool. There are several species of oxygenating plants to choose from but it is usually best to plant a mixture of species as it is difficult to be sure which species will grow fastest in any particular pond. They are usually supplied in bundles with a lead weight with the recommendation just to drop them in the water. However, they will establish themselves more quickly if planted in an aquatic planting basket as for deep water aquatics (Fig. 15.2) which is then placed on the floor of the pond. Three bunches can be planted per basket, making certain that the lead strip is buried. They should be planted in the spring as the water temperature is beginning to rise and the usual planting rate is 3 bunches per m^2 (yd^2) of surface water, excluding shallow margins.

Floating aquatics

Floating aquatics have leaves that lie flat on the surface of the water and roots that do not need any anchorage. They help control algae by reducing the amount of sunlight reaching the surface of the water. Most of them multiply very rapidly once introduced and may become as much of a nuisance as the algae e.g. duckweed, which can cover the entire surface of a pond in a matter of weeks. They are useful to introduce for the first year or two whilst waiting for the deep water aquatics to grow, these will then take over the job of shading the water surface. *Hydrocharis morsus-ranae* (frogbit) is one of the best and the prettiest,

Fig. 15.2 Planting water plants in a container.
First line the container with hessian and then half fill with loam. Place the plant in the centre and then add more loam and firm the plant in well. Cover the surface of the container with gravel before placing in the pond.

Loam

Gravel

and *Azolla caroliniana* (fairy moss) one of the most useful as it spreads rapidly during the first season but is then killed off by frost during the winter.

Deep water aquatics

The name 'deep water' aquatics is rather misleading as the plants include many that flourish in 30 cm (1 ft) depth of water or even less. These plants are essential in the maintenance of a balanced pond system as they reduce the amount of sunlight that reaches the surface of the water. The most popular deep water aquatics are *Nymphaea* spp. (water lilies) and there are a wide range of varieties from which to choose. These range in size from the tiny *Nymphaea × pygmaea* 'Alba' which is suitable for shallow pools where the depth of water is less than 30 cm (1 ft) up to the large *Nymphaea* 'Gladstoniana' which will grow in water up to 2.4 m (8 ft) in depth. The attractiveness, and the efficiency, of these plants lies in the flat expanse of their floating leaves with the cupped blossoms rising above. If a variety is selected which is too vigorous for the pool in which it is planted, then the plant will eventually outgrow the space and the leaves will grow vertically rather than horizontally, overlapping each other in an attempt to find room.

There are water lilies of all sizes and colours but they all share a dislike of moving water or of being splashed, e.g. they will not grow around a fountain. They also need a sunny position to flower well. Many of them are scented but as it is difficult to see how to reach any of the flowers to appreciate the fragrance, it is not an important attribute!

Other useful deep water aquatics include *Aponogeton distachyus* (water hawthorn) which is completely hardy and flowers from spring to autumn with spikes of scented white flowers. It can be planted in water up to 90 cm (3 ft) deep and will tolerate a certain amount of water movement. *Nymphoides peltata* (water fringe) is like a tiny yellow water lily and *Orontium aquaticum* (golden club) has extraordinary yellow spikes of flowers, but neither is really attractive enough to be worth including in any but the largest water garden. *Nuphar* spp. (pond lilies) are less decorative versions of yellow water lilies and can be invasive, but in shaded ponds or large deep ponds might just be worth considering. All deep water aquatics should be planted in containers before being placed in the pool. Plant in spring with one plant per container (see Fig. 15.2. for planting details). In maintaining a balanced pond try to cover about one third of the surface of the water with the leaves of floating or deep water aquatics.

Marginal plants

Marginal plants are those which can be planted in the shallow margins of pools. In natural pools these margins may vary in the depth of water cover between summer and winter, from wet mud in summer to a depth of 15 cm (6 in) or more in winter. Most of them tolerate this variation in depth but virtually all need their roots covered by some water all year round. In the garden pond they are usually planted for their ornamental value but they will also provide useful competition for the algae as they will remove some of the mineral nutrients in the water. In formal pools marginal plants with vertical leaves e.g. *Iris laevigata* can be used to provide a soft contrast to the harsh horizontal lines of the structure. Plant marginal plants in containers or in the soil at the edges of natural ponds. For an informal pool they are best planted in clumps or drifts of one plant using adjacent groups of contrasting foliage. In the wild garden, ponds should be planted with native marginal plants such as *Iris pseudacorus* (yellow flag iris), *Lythrum salicaria* (purple loosestrife) and *Caltha palustris* (marsh marigold). A list of marginal plants can be found in the appendix.

Planting an aquatic plant container

Aquatic plant containers are made of a plastic mesh to allow free movement of water, so to prevent the soil being washed out through the mesh it is advisable to line the container with hessian before planting. The soil used should be a good loam, free of manure or organic matter as these, if present, will dissolve in the pool and add to the amount of nutrients available to the algae. A small amount of bonemeal can be added to the soil to aid rooting or one of the specially produced aquatic fertilizers if necessary.

Plant all roots firmly, taking care not to damage the fleshy roots of water lilies; the crowns of the water lilies should just be exposed above the finished soil level. Make sure the compost is packed firmly down and no gaps are left. Cover the surface of the soil with pea shingle to discourage fish from rooting in, and disturbing, the soil. The containers should then be placed gently into the pool at the correct depth.

The bog garden

The name 'bog garden' is given to an area of ground where the soil is constantly moist but not covered in water, and which is planted with plants that enjoy wet conditions. There are a range of plants available to the gardener that enjoy growing in wet soil and which can be used for planting in damp or boggy places. Some of these plants must have moist soil all year round whilst others are tolerant of both wet and relatively dry conditions. They differ from marginal plants in not liking or needing their roots to be covered in water. In the garden these plants can be grown together, if there is an area of impeded drainage, to create a bog garden. Most of the plants have large leaves and some have very attractive flowers. The plants chosen will depend on the texture and pH of the soil, and many of the loveliest bog garden plants need acid soils that are naturally found in wet woodlands. The selected plants should be planted in drifts or large groups of as many as nine plants to a group. It may be necessary to place stepping stones as a path through the bog garden to give access to the plants without getting wet feet. A list of plants for moist conditions can be found in the appendix.

THE ACID GARDEN

If you have a garden with a lime-free acid soil then there is a whole range of plants that you can grow which are denied to people with lime or chalk in their soil. These plants are mostly members of one family—*Ericaceae*, the heather family, and include all the rhododendrons and azaleas. All the ericaceous plants share with the heathers the same bell-shaped flowers and although ranging in size from small alpines to medium trees, they tend to all look at their best when planted together. A list of ericaceous plants can be found in the appendix.

There are also several very beautiful trees that need acid soil and can be planted to give height and possible focal points in the acid garden. These trees include:

Eucryphia glutinosa
Halesia carolina
Magnolia campbellii
Nyssa sylvatica
Oxydendrum arboreum
Sassafras albidum
Stewartia pseudocamellia
Styrax japonica

Shrubs that need, or prefer, acid soil but are not members of the *Ericaeae* include:

Aronia arbutifolia
Camellia japonica
Clethra alnifolia
Cornus florida
Corylopsis spicata
Crinodendron hookeranum
Desfontainia spinosa
Fothergilla monticola
Hamamelis mollis
Skimmia japonica

There are several very good plants to provide ground cover in the acid garden and these include:

Arctostaphylos uva-ursi — for full sun
Claytonia sibirica — for shade
Cornus canadensis — for shade
Gaultheria procumbens — both sun & shade
Gaultheria shallon — both sun & shade
Linnaea borealis — for shade
Lithospermum diffusum — for sun
Pachysandra terminalis — for shade

Ground cover can also be provided by the heathers, both *Calluna vulgaris* (ling) and *Erica cinerea* (bell heather). There are also a number of herbaceous plants that need lime-free soil including the lovely yellow *Kirengeshoma palmata*, several lilies and the blue himalayan poppy *Meconopsis betonicifolia*.

The above plants need to be selected for aspect and drainage, although most of them prefer damp soils with some shade.

The biggest group of plants that need a lime-free soil are the rhododendrons and azaleas. There are over 800 species of rhododendron and nearly as many hybrids, so they are usually considered as a special group.

Rhododendrons and azaleas

The 800 species of the genus *Rhododendron* include both rhododendrons and azaleas and range from dwarf creeping plants to large shrubs and small trees. Almost all have colourful, showy flowers, many have large beautiful leaves and a few also have very attractive stems. A large number of them come from the Himalayas where they have acid soils, a damp atmosphere and almost continuous rain. As a group of plants they are not used to extremes of climate and dislike intense sunlight, icy winds and drought. For these reasons they grow much better in the western counties of Britain — in fact they grow so well in north Wales that *Rhododendron ponticum* is fast becoming a nuisance where it has naturalized.

The botanical classification of the rhododendrons is immensely complicated and for garden purposes it may be easier to separate them simply into rhododendron species, rhododendron hybrids, and azaleas.

Rhododendron species

These are the rhododendrons which are found growing in the wild in North America, the Himalayas and other parts of Asia. They are almost all evergreen and most of them grow too large to be included in an average-size garden, needing space to be seen to their best advantage. They need deep, humus-rich acid soil and the shade of taller trees.

Garden hybrids have been developed from many of the species which are better garden plants than the parent, but there are some species which are worth growing where you have the right soil and conditions. These include *Rhododendron augustinii*, with early blue flowers; *Rhododendron barbatum*, with crimson flowers and an attractive peeling bark; the smaller *Rhododendron moupinense*, with small leaves and scented pink flowers in early spring; *Rhododendron mucronatum*, which forms a dome of pure white fragrant flowers in late spring; *Rhododendron sinograude*, with huge glossy green leaves, silver underneath and enormous creamy flowers with crimson blotches; the beautiful *Rhododendron williamsianum*, with heart shaped leaves and bell-shaped pink flowers; and the compact *Rhododendron yakushimanum* with young silvery growth in spring, followed by trusses of pink flowers which are borne just above the surface of the leaves, creating a low dome of colour.

Rhododendron hybrids

The first rhododendrons to be brought to Britain were very early flowering with the inherent risk that the blooms would be damaged by frost. To overcome this problem, several nurserymen started hybridizing, crossing the various species to try to get later but still attractive flowers. The results were very successful and gradually a range of hardy hybrids were introduced usually carrying the name of the nursery or its location e.g. Exbury hybrids. Further hybridizing was carried out as each new species was discovered and sent back to Britain, as when *Rhododendron griffithianum* was introduced by Joseph Hooker in 1850. This plant has large trusses of scented white flowers, large beautiful hanging leaves and a reddish peeling bark; unfortunately it is also tender. Nurserymen strived for years to find a hybrid that was as beautiful as the species but also hardy, and finally in 1897 the cross 'Pink Pearl' was produced, with fully hardy pale pink blossoms.

There are literally hundreds of rhododendron hybrids, with blossoms in every conceivable colour, flowering from mid-winter to early summer and ranging in size from dwarf plants suitable for rock gardens, e.g. *Rhododendron* 'Pink Drift'; to medium-sized plants suitable for most gardens, e.g. *Rhododendron* 'Britannia' with large red flowers; up to some very large plants, only suitable where there is a large amount of space, e.g. *Rhododendron* 'Albatross' with fragrant flowers and which will form a small tree if given sufficient room.

Azaleas

Azaleas are species and hybrids of *Rhododendron* but usually listed separately from rhododendrons as they are visually distinctly different in having much more twiggy growth, more open flowers and are either deciduous or if evergreen lose their leaves in spring before the new leaves appear. They also vary in that although they need the same lime-free soil they prefer a sunny position to a shady place. Some of the loveliest azaleas to grow are those which combine scented late spring flowers with magnificent autumn colour e.g. 'Narcissiflorum' and 'Daviesii'. Azaleas are best in beds on their own or with the smaller rhododendrons with perhaps just an edging of another plant e.g. *Alchemilla mollis*. They are also effective as foreground planting in front of some of the larger ericaceous plants noted for their autumn colour e.g. *Enkianthus campanulata* and *Fothergilla monticola*. Many of the azaleas are small, compact plants and adapt well to being grown in containers, which allows them to be grown, in pots of lime-free compost, in gardens where the soil is not acid.

The use of heathers

There are two genera of plants which are both known as heather, *Erica* and *Calluna*. *Erica cinerea* is the plant known as bell heather and *Calluna vulgaris* is commonly called Scottish heather or ling. Amongst the species of *Erica* are some that will tolerate lime in the soil, e.g. *Erica carnea* and *Erica × darleyensis*, whilst others must be planted in lime-free soil e.g. *Erica ciliaris* and *Erica cinerea*.

All heathers prefer a sunny aspect and a moisture retentive soil, they suffer if the soil dries out in the summer. They can be planted as ground cover with other ericaceous plants in the acid garden, with dwarf conifers as mentioned in Chapter 10, or for winter colour with the white stems of *Betula costata* and other birches.

PLANTING FOR WILDLIFE

In recent years there has been a movement towards more natural gardens, with the promotion of wild flower meadows and a much greater awareness of the beauty and fragility of our natural surroundings. As a result many gardeners will now want to include some provision for wildlife in their gardens. This may be the provision of a pond for frogs, newts and dragonflies; it may be the retention or planting of a field hedge as a wildlife corridor; or it may mean including plants to encourage birds, bees and butterflies.

Planting for birds

Birds bring movement, colour and sound into the garden; there are very few sounds as cheerful as the song of the blackbird or robin and very few sights more welcome in spring than the swift flight of the returning swallows. Birds may also help the gardener by eating insects such as caterpillars, or snails; for instance wrens are caterpillar eaters, and blackbirds and thrushes eat insects and snails.

In encouraging birds to visit the garden it

has to be accepted that it is impossible to specify which particular birds are welcome. If wrens, swallows, blackbirds, robins and thrushes feel welcome then so will pigeons, starlings and bullfinches. Starlings are only tiresome in clearing all the food carefully put out on the bird table for other, more ornamental, birds, they are actually beneficial as they feed on insects that damage lawns; whereas pigeons will decimate the vegetable garden and bullfinches will destroy the buds on fruit trees and bushes. If vegetables and fruit can be protected by netting, then the problem is solved.

Birds need perches, food, water, nesting materials and sites, and protection from predators. Perches are best provided by established trees, shrubs and hedges, these will also provide nesting materials and nesting sites for the majority of garden birds. 'Instant meals' for birds can be provided by means of a bird table, but perhaps more helpful is to plant plants that either provide the habitat for the insects that some birds feed on, or the seeds and fruit for other birds. Garden plants that provide food for birds include:

Aster novi-belgii (michaelmas daisies) — seed
Berberis — most provide berries
Calendula officinalis (marigold) — seeds
Cotoneaster — most provide berries
Hedera helix (ivy) — berries
Helianthus annuus (sunflower) — seeds
Lonicera periclymenum — berries
Onorpordum acanthium (Scotch thistle) — seeds
Pyracantha — all provide berries
Pernettya mucronata — berries
Scabiosa caucasica — seeds
Skimmia japonica — berries
Symphoricarpos racemosa — berries
Viburnum opulus — berries

PLANTING FOR BEES AND BUTTERFLIES

There are many insects that should definitely be excluded from the garden if at all possible, these would include sawflies, thrips, aphids, and caterpillars! But amongst the insects are many that are beneficial in the garden, some feeding on the insects listed above, others pollinating flowers, still others that provide food for birds as discussed above. The two groups of insects which are specifically encouraged to visit the garden are the bees and the butterflies. Bees are easy to attract into the garden provided there are plenty of flowers for them to visit. They are fascinating creatures to watch as they work over the flowers collecting pollen and nectar. There are 250 species of bees living in Britain alone, and they vary in the flowers they visit for food depending on the length of their tongue. Whilst collecting food they are also acting as pollinators for the flowers they visit.

In gardens where hives of honey bees are kept, then the specific plants visited by honey bees need to be grown, but otherwise plant any of the bee plants listed and bees will come into the garden.

Garden plants visited by bees for pollen and/or nectar include:

Allium schoenoprasum
Althaea rosea
Aubrieta deltoidea
Borago officinalis
Cotoneaster horizontalis
Daphne mezereum
Echinops ritro
Endymion non-scriptus
Foeniculum vulgare
Hyssopus officinalis
Lavandula spica
Limnanthes douglasii
Lythrum salicaria
Melissa officinalis
Oenothera biennis
Origanum vulgare
Nepeta × faassenii
Phacelia tanacetifolia
Reseda odorata
Rosmarinus officinalis
Salvia officinalis

Symphytum grandiflorum
Thymus vulgaris
Veronica spicata

Not all gardeners will want to encourage bees, particularly if the household includes young children or people allergic to bee stings, but most people would be happy to encourage butterflies, and particularly the large, brightly coloured ones like the Red Admiral, Peacock and Tortoiseshell.

Butterflies have a complex life-cycle, with the adult butterfly laying eggs on a plant which will supply food when the larva emerges. This larva is known as a caterpillar, not all of which can be considered beneficial to garden plants, and after growing sufficiently, pupates before the adult butterfly emerges. The adult butterfly's purpose in life is to mate with another butterfly to produce the eggs which start the cycle all over again.

Adult butterflies will visit any garden which contains the plants which they visit for nectar, providing that the garden is within the area where the food plants of the caterpillar stage are in abundance. The food plants are nearly all native rather than cultivated plants and the caterpillar stage of many butterflies will only feed on one or two species of plants e.g. the brimstone caterpillar will only feed on *Rhamnus* species (buckthorn and alder buckthorn), and the peacock and red admiral larvae will only feed on *Urtica dioica* (stinging nettle). If you intend leaving a clump of nettles as food for larvae than make sure that the clump is in full sun as the adult butterfly will only lay eggs in the sunshine. Some of the best garden plants for attracting butterflies are:

Aubrieta deltoidea — brimstones and orange-tips
Alyssum saxatile — most butterflies
Aster novi-belgii — small coppers & tortoiseshells
Buddleia davidii — peacocks, commas, red admirals, small tortoiseshells
Centranthus ruber — most butterflies and moths

Cheiranthus cheiri — early butterflies
Hesperis matrionalis — orange-tips
Lavandula spica — whites and browns
Lunaria spp. — orange-tips
Lythrum salicaria — most butterflies
Nepeta × faassenii — most butterflies
Sedum spectabile — small tortoiseshells

Lunaria annuum (honesty) and *Hesperis matrionalis* (sweet rocket) are also food plants for the larvae of the orange-tip.

PLANTS FOR PAVED AREAS

Many small gardens have a large proportion of their area paved to give access throughout the year, and larger gardens may have an expanse of paved terrace around the house. These paved areas may be very practical but may also look rather harsh and dull. Plants can be used to soften the paving by being planted in beds and borders beneath the walls of the house, by being planted in containers, or by being planted within the paved surface.

Planting for beds and borders in paved areas

Borders at the base of house walls will frequently contain little soil and what there is is often very impoverished. These areas suffer from the extreme effects of aspect, i.e. north-facing borders are in complete shade; south-facing borders are extremely dry and hot; west-facing borders are fine but may be exposed to strong prevailing winds; and east-facing borders may be completely dry, the house creating a rain-shadow from the wet, west winds. A further problem is where the walls above the border have been constructed with a lime mortar. This may lead to an increase in the alkalinity of the soil below when the lime is washed out of the mortar during wet weather.

Before planting these borders, check the depth and quality of the top soil and add manure and compost where necessary. If the soil is very poor then additional topsoil will need to be brought in either from another part of the garden or from outside. Select plants for the soil, aspect and drainage of each border and try to include some scented plants which will be enjoyed both whilst sitting on the terrace and from inside the house when the windows are open. Winter-flowering plants are a good choice for these areas as they can be enjoyed when looking out through the windows on a cold day.

Try to include as many evergreen plants as possible to give interest throughout the year, using grey-leaved evergreen plants for the south-facing borders. Include areas which can be planted with bedding plants, in both spring and autumn, for extra colour.

Planting within paved areas

There are a few prostrate plants that can be planted within paved areas. These plants need to be able to survive being stepped on occasionally and having their roots contained within gaps in the paving. If you enjoy growing plants within paving it is advisable to leave adequate room for plants by omitting some of the paving whilst it is being laid. Trying to squeeze plants into the joints between paving slabs is not very successful, nor is breaking small corners off individual paving slabs; a few plants may manage to survive in these tiny pockets of soil but most will eventually find the conditions too dry.

Prostrate plants suitable for growing in paving include *Lysimachia nummularia* (creeping jenny) which forms a carpet of rounded leaves providing there is adequate moisture — it is at its best planted in the shade of a north wall — and *Thymus drucei* (creeping thyme) which is ideal for a really hot, dry terrace and will tolerate quite heavy foot traffic. There are several cultivars of this thyme, including golden and gold-variegated leaved forms and white, pink and lavender-coloured flowers.

Plants for containers

Containers for growing plants can be any shape or size from a small plain terracotta flower pot to the most elaborate of swagged and decorated cast iron urns. There are several approaches to planting containers but the basic difference is whether just one plant or clump of plants is planted or whether a mixture of different plants. In the first case the container is being used as a flower pot and the second as a vase in which the planting acts as a flower arrangement.

Plants in pots

Any plant that tolerates having its roots contained can be planted in a container and for some plants it is the best way of growing them. Plants that require winter protection can be grown in a container so that they can be placed outside in the summer and brought inside, into the conservatory or greenhouse, for the winter. Plants suitable for treating in this way include *Laurus nobilis* (bay tree) particularly when grown as a specimen, agaves with their thick, fleshy leaves, *Lippia citriodora* (lemon verbena) and citrus trees.

Herbs are particularly good planted in containers with one herb to each pot, though not necessarily one plant. The herbs can then be given the exact soil they need and be placed for sun or shade as required. Having the herbs raised in containers means that they are above the height of possible contamination by cats and dogs, an essential consideration if the herbs are to be used for cooking!

Other plants that look attractive when planted on their own in pots are hostas, agapanthus and lilies. All make fine clumps of leaves and flowers that flow over and disguise the edge of the container.

Plants that cannot be grown in the garden because the soil doesn't suit them can be grown in containers instead. In a chalk garden, azaleas, camellias and the dwarf rhododendrons can be planted individually in suitable size containers filled with a lime-free

Fig. 15.3 Pots and urns.

(*a*) Pots — suitable containers for planting up with a single plant or groups of plants.

(*b*)Urns — leave unplanted as an ornament or plant as a vase of flowers.

soil. They can then be placed out of direct sunlight with protection from the east wind. All the above plants are best planted in pots rather than urns, and need a container that is large enough for at least a year's growth (Fig. 15.3). Good drainage is essential and good soil. Ordinary garden soil is not good enough without the addition of peat and sand and plenty of fertilizer preferably slow-release. You can make up your own mixture but it is much easier to buy in a proprietary potting mixture; John Innes no.2 is the best all round mixture, but will not be suitable for the plants that need a lime-free soil. These plants will need a special potting compost which will probably be labelled 'Ericaceous' mix.

Planting urns

Many gardeners use planted urns to add a splash of colour to balconies, terraces, or flights of steps. They need to be planted as you would arrange flowers in a vase i.e. so that the flowers dominate, not the container. In summer annuals and half hardy perennials can be planted so that by mid-summer the plants have grown sufficiently to create the impression of a vase full of flowers.

To achieve this effect it is necessary to plant the container in early spring if you can move it into a greenhouse, and late spring if you have to plant it outside. Use small plants and plant them as close together as possible, starting with a central plant chosen for its height. This might be a specimen pelargonium or fuchsia. Next plant a circle of plants around the central plant using plants chosen for their flowers. These might be other smaller pelargoniums and fuchsias or begonias, or petunias and, if the container is in a shady position, then use impatiens. If the urn is very large there may be room for a second circle of these plants. Finally around the rim plant a circle of plants chosen for their ability to grow down to hide the edge of the container, suitable plants are hanging lobelias, ivy-leaved pelargoniums and *Helichrysum petiolaris*.

After planting, the urn will need watering frequently, possibly every day during summer, and will need feeding with a liquid fertilizer every week. The result will be a container overflowing with flowers and foliage from mid-summer right through until the first frosts.

CHAPTER 16

FUNCTIONAL PLANTING

FUNCTIONAL PLANTING

Functional plants are those which are grown because they are useful to the owner, rather than for their contribution to the design of the garden. They are usually grouped together in the vegetable garden, a name given to the area of the garden where vegetables are to be grown but frequently incorporating soft fruit, herbs and flowers for cutting as well as the compost heap and even the bonfire!

Vegetables

Vegetables are usually grown in gardens to provide food which may not be cheaper but is certainly fresher than the vegetables in shops. They may also be grown for exhibition in shows or because the garden owner prefers growing vegetables to other plants. If planted in the formal arrangement of the 'potager' vegetables can be considered an ornamental feature.

Fruit

Fruit is also grown for food, there being two types of fruit, the top fruits and the soft fruits. Top fruits are those usually grown as trees and include apples, pears, plums and cherries; the less hardy peach, nectarine and apricot; and the less frequently grown quinces, medlars, walnuts and damsons. Traditionally top fruit were grown either in orchards or trained onto the walls of the kitchen garden. Soft fruit include bush fruits, red currants, black currants and gooseberry; cane fruits, raspberry, blackberry and loganberry; vines and strawberries. Soft fruits are usually grown in fruit cages to prevent the fruit being taken by birds.

Herbs

Herbs are plants which though not providing food are used by man for a variety of purposes; for flavouring food, for cosmetic use, for medicinal use, and for scenting rooms and repelling insects. Historically they were the first plants to be cultivated in the garden being essential to every aspect of life and, from Roman times right through to the Renaissance, herbs filled the garden, being formally planted in knot gardens or on their own in raised beds. In gardens today herbs may be grown just for their use alone e.g. a clump of mint in the vegetable garden which is used to flavour new potatoes, or for their ornamental value. They can be included as rows of individual herbs in the vegetable garden, grown in pots by the kitchen door, planted in beds and borders with ornamental plants or as a special feature together in a herb garden.

Flowers for cutting and drying

Gardeners have always used the flowers grown in their gardens to decorate their houses. Usually flowers are picked from the ornamental beds and borders but some gardeners will want to be able to pick flowers without denuding their beds, or may need flowers which are the wrong colour or type for the ornamental areas. In this case room should be put aside in the functional area for growing these plants which can then be cut for flower arranging as and when required. The flowers, to be grown, may be just for the house or may need to include enough to allow the owner to arrange flowers for competitions or as a small business. The cut flower area may need to include rows of herbaceous perennials and a separate area for annuals which might be included within the rotation of the vegetable beds. There may also need to be room for carnations, dahlias, gladioli and chrysanthemums, all of which are frequently best grown separately so that their specific needs can be met e.g. being lifted in winter. This group of plants are often cultivated for showing and may require a lot of attention and protection so are best placed where they can be reached easily. Dried flowers have become very popular recently as, once arranged, they look attractive for months or even years. Many of the easiest flowers for drying are annuals e.g. *Helichrysum* and *Acroclinium* which are usually called everlasting flowers. These need to be grown in their own area within the vegetable garden where they can be looked after and then picked daily when ready.

Planning the vegetable garden

Vegetables and fruit need a deep, fertile, well-drained soil in full sun, as do many of the herbs and flowers for cutting, although these last two groups include plants that will tolerate some shade and poorer soils. A supply of water is usually necessary and if a greenhouse is to be included, then an electricity supply may be needed for heating; the route of the water pipe and the electricity cable need to be checked as problems in supplying these services may affect where the vegetable garden can be positioned. The position of the vegetable garden will need to be decided at an early stage in the planning process so that a suitable site can be chosen which can then be screened so that it doesn't detract from the rest of the garden. It is easier to screen a vegetable garden placed to the south of the house as any screen planting will be to the north side of the vegetables and so will not create shade (Fig. 16.1).

Screening the vegetable garden
Any screen which is to hide the vegetable garden from the house needs to be high enough to cover the items which require screening. If

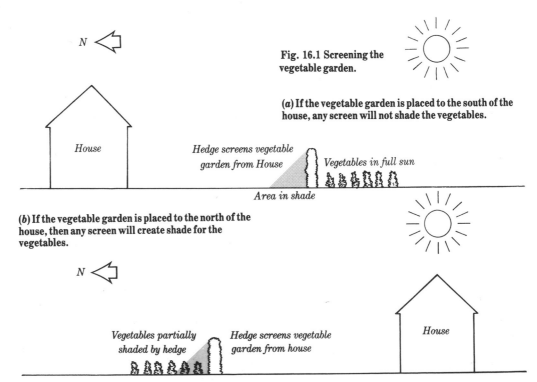

Fig. 16.1 Screening the vegetable garden.

(*a*) If the vegetable garden is placed to the south of the house, any screen will not shade the vegetables.

N

House

Hedge screens vegetable garden from House *Vegetables in full sun*

Area in shade

(*b*) If the vegetable garden is placed to the north of the house, then any screen will create shade for the vegetables.

N

Vegetables partially shaded by hedge *Hedge screens vegetable garden from house*

House

this is a fruit cage which is 2 m (6½ ft) high then the screen needs to be the same height. If the screen is just to hide the decaying stems of Brussels sprout plants then the screen need only be 1 m (3¼ ft) high!

Screens can be fences or walls as in the traditional kitchen garden, or they can be a hedge, trellis with climbers or a row of cordon apple trees supported by horizontal wires. In a small garden where space is limited then cordon fruit trees will screen the area and provide blossom in spring and fruit in autumn. An alternative would be a row of tripods supporting runner beans or a row of Jerusalem artichokes, both of which would give an effective screen in summer but little or no screen in winter.

Hedges make good dense screens where there is more room, beech being a good choice for a formal clipped hedge and where height is required, whereas *Rosa rugosa* is a much prettier hedge where it can be left unpruned.

In some areas vegetable gardens will need to be protected from rabbits and possibly deer. The entire garden may be fenced or, if this is impossible, it is sensible at least to stop them from getting all your vegetables! With both rabbit and deer, some form of boundary fence will be necessary and this may influence the type of screen that is to be used. Fencing for rabbits needs to be a close mesh and to be buried at least 30 cm (1 ft) in the ground. Deer need high fencing, the exact height depending on which type of deer is likely to be a problem.

Size of the vegetable garden

The size of area needed for vegetables will depend on the number of persons in the family to be fed and the time available to grow and look after the crops. It will also depend on whether the gardener or gardeners in the household actually enjoy growing vegetables or would rather be growing roses! If the latter is the case then the space given to vegetables should be the minimum needed for growing the real essentials such as early potatoes or mange-tout peas!

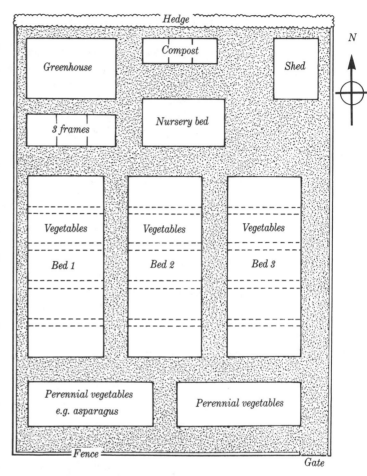

Fig. 16.2 Plan for a vegetable garden.
The greenhouse, shed and compost heaps should be placed to the north of the vegetable beds so that no shade is created. A minimum of three beds are needed to allow for a three-year rotation of vegetables.

The keen vegetable grower will want plenty of space to grow a full range of crops and to allow for rotation. There may well need to be space for a frame, a greenhouse for raising plants from seed and growing tomatoes, and at least one compost heap. For a good rotation at least three separate beds are needed, one for brassicas, one for root crops, and one for peas and beans. There may also need to be another area for perennials crops which might include asparagus, globe artichokes or rhubarb (Fig. 16.2).

For practical reasons it is sensible to have rectangular beds even if the area is an irregular shape. The beds should have paths between them which are wide enough for a wheelbarrow to be easily manoeuvred. If hedges are used to screen the garden then a path should be left between the beds and the hedge to allow for hedge-cutting.

Top fruit and orchards

Many gardens already have some existing fruit trees, usually apples or pears which will continue to produce fruit for 80 years or more. These trees may need pruning to bring into shape and to produce more fruit but may provide enough fruit for the family. Old apple trees whether producing a good crop or not, make ideal trees for climbing and for tree houses, or can be used to support a climbing rose e.g. *Rosa filipes* 'Kiftsgate' which can reach up into the tallest apple tree and produces large clusters of scented white flowers in mid-summer. Where there are no existing fruit trees or where those that are present are not the varieties that are wanted then new trees need to be planted.

If apples or pears are required then there is a range of possible sizes and types of tree available including trees suitable for any size garden (Table 16.1 and Fig. 16.3). There are fewer sizes of plums and cherries but still enough to give plenty of choice. Peaches, nectarines and apricots only produce ripe fruit when planted on a sheltered, sunny wall and are usually planted as fan-trained trees. Traditionally fruit trees were planted in orchards, the trees being well spaced out in a series of parallel rows. The regular lines of fruit trees formed an attractive formal pattern and were at their best in late spring when the trees were covered in blossom.

Most gardens are not large enough to include an orchard, one or two fruit trees, or a row of cordons having to suffice. Where there is room for an orchard, in a large country garden, then a much wider range of fruit than the usual apples and pears can be planted. Some apples and pears, both cooking and eating, will probably still want to be included

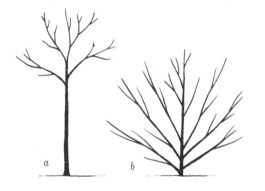

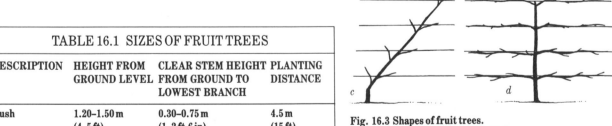

Fig. 16.3 Shapes of fruit trees.
(a) *Standard* see details in Table 16.1.
(b) *Fan* — train against wall
planting distance — 6 m (20ft).
(c) *Cordon* — train on wires
planting distance — 90 cm (3ft).
(d) *Espalier* — train on wires or wall
planting distance — 4 m (13 ft).

TABLE 16.1 SIZES OF FRUIT TREES			
DESCRIPTION	HEIGHT FROM GROUND LEVEL	CLEAR STEM HEIGHT FROM GROUND TO LOWEST BRANCH	PLANTING DISTANCE
Bush	1.20–1.50 m (4–5 ft)	0.30–0.75 m (1–2 ft 6 in)	4.5 m (15 ft)
Half standard	1.80–2.10 m (6–7 ft)	1.20–1.50 m (4–5 ft)	7.2 m (24 ft)
Standard	2.75–3.00 m (9–10 ft)	1.80 m (6 ft)	9.0 m (30 ft)

as will plums and cherries, but you can also include a mulberry, a quince, a medlar, and perhaps a cherry plum, some crab apples, a damson and even a sloe particularly if you like sloe gin! Nuts can also be planted amongst the fruit including walnuts, hazels and filberts, although you may have to fight the squirrels to be able to harvest them. All of these trees are quite hardy and will grow and produce fruit in most soils and locations.

Planting fruit trees

There are several important points to remember when selecting and planting fruit trees including frost-protection and pollination. Late spring frosts will damage fruit blossom and stop the fruit from developing. Avoid planting fruit in hollows where frost collects and in cold areas provide some form of screen. Most varieties of fruit are not self-fertile and need another variety that flowers at the same time for pollination. None of the apple varieties are self-fertile but the pear 'Conference', the plum 'Victoria' and the cherry 'Stella' are. In a small garden where there is only space for a single tree of each fruit these would be the varieties to use.

Most catalogues from fruit tree nurseries include details of the pollination requirements of the varieties of fruit listed.

Soft fruit

Fruit cages are essential if soft fruit is to be grown and enjoyed. They usually consist of wooden or metal uprights which support cross beams to which a net is attached, the net covering the entire structure to prevent even the smallest bird entering to eat the fruit. Fruit cages are quite easy to construct or can be purchased; they are usually of sufficient height to allow a person to stand upright once again inside and come in a range of sizes. First decide on which fruits are to be grown and the area to be planted and then buy or construct a cage to fit the area. Unfortunately most fruit cages are ugly structures which need to be screened from view.

The potager

'Potager' is the name given to a special type of vegetable garden the prime purpose of which is to be enjoyed as a formal garden of pattern and line. Beds are set out in a formal pattern and then planted with vegetables which may be selected for the colour and texture of their leaves rather than for their use in the kitchen. Herbs may be included either in their own area or as edging to the vegetable beds e.g. thyme, chives and parsley. If a very formal garden is wanted then all the beds may be edged with dwarf box and the whole area contained within a trellis, formal hedge or rows of cordon fruit. Fruit trees may be included as features being pruned to create pyramids or trained to form bells.

This form of vegetable garden is great fun to plan and plant but requires a lot of time to keep looking neat and tidy, particularly when you start harvesting the crop; a neat block of red cabbages doesn't look quite the same when one of the cabbages has been removed for dinner! If you want to include a potager then it needs to be planned as part of the overall garden design and should be placed with the other formal elements in the garden.

The herb garden

Herb gardens are areas where all the plants used are herbs i.e. useful plants. They are usually, but not always, formal with the beds of herbs arranged to form a symmetrical pattern. The area chosen should be near the other formal elements in the garden and also near the kitchen door so that the herbs are accessible when needed. The garden should be designed using small size beds so that all the herbs can be picked easily from the paths rather than having to stand on the soil, and the paths should be paved rather than grassed so that the herbs can be reached in all weather (Fig. 16.4). There are several points to remember when selecting the herbs to be planted, firstly herbs include a very wide range

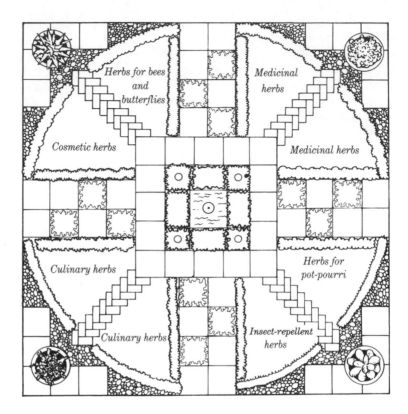

Fig. 16.4 Plan for a formal herb garden.

of plants with some herbs requiring hot, dry conditions like the thymes and lavender; whilst other herbs prefer damp shade like sweet cicely. Secondly, a herb garden is an ornamental feature so the plants used should have either ornamental flowers or foliage. Thirdly, many of the herbs can be invasive; mint, for instance, can take over a small herb garden in an incredibly short space of time. The location and soil of the herb garden will, to a certain extent, decide the herbs that might be included and suitable herbs can then be selected for colour and texture. With a herb garden in full sun it is very easy to plan an attractive scheme based on a purple, yellow and grey harmony.

Plants that could be included are rosemary and lavender both of which have grey foliage and soft purple flowers; there are several varieties of sage that are suitable including both gold and purple leaved forms. Gold marjoram and golden thyme provide more gold and both have pale purple flowers, and cotton lavender and *Phlomis fruticosa* (Jerusalen sage) have grey foliage with yellow flowers. All the above herbs are attractive to bees and butterflies which is an added bonus. Other possible colour schemes for herb gardens are green and gold, white, cream and green, and red, pink and green. In each of these harmonies there are a range of attractive plants to choose from.

APPENDIX: PLANT TABLES

1. Plants for chalk soils
2. Ericaceous plants for lime free soil
3. Plants for dry, sunny positions
4. Plants for shade
5. Evergreen plants for structural planting
6. Plants for use as focal points
7. Winter flowering plants
8. Plants for autumn colour
9. Shrubs for use as ground cover
10. Herbaceous plants for use as ground cover
11. Plants with green/white vareigated foliage
12. Plants with yellow/green variegated foliage
13. Plants with purple foliage
14. Plants with golden foliage
15. Plants with grey foliage
16. Aromatic plants
17. Plants with scented flowers
18. Marginal plants
19. Plants for moist conditions
20. Ferns
21. Climbers

KEY TO SYMBOLS
Height = Mature height
E = Evergreen
D = Deciduous

1 PLANTS FOR CHALK SOILS

NAME	E/D	FLOWERS/FRUIT	FLOWERING SEASON	HEIGHT	
Trees					
Acer campestre	D	yellow	spring	10 m	(33 ft)
Acer negundo	D	yellow	spring	10 m	(33 ft)
Crataegus oxyacantha	D	white, pink or red	late spring	6 m	(20 ft)
Fraxinus ornus	D	white	late spring	12 m	(40 ft)
Malus floribunda	D	pink	mid-late spring	6 m	(20 ft)
Morus nigra	D	purple fruit	early autumn	10 m	(40 ft)
Paulownia tomentosa	D	blue purple	late spring	12 m	(40 ft)
Prunus — flowering cherries	D	white or pink	spring	8 m	(26 ft)
Sophora japonica	D	cream	late summer	8 m	(26 ft)
Sorbus aria	D	white/red fruit	spring	12 m	(33 ft)
Shrubs					
Buddleia davidii	D	pale lavender	late summer	4 m	(13 ft)
Cistus × corbariensis	E	white	summer	60 cm	(2 ft)
Cornus mas	D	yellow	winter	4 m	(13 ft)
Deutzia × rosea	D	pink	late spring	90 cm	(3 ft)
Forsythia suspensa	D	yellow	spring	3 m	(10 ft)
Hebe salicifolia	E	white	summer	1.2 m	(4 ft)
Olearia macrodonta	E	white	mid-late summer	2 m	(6 ft 6 in)
Potentilla fruticosa	D	yellow	summer	90 cm	(3 ft)
Syringa vulgaris	D	lilac	late spring	3 m	(10 ft)
Weigela florida	D	rose-pink	early summer	1.5 m	(5 ft)
Herbaceous					
Acanthus mollis	D	white-purple	mid-late summer	1.2 m	(4 ft)
Campanula latiloba	E	blue	mid-late summer	90 cm	(3 ft)
Dianthus hybrids	E	pink or white	mid summer	30 cm	(12 in)
Eremurus hybrids	D	white yellow or pink	early summer	1.5 m	(5 ft)
Helenium autumnale	D	yellow orange or red	mid-late summer	60–120 cm	(2–4 ft)
Helleborus orientalis	E	white to crimson	early spring	45 cm	(18 in)
Iris germanica	semi E	wide colour range	late spring	90 cm	(3 ft)
Kniphofia hybrids	E	yellow orange or red	late summer	90 cm	(3 ft)
Rudbeckia fulgida	D	yellow	mid-late summer	60–90 cm	(2–3 ft)
Verbascum phoeniceum	E	yellow	mid-summer	1.5 m	(5 ft)

2 ERICACEOUS PLANTS FOR LIME FREE SOIL

NAME	E/D	FLOWERS/FOLIAGE	FLOWERING SEASON	HEIGHT	
Andromeda polifolia	E	pink	spring	60 cm	(2 ft)
Arctostaphylos uva-ursi	E	pink/red berries	spring	30 cm	(12 in)
Calluna vulgaris	E	white, pink or purple	summer	60 cm	(2 ft)
Daboecia cantabrica	E	white or purple	summer to autumn	60 cm	(2 ft)
Erica arborea	E	white	early spring	3 m	(10 ft)
Erica cinerea	E	white, crimson purple	mid-late summer	30 cm	(12 in)
Erica vagans	E	white or pink	late summer	60 cm	(2 ft)
Gaultheria shallon	E	pinky white	summer	90 cm	(3 ft)
Kalmia latifolia	E	pink	mid-spring	3 m	(10 ft)
Kalmia polifolia	E	rose purple	mid-spring	45 cm	(18 in)
Leucothoe fontanesiana	E	white	mid-late spring	1.2 m	(4 ft)
Oxydendrum arboreum	D	white/red & orange in autumn	late summer autumn	6 m	(20 ft)
Pernettya mucronata	E	white/pink or white berries	late spring	90 cm	(3 ft)
Pieris formosa forrestii	E	white/red new leaves	mid-late spring	2 m	(6 ft 6 in)
Pieris japonica	E	white/coppery young leaves	mid-late spring	1.5 m	(5 ft)
Rhododendron — large flower hybrids	E	wide range of colours	early-late spring	2–3 m	(6–10 ft)
Rhododendron species	E	wide range of colours	early-late spring	up to 4 m	(13 ft)
Rhododendron — Azaleas	E/D	wide range of colours	mid-late spring	1.2 m	(4 ft)
Vaccinium corymbosum	D	white/scarlet autumn colour	late spring	1.2 m	(4 ft)
Zenobia pulverulenta	D	white	early summer	1.2 m	(4 ft)

3 PLANTS FOR DRY, SUNNY POSITIONS

NAME	E/D	FLOWERS/FOLIAGE	FLOWERING SEASON	HEIGHT	
Abutilon vitifolium	D	mauve/grey	mid summer	3 m	(10 ft)
Callistemon citrinus	E	scarlet	summer	1.8 m	(6 ft)
Carpenteria californica	E	white	mid-summer	1.5 m	(5 ft)
Caryopteris × clandonensis	D	violet blue/green grey	early autumn	75 cm	(2 ft 6 in)
Ceanothus spp.	D/E	blue	most late summer	up to 3 m	(10 ft)
Cistus spp.	E	white/sage grey	summer	up to 1.5 m	(5 ft)
Convolvulus cneorum	E	white/silvery	summer onwards	45 cm	(18 in)
Coronilla glauca	E	yellow/glaucous	early summer & autumn	1.8 m	(6 ft)
Cytisus battandieri	D	yellow/silvery	early summer	3 m	(10 ft)
Fremontodendron 'California Glory'	E	yellow/grey green	late spring-autumn	4 m	(13 ft)
Genista hispanica	D	yellow	early summer	60 cm	(2 ft)
Helianthemum nummularium	E	yellow & orange	all summer	30 cm	(12 in)
Hibiscus syriacus	D	blue white pink	late summer	1.8 m	(6 ft)
Hyssopus officinalis	D	blue	summer	45 cm	(18 in)
Lavandula angustifolia	E	lavender	summer onwards	45 cm	(18 in)

3 PLANTS FOR DRY, SUNNY POSITIONS (*continued*)

NAME	E/D	FLOWERS/FOLIAGE	FLOWERING SEASON	HEIGHT	
Lippia citriodora	D	mauve	late summer	2 m	(6 ft 6 in)
Myrtus communis	E	white	late summer	3 m	(10 ft)
Perovskia atriplicifolia	D	blue/grey	late summer	90 cm	(3 ft)
Phlomis fruticosa	E	yellow/grey	mid summer	60 cm	(2 ft)
Poncirus trifoliata	D	white	late spring	1.8 m	(6 ft)
Romneya coulteri	D	white/grey green	summer	1.2 m	(4 ft)
Rosmarinus officinalis	E	pale lavender	late spring	1.2 m	(4 ft)
Ruta graveolens	E	yellow/glaucous	summer onwards	45 cm	(18 in)
Salvia officinalis	E	lavender blue/grey green	mid summer	45 cm	(18 in)
Teucrium fruticans	E	pale blue/grey	summer	1.5 m	(5 ft)
Thymus vulgaris	E	pale lilac	summer	20 cm	(10 in)

4 PLANTS FOR SHADE

NAME	E/D	FLOWERS/FRUIT	FLOWERING SEASON	HEIGHT	
Aucuba japonica	E	pale yellow/red berries	autumn-early spring	1.2 m	(4 ft)
Bergenia cordifolia	E	pink	spring	30 cm	(12 in)
Buxus sempervirens	E	sulphur yellow	spring	2 m	(6 ft 6 in)
Camellia japonica	E	white, pink or red	early spring	1.8 m	(6 ft)
Crinodendron hookeranum	E	red	early summer	3 m	(10 ft)
Danae racemosa	E	orange berries	fruit in autumn	90 cm	(3 ft)
Daphne laureola	E	yellowish green/black fruit	early spring	90 cm	(3 ft)
Epimedium perralderianum	E	yellow	spring	45 cm	(18 in)
Euonymus fortunei	E	pale green	spring	60 cm	(2 ft)
Fatsia japonica	E	cream/black fruit	spring & summer	3 m	(10 ft)
Gaultheria procumbens	E	red berries	winter fruit	15 cm	(6 in)
Helleborus foetidus	E	green	late winter	60 cm	(2 ft)
Hosta spp.	D	pale lilac	summer	up to 90 cm	(3 ft)
Hypericum calycinum	E	yellow	all summer	30 cm	(12 in)
Ilex aquifolium	E	white/red berries	fruit in autumn/winter	6 m	(20 ft)
Iris foetidissima	E	pale lilac/orange berries	early summer	45 cm	(18 in)
Lamium galeobdolon	E	yellow	early summer	30 cm	(12 in)
Ligustrum japonicum	E	white	late summer	1.2 m	(4 ft)
Lonicera pileata	E	yellow/violet berries	spring	1.2 m	(4 ft)
Mahonia aquifolium	E	yellow/black fruit	early spring	75 cm	(2 ft 6 in)
Pachysandra terminalis	E	greenish white	early spring	30 cm	(12 in)
Prunus laurocerasus	E	white/black fruit	mid spring	4 m	(13 ft)
Pulmonaria officinalis	E	pink turning blue	early spring	30 cm	(12 in)
Rubus odoratus	D	rose	mid-late summer	2 m	(6 ft 6 in)

4 PLANTS FOR SHADE (*Continued*)

NAME	E/D	FLOWERS/FRUIT	FLOWERING SEASON	HEIGHT	
Ruscus aculeatus	E	red fruit	fruit in autumn	1 m	(3 ft 3 in)
Sarcococca hookerana	E	white/black fruits	late winter	1.5 m	(5 ft)
Skimmia japonica	E	white/red fruit	late spring	1.5 m	(5 ft)
Viburnum davidii	E	white/turquoise berries	early summer	1.2 m	(4 ft)
Vinca major	E	blue	summer	30 cm	(12 in)
Vinca minor	E	blue	summer	15 cm	(6 in)

5 EVERGREEN PLANTS FOR STRUCTURAL PLANTING

NAME	FLOWERS/FRUIT	SEASON	HEIGHT	
Aucuba japonica	pale yellow/red berries	fruit in autumn-early spring	1.2 m	(4 ft)
Berberis julianiae	yellow/leaves red in autumn	late spring	1.8 m	(6 ft)
Choisya ternata	white	late spring	1.8 m	(6 ft)
Cotoneaster 'Cornubia'	white/red berries	early summer	3 m	(10 ft)
Elaeagnus × ebbingei	pale yellow	late summer	3 m	(10 ft)
Euonymus japonicus	green yellow/pink fruit	late spring	2 m	(6 ft 6 in)
Ilex × altaclarensis	white/red berries	fruit in autumn/winter	5 m	(16 ft 6 in)
Ilex aquifolium	white/red berries	fruit in autumn/winter	6 m	(20 ft)
Kalmia latifolia	pink	mid spring	3 m	(10 ft)
Ligustrum lucidum	cream/blue black fruit	late summer	2.4 m	(8 ft)
Mahonia japonica	yellow	winter	2.4 m	(8 ft)
Osmanthus × burkwoodi	white	early-mid spring	1.8 m	(6 ft)
Photinia × fraseri	white/red new leaves	late spring	2 m	(6 ft 6 in)
Pieris formosa forrestii	white/red new leaves	mid-late spring	2 m	(6 ft 6 in)
Piptanthus laburnifolius	yellow	mid-late spring	4 m	(13 ft)
Prunus laurocerasus	white/black fruit	mid-spring	4 m	(13 ft)
Prunus lusitanica	white/black fruit	early summer	4 m	(13 ft)
Pyracantha coccinea	white/orange red fruit	early summer	3 m	(10 ft)
Rhododendron ponticum	mauve	late spring	3 m	(10 ft)
Viburnum tinus	white	winter-mid spring	3 m	(10 ft)

6 PLANTS FOR USE AS FOCAL POINTS

NAME	E/D	FLOWERS/FRUIT	FLOWERING SEASON	HEIGHT	
Plants with a Fastigiate Shape					
Calocedrus decurrens	E	cones	—	20 m	(66 ft)
Cupressus sempervirens 'Stricta'	E	cones	—	16 m	(53 ft)
Fagus sylvatica 'Dawyck'	D	—	—	20 m	(66 ft)
Juniperus virginiana 'Skyrocket'	E	—	—	4 m	(13 ft)
Liriodendron tulipifera 'Fastigiatum'	D	greeny yellow	summer	20 m	(66 ft)
Malus 'Van Eseltine'	D	pink/yellow fruit	late spring	6 m	(20 ft)
Populus nigra 'Italica'	D	catkins	early spring	25 m	(80 ft)
Prunus 'Amanogawa'	D	pale pink	mid spring	6 m	(20 ft)
Sorbus aucuparia 'Fastigiata'	D	white/red fruit	late spring	10 m	(33 ft)
Taxus baccata 'Fastigiata'	E	red 'berries'	winter	5 m	(16 ft 6 in)
Plants with a Spiky Shape					
Cordyline australis	E	white	early summer	3.6 m	(12 ft)
Phormium tenax	E	red bracts	early summer	2.1 m	(7 ft)
Trachycarpus fortunei	E	cream	summer	4 m	(13 ft)
Yucca filamentosa	E	cream	late summer	1.5 m	(5 ft)
Trees with a Weeping Habit					
Alnus incana 'Pendula'	D	catkins	early spring	10 m	(33 ft)
Betula pendula 'Youngii'	D	catkins	early spring	8 m	(26 ft)
Caragana arborescens 'Pendula'	D	yellow	late spring	6 m	(20 ft)
Cotoneaster 'Hybridus Pendulus'	E	white/red fruit	late spring	3 m	(10 ft)
Fagus sylvatica 'Pendula'	D	—	—	15 m	(50 ft)
Ilex aquifolium 'Pendula'	E	white/red fruit	summer	6 m	(20 ft)
Malus 'Red Jade'	D	white/red fruit	late spring	3 m	(10 ft)
Morus alba 'Pendula'	D	—	—	8 m	(26 ft)
Prunus 'Kiku-Shidare Sakura'	D	pink	late spring	5 m	(16 ft 6 in)
Prunus subhirtella 'Pendula'	D	pink	early spring	2.4 m	(8 ft)
Prunus × yedoensis 'Shidare Yoshino'	D	blush white	mid spring	5 m	(16 ft 6 in)
Salix caprea 'Kilmarnock'	D	yellow catkins	spring	3 m	(10 ft)
Salix × chrysocoma	D	yellow catkins	spring	20 m	(66 ft)
Plants with a Horizontal Habit					
Cedrus libani	E	cones	—	20 m	(66 ft)
Cornus controversa	D	white/blue black fruit	late spring	6 m	(20 ft)
Juniperus × media 'Pfitzerana'	E	—	—	1.8 m	(6 ft)
Prunus laurocerasus 'Zabeliana'	E	white/black fruit	mid spring	1.8 m	(6 ft)
Taxus baccata 'Dovastoniana'	E	—	—	1.5 m	(5 ft)
Viburnum plicatum 'Mariesii'	D	white/red fruit	late spring	3 m	(10 ft)

7 WINTER-FLOWERING PLANTS

NAME	E/D	FLOWERS/FRUIT	HEIGHT		SCENT
Abeliophyllum distichum	D	white	1.2 m	(4 ft)	✓
Chimonanthus praecox	D	waxy yellow	1.8 m	(6 ft)	✓
Clematis cirrhosa balearica	E	pale yellow	4 m	(13 ft)	x
Cornus mas	D	yellow	4 m	(13 ft)	x
Corylus avellana	D	yellow catkins	6 m	(20 ft)	x
Daphne mezereum	D	purple red/red berries	75 cm	(2 ft 6 in)	✓
Daphne odora	E	purple pink	1.5 m	(5 ft)	✓
Erica carnea	E	white pink & purple	45 cm	(18 in)	x
Erica × darleyensis	E	white pink & crimson	45 cm	(18 in)	x
Garrya elliptica	E	grey-green catkins	3.6 m	(12 ft)	x
Hamamelis × intermedia	D	yellow	3 m	(10 ft)	✓
Hamamelis mollis	D	yellow	3 m	(10 ft)	✓
Helleborus niger	E	white	30 cm	(12 in)	x
Jasminum nudiflorum	D	yellow	2 m	(6 ft 6 in)	x
Lonicera × purpusii	D	cream	2 m	(6 ft 6 in)	✓
Mahonia japonica	E	yellow	2.4 m	(8 ft)	✓
Prunus subhirtella 'Autumnalis'	D	white	6 m	(20 ft)	x
Rhododendron 'Praecox'	E	rose purple	3 m	(10 ft)	x
Sarcococca confusa	E	white	1.2 m	(4 ft)	✓
Skimmia japonica 'Fragrans'	E	white	90 cm	(3 ft)	✓
Viburnum × burkwoodii	E	white	3 m	(10 ft)	✓
Viburnum farreri	D	white	3 m	(10 ft7	✓
Viburnum tinus	E	white	3 m	(10 ft)	x

8 PLANTS FOR AUTUMN COLOUR

NAME	FOLIAGE/FRUIT	HEIGHT	
Acer japonicum	brilliant red and orange leaves	3 m	(10 ft)
Acer palmatum	red, orange and yellow leaves	3 m	(10 ft)
Aesculus flava	bright orange and red leaves	12 m	(40 ft)
Amelanchier lamarckii	orange and red; crimson fruit	6 m	(10 ft)
Aronia melanocarpa	bright red; black fruit	1.8 m	(6 ft)
Berberis wilsoniae	red and orange; coral fruit	1.2 m	(4 ft)
Callicarpa bodinieri	rose purple; violet fruit	4 m	(13 ft)
Ceratostigma willmotianum	purplish red leaves	1 m	(3 ft 3 in)
Cercidiphyllum japonicum	pink, red and yellow leaves	12 m	(40 ft)
Cornus florida	brilliant orange and scarlet	5 m	(16 ft 6 in)

8 PLANTS FOR AUTUMN COLOUR (*Continued*)

NAME	FOLIAGE/FRUIT	HEIGHT	
Cotinus coggygria	orange and yellow leaves	5 m	(16 ft 6 in)
Cotoneaster divaricatus	scarlet; crimson fruit	3 m	(10 ft)
Crataegus prunifolia	orange and scarlet; crimson fruit	8 m	(26 ft)
Euonymus alatus	rose scarlet leaves	1.8 m	(6 ft)
Ginkgo biloba	bright yellow leaves	20 m	(66 ft)
Hamamelis × intermedia	coppery red leaves	3 m	(10 ft)
Liquidambar styraciflua	crimson and gold leaves	15 m	(50 ft)
Malus tschonoskii	orange and red; crimson fruit	12 m	(40 ft)
Metasequoia glyptostroboides	pink and old gold leaves	10 m	(33 ft)
Nandina domestica	crimson and scarlet leaves	1 m	(3 ft 3 in)
Nyssa sylvatica	scarlet, orange and yellow leaves	10 m	(33 ft)
Parrotia persica	crimson and gold leaves	10 m	(33 ft)
Parthenocissus quinquefolia	orange and scarlet leaves	climber 7 m	(23 ft)
Prunus sargentii	bright red and orange leaves	9 m	(30 ft)
Rhododendron — deciduous Azaleas	gold and flame leaves	1.2 m	(4 ft)
Rhus typhina	orange, red and purple leaves	4 m	(13 ft)
Ribes odoratum	yellow; black berries	2 m	(6 ft 6 in)
Sorbus 'Joseph Rock'	copper and orange; yellow fruit	9 m	(30 ft)
Viburnum opulus	scarlet; red berries	4 m	(13 ft)

9 SHRUBS FOR USE AS GROUND COVER

NAME	E/D	FLOWERS/FRUIT	FLOWERING SEASON	HEIGHT	
Calluna vulgaris	E	white pink & purple	summer	60 cm	(2 ft)
Cornus canadensis	D	white	early summer	15 cm	(6 in)
Cotoneaster dammeri	E	white/red berries	late spring	10 cm	(4 in)
Cotoneaster horizontalis	D	white/red berries	late spring	60 cm	(2 ft)
Erica carnea	E	white pink & purple	winter	45 cm	(18 in)
Euonymus fortunei	E	pale green	spring	60 cm	(2 ft)
Gaultheria procumbens	E	red berries	fruit in winter	15 cm	(6 in)
Hedera helix	E	lime green/black fruit	spring	30 cm	(12 in)
Helianthemum nummularium	E	yellow & orange	all summer	30 cm	(12 in)
Hypericum calycinum	E	yellow	all summer	30 cm	(12 in)

9 SHRUBS FOR USE AS GROUND COVER (*Continued*)

NAME	E/D	FLOWERS/FRUIT	FLOWERING SEASON	HEIGHT
Lonicera pileata	E	yellow/violet fruit	spring	1.2 m (4 ft)
Mahonia aquifolium	E	yellow/black fruit	early spring	75 cm (2 ft 6 in)
Pachysandra terminalis	E	greenish white	early spring	30 cm (12 in)
Prunus laurocerasus 'Zabeliana'	E	white/black fruit	spring	1.8 m (6 ft)
Rubus tricolor	E	white/red fruit	late summer	45 cm (18 in)
Salix lanata	D	yellow catkins	spring	90 cm (3 ft)
Sarcococca humilis	E	white/black fruit	winter	40 cm (16 in)
Symphoricarpos 'Hancock'	D	white/pink fruit	late summer	30 cm (12 in)
Vaccinium vitis-idaea	E	white/red berries	late summer	25 cm (10 in)
Viburnum davidii	E	white/turquoise fruit	early summer	1.2 m (4 ft)
Vinca major	E	blue	summer	30 cm (12 in)
Vinca minor	E	blue	summer	15 cm (6 in)

10 HERBACEOUS PLANTS FOR USE AS GROUND COVER

NAME	E/D	FLOWERS/FRUIT	FLOWERING SEASON	HEIGHT
Ajuga reptans	E	blue	spring	15 cm (6 in)
Alchemilla mollis	D	yellow	summer	45 cm (18 in)
Asperula odorata	D	white	late spring	20 cm (8 in)
Bergenia cordifolia	E	pink	spring	30 cm (12 in)
Brunnera macrophylla	D	blue	spring	45 cm (18 in)
Campanula poscharskyana	E	blue	mid summer	20 cm (8 in)
Epimedium pinnatum	E	yellow	spring	38 cm (15 in)
Euphorbia griffithii	D	brich red	summer	60 cm (2 ft)
Fragaria vesca	E	white/red fruit	all summer	20 cm (8 in)
Geranium sanguineum	D	magenta	mid summer	30 cm (12 in)
Geum × borisii	D	orange	late spring	45 cm (18 in)
Helleborus viridis	D	green	late winter	40 cm (14 in)
Hemerocallis flava	D	yellow	summer	75 cm (2 ft 6 in)
Hosta spp.	D	pale lilac	summer	to 90 cm (3 ft)
Lamium galeobdolon	E	yellow	early summer	30 cm (12 in)
Lysimachia nummularia	E	yellow	summer	5 cm (2 in)
Nepeta × faassenii	D	lavender blue	all summer	45 cm (18 in)
Omphalodes cappaodocica	D	blue	early summer	25 cm (10 in)
Polygonatum multiflorum	D	green & white	late spring	90 cm (3 ft)
Polygonum affine	D	pink	summer onwards	25 cm (10 in)
Prunella grandiflora	E	pink	summer	20 cm (8 in)
Pulmonaria angustifolia	D	blue	early spring	20 cm (8 in)

10 HERBACEOUS PLANTS FOR USE AS GROUND COVER (*Continued*)

NAME	E/D	FLOWERS/FRUIT	FLOWERING SEASON	HEIGHT
Saxifraga umbrosa	E	pink	early summer	25 cm (10 in)
Sedum spectabile	D	pink	late summer	45 cm (18 in)
Symphytum grandifolrum	E	cream	spring	25 cm (10 in)
Tiarella cordifolia	E	cream	spring	25 cm (10 in)

11 PLANTS WITH GREEN/WHITE VARIEGATED FOLIAGE

NAME	E/D	FLOWERS/FRUIT	FLOWERING SEASON	HEIGHT
Ajuga reptans 'Variegata'	E	blue	spring	10 cm (4 in)
Euonymus fortunei 'Silver Queen'	E	—	—	60 cm (2 ft)
Fatsia japonica 'Variegata'	E	cream/black fruit	spring & summer	3 m (10 ft)
Fragaria vesca 'Variegata'	E	white/red fruit	all summer	20 cm (8 in)
Hebe × andersonii 'Variegata'	E	lavender blue	all summer	1.2 m (4 ft)
Hedera colchica 'Dentata Variegata'	E	green	winter	4 m (13 ft)
Hedera helix 'Glacier'	E	green yellow	early spring	3 m (10 ft)
Ilex aquifolium 'Silver Milkboy'	E	—	—	3 m (10 ft)
Leucothoe fontanesiana 'Rainbow'	E	white	spring	1.2 m (4 ft)
Lamium maculatum 'Beacon Silver'	E	mauve pink	early summer	20 cm (8 in)
Pachysandra terminalis 'Variegata'	E	greenish white	early spring	30 cm (12 in)
Pieris japonica 'Variegata'	E	white	spring	1.2 m (4 ft)
Pittosporum tenuifolium 'Silver Queen'	E	chocolate brown	late spring	3 m (10 ft)
Prunus lusitanica 'Variegata	E	white	early summer	1.8 m (6 ft)
Aralia elata 'Variegata'	D	white	late summer	3 m (10 ft)
Astrantia major 'Sunningdale Variegated'	D	rose pink	summer	45 cm (18 in)
Brunnera macrophylla 'Hadspen Cream'	D	blue	spring	45 cm (18 in)
Buddleia davidii 'Harlequin'	D	red violet	late summer	2.7 m (9 ft)
Cornus alba 'Elegantissima'	D	white/blue white fruit	spring	2.4 m (8 ft)
Cornus controversa 'Variegata'	D	white/blue black fruit	late spring	5 m (16 ft 6 in)
Cotoneaster horizontalis 'Variegatus	D	white/red berries	late spring	60 cm (2 ft)
Fuchsia magellanica 'Versicolor'	D	crimson & purple	summer & autumn	75 cm (2 ft 6 in)
Hosta fortunei 'Marginata Alba'	D	pale lilac	summer	60 cm (2 ft)
Hydrangea macrophylla 'Tricolor'	D	pale pink	late summer & autumn	1.2 m (4 ft)
Kerria japonica 'Variegata'	D	yellow	spring	1.2 m (4 ft)
Philadelphus coronarius 'Variegatus'	D	white	summer	2 m (6 ft 6 in)

12 PLANTS WITH YELLOW/GREEN VARIEGATION

NAME	E/D	FLOWERS/FRUIT	FLOWERING SEASON	HEIGHT	
Arundinaria viridistriata	E	—	—	1.2 m	(4 ft)
Aucuba japonica 'Crotonifolia'	E	yellow	spring	1.2 m	(4 ft)
Buxus sempervirens 'Aureovariegata'	E	—	—	1.8 m	(6 ft)
Cortaderia selloana 'Gold Band'	E	silver white	autumn	1.8 m	(6 ft)
Elaeagnus pungens 'Maculata'	E	pale yellow	autumn	2.4 m	(8 ft)
Euonymus fortunei 'Emerald 'n' Gold'	E	—	—	60 cm	(2 ft)
Euonymus japonicus 'Aureopictus'	E	green white	late spring	2.4 m	(8 ft)
Hebe × franciscana 'Variegata'	E	violet purple	all summer	90 cm	(3 ft)
Hedera canariensis ' 'Variegata'	E	green	late winter	9 m	(30 ft)
Hedera helix 'Goldheart'	E	lime green	spring	6 m	(20 ft)
Ilex aquifolium 'Golden Milkboy'	E	—	—	3 m	(10 ft)
Lonicera japonica Aureo-reticulata'	E	yellow	summer	6 m	(20 ft)
Phormium cookianum 'Cream Delight'	E	red bracts	early summer	90 cm	(3 ft)
Salvia officinalis 'Icterina'	E	lavender blue	mid summer	45 cm	(18 in)
Abelia × grandiflora 'Frances Mason'	D	pale pink	late summer	1.2 m	(4 ft)
Abutilon megapotamicum 'Variegatum'	D	yellow red	late summer	2.1 m	(7 ft)
Aralia elata 'Aureovariegata'	D	white/maroon fruit	late summer	3 m	(10 ft)
Cornus alba 'Spaethii'	D	white/blue-white fruit	spring	2.4 m	(8 ft)
Hakonechloa macra 'Aureola'	D	yellowish	late summer	30 cm	(1 ft)
Hosta fortunei 'Albo Picta'	D	lilac	summer	60 cm	(2 ft)
Hosta sieboldiana 'Frances Williams'	D	lilac white	summer	60 cm	(2 ft)
Hypericum × moseranum 'Tricolor'	D	yellow	all summer	90 cm	(3 ft)
Iris pseudacorus 'Variegata'	D	yellow	early summer	60 cm	(2 ft)
Melissa officinalis 'Variegata'	D	white	summer	45 cm	(18 in)
Mentha × gentilis 'Variegata'	D	mauve	summer	60 cm	(2 ft)
Miscanthus sinensis 'Zebrinus'	D	cream	summer	1.2 m	(4 ft)
Sambucus nigra 'Aureomarginata'	D	cream/black berries	early summer	4 m	(13 ft)
Symphoricarpus orbiculatus 'Variegatus'	D	pink	late spring	1.5 m	(5 ft)

13 PLANTS WITH PURPLE FOLIAGE

NAME	E/D	FLOWERS/FRUIT	FLOWERING SEASON	HEIGHT	
Acer palmatum 'Atropurpureum'	D	reddish/reddish fruit	spring	3 m	(10 ft)
Acer platanoides 'Crimson King'	D	yellow/reddish fruit	spring	18 m	(60 ft)
Berberis × ottawensis 'Purpurea'	D	yellow/red berries	spring	2 m	(6 ft 6 in)
Corylopsis willmottiae 'Spring Purple'	D	pale yellow	early spring	1.8 m	(6 ft)
Corylus maxima 'Purpurea'	D	catkins	spring	2.7 m	(9 ft)
Fagus sylvatica 'Riversii'	D	—	—	27 m	(90 ft)
Hebe 'Purple Queen'	E	purple	summer	1.2 m	(4 ft)
Malus 'Royalty'	D	crimson/dark red fruit	mid spring	8 m	(26 ft)
Phormium tenax 'Purpureum'	E	red bracts	summer	1.5 m	(5 ft)
Pittosporum tenuifolium 'Purpureum'	E	chocolate	spring	3 m	(10 ft)
Prunus 'Cistena'	D	white	spring	1.8 m	(6 ft)
Prunus cerasifera 'Pissardii'	D	blush white	early spring	8 m	(26 ft)
Sambucus nigra 'Purpurea'	D	cream/black fruit	early summer	4 m	(13 ft)
Vitis vinifera 'Purpurea'	D	black fruit	autumn	5 m	(16 ft 6 in)
Weigela florida 'Foliis Purpureis'	D	pink	summer	1.5 m	(5 ft)

14 PLANTS WITH GOLDEN FOLIAGE

NAME	E/D	FLOWERS/FRUIT	FLOWERING SEASON	HEIGHT	
Acer japonicum 'Aureum'	D	red/reddish fruit	spring	3 m	(10 ft)
Berberis thunbergii 'Aurea'	D	yellow red berries	spring	90 cm	(3 ft)
Catalpa bignonioides 'Aurea'	D	pinky white	late summer	6 m	(20 ft)
Gleditsia triacanthos 'Sunburst'	D	green	summer	9 m	(30 ft)
Hedera helix 'Buttercup'	E	lime green	autumn	3 m	(10 ft)
Ligustrum 'Vicaryi'	E	white/black fruits	late summer	2.4 m	(8 ft)
Lonicera nitida 'Baggesen's Gold'	E	—	—	1.2 m	(4 ft)
Philadelphus coronarius 'Aureus'	D	white	summer	1.8 m	(6 ft)
Physocarpus opulifolius 'Dart's Gold'	D	white	mid summer	1.8 m	(6 ft)
Ribes sanguineum 'Brocklebankii'	D	pink	spring	1.8 m	(6 ft)
Robinia pseudoacacia 'Frisia'	D	white	summer	15 m	(50 ft)
Sambucus racemosa 'Plumosa Aurea'	D	cream/red fruits	summer	4 m	(13 ft)
Spiraea japonica 'Gold Flame'	D	pink	mid summer	60 cm	(2 ft)
Weigela 'Looymansii Aurea'	D	pink	summer	1.8 m	(6 ft 6 in)
Humulus lupulus 'Aureus'	D	green 'hops'	autumn	6 m	(20 ft)

15 PLANTS WITH GREY FOLIAGE

NAME	E/D	FLOWERS/FRUIT	FLOWERING SEASON	HEIGHT	
Trees					
Eucalyptus niphophila	E	cream	late autumn	20 m	(66 ft)
Populus alba	D	green catkins	spring	18 m	(60 ft)
Pyrus nivalis	D	white	spring	6 m	(20 ft)
Pyrus salicifolia 'Pendula'	D	white/green fruit	spring	4.5 m	(15 ft)
Salix alba 'Sericea'	D	yellow catkins	spring	15 m	(50 ft)
Sorbus aria 'Lutescens'	D	white/red berries	spring	12 m	(40 ft)
Shrubs					
Artemisia 'Powis Castle'	E	grey	summer	90 cm	(3 ft)
Atriplex halimus	D	—	—	1.8 m	(6 ft)
Ballota pseudodictamnus	E	lilac pink	mid summer	45 cm	(18 in)
Berberis dictyophylla	D	yellow/red fruit	spring	1.8 m	(6 ft)
Buddleia alternifolia	D	lilac	early summer	3 m	(10 ft)
Buddleia fallowiana	D	lavender blue	late summer	2.4 m	(8 ft)
Caryopteris × clandonensis	D	violet blue	early autumn	60 cm	(2 ft)
Cistus 'Sunset'	E	pink	summer	60 cm	(2 ft)
Convolvulus cneorum	E	white	summer onwards	45 cm	(18 in)
Dorycnium hirsutum	D	pink	late summer	45 cm	(18 in)
Elaeagnus angustifolia	D	yellow	spring	3 m	(10 ft)
Feijoa sellowiana	E	crimson and white	summer	3 m	(10 ft)
Halimum ocymoides	E	yellow	early summer	30 cm	(12 in)
Hebe albicans	E	white	summer	30 cm	(12 in)
Helianthemum nummularium					
'Wisley Primrose'	E	yellow	all summer	30 cm	(12 in)
Hippophae rhamnoides	D	orange berries	autumn & winter	5 m	(16 ft 6 in)
Helichrysum plicatum	E	yellow	late summer	60 cm	(2 ft)
Lavandula spica	E	lavender	summer onwards	45 cm	(18 in)
Olearia × scilloniensis	E	white	early summer	2 m	(6 ft 6 in)
Perovskia atriplicifolia	D	blue	late summer	90 cm	(3 ft)
Phlomis fruticosa	E	yellow	midsummer	60 cm	(2 ft)
Salix exigua	D	catkins	early spring	3 m	(10 ft)
Salvia officinalis	E	lavender	midsummer	45 cm	(18 in)
Santolina chamaecyparissus	E	yellow	summer	45 cm	(18 in)
Senecio greyi	E	yellow	early summer	1.2 m	(4 ft)

16 AROMATIC PLANTS

NAME	E/D	FLOWERS/FRUIT	FLOWERING SEASON	HEIGHT
Artemisia abrotanum	D	silver	early summer	90 cm (3 ft)
Callistemon citrinus	E	scarlet	summer	1.8 m (6 ft)
Caryopteris × clandonensis	D	violet blue	early autumn	60 cm (2 ft)
Cercidiphyllum japonicum	D	red tassels	spring	12 m (40 ft)
Choisya ternata	E	white	late spring	1.8 m (6 ft)
Cistus ladanifer	E	white	summer	1.8 m (6 ft)
Escallonia macrantha	E	pink	late spring	2.4 m (8 ft)
Eucalyptus gunnii	E	white	late autumn	20 m (66 ft)
Helichrysum plicatum	E	yellow	late summer	60 cm (2 ft)
Hyssopus officinalis	D	blue	summer	45 cm (18 in)
Laurus nobilis	E	creamy white	spring	4 m (13 ft)
Lavandula spica	E	lavender	summer onwards	45 cm (18 in)
Lippia citriodora	D	mauve	late summer	2 m (6 ft 6 in)
Myrica gale	D	yellow	early spring	90 cm (3 ft)
Myrtus communis	E	white	late summer	3 m (10 ft)
Olearia macrodonta	E	white	summer	2 m (6 ft 6 in)
OPerovskia atriplicifolia	D	blue	late summer	90 cm (3 ft)
Phlomis fruticosa	E	yellow	mid summer	60 cm (2 ft)
Populus × candicans	D	catkins	early spring	20 m (66 ft)
Ribes sanguineum	D	pink	spring	1.8 m (6 ft)
Rosa eglanteria	D	pink/red hips	summer	2 m (6 ft 6 in)
Rosmarinus officinalis	E	pale lavender	late spring	1.2 m (4 ft)
Ruta graveolens	E	yellow	summer onwards	45 cm (18 in)
Salvia officinalis	E	lavender blue	mid summer	45 cm (18 in)
Santolina virens	E	yellow	mid summer	45 cm (18 in)
Skimmia laureola	E	green/red fruit	spring	60 cm (2 ft)

17 PLANTS WITH SCENTED FLOWERS

NAME	E/D	FLOWERS/FRUIT	FLOWERING SEASON	HEIGHT
Azara lanceolata	E	yellow	early summer	2.4 m (8 ft)
Buddleia alternifolia	D	lilac	early summer	3 m (10 ft)
Chimonanthus praecox	D	waxy yellow	winter	1.8 m (6 ft)
Clethra alnifolia	D	white	late summer	2.1 m (7 ft)
Coronilla glauca	E	yellow	early summer and autumn	1.8 m (6 ft)
Cytisus battandieri	D	yellow	early summer	3 m (10 ft)
Daphne collina	E	rose pink	late spring	60 cm (2 ft)
Daphne mezereum	D	purple-red/red berries	winter	75 cm (2 ft 6 in)
Daphne odora	E	purple-pink	winter	1.5 m (5 ft)

17 PLANTS WITH SCENTED FLOWERS (*Continued*)

NAME	E/D	FLOWERS/FRUIT	FLOWERING SEASON	HEIGHT	
Elaeagnus commutata	D	small yellow	mid summer	2.4 m	(8 ft)
Elaeagnus × ebbingei	E	pale yellow	late summer	3 m	(10 ft)
Erica arborea	E	white	early spring	3 m	(10 ft)
Hamamelis mollis	D	yellow	winter	3 m	(10 ft)
Jasminum officinale	D	white	summer	9 m	(30 ft)
Lonicera fragrantissima	E	cream	winter	2 m	(6 ft 6 in)
Lonicera japonica	E	cream	late summer	9 m	(30 ft)
Lonicera syringantha	D	pinky lilac	late spring	2 m	(6 ft 6 in)
Mahonia japonica	E	yellow	winter	2.4 m	(8 ft)
Osmanthus delavayi	E	white	early spring	3 m	(10 ft)
Philadelphus coronarius	D	white	summer	1.8 m	(6 ft)
Pittosporum tobira	E	cream	mid summer	1.8 m	(6 ft)
Robinia pseudoacacia	D	white	summer	15 m	(50 ft)
Sarcococca humilis	E	white/black berries	winter	40 cm	(16 in)
Syringa vulgaris	D	lilac	late spring	3 m	(10 ft)
Tilia × europaea	D	yellow-white	mid summer	20 m	(66 ft)
Viburnum carlesii	E	white	mid spring	1.2 m	(4 ft)
Viburnum × bodnantense	D	rose white	winter to early spring	3 m	(10 ft)
Wisteria sinensis	D	mauve	late spring	9 m	(30 ft)

18 MARGINAL PLANTS

Plants which need to be grown in wet soil and up to a depth of 15 cm (6 in) of water.

All can be planted in containers or in soil allowing 45 cm (18 in) spacing.

NAME	FLOWERS/FOLIAGE	SEASON	HEIGHT	
Acorus calamus 'Variegatus'	green & cream aromatic foliage	summer	60 cm	(2 ft)
* Alisma plantago-aquatica	pink flowers	summer	60–90 cm	(2–3 ft)
Butomus umbellatus	pink flowers	late summer	60 cm	(2 ft)
Calla palustris	white flowers; red fruits	spring/autumn	15 cm	(6 in)
Caltha palustris	golden flowers	spring	30–45 cm	(12–18 in)
* Cyperus longus	brown flowers	summer	1.2 m	(4 ft)
Eriophorum angustifolium	white flowers	early summer	45 cm	(18 in)
Glyceria aquatica 'Variegata'	green & cream foliage	summer	60 cm	(2 ft)
Iris laevigata	blue flowers	early summer	60 cm	(2 ft)
Iris pseudacorus	yellow flags	early summer	90 cm	(3 ft)
Juncus effusus 'Spiralis'	green twisted foliage	summer	30–45 cm	(12–18 in)
* Mentha aquatica	pale purple flowers	summer	30–45 cm	(12–18 in)
Menyanthes trifoliata	white scented flowers	spring	25 cm	(10 in)
Myosotis palustris	blue flowers	early spring	25 cm	(10 in)

18 MARGINAL PLANTS (*Continued*)

NAME	FLOWERS/FOLIAGE	SEASON	HEIGHT	
Pontederia cordata	blue flowers; large green leaves	late summer	60 cm	(2 ft)
* Ranunculus lingua	yellow flowers	early summer	90 cm	(3 ft)
Sagittaria sagittifolia	white flowers; large green leaves	late summer	60 cm	(2 ft)
Saururus cernuus	cream foliage	summer	30 cm	(1 ft)
* Typha latifolia	brown 'maces'	late summer	1.8 m	(6 ft)
Veronica beccabunga	blue flowers	summer	25 cm	(10 in)

* plants that are invasive and must be planted in containers.

19 PLANTS FOR MOIST CONDITIONS

NAME	FLOWERS/FOLIAGE	FLOWERING SEASON	HEIGHT	
Aruncus sylvester	cream	summer	1.5 cm	(5 ft)
Astible × arendsii	white pink or red	summer	60–90 cm	(2–3 ft)
Filipendula ulmaria	cream	summer	1.2 m	(4 ft)
Gunnera manicata	brown/enormous leaves	summer	2.4 cm	(8 ft)
Hosta glauca	lavender	summer	60 cm	(2 ft)
Iris kaempferi	purple and blue	mid summer	60 cm	(2 ft)
Iris sibirica	blue	mid summer	90 cm	(3 ft)
Ligularia clivorum	orange	late summer	1.2 cm	(4 ft)
Lobelia cardinalis	red	late summer	60 cm	(2 ft)
Lysichiton americanus	yellow/huge leaves	spring	75 cm	(2 ft 6 in)
Lysimachia punctata	yellow	summer	60 cm	(2 ft)
Lythrum salicaria	rose purple	summer	1.2 m	(4 ft)
Mimulus cardinalis	scarlet	late summer	45 cm	(18 in)
Peltiphyllum peltatum	pink	spring	60 cm	(2 ft)
Primula florindae	yellow	summer	60 cm	(2 ft)
Primula japonica	deep red	late spring	60 cm	(2 ft)
Ranunculus acontifolius 'Flore Pleno'	white	early summer	60 cm	(2 ft)
Rheum palmatum	cream/huge leaves	early summer	1.8 m	(6 ft)
Rodgersia aesculifolia	cream	mid summer	1.5 m	(5 ft)
Trollius europaeus	yellow	late spring	60 cm	(2 ft)

20 FERNS

NAME	E/D	FROND COLOUR	HEIGHT	PLANTING DISTANCE
Adiantum pedatum	D	soft green	30 cm (12 in)	45 cm (18 in)
Asplenium scolopendrium	E	rich green	45 cm (18 in)	45 cm (18 in)
Athyrium filix-femina	D	light green	90 cm (3 ft)	60 cm (2 ft)
Blechnum tabulare	E	dark green	90 cm (3 ft)	60 cm (2 ft)
Cystopteris bulbifera	D	bright green	30 cm (12 in)	45 cm (18 in)
Dryopteris filix-mas	D	dull green	1.2 m (4 ft)	60 cm (2 ft)
Matteucia struthopteris	D	light green	60 cm (2 ft)	60 cm (2 ft)
Onoclea sensibilis	D	light green	1 m (3 ft 3 in)	90 cm (3 ft)
Osmunda regalis	D	fresh green	1 m (3 ft 3 in)	90 cm (3 ft)
Polypodium vulgare	E	dull green	25 cm (10 in)	30 cm (12 in)
Polystichum aculeatum	E	dark green	60 cm (2 ft)	60 cm (2 ft)
Polystichum setiferum	E	green	90 cm (3 ft)	60 cm (2 ft)

21 CLIMBERS

NAME	E/D	FLOWERS/FOLIAGE	FLOWERING SEASON	ASPECT	HEIGHT
Actinindia kolomikta	D	white/pink, white & green	early summer	S & W	4 m (13 ft)
Akebia quinata	D	purple	spring	N, E & W	6 m (20 ft)
Berberidopsis corallina	E	crimson	summer	W	4.5 m (15 ft)
Campsis grandiflora	D	orange & red	late summer	S	9 m (30 ft)
Celastrus orbiculatus	D	yellow orange fruit	fruit in autumn	any	7 m (23 ft)
Clematis armandii	E	white	mid spring	S	6 m (20 ft)
Clematis montana	D	white	spring	any	9 m (30 ft)
Clematis large flower hybrids	D	wide range of colours	summer & autumn	any	4 m (13 ft)
Eccremocarpus scaber	E	orange	summer onwards	S or W	3 m (10 ft)
Hedera canariensis	E	green/black fruit	late winter	any	9 m (30 ft)
Hedera helix	E	lime green/black fruit	spring	any	6 m (20 ft)
Hydrangea petiolaris	D	white	summer	N, E, W	6 m (20 ft)
Jasminum officinale	D	white	summer	any	9 m (30 ft)
Lonicera japonica	E	cream	late summer	any	9 m (30 ft)
Lonicera periclymenum	D	purple & cream	early summer	any	6 m (20 ft)
Parthenocissus henryana	D	bright red autumn colour	autumn leaves	any	6 m (20 ft)
Parthenocissus quinquefolia	D	scarlet autum colour	autumn leaves	any	7 m (23 ft)
Passiflora caerulea	D	white/orange fruit	summer	S	6 m (20 ft)
Pileostegia viburnoides	E	creamy white	late summer	any	4 m (13 ft)
Polygonum baldschuanicum	D	cream	summer & autumn	any	12 m (40 ft)
Schisandra propinqua sinensis	D	deep crimson	late spring	any	4 m (13 ft)
Schizophragma hydrangioides	D	white	late summer	any	6 m (20 ft)
Solanum crispum	D	purple	late summer	S & W	4 m (13 ft)
Trachelospermum jasminoides	E	white	late summer	S & W	3 m (10 ft)
Vitis coignetiae	E	green/brilliant autumn colour	autumn	any	9 m (30 ft)
Wisteria floribunda	D	violet blue	late spring	S or W	9 m (30 ft)

INDEX

gardens, 117; steps, 104; walls, 61–4, *62–4*
Stone veneer walls, 62, *62*
Stoneware pots, 134
Streams, 112, *113*, 118
Stretcher bond, 54, *55*, 60, *93*, 94
Strimmers, 188
Structural planting, 154–6; backgrounds, 155, *155*; conifers, 174; delineating areas, 155, *156*; evergreens, 155–6, 239; screens, 154–5; shrubs, 178–9; trees, 166–8; vistas, 155
Style, 22–3, 24–5, 143
Summer interest: colour, 204; scented plants, 217; shrubs, 182; trees for, 169–70
Summerhouses, 123, 126
Sunken gardens, 65
Sunny positions, plants for, 195, 237–8
Supports: climbing plants, 215–16; staking trees, 170–1, *171*
Surprise, 28
Surveys, 11–19, *12–13*
Swimming pools, 115–16, *115*
Swings, 128
Symmetry, 24
Synthetic turf, 188

Tables, 132
'Tapestry' hedges, 180
Tarmac drives, 97, *97*, 99
Telegraph poles, retaining walls, 68
Tender plants, 149, 216
Terraces, on banks, 64–5, *65*, 66; *see also* Patios
Terracotta pots, 134
Thyme 'lawns', 189
Thyme seats, *189*
Tile drains, 40–1, *41*
Timber: containers, 134; decking, 91, *91*; edge restraints and trim, 102–3, *102*; furniture, 132; gates, 81, *81*, 138; paths, 96; pergolas and arbours, 121, 122–3, *122*; preservatives, 137, 138; raised beds, 103;

retaining walls, 68; sheds, 124–5, *124*; steps, 105
Timber profiles, building stone walls, 63, *64*
Tools, 139–41
Topiary, 175
Topsoil, 16, 37, 144
Tortuous habit, 165
Tree preservation orders, 171–2
Tree ties, 170, 171
Trees: acid soils, 222; avenues, 167–8; buying, 152; climbing plants in, 215; conifers, 173–7; fences and, 71; focal points, 156–7, *157*, 168; framing views with, 168; fruit, 148, 229, 231, 232–3, *232*; ground cover under, 195; grouping, 168–9; habits, 164–5, *165*; levels around, 39, *39*; native, 166; ornamental value, 168–70; planting, 170–1, *171*; shapes, 163–4, *164*; structural planting, 154, 155–6; tree belts and screens, 148, *148*, 166–7, *167*; tree seats, 131; woodland planting, 167
Trellis, 70, 216
Triangular gardens, 32, *33*
Triangulation, 13, *13*
Troughs, 133, 134, 219
Tubs, 133, 134
Turf, 185–7, *187*; mazes, 194; synthetic, 188

Umbrellas, 133
Unity, design, 23
Urns, 133, 228, *228*
Utility areas, 18, 82, 123

Variegated foliage, 151, 244–5
Vases, 133
Vegetables, 159, 229, 230–2, *230–1*, 233
Versailles tubs, 134
Vertical habit, 165
Victorian roses, 212
Views and vistas, 14–15, 155, *156*, 168

Walls: advantages and disadvantages, 45–6; behind borders, 208; brick, 52–8, *54–9*; concrete blocks, 58–60, *60*; construction, 48–52, *48–50*; copings, 54, 56–7, *57*, 63, 64, *64*; costs, 45; damp proof courses, 54, *54*; expansion joints, 54, 67; footings, 48–50, *49–50*, 63, *63*; joints, 55–6, *56*, 137; maintenance, 137; mortar, 52; pointing, 55; retaining, 64–8, *65–8*; stone, 61–4, *62–4*; wall shrubs, 214, 216
Water: children's safety, 128; fountains, 113, *113*; irrigation, 43; marginal plants, 221, 249–50; millstone features, 114, *114*, 128; paddling pools, 114–15, 128; pools, 106–10, *108–9*; streams, 112, *113*, 118; swimming pools, 115–16, *115*; water gardens, 220–2, *220*; water table, 17, 39, 65; waterfalls, 110–12, *110–11*, 118; *see also* Drainage water lilies, 221, 222
Wattle hurdles, 74, *75*
Weeds, 158; ground cover plants, 196; lawns, 186; in rock gardens, 218–19
'Weep holes', retaining walls, 67
Weeping trees, 165, *165*
White gardens, 202–3
Wild flower meadows, 190
Wildlife gardens, 224–6
Wind: and aspect, 146; prevailing, 15; protection from, 69, 148, *148*; tree belts, 166, *167*
Window boxes, 135
Winter interest: colour, 203; conifers, 176; flowering plants, 241; scented plants, 217; shrubs, 181; trees for, 169
Wood *see* Timber
Woodland planting, 167, 192

Yellow, colour harmony, 201–2, *201*